Lecture Notes in Computer Science   13071

More information about this subseries at http://www.springer.com/series/7408

Shengchao Qin · Jim Woodcock ·
Wenhui Zhang (Eds.)

Dependable
Software Engineering

Theories, Tools, and Applications

7th International Symposium, SETTA 2021
Beijing, China, November 25–27, 2021
Proceedings

 Springer

Editors
Shengchao Qin 🄳
Teesside University
Middlesbrough, UK

Jim Woodcock 🄳
University of York
York, UK

Wenhui Zhang 🄳
Institute of Software, Chinese Academy
of Sciences
Beijing, China

ISSN 0302-9743   ISSN 1611-3349   (electronic)
Lecture Notes in Computer Science
ISBN 978-3-030-91264-2   ISBN 978-3-030-91265-9   (eBook)
https://doi.org/10.1007/978-3-030-91265-9

LNCS Sublibrary: SL2 – Programming and Software Engineering

This Springer imprint is published by the registered company Springer Nature Switzerland AG
The registered company address is: Gewerbestrasse 11, 6330 Cham, Switzerland

Preface

This volume contains the papers presented at SETTA 2021: the 7th International Symposium on Dependable Software Engineering Theories, Tools and Applications held during November 25–27, 2021 in Beijing.

The purpose of SETTA is to bring international researchers together to exchange research results and ideas on bridging the gap between formal methods and software engineering. The interaction with the Chinese computer science and software engineering community is a central focus point. The aim is to show research interests and results from different groups so as to initiate interest-driven research collaboration. Past SETTA symposiums were successfully held in Nanjing (2015), Beijing (2016), Changsha (2017), Beijing (2018), Shanghai (2019), and Guangzhou (2020).

SETTA 2021 included a main track and a journal first track. Its main track attracted 39 submissions co-authored by researchers from 12 countries. Each submission was reviewed by at least 3 Program Committee members with help from additional reviewers. The Program Committee discussed the submissions online and 16 papers were finally accepted for presentation at the conference. The journal first track of SETTA 2021 was organized in partnership with the Journal of Computer Science and Technology. It attracted 14 eligible submissions. Those accepted by the journal following a standard review process were expected to be presented as part of the SETTA 2021 conference program. The program also included three keynote speeches given by Joost-Pieter Katoen from RWTH Aachen University, Frits Vaandrager from Radboud University, and Charles Zhang from the Hong Kong University of Science and Technology.

SETTA 2021 was sponsored and organized by the Institute of Software, Chinese Academy of Sciences. We are grateful to the local organizing committee for their hard work in making SETTA 2021 a successful event. Our warmest thanks go to the authors for submitting their papers to the conference. We thank the members of the steering committee for their support in organizing this event. We thank all the members of Program Committee for completing reviews on time, and being active in discussions during the review process. We also thank the additional reviewers for their effort that helped the Program Committee to decide which submissions to accept. Special thanks go to our invited speakers for presenting their research at the conference. Finally, we thank the conference general chair, Chen Zhao, the publicity chair, Fu Song, and the local organization chair, Zhilin Wu.

October 2021

Shengchao Qin
Jim Woodcock
Wenhui Zhang

Preface

This volume contains the papers presented at SETTA 2021, the 7th International Symposium on Dependable Software Engineering Theories, Tools and Applications, ...

Organization

Program Committee

Yamine Ait Ameur	IRIT/INPT-ENSEEIHT, France
Richard Banach	The University of Manchester, UK
Lei Bu	Nanjing University, China
Milan Ceska	Faculty of Information Technology, Brno University of Technology, Czech Republic
Sudipta Chattopadhyay	Singapore University of Technology and Design, Singapore
Liqian Chen	National University of Defense Technology, China
Yu-Fang Chen	Academia Sinica, Taiwan, China
Alessandro Cimatti	Fondazione Bruno Kessler, Italy
Florin Craciun	Babes-Bolyai University, Rome
Yuxin Deng	East China Normal University, China
Wei Dong	National University of Defense Technology, China
Hongfei Fu	Shanghai Jiao Tong University, China
Jan Friso Groote	Eindhoven University of Technology, The Netherlands
Nan Guan	City University of Hong Kong, China
Dimitar Guelev	Bulgarian Academy of Sciences, Bulgaria
Thai Son Hoang	University of Southampton, UK
Chao Huang	University of Liverpool, UK
Yu Jiang	Tsinghua University, China
Sebastian Junges	University of California, Berkeley, USA
Guoqiang Li	Shanghai Jiao Tong University, China
Yi Li	Nanyang Technological University, Singapore
Yang Liu	Nanyang Technological University, Singapore
Zhiming Liu	Southwest University, China
Tiziana Margaria	Lero, Ireland
Dominique Mery	Université de Lorraine, LORIA, France
Stefan Mitsch	Carnegie Mellon University, USA
Jun Pang	University of Luxembourg, Luxembourg
Dave Parker	University of Birmingham, UK
Yu Pei	The Hong Kong Polytechnic University, China
Shengchao Qin (Co-chair)	Teesside University, UK
Mickael Randour	F.R.S.-FNRS/Université de Mons, Belgium
Stefan Schupp	TU Wien, Austria
Zhiping Shi	Capital Normal University, China
Fu Song	School of Information Science and Technology, Shanghai Tech University, China
Jeremy Sproston	University of Turin, Italy

Ting Su	East China Normal University, China
Jun Sun	Singapore Management University, Singapore
Meng Sun	Peking University, China
Andrea Turrini	Institute of Software, Chinese Academy of Sciences, China
Tarmo Uustalu	Reykjavik University, Iceland
Jaco van de Pol	Aarhus University, Danmark
Jim Woodcock (Co-chair)	University of York, UK
Xiaofei Xie	Kyushu University, Japan
Zhiwu Xu	Shenzhen University, China
Bai Xue	Institute of Software, Chinese Academy of Sciences, China
Chenyi Zhang	Jinan University, China
Wenhui Zhang (Co-chair)	Institute of Software, Chinese Academy of Sciences, China

Additional Reviewers

Bouwman, Mark	van Spaendonck, Flip
Chen, Zhe	Vandenhove, Pierre
Cheng, Zheng	Wang, Jiawan
Cui, Zhanqi	Wang, Rui
Dupont, Guillaume	Wu, Hongjun
Li, Ming	Wu, Xiuheng
Li, Renjue	Yang, Dong
Liu, Bo	Zhan, Bohua
Luan, Xiaokun	Zhang, Qianying
Maarand, Hendrik	Zhao, Ying
Martens, Jan	Zheng, Wei
Shi, Hao	Zhu, Xue-Yang
Tsai, Wei-Lun	Zhuo, Zhang

Abstracts of Keynote Speeches

Mechanically Finding the Right Probabilities in Markov Models

Joost-Pieter Katoen

Modelling and Verification of Software Group, RWTH Aachen University,
Aachen, Germany

Markov chains are central in performance and dependability analysis, whereas Mark-ov decision processes are key in stochastic decision making and planning in AI. A standard assumption in these models is that all probabilities are precisely known a priori. In many cases, this assumption is too severe. System quantities such as component fault rates, molecule reaction rates, packet loss ratios, etc. are often not, or at best partially, known.

This talk surveys the analysis of parametric Markov models whose transitions are labelled with functions over a finite set of parameters. These models are symbolic representations of uncountably many concrete probabilistic models, each obtained by instantiating the parameters. We consider various analysis problems for a given logical specification φ: do all parameter instantiations within a given region of parameter values satisfy φ?, which instantiations satisfy φ and which ones do not?, and how can all such instantiations be characterised, either exactly or approximately?

We address theoretical complexity results and describe the main ideas underlying state-of-the-art algorithms that established an impressive leap over the last decade enabling the fully automated analysis of models with millions of states and thousands of parameters. Examples from distributed computing, satellites and AI illustrate the applicability of these parameter synthesis techniques.

A New Approach for Active Automata Learning Based on Apartness

Frits W. Vaandrager

Institute for Computing and Information Sciences, Radboud University,
Netherlands

We present $L^{\#}$, a new and simple approach to active automata learning. Instead of focusing on equivalence of observations, like the L^{*} algorithm and its descendants, $L^{\#}$ takes a different perspective: it tries to establish apartness, a constructive form of inequality. $L^{\#}$ does not require auxiliary notions such as observation tables or discrimination trees, but operates directly on tree-shaped automata. $L^{\#}$ has the same asymptotic query and symbol complexities as the best existing learning algorithms, but we show that adaptive distinguishing sequences can be naturally integrated to boost the performance of $L^{\#}$ in practice. Experiments with a prototype implementation, written in Rust, suggest that $L^{\#}$ outperforms existing algorithms.[1]

---

[1] (Based on joint work with Bharat Garhewal, Jurriaan Rot & Thorsten Wissmann)

Enterprise-Scale Static Analysis: A Pinpoint Experience

Charles Zhang

Department of Computer Science and Engineering, HKUST, Hong Kong

Despite years of research and practice, modern static analysis techniques still cannot detect oldest and extremely well understood software bugs such as the Heartbleed, one of the most spectacular security flaws of the recent decade. A remedy, as what we have attempted through the successful commercialization of the Pinpoint platform (PLDI s18), is to make static program analysis aware of the basic characteristics of the modern enterprise-scale software system. The talk focuses on discussing these characteristics and how Pinpoint addresses them pragmatically as well as its future directions. Pinpoint is a LLVM-based cross-language static analysis platform and deployed in major Chinese tech companies such as Tencent, Baidu, Huawei, and Alibaba.

Contents

Systems Development

Translating a Large Subset of Stateflow to Hybrid CSP with Code Optimization

Panhua Guo[1], Bohua Zhan[2,3(✉)], Xiong Xu[2,3], Shuling Wang[2,3], and Wenhui Sun[1]

[1] Beijing Jiaotong University, Beijing, China
{phguo1,whsun1}@bjtu.edu.cn
[2] SKLCS, Institute of Software, Chinese Academy of Sciences, Beijing, China
{bzhan,xux,wangsl}@ios.ac.cn
[3] University of Chinese Academy of Sciences, Beijing, China

Abstract. Stateflow is a graphical language for modeling hierarchical transition systems, well-known for the complexity of its semantics, which is only informally explained in its user manual. Formal analysis and verification of Stateflow models usually proceed by first translating a subset of Stateflow to a formal language with precise semantics. Most existing work address only "safe" subset of Stateflow and ignore the most complex semantic issues. Moreover, it is difficult to balance simplicity of the translation algorithm with conciseness of the resulting model. In this paper, we describe a two-stage process for translating a large subset of Stateflow to Hybrid CSP, where the first stage is mostly syntax-directed and addresses each feature of Stateflow separately, and the second stage is a code optimization step that simplifies the resulting model using information from static analysis. We thoroughly validate the translation process using a hand-designed set of benchmarks, as well as larger case studies from existing work.

1 Introduction

Model-based design (MBD) is a software engineering practice for building complex systems. Instead of implementing the system directly, one first builds an abstract model of the system. The model is then subjected to simulation and analysis. Afterwards the concrete system may be produced by code generation from the model. This approach helps engineers catch design-errors early, avoiding costly changes later in the project as result of mistakes in design that are discovered only during testing.

Simulink/Stateflow is a modeling tool developed by MathWorks, considered as a de-facto industry standard for model-based design of embedded systems. Simulink [16] is well-suited for modeling dynamical systems and control laws. Stateflow [17] is a toolbox in Simulink for modeling hierarchical transition systems. Stateflow is well-known for the complexity of its semantics. Recent versions of its user manual run over 1400 pages, which still cannot cover its semantics with full precision. The semantics is ultimately defined by the behavior of simulation within Matlab/Simulink.

© Springer Nature Switzerland AG 2021
S. Qin et al. (Eds.): SETTA 2021, LNCS 13071, pp. 3–21, 2021.
https://doi.org/10.1007/978-3-030-91265-9_1

For formal analysis of Stateflow, through either model checking or theorem proving, it is necessary to obtain a formal description of Stateflow models, at least for the subset of Stateflow intended to be handled. The formal semantics is often associated with a translation procedure to a formal language. There have been many works studying the semantics of Stateflow and its translation to various formal languages. All these work necessarily concerns only a subset of Stateflow. Moreover, the translation procedures are usually quite involved, and it is difficult to balance the simplicity of translation algorithm with conciseness of the resulting model.

In this work, we address the above challenge by proposing a method of translation that consists of two stages. The first stage is mostly syntax-directed, considering each feature of Stateflow separately. The second stage performs whole-program code optimization on the resulting model using information from static analysis. We necessarily still consider a subset of features in Stateflow, but the subset is larger compared to existing work. The translation procedure is both relatively easy to understand as well as yielding concise results.

For the formal language, we choose Hybrid CSP (HCSP) [13,25]. The language has the advantage of having all the necessary features for modeling synchronous and asynchronous hybrid systems, in particular those expressed using Simulink/Stateflow. In addition to the usual program constructs, HCSP contains constructs for communication, evolution by ODEs, internal and external choice, and interrupt of ODEs by communications. A Hoare logic has been defined for verifying HCSP programs using theorem proving [15,21]. Existing work (which the current work is based on) defined translation of a limited subset of Simulink/Stateflow to HCSP along with verification of the resulting models [26,27]. This has been applied to the verification of controlled descent of a lunar lander [24], and part of the Chinese Train Control System [1]. However, the translation algorithm is quite complicated, involving a large number of extra communications. For translation to HCSP, it is especially important that the resulting model is concise and easy to understand, as the main verification tool is theorem proving, which requires the human user to understand details of the model and why it is correct.

After defining and implementing the translation algorithm, we validate the translation process using a large number of benchmark examples. Each example is hand-designed, and intended to illustrate some aspect of the Stateflow semantics. In full, we constructed a benchmark set consisting of 100 examples, covering a wide range of semantic issues. We also evaluate the translation using larger case studies from existing work.

In summary, the contributions of this paper are as follows:

1. We propose a two-stage translation procedure from a large subset of Stateflow to Hybrid CSP, that is both relatively simple to understand, as well as producing concise results.
2. As part of the process, we describe code optimization of Hybrid CSP programs based on information from static analysis.

3. We introduce a large set of benchmark examples which serve to clarify various aspects of Stateflow semantics, that can be used to validate this as well as other translation procedures from Stateflow.

The remainder of this paper is organized as follows. Section 2 reviews Hybrid CSP, including some small language extensions that are used in this paper. Section 3 explains the semantics for the subset of Stateflow that we consider, with a focus on tricky semantical aspects and restrictions on models. In Sect. 4, we describe the first stage of the translation, considering each semantic feature in turn. Section 5 presents the second stage, using code optimization for Hybrid CSP. We describe the validation of the translation procedure in Sect. 6, related work in Sect. 7 and conclude in Sect. 8 with a discussion of future work.

2   Hybrid CSP

First, we briefly introduce the target of translation: Hybrid CSP (HCSP), including some language extensions that are used in this paper. HCSP [13,25] is an extension of CSP (Communicating Sequential Processes) [11] for modeling the concurrent execution of multiple processes with synchronizing communication between them. HCSP extends CSP by adding continuous evolution following an ordinary differential equation, as well as the possibility to interrupt execution with communication. A detailed explanation of HCSP can be found in [23].

Extensions to HCSP that are used in this paper are as follows.

- First, whereas the original HCSP allow only real numbers as values, we allow values to also be strings, lists, and records (dictionary mapping from strings to values). String values are used to give a more convenient representation of state activity. Lists (which also appear in [26]) are used to represent the stack of event broadcasts, as well as to emulate Matlab arrays and matrices. Records are used to represent messages in Stateflow. Only real numbers can be involved in continuous evolution following ODEs.
- Second, we allow explicit declaration of procedures. Procedures are already allowed implicitly through recursions in the original HCSP. In this paper, we permit declaring named procedures before the main process. To reduce complexity, procedure arguments and return values are not allowed. Procedure arguments can be emulated using stacks represented by lists, and return values can be emulated by setting a special variable _ret.

In summary, the syntax of HCSP is as follows:

$$lname :: = var \mid lname[e] \mid lname.field$$
$$P :: = \text{skip} \mid lname := e \mid ch?lname \mid ch!e \mid P; Q \mid P \sqcup Q \mid P^* \mid \text{if } B \text{ then } P_1 \text{ else } P_2 \mid$$
$$[]_{i \in I}(io_i \to Q_i) \mid \langle \dot{x} = e \& B \rangle \mid \langle \dot{x} = e \& B \rangle \unrhd []_{i \in I}(io_i \to Q_i) \mid @proc$$
$$proc :: = \textbf{proc } name = P$$
$$ps :: = (proc)^* P$$
$$S :: = ps \mid ps \|_{cs} ps$$

Here *lname* are terms that can occur on the left side of assignments, including variables, array indices, and fields. *e* are expressions, whose syntax we omit, but includes the usual arithmetic operators as well as operations on lists. HCSP commands, in the order listed above, are skip, assignment, input, output, sequence, internal choice, repetition, conditional, external choice, evolution by ODE, interrupt, and procedure calls. Using these, we can define additional constructs such as one-sided condition $B \to P$ and delay wait(e) [23]. Procedure definition $proc$ follow the syntax **proc** $name = P$, where P is a command. A sequential process ps is given by a list of procedure definitions followed by the main command. Finally, an HCSP program S is formed by parallel composition of sequential processes.

3   A Brief Tour of Stateflow Semantics

In this section, we give an overview of the subset of Stateflow that we cover. This is necessarily brief, as Stateflow is a very rich language. We will focus on the particularly tricky aspects of the semantics, illustrated by examples. We will also describe the restrictions we put on the model along with their justifications. Most of these restrictions are also checked by Matlab, and will produce a warning or error if violated.

3.1   States

The core of a Stateflow model is the hierarchy of states. Each state is either at the top level or is contained in another state, and is one of two types: AND-state or OR-state. States that are siblings (contained in the same parent state) must have the same type. During the course of execution of the system, each state is either active or inactive. If the children of a state are AND-states, then if the state is active all its children are active. Otherwise, if the state is active, exactly one of its children is active.

Each state specifies three actions: *entry*, *during*, and *exit* (abbreviated as en, du, and ex). *Entry* action is executed when the state is entered. *During* action is executed when the state remains active for one iteration (that is, no outgoing transitions can be carried out). *Exit* action is executed when the state exits. We will discuss this point more thoroughly in Sect. 3.4.

3.2   Transitions

Transitions are edges that go between states. Each transition specifies a label of the form $E[C]\{ca\}/\{ta\}$, where E is an *event*, C is the condition (boolean expression), ca is the *condition action*, and ta is the *transition action*. All four components are optional. If event E is specified, then the transition can be carried out only if E is present. Broadcast of events will be discussed in more detail in Sect. 3.5. If condition C is specified, the transition can be carried out only if C holds. After passing the checks for E and C, the condition action ca is executed immediately. The transition action ta is executed at the end of the transition (this will become more clear when we discuss junctions in Sect. 3.3).

Transitions are further divided into *outer transitions* and *inner transitions*. The distinction can be seen from the drawing of the Stateflow diagram: outer transitions leave from the outer boundary of a state, whereas inner transitions leave from the inner boundary of a state.

Transition edges can cross levels of the state hierarchy. These are called inter-level transitions (or super-transitions). For any transition, we define the *parent* of the transition as follows. For a transition from state s to state t, its parent is the lowest common ancestor between s and t, with exactly one exception: if the transition is an outer transition from state s to itself, then its parent is the parent of s. Let a be the parent of a transition from s to t, carrying out the transition exits all states between s and a, including s but not a, and enters all states between a and t, including t but not a. We impose the restriction that for an inter-level transition, all states along the path from s to a and from a to t, but not including a, are OR-states. If this condition does not hold, exiting the chain from s to a and entering the chain from a to t will require entry and exit from siblings, which significantly complicates the semantics and can lead to various ambiguities.

3.3 Junctions

Junctions can be considered as intermediate points in a multi-step transition. Traversal through junctions proceed in a depth-first manner: at the initial state and at each junction, the outgoing transitions are tried in order. The search stops the first time another state is reached. During the traversal, condition actions are executed, and their effects are not reverted even if search along the corresponding path fails. The transition actions are executed in the order they are encountered, *after* reaching a final state. More precisely, it happens between exiting from the starting states and entering the final states.

Junctions can form loops. However, we impose the restriction that all transitions within a loop do not have transition actions. If this restriction is not imposed, quite complex scenarios can be constructed which are difficult for code generation (see Fig. 1).

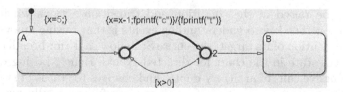

Fig. 1. An example of an invalid junction loop. Simulink reports an error on this example and would not permit simulation. The natural interpretation would be that the junction loop will be traversed 5 times, each time outputting c and adding an output of t to the transition action. Then the overall behavior is output c 5 times, followed by output t 5 times. An unbounded number of transition actions can be accumulated in the loop, which poses difficulty in model transformation and code generation.

There can be inter-level transitions to a junction. Hence junctions do not have to be located in the same parent state as the starting and ending states. We observe that if a junction is located in another state, going through the junction will not induce entry or exit of that state. This is illustrated in Fig. 2.

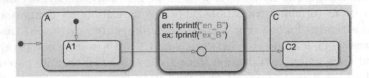

Fig. 2. This example shows going through a junction located in another state will not induce entry or exit of that state. While the middle junction is located within state B, carrying out the transition from $A1$ to $C2$ does not involve entering or exiting B.

3.4 State Lifecycle

We are now ready to describe the execution of a state, and its entry and exit procedures. When a state is entered, first execute its **en** action. Then, recursively enter its child states. If the child states are AND-states, all of them will be entered in a pre-defined order. Otherwise, the default transition is entered. The one exception is when the state has been entered previously and has a history junction. In that case the child state that is active last time is entered again.

For executing a state in each iteration, first the outer transitions are attempted in order. If one of the outer transitions can be carried out, execution of the state finishes. Otherwise, the **du** action of the state is executed, followed by attempting each of the inner transitions. If one of the inner transitions can be carried out, execution of the state finishes here. Otherwise, the active child states are executed in order.

To exit from a state, first exit from the active child states. If the child states are AND-states, the order of exit is in reverse to that of entry. Then perform the **ex** action of the state, and finally set the state to be inactive.

3.5 Events and Temporal Events

Events may be raised in the condition and transition actions when carrying out a transition. The key to understanding events is that raising an event causes immediate execution of its target: the entire Stateflow chart for broadcast events, and the target state in the chart for directed events. Hence, raising events can result in recursive calls of arbitrary depth, and changes to status of states in the chart. Infinite recursion can occur if one is not careful, especially for broadcast events. For this reason, it is usually advised to use directed events to a small part of a chart. However, we consider the semantics of both broadcast and directed events in full in this paper.

Temporal events are used to specify that a transition can be carried out a certain number of ticks or seconds after entering into a state. If the condition is specified by the number of ticks, it is called *implicit events*. If the condition is specified by the number of seconds, it is called *absolute time events*.

3.6   Early Return

Early return is one of the most complicated semantic feature of Stateflow. It concerns the possibility that event handling during the execution of an action can modify the context of execution, so that it no longer makes sense to carry out the remainder of the action. Most of the time, explanation of early return is associated with condition actions, as illustrated in Fig. 3.

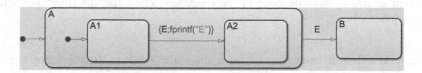

Fig. 3. Simple example of early return. In this example, when the transition from $A1$ to $A2$ occurs, event E is broadcast, which results in a transition from A to B. So when broadcasting E returns, the state $A1$ is no longer active, and it no longer makes sense to continue the transition to $A2$.

However, early return can happen in other contexts as well, and interacts with the traversal through junctions. The full list of scenarios is given in the Stateflow user manual [17], but appears to not be covered in existing research studying translation of Stateflow. We handle all of the following cases:

- *Entry, during* and *exit* actions: early return occurs when the state is no longer active.
- Condition action: early return occurs when the *original source state* is no longer active.
- Transition action: early return occurs when either the parent of the transition is no longer active, or when the parent already has an active child (since transition actions occur after the source state of the transition has exited, its parent should have no active child at the time).

In summary, early return from an action occurs after handling an event, if the context for executing the action is no longer present. It should be noted that early return cares only whether a state is active *at the end* of handling an event, not whether it is left in the middle. This is illustrated in Fig. 4.

3.7   Data and Messages

A Simulink model can contain multiple Stateflow charts, and data can be transmitted between charts using either input/output ports, data store memory, or messages. Each chart specify its input/output ports, and lines are drawn from output of one chart to input of another chart to specify data channels. Data store memory represents global data that can be accessed by all charts.

Messages is another feature of Stateflow that is rarely covered in existing work on translation. Similar to data and events, messages can be used to transmit information between charts or within a chart. However, the semantics of

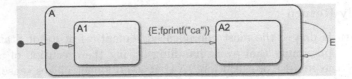

Fig. 4. Lack of early return when source state is left in the middle. In this example, the event broadcast of E leads to exit and re-entry of state A and $A1$. When it returns, $A1$ is still active, so the remainder of the condition action and the transition action will be carried out.

messages is different from that of both data and events. Messages are kept in queues. When a transition specifies the name of a message in its event, one message is consumed from the queue. This message will be active until the end of iteration, so other transitions specifying the same type of message will not consume another message from the queue. Data in the message can then be referred to in conditions, either in the same transition or in another transition. The same data will be used in future iterations, as long as it is not covered by consuming another message of the same type.

3.8 Functions and Graphical Functions

Any condition or action in a Stateflow chart can invoke functions defined in Matlab or within the chart. It is possible to include regular Matlab functions inside Stateflow charts. It is also possible to define functions using a transition system consisting of junctions, called *graphical functions*.

We consider translation of graphical functions as well as a limited language of Matlab functions. We aim at supporting the most-often used features in Matlab, including assignments, conditionals, arrays, and some basic functions (such as `min` and `max`). The behavior of graphical functions is similar to that of ordinary junctions, as described in Sect. 3.3.

3.9 Continuous Evolution

Stateflow can also be used to specify continuous evolution, independent from the use of Simulink blocks outside the chart. This is done by adding assignments of the form `x_dot = e` to the during action of states, indicating that the derivative of x is e. Arbitrary combination of differential equations with other features of Stateflow can easily lead to semantic problems, so a large number of restrictions on the use of continuous evolution are imposed by Matlab. For example, evaluation of e should be free of side-effects, as is evaluation of conditions in transitions out of a state. Moreover, there should not be condition actions in a transition that does not immediately lead to another state. Violating any of these rules can cause actions with side effects to be executed arbitrary number of times. We impose the same restrictions in our work, but cover the most frequently used cases in our translation.

4 Translation from Stateflow

In this section, we describe the method of translation from Stateflow to HCSP. Each Stateflow chart is translated into a single HCSP process. Sharing of data between charts, including the use of input/output ports, data store memory, and messages, are translated to communications in HCSP. For each chart, we produce two main procedures: initialization init_Chart and iteration exec_Chart. So the overall process for each chart is @init_Chart; (@exec_Chart)*. For charts with differential equations, ODE commands with boundary are used in @exec_Chart, and the time length of each iteration is not fixed. Otherwise, each @exec_Chart contains a wait command indicating waiting for a duration equal to the sample time of the chart.

Due to space constraints, we cannot cover all aspects of the translation in detail. Instead, we will discuss the key aspects, in order to illustrate the general approach.

4.1 Variables

Each variable that appears in the Stateflow chart will be translated to variables of the same name in the HCSP program. There are further *control variables* in the HCSP program serving various functions. These are summarized in Table 1. We use $\langle name \rangle$ to denote the name of the state currently referred to.

Table 1. Description of control variables

Role	Name	Range	Description
Activity	$\langle name \rangle$_st	States with OR-state children	Empty string indicates no active child, otherwise name of the active child
Event stack	EL	Global	Stack of broadcast and directed events
Input queue	IQU	Global	Queue for input messages
Local queue	LQU	Global	Queue for local messages
History variable	$\langle name \rangle$_hist	States with history junction	Empty string indicates never entered before, otherwise name of the last entered child state
Tick counter	$\langle name \rangle$_tick	States with implicit event	-1 if state is not active, otherwise number of ticks since last entry
Time counter	$\langle name \rangle$_time	States with absolute time event	-1 if state is not active, otherwise number of seconds since last entry
Return value	_ret	Global	Return value for procedures

The global variables include EL for the event stack, and IQU and LQU for queue of input and local messages. _ret is used for return value from procedures.

For representing activity of states in the Stateflow diagram, we opt for a different approach than what is usual in the past. Instead of using one boolean variable for each state to represent whether it is active, we use one variable ⟨name⟩_st of type string for each state that has OR-states as children. The string is empty if none of the child states is active. Otherwise, it is set to the name of the child state that is active. Using this approach, we reduce both the number of variables used and the number of assignments necessary for transition between states.

Several variables are used for states with additional features: ⟨name⟩_hist for states with history junctions, ⟨name⟩_tick for states with an outgoing transition guarded by an implicit event, and ⟨name⟩_time for states with an outgoing transition guarded by an absolute time event.

4.2 States

For each state, we create three procedures entry_⟨name⟩, during_⟨name⟩ and exit_⟨name⟩ corresponding to entry, during, and exit of the state. The content of these procedures are described below. They reflect the state lifecycle in Sect. 3.4, along with additional bookkeeping for history junctions and temporal events.

Entry. The following actions are performed in order for entering into a state. **1.** If the current state is an OR-state, set the activity variable of the parent state. **2.** If the parent state has history junction, set the history variable of the parent state. **3.** If the state has implicit (resp. absolute time event) on an outgoing transition, reset the tick counter (resp. time counter) of the state to 0. **4.** Perform the **en** action of the state. **5.** Enter into child states by calling corresponding entry procedures. If the child states are AND-states, enter each child state in sequence. Otherwise, enter according to history variable (if present) or by taking the default transition.

During. The following actions are performed for execution on a state. **1.** Initialize a variable ⟨name⟩_done to zero. **2.** As long as ⟨name⟩_done is zero, perform each of the outgoing transitions by calling the procedure given in Sect. 4.3, assigning ⟨name⟩_done to the return value of the call. **3.** If ⟨name⟩_done is zero, perform the during action of the state. **4.** As long as ⟨name⟩_done is zero, perform each of the inner transitions of the state. **5.** If ⟨name⟩_done is still zero, recursively call the during procedure of active child states.

Exit. The following actions are performed for exiting from a state. **1.** Perform the **ex** action of the state. **2.** If there are implicit (resp. absolute time events), reset the tick counter (resp. time counter) of the state to −1. **3.** Exit from child states by calling appropriate exit procedures. **4.** Set the activity variable of the parent state to the empty string.

Example. We give an example illustrating the order of steps. Suppose a state A has entry action $x = 1$ and exit action $x = 0$, and two child AND-states $A1$ and $A2$. It also has implicit events. Then the entry procedure is:

```
Chart_st := "A"; A_tick := 0; x := 1; @entry_A1; @entry_A2
```

and the exit procedure is:

```
@exit_A2; @exit_A1; x := 0; A_tick := -1; Chart_st := ""
```

4.3 Transitions and Junctions

We now consider the translation for transitions, junctions, and early return. As discussed in Sect. 3, traversal through junctions follows a depth-first-search: at the starting state and each intermediate junction, test each of the transitions in order and with backtracking, stopping when another state is reached. From this point of view, it is natural to assign a procedure for each junction. However, there are further complications: during the traversal, the ensuing behavior is influenced by the state we started from, as well as the list of accumulated transition actions. This difficulty is addressed in [6] using the concept of continuations. We follow similar ideas in our work.

We maintain a dictionary whose keys are triples consisting of the current junction, starting state, and list of accumulated transition actions, and values are names of corresponding HCSP procedures. During the translation process, whenever a new combination of junction, starting state, transition actions is encountered, a new entry is created in the dictionary with a fresh procedure name, and the corresponding procedure is generated. Note that this works only if there are no junction loops that contain transition actions (so the example in Fig. 1 must be excluded).

The content of the junction procedures are as follows: **1.** If an ending state is reached, carry out the transition by first exiting from the source states, execute the transition actions with detection of early return, and finally entering the target states. **2.** Otherwise, initialize a variable $\langle name \rangle$_done to zero. **3.** As long as $\langle name \rangle$_done is zero, perform each of the outgoing transitions, with detection of early return on the condition action. New procedures are created for the situation after transition if necessary. Then assign $\langle name \rangle$_done to the return value of the call. **4.** Set return value _ret to the value of $\langle name \rangle$_done at the end.

4.4 Events

Raising events are performed by first pushing the name of the event onto the stack EL, call the procedure for executing either the full chart or the state the event is directed to, and finally popping the stack EL. Care need to be taken to test for early return conditions.

For example, suppose the chart consists of simple OR-states A and B, with a transition from A to B having label $\{E; x = 1\}/\{y = 1\}$. This will be translated to the following HCSP code:

```
EL := push(EL,"E"); @during_Chart; EL := pop(EL);
Chart_st == "A" -> x := 1; @exit_A; y := 1; @entry_B
```

4.5 Order of Execution of Charts

When there are multiple Stateflow charts in the model, a subtle question arises as to the order of execution between these charts. Different orders of execution can result in different behavior due to sharing and transmission of data between charts. We implement the following order of execution which works in all our examples (although the "official" semantics remains to be clarified): if chart B receives data or messages from chart A, then B is executed after A. Otherwise, follow the alphabetical order according to the name of charts. The correct order is ensured in the HCSP program using a *control process*, which sends starting and ending signals to processes for each chart in the above order, using the communication commands in HCSP.

4.6 Translation of Continuous Evolution

Specifying continuous evolution within *during* actions of states (Sect. 3.9) allows one to model mix of discrete and continuous behaviors. Most works on formal semantics and translation of Stateflow consider only its discrete aspects [6,7,19]. C2E2 [4,5] handles continuous evolution in Stateflow, but not its more complex discrete features. In this work, we handle both aspects of Stateflow at the same time, making use of the ODE with boundary construct in HCSP.

For each state with continuous evolution, we first collect all ODEs (specified as du action of the state and its ancestors) as $\dot{x} = e$. Next, we collect all conditions on transitions out of the state or its ancestors, and let B be the disjunction of all these conditions. Then, at the end of iteration, we add a command stating that if the state is active (and no descendent state containing ODEs is active), then the continuous evolution $\langle \dot{x} = e \& B \rangle$ is executed, so that evolution follows $\dot{x} = e$ until one of the outgoing transitions from the state can possibly be carried out.

5 Code Optimization

In this section, we present the code optimization process for HCSP. We perform four kinds of code optimization: inlining of procedures, peephole optimization, constant propagation, and dead code elimination. These are among the most standard code optimization steps performed by compilers, and are presented, for example, in [2,18] for ordinary programming languages. However, as far as we know this is the first time the process is presented for HCSP.

5.1 Inlining of Procedures

During the translation process, we are free with the creation of procedures. For example, three procedures are created for entry, during and exit of each state, and one procedure is created for each possible combination of junction, initial state, and list of accumulated transition actions. This allows a simple description of the translation, but makes the resulting code difficult to follow. This is addressed by *inlining*, where calls to a procedure is replaced by its body. Not all procedures can be inlined – the obstacle coming from recursive definitions that are results of broadcast events and junction loops. For the remaining cases, heuristics are needed to avoid blowing up the size of the code. For our purpose, we use the heuristic that a procedure will be inlined if it does not have recursive calls, and is either called at most once, or consists of at most two commands. Note as the ensuing simplifications reduce the size of some procedures, more procedures can be inlined following this rule.

5.2   Peephole Optimization

Peephole optimization concerns optimizations that can be performed locally, without analyzing the context in which the code appears. In our case, we perform the following peephole optimizations:

1. Remove appearances of skip within a sequence of commands.
2. Evaluate constant expressions (for example, $3 < 5$ to true).
3. If the guard in a condition command is true (resp. false), remove the guard (resp. the entire command).
4. Likewise, if the guard in an if-then-else command is constant true (resp. false), take the if branch (resp. the else branch).

For example, the command

```
if 0 = 1 then x := x + 1 else skip; y := y + 1
```

is simplified to y := y + 1, using the above rules 2, 4, and 1 in sequence.

The use of peephole optimizations mean that we do not need to consider special cases (such as transitions without condition action) to generate concise code. Such cases (which results in a condition command with guard true) will be simplified at this stage. Peephole optimization is also effective when combined with the following two steps.

5.3   Constant Propagation

Constant propagation consists in replacing variables appearing in commands with constants, when it can be shown that it is the only assignment to the variable that can reach the command. For example, in the following code fragment, which may result from translating a chart where the only child state of A is $A1$:

```
A_st := "A1"; A_st == "A1" -> P
```

Constant propagation will change the condition A_st == "A1" into "A1" == "A1", which is then simplified to true, so the guard can be eliminated altogether, resulting in simplified code A_st := "A1"; P.

Implementation of constant propagation requires building the control flow graph of an HCSP program, then computing the *reaching definitions*, which records for each atomic command and test in conditional statement, what are the assignments that can potentially reach it. Such computations are standard [18]. In the context of HCSP, we need to be careful that in addition to regular assignments, variables can also be modified by input communication, ODEs, external choice and interrupt. We also assume that any variable may be assigned during procedure calls (that is, no interprocedural analysis is implemented).

5.4 Dead Code Elimination

Dead code elimination concerns elimination of code whose execution will not have any effect. In particular, this includes assignments to variables that will never be read. In the previous example, after simplifying the program to A_st := "A"; P, if there is no more reference to A_st in the ensuing code (more precisely, before another assignment to A_st), then the assignment can be removed altogether, simplifying the code to P.

Dead code elimination requires performing *live variable analysis*, which computes for each position in the code, which variables are potentially read after this position. Again, this is a standard computation by backward propagation from locations where variables are read. Then, any assignment whose assigned variable will certainly not be read can be removed. Note that unlike constant propagation, we cannot remove input communications, ODEs and interrupts in this way, as they have effect that is observable from outside the process.

6 Evaluation

We implemented the translation and code optimization procedure in Python, as part of the MARS toolchain[1]. As input to the procedure, we use XML files exported by Matlab/Simulink. This is a structured textual representation of the graphical Stateflow model. The representation already includes information about ordering between transitions from a state/junction, as well as ordering of execution for AND-states. The implementation is based on the existing work of [26], sharing the method of reading XML files, as well as the infrastructure of building HCSP programs. However, the translation procedure is completely redone, and the code optimization process is new.

6.1 Benchmarks

When designing translating procedures from a language as complex as Stateflow, it is important to validate the process by testing it on a large variety of test cases, comparing the execution results in Stateflow with the result of executing the translated HCSP program. For this purpose, we hand-designed a set of benchmark examples, covering various aspects of the semantics that we described in Sect. 3. The benchmarks are listed in Table 2. They are divided into

---

[1] Source code and examples available at https://gitee.com/bhzhan/mars.

Table 2. Description of benchmark examples. N_{raw} is the average size of HCSP program before code optimization. N_{simp} is the average size after code optimization, with ratio $(N_{raw} - N_{simp})/N_{raw}$ in brackets.

Name	#Tests	Description	N_{raw}	N_{simp}
States	8	*Entry, during, exit* action of states; order of entry and exit for hierarchical states; history junctions; OR-states and AND-states; self loops	150	67 (55%)
Transitions	8	Inter-level transitions; outer and inner transitions, ordering between transitions; condition and transition actions	149	61 (59%)
Junctions	8	Branches and loops in junctions; effect of location of junctions; backtracking; condition and transition actions with junctions	209	59 (72%)
EarlyReturn	20	Early return logic, including those for entry and exit action, condition and transition actions. Early return logic in the presence of junctions	174	81 (53%)
Events	12	Broadcast and directed events; nested events; implementing recursion using events; combination of directed event with early return	259	121 (53%)
Temporal	8	Implicit and absolute time events; waiting for a random amount of time; *after*, *before*, and *at*. Reset of counter by transitions	111	68 (39%)
Messages	8	Sending and processing of messages: expiration, queuing, and skipping of messages	184	86 (53%)
Functions	10	Matlab functions and graphical functions: functions with multiple inputs and outputs; arrays; conditionals; graphical functions with loops	114	47 (59%)
Data	12	Communication between charts; data store memory; order of execution between charts	180	94 (48%)
Continuous	6	Continuous evolution following ODEs; combination with multiple outer transitions and hierarchical states	158	92 (42%)
Total	100		173	80 (54%)

several groups, according to the aspect of semantics they are intended to test. The table contains a detailed description of each group, showing the variety of cases that are tested. Moreover, the table shows size of HCSP program generated (in number of commands) before and after code optimization. Overall, we see that code optimization is fairly effectively, reducing average code size by more than half.

We briefly describe the validation process. In the Stateflow examples, we insert print commands that output messages to the console at certain steps, as well as show values of variables. These are translated to `log` commands in the HCSP program. By placing print commands at locations of interest and observing the output on the two sides, we can compare the behavior of models before and after translation, including fine details about the order of execution of steps. This allows us to automatically validate the translation on all benchmark examples.

6.2 Case Studies

In addition to the benchmarks, we also tested the translation on larger case studies from existing work. This includes the stop watch example from [6,7]. A more complex case study comes from [14], which models the Real-Time Publish and Subscribe Protocol (RTPS) using Stateflow. The model contains many of the advanced features described in Sect. 3, including junctions, directed events, temporal events, functions and graphical functions, probabilistic choice, communication between charts, and so on. Several of these features are not supported in the translation described in [26], so it cannot process this model. Using the translation procedure described in this paper, we are able to successfully translate the model, and the result of simulation of the resulting HCSP program agrees with that using Simulink (all messages are successfully sent after interaction between the sender and receiver using heartbeats, acknacks, and resends).

7   Related Work

There is a long series of work on formal semantics, translation, and verification of Stateflow and similar hierarchical modeling languages. The precursor to Stateflow is Statecharts, introduced by Harel in [8]. Formal semantics of Statecharts is studied in detail in [9,12]. A version of the semantics, in terms of hierarchical automata, is formalized by Helke et al. in Isabelle/HOL [10].

The semantics of Stateflow, however, is significantly different from that of Statecharts. In particular, the former is deterministic while the latter is highly nondeterministic. Tiwari et al. [20] presented a translation of Stateflow models to communicating pushdown automata, using the stack to record event broadcasts. Hamon and Rushby proposed an operational semantics for Stateflow in [7], and Hamon followed it by introducing a denotational semantics [6]. The denotational semantics is more complete, supporting inter-level transitions in full, as well as directed events. It also makes key use of continuations to deal with transition actions, and we follow a similar technique in Sect. 4.3.

Scaife et al. introduced a "safe" subset of Simulink/Stateflow and described the translation of this subset into Lustre [19]. This definition of safe subset is intended to correspond to common industrial guidelines, and avoids constructs that could result in semantic ambiguities. Notably, it excludes unbounded event broadcasting. In comparison, our work imposes fewer such limits, in particular unbounded event broadcasting and certain loops in junctions are allowed. Chen et al. [3] proposed a translation from a larger subset of Stateflow into CSP#, allowing verification using the PAT model checker. The work handles broadcasting in full, history junctions, and temporal events. However, it does not consider early return, nor is there any discussion of how functions, data exchange, and messages are handled. Yang et al. [22] proposed a translation of Stateflow to timed automata, covering features such as temporal events and interrupts. The procedure is quite complex, translating a general state into four timed automata, handling respectively the event stack, state actions, condition action, and transition action.

C2E2 [4,5] is a verification tool for hybrid systems, which takes as input Stateflow models, and interprets the ODEs located in the during action of states. However, the tool does not handle the more complex features of Stateflow.

The current work can be seen as an extension the work of Zou et al. [26,27], which proposed translation of Simulink/Stateflow to HCSP, followed by verification using hybrid Hoare logic. Compared to these work, we streamlined the translation process by dividing it into two stages, and made several simplifying changes, including the encoding of state activity and the treatment of event broadcasts. These yields translated results that are easier to understand. In addition, we cover more features of Stateflow, including complete treatment of inter-level transitions and early return, as well as messages, functions, and continuous evolution.

8 Conclusion and Future Works

In this paper, we presented a procedure for translating Stateflow models to the formal language Hybrid CSP. The procedure is distinguished by having two stages. The first stage has a modular design, handling each feature of Stateflow relatively independently. The second stage is a code optimization step for Hybrid CSP, which simplifies some of the verbosity introduced in the first stage. The result is a translation process that covers a large subset of Stateflow, but still easy to understand, as well as yielding concise Hybrid CSP models.

Based on the current work, we intend to explore several future directions:

- First, much improvement can be made to the code optimization process, e.g. by considering interprocedural analysis, to compute which variables may be changed during a procedural call. This would allow us to perform further simplifications by analyzing what could not change during event handling or other procedure calls. Along similar lines, we will also consider allowing parameters and return values for procedures, which could lead to more natural translation results as well as more powerful optimizations.
- For some of the simpler examples, the translation result does not contain arrays or procedure definitions. Hence they can be verified using hybrid Hoare logic, although it still requires substantial effort to verify programs of moderate length. For other examples, the result of translation contains newer elements in Hybrid CSP, including records and procedure definitions, which

is not supported in the current version of hybrid Hoare logic. In the future, we intend to further reduce the effort of proofs using hybrid Hoare logic, as well as extending it to handle the newer elements.
- While we have thoroughly validated the translation procedure using benchmark examples, it is still possible that errors remain in the description of the procedure or its implementation. Much stronger confidence in the correctness of translation can be obtained by formalizing the semantics of Stateflow in a proof assistant such as Coq or Isabelle, and then verifying the correctness of translation by proving that the behavior of the model before and after translation always agree according to the semantics on the two sides.

Acknowledgement. This work was partially supported by the National Natural Science Foundation of China under Grant Nos. 61972385, 62032024, and the Chinese Academy of Sciences Pioneer 100 Talents Program under Grant No. Y9RC585036.

References

1. Ahmad, E., Dong, Y., Larson, B.R., Lü, J., Tang, T., Zhan, N.: Behavior modeling and verification of movement authority scenario of Chinese train control system using AADL. Sci. China Inf. Sci. **58**(11), 1–20 (2015)
2. Aho, A.V., Sethi, R., Ullman, J.D.: Compilers: Principles, Techniques, and Tools. Addison-Wesley Series in Computer Science. World Student Series Edition. Addison-Wesley, Boston (1986)
3. Chen, C., Sun, J., Liu, Y., Dong, J.S., Zheng, M.: Formal modeling and validation of stateflow diagrams. Int. J. Softw. Tools Technol. Transf. **14**(6), 653–671 (2012)
4. Duggirala, P.S., Mitra, S., Viswanathan, M., Potok, M.: C2E2: a verification tool for stateflow models. In: Baier, C., Tinelli, C. (eds.) TACAS 2015. LNCS, vol. 9035, pp. 68–82. Springer, Heidelberg (2015). https://doi.org/10.1007/978-3-662-46681-0_5
5. Fan, C., Qi, B., Mitra, S., Viswanathan, M., Duggirala, P.S.: Automatic reachability analysis for nonlinear hybrid models with C2E2. In: Chaudhuri, S., Farzan, A. (eds.) CAV 2016. LNCS, vol. 9779, pp. 531–538. Springer, Cham (2016). https://doi.org/10.1007/978-3-319-41528-4_29
6. Hamon, G.: A denotational semantics for stateflow. In: Proceedings of the 5th ACM International Conference on Embedded Software EMSOFT 2005, Jersey City, NJ, USA, 18–22 September 2005, pp. 164–172 (2005)
7. Hamon, G., Rushby, J.M.: An operational semantics for stateflow. Int. J. Softw. Tools Technol. Transf. **9**(5–6), 447–456 (2007)
8. Harel, D.: Statecharts: a visual formalism for complex systems. Sci. Comput. Program. **8**(3), 231–274 (1987)
9. Harel, D., Naamad, A.: The STATEMATE semantics of statecharts. ACM Trans. Softw. Eng. Methodol. **5**(4), 293–333 (1996)
10. Helke, S., Kammüller, F.: Formalizing statecharts using hierarchical automata. Archive of Formal Proofs 2010 (2010)
11. Hoare, C.A.R.: Communicating Sequential Processes. Prentice-Hall, Hoboken (1985)
12. Hooman, J., Ramesh, S., de Roever, W.P.: A compositional axiomatization of statecharts. Theor. Comput. Sci. **101**(2), 289–335 (1992)

13. Jifeng, H.: From CSP to Hybrid Systems, pp. 171–189. Prentice Hall International (UK) Ltd., Great Britain (1994)
14. Lin, Q., Wang, S., Zhan, B., Gu, B.: Modelling and verification of real-time publish and subscribe protocol using Uppaal and Simulink/Stateflow. J. Comput. Sci. Technol. **35**(6), 1324–1342 (2020)
15. Liu, J., et al.: A calculus for hybrid CSP. In: Ueda, K. (ed.) APLAS 2010. LNCS, vol. 6461, pp. 1–15. Springer, Heidelberg (2010). https://doi.org/10.1007/978-3-642-17164-2_1
16. MathWorks: Simulink® User's Guide (2018). http://www.mathworks.com/help/pdf_doc/simulink/sl_using.pdf
17. MathWorks: Stateflow® User's Guide (2018). http://www.mathworks.com/help/pdf_doc/stateflow/sf_ug.pdf
18. Nielson, F., Nielson, H.R., Hankin, C.: Principles of Program Analysis. Springer, Heidelberg (1999). https://doi.org/10.1007/978-3-662-03811-6
19. Scaife, N., Sofronis, C., Caspi, P., Tripakis, S., Maraninchi, F.: Defining and translating a "safe" subset of Simulink/Stateflow into Lustre. In: Proceedings of the Fourth ACM International Conference on Embedded Software, EMSOFT 2004, Pisa, Italy, 27–29 September 2004, pp. 259–268 (2004)
20. Tiwari, A., Shankar, N., Rushby, J.M.: Invisible formal methods for embedded control systems. Proc. IEEE **91**(1), 29–39 (2003)
21. Wang, S., Zhan, N., Zou, L.: An improved HHL prover: an interactive theorem prover for hybrid systems. In: Butler, M., Conchon, S., Zaïdi, F. (eds.) ICFEM 2015. LNCS, vol. 9407, pp. 382–399. Springer, Cham (2015). https://doi.org/10.1007/978-3-319-25423-4_25
22. Yang, Y., Jiang, Y., Gu, M., Sun, J.: Verifying simulink stateflow model: timed automata approach. In: Proceedings of the 31st IEEE/ACM International Conference on Automated Software Engineering, ASE 2016, Singapore, 3–7 September 2016, pp. 852–857 (2016)
23. Zhan, N., Wang, S., Zhao, H. (eds.): Formal Verification of Simulink/Stateflow Diagrams, A Deductive Approach. Springer, Cham (2017). https://doi.org/10.1007/978-3-319-47016-0
24. Zhao, H., Yang, M., Zhan, N., Gu, B., Zou, L., Chen, Y.: Formal verification of a descent guidance control program of a lunar lander. In: Jones, C., Pihlajasaari, P., Sun, J. (eds.) FM 2014. LNCS, vol. 8442, pp. 733–748. Springer, Cham (2014). https://doi.org/10.1007/978-3-319-06410-9_49
25. Chaochen, Z., Ji, W., Ravn, A.P.: A formal description of hybrid systems. In: Alur, R., Henzinger, T.A., Sontag, E.D. (eds.) HS 1995. LNCS, vol. 1066, pp. 511–530. Springer, Heidelberg (1996). https://doi.org/10.1007/BFb0020972
26. Zou, L., Zhan, N., Wang, S., Fränzle, M.: Formal verification of simulink/stateflow diagrams. In: Finkbeiner, B., Pu, G., Zhang, L. (eds.) ATVA 2015. LNCS, vol. 9364, pp. 464–481. Springer, Cham (2015). https://doi.org/10.1007/978-3-319-24953-7_33
27. Zou, L., Zhan, N., Wang, S., Fränzle, M., Qin, S.: Verifying simulink diagrams via a hybrid hoare logic prover. In: Proceedings of the International Conference on Embedded Software, EMSOFT 2013, Montreal, QC, Canada, 29 September–4 October 2013, pp. 9:1–9:10 (2013)

DeepGlobal: A Global Robustness Verifiable FNN Framework

Weidi Sun, Yuteng Lu, Xiyue Zhang, and Meng Sun[(✉)]

School of Mathematical Sciences, Peking University, Beijing, China
{weidisun,luyuteng,zhangxiyue,sunm}@pku.edu.cn

Abstract. Feed forward neural networks (FNNs) have been deployed in a variety of domains, though achieving great success, also pose severe safety and reliability concerns. Existing adversarial attack generation and automatic verification techniques cannot formally verify a network globally, i.e., finding all adversarial dangerous regions (ADRs) of a network is out of their reach. To address this problem, we develop a global robustness verifiable FNN framework DeepGlobal with three components: 1) a rule-generator finding all potential boundaries of a network by logical reasoning; 2) a new network architecture *Sliding Door Network (SDN)* enabling rule generation in a feasible way; 3) a selection approach which selects real boundaries from the generated potential boundaries. The ADRs can be further represented by the identified real boundaries. We demonstrate the effectiveness of our approach on both synthetic and real datasets.

Keywords: Feed forward neural networks · Robustness · Global verification

1 Introduction

Feed forward neural networks (FNNs) have been applied to a variety of domains and achieved great success. Reliance on FNNs' decisions in safety-critical applications makes their behaviour correctness of high importance. Recent researches have shown that the correctness of FNNs is threatened by their susceptibility to human-imperceptible adversarial perturbations [1,6,21].

To explore FNNs' robustness, existing research attempts mainly fall into three categories: *crafting adversarial examples, automatic verification,* and *prediction explanation.* Given an input sample, adversarial example generation techniques [2,9,15,20,22] cannot guarantee that no adversarial example exists around the given input, when they fail to generate adversarial examples. *Automatic verification* mainly focuses on the guarantee of local robustness [4,8,14,18,23], i.e., the robustness of a single input's neighbourhood. These verification approaches can provide a rigorous local robustness proof that adversarial examples do not exist in a local region. However, the local robustness only takes a small part of the input space into account, and thus cannot guarantee the robustness of the

© Springer Nature Switzerland AG 2021
S. Qin et al. (Eds.): SETTA 2021, LNCS 13071, pp. 22–39, 2021.
https://doi.org/10.1007/978-3-030-91265-9_2

whole network for every possible input. Along with the *automatic verification* thread of local robustness, the technique developed in [19] goes a step further. It evaluates the local robustness of each sample in a test dataset and treats the expected value of evaluation results as the indicator of "global robustness". The technique in [19] can be considered as finding expected maximum safe radius over the test dataset. However, the selection of the test dataset would directly influence the estimation of global robustness. The efforts in *prediction explanation* related to our work focus on attributing predictions to input features. They are based on reachable set computation [24], back-propagating the prediction score [10], computing local linear approximations [17] or cooperative game theory [13]. The closest work to ours, focuses on inferring input-output properties of neural networks [7]. Nevertheless, these techniques cannot provide a comprehensive and formal analysis for the whole input space. We can easily identify two stumbling blocks on the path of FNNs' global verification: the *complex activation patterns*[1] and the *large input space*. It is computationally unacceptable to analyse all possible activation patterns or traverse input space to provide evidence for FNNs' dependable operation.

In this paper, we develop a global robustness verifiable FNN framework named DeepGlobal which can perform in the role of FNNs and explicitly present the decision boundaries. With the help of these boundaries, we can warn the machine learning engineers of all DeepGlobal's adversarial dangerous regions (ADRs, i.e., the input regions consisting of inputs which are susceptible to small adversarial perturbations). DeepGlobal consists of three components:

- a rule generator which is used for mapping classification rules from output to input to find potential boundaries;
- a new network design *Sliding Door Network (SDN)* that enables feasible rule-generation
- a selection approach which selects real boundaries from the generated potential boundaries.

Real boundaries are the decision boundaries of classification which divide the inputs into different classes. The ADRs can be represented as the neighbourhood of real boundaries, since adversarial examples only appear around these boundaries.

Particularly, we address the "two stumbling blocks" by means of the following methods, respectively. Firstly, we design a new activation function *Sliding Door Activation (SDA)*, with which the number of possible activation patterns is dramatically reduced to circumvent the complexity issue. Secondly, instead of treating inputs as the basis of robustness analysis like existing works, we cluster the input space into multiple regions to address the input space explosion challenge. To the best of our knowledge, this is the first work that can verify global robustness formally. We evaluate the effectiveness of our framework on the MNIST [12] and Fashion-MNIST [16] datasets. We also design a synthetic case study to show the feasibility of our global verification method.

---

[1] Activation pattern is the state about which neurons are activated during the execution of a FNN.

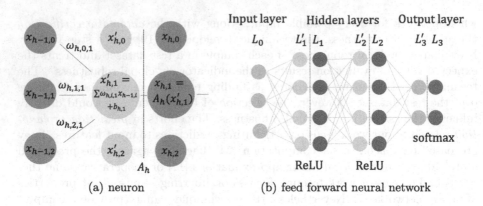

Fig. 1. Architectures of neuron and a FNN.

The rest of this paper is structured as follows. We firstly provide the background of FNNs and ADRs in Sect. 2. Secondly, we introduce the naive rule-generation method in Sect. 3. The SDN network design and the corresponding rule-generator are elaborated in Sect. 4. Section 5 then presents the selection approach for SDN's rule-generation result. We demonstrate SDNs' effectiveness in reducing rule-generation cost and the feasibility of global verification in Sect. 6. Finally, we conclude our paper and present the possible future work in Sect. 7.

2   Background

2.1   Feed Forward Neural Networks

A FNN consists of an input layer, some hidden layers, and an output layer. Each layer is composed of neurons and these neurons connect the adjacent layers by weighted edges. In this paper, each neuron (layer) is treated as two virtual neurons (layers): pre-activation and activation neuron (layer), denoted by $x'_{h,i}$ (L'_h) and $x_{h,i}$ (L_h), respectively. An example is shown in Fig. 1. In Fig. 1(a), the activation neurons in $Layer_h$ are $x_{h,0}, x_{h,1}, x_{h,2}$ and the pre-activation neurons are $x'_{h,0}, x'_{h,1}, x'_{h,2}$. In Fig. 1(b), the activation layers are L_1, L_2, L_3 and the pre-activation ones are L'_1, L'_2, L'_3. The formal definition of FNN is shown as follows:

Definition 1 (Feed Forward Neural Networks). *A FNN can be defined as a quaternion (L, L', W, A) where*

- $L = \{L_h \mid h \in \{0, ..., N\}\}$ *is the set of layers in which L_0 is the input layer, $L_h s$ $(0 < h < N)$ are the activation hidden layers, and L_N is the activation output layer. The neurons in these layers are represented as $x_{h,i}$, which means the i-th neuron in L_h.*
- $L' = \{L'_h \mid h \in \{1, ..., N-1\}\}$ *is the set of pre-activation layers. The neurons in these layers are represented as $x'_{h,i}$, which means the i-th neuron in L'_h.*

- $W = \{(W_h, B_h) \mid h \in \{1, ..., N\}\}$ *include matrices of weights W_hs and bias arrays B_hs. Each W_h represents the matrix that consists of the weights $\omega_{h,i,j}$s connecting the neurons $x_{h-1,i}$ in L_{h-1} and $x'_{h,j}$ in L'_h. Each B_h represents the biases of L'_h, and the i-th element of B_h is denoted by $b_{h,i}$.*
- $A = \{A_h \mid h \in \{1, ..., N\}\}$ *is a set of activation functions $A_h : L'_h \to L_h$ such as ReLU or softmax.*

The forward-propagation can be defined as a function whose input x is a vector:
$$F(x) = A_N(W_N A_{N-1}(...A_1(W_1 x + B_1)...) + B_N)$$

There is an ideal classification function $f : X \to C$ for every classification task, where X and C are used to represent the input set and class set, respectively. This function f maps every input to the correct class, and $F(x)$ is trained to approximate f.

2.2 Adversarial Dangerous Regions

FNNs have been deployed to a range of safety-critical applications which makes their robustness of high importance. A robust FNN F must satisfy the *smoothness* assumption [5], i.e., for any input x, and a small perturbation δ, $F(x+\delta) \approx F(x)$. This assumption is in line with the actual human visual capabilities. For humans, if A looks similar to B, A and B should belong to the same class.

However, FNNs are susceptible to adversarial perturbations, in other words, not robust. To introduce FNNs' susceptibility more intuitively, we provide Fig. 2 which shows a binary classification task where the inputs in orange regions C_1 are classified as "0" and the inputs in blue region C_2 are classified as "9". As shown in Fig. 2, I_1, I_2, I_3, I_4 are four inputs, and the black line between C_1 and C_2 is FNN's boundary. The input I_3 near the boundary is correctly classified as "9" by the FNN. We slightly perturb I_3 by $I_4 - I_3$. Though the result I_4 looks like I_3, I_4 is wrongly classified as "0". If we limit the size of perturbation δ to $||\delta||_2 \leq \varepsilon$,

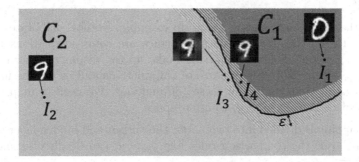

Fig. 2. A binary classification task where the inputs in orange regions C_1 are classified as "0" and the inputs in blue region C_2 are classified as "9". I_is $(0 < i < 5)$ are the inputs. (Color figure online)

all inputs belonging to the shadow region in Fig. 2 are susceptible to adversarial perturbations. Since the shadow region is the boundary's neighborhood and the neighborhood radius is ε. ADRs can be defined as $\{x|\|x-y\|_k < \epsilon, y \in B\}$ where $k \geq 1$, ϵ is the given dangerous distance and B is the set of inputs in real boundaries. In this paper, we focus on finding all the boundaries, so as to find all ADRs.

3   Naive Rule-Generation

FNNs compare the output values to classify the inputs, e.g., if a output value y_k is bigger than other outputs $\bigwedge_{j\neq k} y_k > y_j$, the corresponding input belongs to class k. It is natural to use some inequations like $y_k > y_j$ to divide the input space into several regions, so as to address the input space explosion challenge. These inequations named classification rules in the input space could be achieved by the rule-generation method, as elaborated below. Before introducing the classification rules in detail, we first present a warm up example.

Example 1. Considering the one-layer network in Fig. 3(a), a classification rule in the output space is $(y_0 > y_1)$ which represents a blue region in output space shown as Fig. 3(b). The rule-generation method we proposed aims for mapping classification rules to the input space. For example, the activation pattern "all neurons are active" means that $(y_0 = y'_0 \wedge y_1 = y'_1 \wedge y'_0 > 0 \wedge y'_1 > 0)$. As $(y'_0 = x_1 \wedge y'_1 = x_0)$, $(y_0 > y_1)$ and $(y'_0 > 0 \wedge y'_1 > 0)$ are equivalent to $(x_1 > x_0)$ and $(x_1 > 0 \wedge x_0 > 0)$, respectively. Thus $(y_0 > y_1)$'s mapping result under this activation pattern is $(x_0 > 0 \wedge x_1 > 0 \wedge x_1 > x_0)$. If we change the activation pattern to "y_0 is active and y_1 is inactive", the equivalent condition of this activation pattern is $(y_0 = y'_0 \wedge y_1 = 0 \wedge y'_0 > 0 \wedge y'_1 < 0)$, because ReLU assigns 0 to y_1. Thus $(y'_0 > 0 \wedge y'_1 < 0)$ is equivalent to $(x_1 > 0 \wedge x_0 < 0)$; $(y_0 > y_1)$ is equivalent to $(x_1 > 0)$; the mapping result is $(x_0 < 0 \wedge x_1 > 0)$. Obviously, the activation pattern determines the mapping result. The mapping result $(x_0 > 0 \wedge x_1 > 0 \wedge x_1 > x_0)$ represents a blue region in input space shown in Fig. 3(c).

With the intuition from the warm up example, we now elaborate the rule-generation for FNNs. The classification rules are some inequations recorded as $P_{h,\gamma,\eta}$ in $Layer_h$. These inequations make up the disjunctive normal form[2] $\bigvee_\gamma \bigwedge_\eta P_{h,\gamma,\eta}$ where γs are the indexes of conjunctions and ηs are the indexes of propositions, i.e., inequations in these conjunctions. We need to map the rules in output space like $\bigwedge_{j\neq k} y_k > y_j$ to input space.

The mapping is divided into two parts: the output and hidden layer part. For the output layer, the comparison rules like $y_k > y_j$ can be directly mapped to

---

[2] In boolean logic, a disjunctive normal form (DNF) is a canonical normal form of a logical formula consisting of a disjunction of conjunctions; it can also be described as an OR of ANDs. For example, $(A \wedge B) \vee C$ (A, B, C are three propositions) is a DNF meaning (A and B) or C.

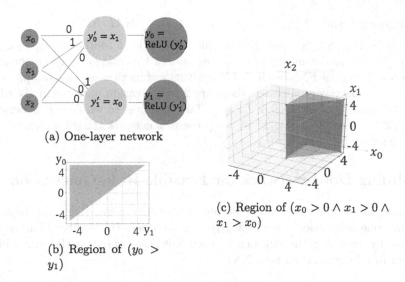

(a) One-layer network

(b) Region of ($y_0 > y_1$)

(c) Region of ($x_0 > 0 \wedge x_1 > 0 \wedge x_1 > x_0$)

Fig. 3. The one-layer network and regions of classification rules. (Color figure online)

the corresponding pre-activation layer based on the order-preserving activation function. Taking softmax as an example, $y_j = softmax(\sum_i \omega_{N,i,j} x_{N-1,i} + b_{N,j})$ and $y_k = softmax(\sum_i \omega_{N,i,k} x_{N-1,i} + b_{N,k})$ lead to a result:

$$y_k > y_j \Leftrightarrow (\sum_i \omega_{N,i,k} x_{N-1,i} + b_{N,k} > \sum_i \omega_{N,i,j} x_{N-1,i} + b_{N,j})$$

Thus, we replace every variable y_j in inequations with the corresponding polynomial $\sum_i \omega_{N,i,j} x_{N-1,i} + b_{N,j}$ to obtain the classification rules in $Layer_{N-1}$. Generally, the derived rules for the output layer can be formalized by the following function

$$MAP\text{-}OUT(y_k > y_j) = (\sum_i \omega_{N,i,k} x_{N-1,i} + b_{N,k} > \sum_i \omega_{N,i,j} x_{N-1,i} + b_{N,j})$$

and the mapping result of $\bigwedge_{j(j \neq k)} y_k > y_j$ is $\bigwedge_{j(j \neq k)} MAP\text{-}OUT(y_k > y_j)$, i.e., the classification rules in $Layer_{N-1}$. The mapping function for the hidden layer is formalized as $MAP\text{-}HIDDEN$. Hidden layers cannot be processed in the same way as output layer because the activation patterns influence the mapping result as shown in Example 1. We denote the set of active neurons' indexes by Θ and use Θ to represent the activation pattern. For simplicity, we record $P_{h,\gamma,\eta}$ as P_h and the mapping result of P_h under Θ_h as $MAP\text{-}FIX(\Theta_h, P_h)$ where Θ_h is the activation pattern of $Layer_h$. $MAP\text{-}FIX(\Theta_h, P_h)$ is the conjunction of some classification rules in $Layer_{h-1}$. $MAP\text{-}FIX$ works like the rule-generation with fixed activation pattern in Example 1. The function $MAP\text{-}HIDDEN$ is shown as follows where Δ_h denotes all activation patterns of $Layer_h$:

$$MAP\text{-}HIDDEN(\Delta_h, P_h) = \bigvee_{\Theta_h \in \Delta_h} MAP\text{-}FIX(\Theta_h, P_h)$$

The mapping result of $\vee_\gamma \wedge_\eta P_{h,\gamma,\eta}$ is $\vee_\gamma \wedge_\eta \bigvee_{\Theta_h \in \Delta_h} MAP\text{-}FIX(\Theta_h, P_{h,\gamma,\eta})$, i.e., all possible $Layer_{h-1}$'s classification rules which lead to the $\vee_\gamma \wedge_\eta P_{h,\gamma,\eta}$ in $Layer_h$. However, the immense time cost makes the rule-generation infeasible for FNNs. Taking a FNN with ReLU activation function as an example, each neuron has two activation states, there are 2^{m_h} activation patterns in Δ_h where m_h is the number of neurons in $Layer_h$. The time cost of whole rule-generation is $O(\Pi_h 2^{m_h}) = O(2^{\sum_h m_h})$. Thus, we present a network design which enables rule-generation in a feasible way.

4   Sliding Door Network for Feasible Rule-Generation

To handle the complexity issue, we present a network design, SDN, and the corresponding rule-generation method M_{SDN}. SDN reduces the number of activation patterns by grouping the neurons in each layer to overcome the infeasibility problem in rule-generation for FNNs.

4.1   Sliding Door Network

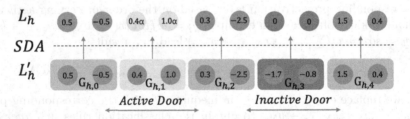

Fig. 4. Sliding door activation. $G_{h,1}$ and $G_{h,3}$ are active door and inactive door respectively and other activation results are the copy of other groups.

Compared with FNNs, SDN has two different components: an activation function SDA and the loss function design for supporting SDA.

Sliding Door Activation. SDA takes a pre-activation layer into account and divides neurons into several groups evenly. The grouping bases on neurons' subscripts, e.g., if we divide the layer L'_h in Fig. 4 with 10 neurons into 5 groups, the adjacent neurons are in the same group and the grouping result is $G_{h,j} = \{x'_{h,i} | 2j \leq i < 2j+2\}$ ($0 \leq j < 5$). Neurons in the same group behave the same way, i.e., they are in the same activation state, so as to relieve the explosion of activation pattern number, which is caused by the combination of neurons' activation states. These groups are classified by SDA into three categories: *active group* with all positive neurons (e.g., $G_{h,1}$ and $G_{h,4}$ in Fig. 4), *inactive group* in which all neurons are negative (e.g., $G_{h,3}$ in Fig. 4), and *trivial groups* with mixing of both positive and negative neurons (i.e., $G_{h,0}$ and $G_{h,2}$ in Fig. 4).

In order to reduce the complexity, SDA selects the first active (inactive) group as *active (inactive) door* for each pre-activation layer. For example in Fig. 4, $G_{h,1}$ and $G_{h,3}$ are active door and inactive door respectively. Based on the assigned doors, we define SDA as:

$$x_{h,i} = SDA(x'_{h,i}) = \begin{cases} 0 & \text{if } x'_{h,i} \text{ belongs to inactive door;} \\ \alpha x'_{h,i} & \text{if } x'_{h,i} \text{ belongs to active door;} \\ x'_{h,i} & \text{otherwise.} \end{cases}$$

To increase the network expressiveness, SDA strengthens the active door by α and assigns 0 to inactive door's neurons. Other groups are sent to the corresponding pre-activation layer directly. During execution, for each pre-activation layer, the position of the two doors might change instantly up to the states of the groups, behaving like a sliding door, thus the name of our activation function. Figure 5 shows the entire network architecture, replacing the ReLU in FNNs with the proposed SDA for each layer.

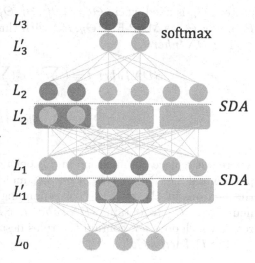

Fig. 5. Architecture of SDN

Loss Function Design. If a pre-activation layer cannot provide *active* or *inactive* door, the expressiveness of SDN will be weakened. To avoid this issue, we design a regularization term to penalize the absence of either of the two doors. If the active (inactive) door does not appear in L'_h, we will find the group $G_{h,\alpha}$ $(G_{h,\beta})$ in L'_h with most active (inactive) neurons, and adjust the weights to make the negative (positive) neurons in $G_{h,\alpha}$ $(G_{h,\beta})$ tend to be positive (negative) so as to create active (inactive) groups. Thus, besides the typical data fitting loss, we add a regularization term to encourage the emergence of such groups, defined as:

$$Loss(W) = \left(\sum_{i=1}^{n}(y_i - \hat{y}_i)^2 + \lambda \sum_h \left(\sum_{x'_{h,i} \in G_{h,\alpha}, x'_{h,i}<0} -x'_{h,i} \right. \right.$$
$$\left. \left. + \sum_{x'_{h,i} \in G_{h,\beta}, x'_{h,i}>0} x'_{h,i} \right) \right)$$

where W denotes all the weights and biases to be trained, and λ is the user-given penalty parameter, $(\sum_{x'_{hb_{i,h-1}i} \in G_{h,\alpha}, x'_{h,i}<0} -x'_{h,i})$ forces $G_{h,\alpha}$ to become an active door and $(\sum_{x'_{h,i} \in G_{h,\beta}, x'_{h,i}>0} x'_{h,i})$ forces $G_{h,\beta}$ to become an inactive door.

4.2   Rule-Generation for SDN

As there is no difference between FNNs' and SDNs' output layer activation functions, *MAP-OUT* can be reused for the rule-generation of SDN's output layer. Thus, we focus on mapping between hidden layers in this section. The construction process of *MAP-HIDDEN* for SDN is as follows.

We denote the set of neurons in the active door of layer L'_h as Θ_h^A, the set of neurons in the inactive door as Θ_h^I, and other neurons are in Θ_h^T. Considering the condition that a rule in L_h is $P_h = \sum_i c_i x_{h,i} + b > 0$, and the activation pattern Θ_h is fixed where $\Theta_h = \{\Theta_h^A, \Theta_h^I, \Theta_h^T\}$, we record the mapping result of P_h under Θ_h as MAP-FIX(Θ_h, P_h) with three components:

1) *SDNInherit*.

$$
SDNInherit = (\sum_{i \in \Theta_h^A} \alpha c_i (\sum_t \omega_{h,t,i} x_{h-1,t} + b_{h,i})
$$

$$
+ \sum_{i \in \Theta_h^T} c_i (\sum_t \omega_{h,t,i} x_{h-1,t} + b_{h,i}) + b > 0)
$$

where we replace the neurons in P_h belonging to Θ_h^A with the corresponding polynomial, i.e., $\sum_t \omega_{h,t,i} x_{h-1,t} + b_{h,i}$ multiplied by α due to SDA activation, the neurons in Θ_h^T with the corresponding polynomial meanwhile remove the neurons in Θ_h^I to obtain *SDNInherit*. *SDNInherit* is P_h's direct mapping result which does not contain the rules describing activation states.

2) *SDNActiveCon*.

$$
SDNActiveCon = \bigwedge_{i \in \Theta_h^A} (\sum_t \omega_{h,t,i} x_{h-1,t} + b_{i,h-1} > 0)
$$

It describes the activation state that "all the corresponding pre-activation neurons of Θ_h^A are greater than 0" and we replace these pre-activation neurons with corresponding polynomial.

3) *SDNInactiveCon*.

$$
SDNInactiveCon = \bigwedge_{i \in \Theta_h^I} (\sum_t -\omega_{h,t,i} x_{h-1,t} - b_{h,i} > 0)
$$

It describes the activation state that "all the corresponding pre-activation neurons in Θ_h^I are less than 0" and we replace these pre-activation neurons with corresponding polynomial. The function *MAP-FIX* can be further represented as follows:

$$
MAP\text{-}FIX(\Theta_h, P_h) = SDNInherit \wedge SDNActiveCon \wedge SDNInactiveCon
$$

Taking all the activation patterns into account, we can obtain the function *MAP-HIDDEN*.

$$
MAP\text{-}HIDDEN(\Delta_h, P_h) = \bigvee_{\Theta_h \in \Delta_h} MAP\text{-}FIX(\Theta_h, P_h)
$$

The combination of *MAP-OUT* and *MAP-HIDDEN* is the complete rule-generation function M_{SDN}:

$$M_{SDN}(\Delta_h, P_h) = \begin{cases} MAP\text{-}OUT(P_h) & h = N \\ MAP\text{-}HIDDEN(\Delta_h, P_h) & h < N \end{cases}$$

Thus the mapping result of all the rules $\vee_\gamma \wedge_\eta P_{h,\gamma,\eta}$ in $Layer_h$ is $\vee_\gamma \wedge_\eta M_{SDN}(\Delta_h, P_{h,\gamma,\eta})$ which is the collection of rules for $Layer_{h-1}$. Each $|\Delta_h|$ equals to $m_h{}^2 + m_h + 1$ where m_h is the number of groups in L'_h.

Compared with the naive rule-generation, the SDN has $O(\Pi_i m_i{}^2)$ activation patterns which is greatly less than the number of FNN's activation patterns $O(2^{\sum_h m_h})$, enabling the classification rules to be generated in a more feasible manner.

5   Selection Approach for Generated Rules

This section is divided into two parts: 1) the pre-processing of generated rules; 2) the real boundaries selection approach.

5.1   Pre-processing of Generated Rules

The generated rules are in the form of $\vee_\gamma \wedge_\eta P_{0,\gamma,\eta}$ where each conjunction form $\wedge_\eta P_{0,\gamma,\eta}$ corresponds to an activation pattern of SDN. We define a strict total order $\prec$ for these conjunction forms, and assign serial numbers to the conjunction forms according to the order.

Definition 2 (Strict total order $\prec$ of conjunction forms). *Given two conjunction forms of rules R_1 and R_2 the corresponding activation patterns are Θ_1 and Θ_2. $Layer_h$ is the bottom layer where Θ_1 is different from Θ_2. $G_{h,i}$ and $G_{h,j}$ are the active doors of Θ_1 and Θ_2 in $Layer_h$ respectively. $G_{h,i'}$ and $G_{h,j'}$ are the inactive doors respectively. If an activation pattern does not have active door (inactive door) in $Layer_h$, the active door (inactive door) will be recorded as $G_{h,num}$ ($G_{h,num'}$) where num (num') is the number of groups in $Layer_h$. $R_1 \prec R_2$ iff $i < j \vee (i = j \wedge i' < j')$.*

As regions and activation patterns are in one-to-one correspondence to conjunction forms, we use the serial numbers to represent regions and activation patterns. In this way, these serial numbers can help us to store the rules in a B+ tree and retrieve the conjunction forms. Specially, the coverage relationship of regions is implied in serial numbers which serves as the basis of the searching scope narrowing strategy in real boundaries selection.

5.2 Real Boundaries Selection Approach

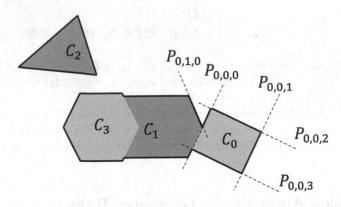

Fig. 6. The regions represented by $\vee_\gamma \wedge_\eta P_{0,\gamma,\eta}(0 \leqslant \gamma \leqslant 3)$

Before presenting the real boundaries selection approach, we need to answer two questions: 1) what is the relation between the rules and the potential boundaries of SDNs; 2) how can we select the real boundaries from the potential boundaries.

• *Question 1: what is the relation between the rules and the potential boundaries of SDNs?*

The classification rules $\vee_\gamma \wedge_\eta P_{0,\gamma,\eta}$ represent some regions in input space as shown in Fig. 6. Each region corresponds to a conjunctive form in DNF, e.g., C_0 corresponds to $\wedge_\eta P_{0,0,\eta}(0 \leqslant \eta \leqslant 3)$. The four inequations $P_{0,0,0}, P_{0,0,1}, P_{0,0,2}, P_{0,0,3}$ are four boundaries of C_0. These boundaries (inequations) are the potential boundaries, namely that

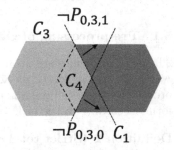

Fig. 7. C_3 is the region formed by conjunction form R_i and $C_4 \cup C_1$ is formed by R_j, the region C_4 satisfying R_j is covered by R_i's region.

the rules are the potential boundaries. However, only some of potential boundaries are real boundaries indicated by solid lines in Fig. 6.

• *Question 2: how can we select the real boundaries from the potential boundaries?*

To answer this question, we should figure out what kind of potential boundaries cannot be real. A potential boundary is not real if it is inside the regions. More specifically, given a region C and its potential boundary P_0, P_0 is not real in two cases:

1. P_0 is covered by C's connected region;
2. P_0 is the common boundary of C and C's connected region.

The first case is caused by the overlapping of regions. The regions represented by conjunction forms may cover each other as shown in Fig. 7 (Fig. 7 is a part of Fig. 6, i.e., $C_1 \cup C_3$ in Fig. 6). C_3 is the region formed by R_i and $C_4 \cup C_1$ is formed by R_j (R_i and R_j are conjunction forms like $\wedge_\eta P_{0,\gamma,\eta}$ in the generated rules $\vee_\gamma \wedge_\eta P_{0,\gamma,\eta}$). The dashed lines are potential boundaries in R_j, however, they are covered by C_3. That is why dashed lines are not real. The second case is shown in Fig. 6. The common boundary of C_0 and C_1 is not real, since it is inside the $C_0 \cup C_1$.

The three steps of real boundary selection are as follows:

1. ***Find the connected regions for every region.*** Both cases for a region's unreal boundaries are caused by its connected regions. Thus, we firstly use simplex method [3] to find the connected regions for every region. To judge whether the regions of R_i and R_j are connected, we apply simplex method to $R_i \wedge R_j{}^3$. If the result of simplex method is nonempty, R_i and R_j are connected. In addition, we narrow the searching scope for this step by Theorem 1. For every R_j, only R_is satisfying the necessary condition in Theorem 1 are possible to be connected to R_j. Thus, we do not need to search all conjunction forms for finding R_j's connected regions which greatly reduces the time cost.
2. ***Remove the covered parts of regions.*** If the covered parts of regions are removed, unreal boundaries in the first case are removed as well. For each R_i, we "flip" the potential boundaries of its connected regions and conjunct these flipped boundaries with R_i to cut the covered parts out of R_i's region. Taking Fig. 7 as an example, we flip the boundaries P_hs of C_3 to get $\neg P_h$s and conjunct each $\neg P_h$ with R_j to form new regions $\neg P_h \wedge R_j$s. Then we abandon the empty new regions and merge the others. Cut by $\neg P_{0,3,0}$ and $\neg P_{0,3,1}$, the merged new region is C_1 which does not include the covered part.
3. ***Remove the common boundaries.*** We realize this step in a similar way like step 2. For example, in Fig. 6, $P_{0,0,0}$ is the common potential boundary of C_0, C_1. If we want to remove the common part to get C_0's real boundary, we flip the boundaries of C_1 and use them to cut the dashed common part out of $P_{0,0,0}$. Then we merge the nonempty segment to get the real boundary. Cut by $P_{0,1,0}$, the solid part of $P_{0,0,0}$ is the selection result and the dashed common part is removed.

Theorem 1. *Given regions C_i and C_j ($j > i$) with activation patterns Θ_i and Θ_j respectively, $Layer_h$ is the bottom layer where Θ_i is different from Θ_j. $G_{h,k}$ and $G_{h,t}$ are the active doors of Θ_i and Θ_j in $Layer_h$ respectively and $G_{h,k'}$ and $G_{h,t'}$ are the inactive doors.*

$$C_i \text{ and } C_j \text{ are connected} \Rightarrow (k \neq t \wedge k' = t') \vee (k = t \wedge k' \neq t')$$

Algorithm 1 is the real boundaries selection approach. We explain Algorithm 1 to show how the selection approach works. The first part (Line 1 to 2) pre-processes the classification rules. With the help of the order in Definition 2,

---

^{3} We replace $>$ in $R_i \wedge R_j$ with $\geq$ to make simplex method feasible.

Algorithm 1. Selection Approach

Require: an SDN N, classification rules $Cons$
Ensure: real boundaries set T
  1: $T \leftarrow Cons$
  2: $T \leftarrow \text{PreProcess}(T)$
  3: **for** $leaf$ in T **do**
  4:     **if** ValidSimplex($leaf$) **then**
  5:         $leaf \leftarrow$ None
  6:     **end if**
  7: **end for**
  8: **for** $leaf$ in T **do**
  9:     **if** $leaf$!= None **then**
 10:         **for** potential connected R in $T[: leaf.index]$ **do**
 11:             $leaf \leftarrow$ RemoveCover($leaf,R$)
 12:             $leaf.connect$.append(R)
 13:         **end for**
 14:     **end if**
 15: **end for**
 16: **for** $leaf$ in T **do**
 17:     **for** R in $leaf.connect$ **do**
 18:         $leaf \leftarrow$ RemoveCommon($leaf,R$)
 19:         $R \leftarrow$ RemoveCommon($R,leaf$)
 20:     **end for**
 21: **end for**
 22: **return** T

---

we assign serial numbers to conjunction forms and store them in a B+ tree T. The second part (Line 3 to 7) eliminates the conjunction forms without feasible region to reduce the time cost. We apply simplex algorithm to R_is. If the result is **None**, the corresponding region of R_i is empty, i.e., R_i is invalid. Then we assign **None** to invalid R_is to eliminate them. The third part (Line 8 to 15) corresponds to step 1 and 2. It finds the connected regions according to step 1 and uses step 2 to remove the covered parts for each valid R_i. The connected regions for each R_i are recorded in this part as well. The fourth part (Line 16 to 21) is step 3 which removes the common boundaries. If R_i shares a common boundary with its connected region, we remove the common part for both of them. Line 22 finally returns the real boundaries.

6   Experiments

The evaluation of our work concentrates on two aspects: 1) the effectiveness of reducing rule-generation cost based on SDNs, 2) the feasibility of global verification. In the first part, we compare our method with the FNNs on *MNIST* and *Fashion-MNIST*. In the second part, we show the effectiveness of global verification.

6.1 Effectiveness of Reducing Rule-Generation Cost

We compare 1) the rule-generation cost of SDNs and FNNs with same capability (evaluated by accuracy on train set); 2) the capability of SDNs and FNNs with same rule-generation cost (evaluated by number of conjunction forms in generated rules). Table 1 and Table 2 are the comparison results on *MNIST* dataset and *Fashion-MNIST* dataset respectively. The details of SDNs are shown as follows:

- Each SDN has two hidden layers $Layer_1$ and $Layer_2$;
- These SDNs have 15, 21, 21, 31 groups in $Layer_1$, respectively and 11, 11, 16, 22 groups in $Layer_2$, respectively. We name these SDNs as (15,11), (21,11), (21,16), and (31,22) based on their architecture features;
- Each group in $Layer_1$ and $Layer_2$ has two neurons.
- The α in these SDNs are 2.

Each FNN has two hidden layers. The structure is represented in a tuple, e.g., (20,20) represents a FNN with 20 neurons in two layers respectively. Cross entropy loss and Adam [11] are used to train all the networks.

The evaluation results in Table 1 show that compared with the FNNs which have roughly the same rule-generation cost, SDNs have greater capability. The accuracy of SDNs on train set are 2.18, 1.99, 2.01, 1.55% higher than FNNs respectively.

Besides, the accuracies of SDNs and the *sat-rate* increase as the numbers of groups in each layer increase.

If the capability of SDNs and FNNs are roughly the same, the rule-generation costs of FNNs are 8374, 17436, 33979, 34124 times as SDNs'. The performance of SDNs is even better on Fashion-MNIST which is more complicated than MNIST. Compared with the

Fig. 8. Adversarial examples are in the first line and the samples in second line are classified correctly

FNNs with roughly the same rule-generation cost, accuracies of SDNs are 11.08, 11.36, 11.30, 1.62% higher respectively. Compared with the FNNs with roughly the same capability, the rule-generation costs of FNNs are 33498, 1115956, 2174684, 2183949 times as SDNs'.

Table 1 and Table 2 show that SDNs greatly reduce the cost of rule-generation which makes the global robustness verification more feasible.

6.2 Feasibility of Global Verification

We show some adversarial examples selected from the ADRs of SDN (21,11) in Fig. 8. To draw an visualized conclusion about whether our method correctly finds all the real boundaries in input space, we visually demonstrate the feasibility of our approach on a two-dimensional synthetic dataset (as conclusion on

Table 1. Evaluation on MNIST where sat-rate is the frequency of layers which can provide both active door and inactive door in evaluation

SDN	Structure	(15,11)	(21,11)	(21,16)	(31,22)
	Accuracy (%)	94.92	95.02	95.28	95.42
	Sat-rate (%)	87.22	90.05	98.32	99.79
	Cost	32053	61579	126399	503451
FNNs (with same cost)	Structure	(8,7)	(10,6)	(10,7)	(10,9)
	Accuracy (%)	92.74	93.03	93.26	93.87
	Cost	32768	65536	131072	524288
FNNs (with same capability)	Structure	(14,14)	(15,15)	(16,16)	(17,17)
	Accuracy (%)	94.69	94.97	95.28	95.42
	Cost	$2.68 * 10^8$	$1.07 * 10^9$	$4.29 * 10^9$	$1.71 * 10^{10}$

Table 2. Evaluation on fashion-MNIST

SDN	Structure	(15,11)	(21,11)	(21,16)	(31,22)
	Accuracy (%)	86.04	86.35	86.42	86.51
	Sat-rate (%)	90.48	92.36	95.13	99.81
	Cost	32053	61579	126399	503451
FNNs (with same cost)	Structure	(8,7)	(10,6)	(10,7)	(10,9)
	Accuracy (%)	74.96	74.99	75.12	84.89
	Cost	32768	65536	131072	524288
FNNs (with same capability)	Structure	(15,15)	(18,18)	(19,19)	(20,20)
	Accuracy (%)	85.97	86.31	86.43	86.51
	Cost	$1.07 * 10^9$	$6.87 * 10^{10}$	$2.74 * 10^{11}$	$1.09 * 10^{12}$

high-dimensional space is hard to be visualized) shown in Fig. 9(a) where the top-right inputs belongs to the first class and others belong to the second class.

We train a SDN with 100 neurons[4] on the synthetic dataset and generate SDN's boundaries. The generation is conducted using a laptop with 1 Intel i7-9750H 2.60 GHz CPU and 1 NVIDIA Rtx 2080Max-Q GPU which takes 193.61 s. The results of the trained SDN are visually shown in Fig. 9(b) where the inputs in the top-right region are classified as the first class and other inputs are classified as the second class.

The potential boundaries found by our method are in Fig. 10(a). These potential boundaries are the boundaries of regions. Some of potential boundaries are real and the others are inside the top right region. The real boundaries selected by our approach are in Fig. 10(b). Given a danger distance, the ADR is shown as the shadow region around real boundaries. The results show that the proposed DeepGlobal framework is effective to identify the real boundaries and the ADRs.

---

[4] Each hidden layer has ten doors and each door has five neurons. The α in this SDN is 2.

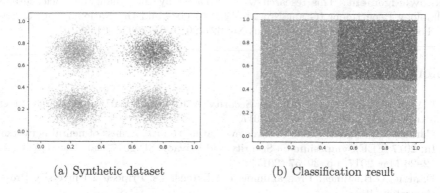

(a) Synthetic dataset   (b) Classification result

Fig. 9. Synthetic dataset and classification result

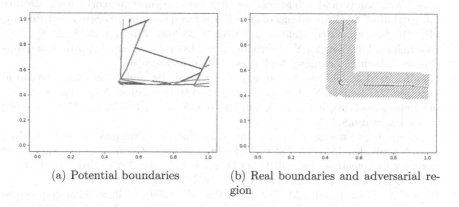

(a) Potential boundaries   (b) Real boundaries and adversarial region

Fig. 10. Potential boundaries, real boundaries, and adversarial region

7   Conclusion

In this paper, we present a global robustness verifiable FNN framework Deep-Global. To the best of our knowledge, this is the first work that provides a complete solution to achieving global robustness verification for neural networks. Based on the rule-generation, we analyse the relationship between activation patterns and classification rules, and design a new network SDN to generate rules in a feasible way. The proposed selection approach further reduces computational complexity and makes the global robustness verification more efficiently. Our evaluation results show that the SDN can greatly reduce the rule-generation cost. Moreover, the global verification can be achieved, which is unattainable by existing techniques. The proposed global verification framework and the SDN network design are particularly useful for safety-critical applications, especially for classification tasks that are eager for rigorous robustness. Developing verifiable framework for large-scale networks is our further research direction.

Acknowledgement. This research was supported by the Guangdong Science and Technology Department (Grant No. 2018B010107004) and the National Natural Science Foundation of China under Grant No. 62172019, 61772038, 61532019.

References

1. Biggio, B., Fumera, G., Roli, F.: Security evaluation of pattern classifiers under attack. CoRR abs/1709.00609 (2017)
2. Carlini, N., Wagner, D.A.: Towards evaluating the robustness of neural networks. In: 2017 IEEE Symposium on Security and Privacy, SP 2017, San Jose, CA, USA, 22–26 May 2017, pp. 39–57 (2017)
3. Dantzig, G.B.: Linear Programming and Extensions. Princeton University Press, Princeton (1998)
4. Gehr, T., Mirman, M., Drachsler-Cohen, D., Tsankov, P., Chaudhuri, S., Vechev, M.T.: AI2: safety and robustness certification of neural networks with abstract interpretation. In: Proceedings of 2018 IEEE Symposium on Security and Privacy, SP 2018, San Francisco, California, USA, 21–23 May 2018, pp. 3–18 (2018)
5. Goodfellow, I.J., Bengio, Y., Courville, A.C.: Deep Learning. Adaptive Computation and Machine Learning. MIT Press, Cambridge (2016)
6. Goodfellow, I.J., Shlens, J., Szegedy, C.: Explaining and harnessing adversarial examples. In: Bengio, Y., LeCun, Y. (eds.) 3rd International Conference on Learning Representations, ICLR 2015, San Diego, CA, USA, 7–9 May 2015. Conference Track Proceedings (2015)
7. Gopinath, D., Converse, H., Pasareanu, C.S., Taly, A.: Property inference for deep neural networks. In: 34th IEEE/ACM International Conference on Automated Software Engineering, ASE 2019, San Diego, CA, USA, 11–15 November 2019, pp. 797–809 (2019). https://doi.org/10.1109/ASE.2019.00079
8. Huang, X., Kwiatkowska, M., Wang, S., Wu, M.: Safety verification of deep neural networks. In: Majumdar, R., Kunčak, V. (eds.) CAV 2017. LNCS, vol. 10426, pp. 3–29. Springer, Cham (2017). https://doi.org/10.1007/978-3-319-63387-9_1
9. Katz, G., Barrett, C., Dill, D.L., Julian, K., Kochenderfer, M.J.: Reluplex: an efficient SMT solver for verifying deep neural networks. In: Majumdar, R., Kunčak, V. (eds.) CAV 2017. LNCS, vol. 10426, pp. 97–117. Springer, Cham (2017). https://doi.org/10.1007/978-3-319-63387-9_5
10. Kindermans, P., et al.: Learning how to explain neural networks: patternnet and patternattribution. In: 6th International Conference on Learning Representations, ICLR 2018, Vancouver, BC, Canada, 30 April–3 May 2018. Conference Track Proceedings (2018)
11. Kingma, D.P., Ba, J.: Adam: a method for stochastic optimization. In: 3rd International Conference on Learning Representations, ICLR 2015, San Diego, CA, USA, 7–9 May 2015. Conference Track Proceedings (2015)
12. LeCun, Y., Cortes, C., Burges, C.J.: The MNIST database of handwritten digits (1998). http://yann.lecun.com/exdb/mnist/. Accessed 4 Jan 2020
13. Lundberg, S.M., Lee, S.: A unified approach to interpreting model predictions. In: Advances in Neural Information Processing Systems 30: Annual Conference on Neural Information Processing Systems 2017, Long Beach, CA, USA, 4–9 December 2017, pp. 4765–4774 (2017)

14. Mirman, M., Gehr, T., Vechev, M.T.: Differentiable abstract interpretation for provably robust neural networks. In: Proceedings of the 35th International Conference on Machine Learning, ICML 2018, Stockholmsmässan, Stockholm, Sweden, 10–15 July 2018, pp. 3575–3583 (2018)

15. Papernot, N., McDaniel, P.D., Jha, S., Fredrikson, M., Celik, Z.B., Swami, A.: The limitations of deep learning in adversarial settings. In: IEEE European Symposium on Security and Privacy, EuroS&P 2016, Saarbrücken, Germany, 21–24 March 2016, pp. 372–387 (2016)

16. Research, Z.: Fashion MNIST: an MNIST-like dataset of 70,000 28x28 labeled fashion images (2017). https://github.com/zalandoresearch/fashion-mnist

17. Ribeiro, M.T., Singh, S., Guestrin, C.: "Why should I trust you?": explaining the predictions of any classifier. In: Proceedings of the 22nd ACM SIGKDD International Conference on Knowledge Discovery and Data Mining, San Francisco, CA, USA, 13–17 August 2016, pp. 1135–1144 (2016). https://doi.org/10.1145/2939672.2939778

18. Ruan, W., Huang, X., Kwiatkowska, M.: Reachability analysis of deep neural networks with provable guarantees. In: Proceedings of the Twenty-Seventh International Joint Conference on Artificial Intelligence, IJCAI 2018, Stockholm, Sweden, 13–19 July 2018, pp. 2651–2659 (2018)

19. Ruan, W., Wu, M., Sun, Y., Huang, X., Kroening, D., Kwiatkowska, M.: Global robustness evaluation of deep neural networks with provable guarantees for the hamming distance. In: Proceedings of the Twenty-Eighth International Joint Conference on Artificial Intelligence, IJCAI 2019, Macao, China, 10–16 August 2019, pp. 5944–5952 (2019)

20. Suya, F., Chi, J., Evans, D., Tian, Y.: Hybrid batch attacks: finding black-box adversarial examples with limited queries. CoRR abs/1908.07000 (2019)

21. Szegedy, C., et al.: Intriguing properties of neural networks. In: 2nd International Conference on Learning Representations, ICLR 2014, Banff, AB, Canada, 14–16 April 2014. Conference Track Proceedings (2014)

22. Wicker, M., Huang, X., Kwiatkowska, M.: Feature-guided black-box safety testing of deep neural networks. In: Beyer, D., Huisman, M. (eds.) TACAS 2018. LNCS, vol. 10805, pp. 408–426. Springer, Cham (2018). https://doi.org/10.1007/978-3-319-89960-2_22

23. Wu, M., Wicker, M., Ruan, W., Huang, X., Kwiatkowska, M.: A game based approximate verification of deep neural networks with provable guarantees. Theor. Comput. Sci. **807**, 298–329 (2020)

24. Xiang, W., Tran, H., Johnson, T.T.: Reachable set computation and safety verification for neural networks with ReLU activations. CoRR abs/1712.08163 (2017)

Leveraging Event-B Theories for Handling Domain Knowledge in Design Models

Ismail Mendil[1]([✉]), Yamine Aït-Ameur[1], Neeraj Kumar Singh[1],
Dominique Méry[2], and Philippe Palanque[3]

[1] INPT-ENSEEIHT/IRIT, University of Toulouse, Toulouse, France
`{ismail.mendil,yamine,nsingh}@enseeiht.fr`
[2] Telecom Nancy, LORIA, Université de Lorraine, Metz, France
`dominique.mery@loria.fr`
[3] IRIT, Université de Toulouse, Toulouse, France
`palanque@irit.fr`

Abstract. Formal system modelling languages lack explicit constructs to model domain knowledge, hindering clear separation of this knowledge from system design models. Indeed, in many cases, this knowledge is hardcoded in the system formal specification or is simply overlooked. Providing explicit domain knowledge constructs and properties would yield a significant improvement in the robustness and confidence of the system design models. Therefore, it speeds up formal verification of safety properties and advances system certification since certification standards and requirements rely on domain knowledge models. The purpose of this paper is to show how formal system design models can benefit from explicit handling of domain knowledge, represented as ontologies. To this end, state-based Event-B modelling language and theories are used to model system models and domain knowledge ontologies, respectively. Our proposition is exemplified by the TCAS (Traffic Collision Avoidance System) system, a critical airborne avionic component. Finally, we provide an assessment highlighting the overall approach.

Keywords: Domain knowledge · Ontologies · System engineering · State-based formal methods · Safety proofs · Invariant preservation · Event-B

1 Introduction

Context. Due to the high level of confidence required, critical systems are subjected to a variety of validation and verification (V&V) activities. Engineering these critical systems requires the use of numerous engineering techniques and methods, standards and certification processes, etc. Formal methods have proved their capability to handle complex verification and validation techniques set up at different development phases. They are grounded on mathematical and logic theories and are equipped with a proof system used to check formalised properties. They advocate the design of a formal model specifying the desired system

S. Qin et al. (Eds.): SETTA 2021, LNCS 13071, pp. 40–58, 2021.
https://doi.org/10.1007/978-3-030-91265-9_3

behaviours and the description of a set of properties expressing requirements, usually safety and security requirements. The underlying proof system allows to check the properties on the formalised system model. Various formal methods are available and several tools have been developed to support both system modelling and property verification using automatic verification procedures like model checking techniques (e.g. Promela/SPIN, NuSMV, Uppaal) or SMT and SAT solvers (e.g. Z3, CVC4), interactive theorem proving based on higher order logic or type theory (e.g. Isabelle/HOL [35], Coq [11]).

If we consider a system specification S and a set of property requirements R, then property verification consists in proving that requirements can be proved from the specification by establishing $S \vdash R$.

In this case, the designed formal model associated to a specification S must make explicit all the knowledge required to write a specification, in particular the domain knowledge provided by the domain and the context where the system is supposed to evolve i.e. S encapsulates the whole formal system description needed to establish R. The seminal work of [46] and [12,13] suggests to separate so called *Domain Knowledge* from the specification and proposes the well-known triptych $K, S \vdash R$ where K formalises domain knowledge. This separation is motivated by two main arguments: first domain knowledge is usually stable and reusable and second its formalisation is made explicit through K.

Motivation. In general, system engineering approaches, particularly formal methods, do not offer *explicit* constructs allowing the designer to define formal models of domain knowledge, nor mechanisms to import such existing models. However, there exist formal modelling languages and/or meta-models, sometimes standardised [18], that support the formalisation of such domain knowledge. It is often the case that transformations are required to reuse, in the set up formal method, already defined knowledge domain formalisations. As a result, heterogeneous formalisations are obtained, so sharing and reuse are compromised.

Our Claim. We believe that ontologies, seen as *an explicit shared specification of a conceptualisation* [25] suit with the requirement of domain knowledge *sharing* and *reuse*. We advocate that domain knowledge must be formalised as an ontology formally modelled as datatypes theories with axioms, theorems and reasoning capabilities, *once and for all*, in the used system development formal method. Moreover, we claim that this formalisation shall not impact system modelling languages nor system models. Last, to avoid semantic heterogeneity, both ontologies, system specifications and requirements shall be formalised in a single *shared* mathematical setting, Event-B [1] with set theory and First order logic in our case.

Objective of This Paper. We propose to use the Event-B [1] proof and refinement formal method to express both domain knowledge as ontologies formalised using Event-B theories, and system specification and requirements formalised as Event-B models (machines and invariants). As ontologies constructs are not present as first order concepts in Event-B, we introduce an Event-B meta-theory, based on generic and abstract datatypes and operators, describing an ontology model formalising an ontology modelling language (e.g. OWL [6]), further instantiated to derive specific domain ontologies. These ontologies become *shareable*, *reusable* and *referencable* by any Event-B model using typing, operators and properties guaranteed by proving both ontology instantiated theorems and Well-Definedness (WD) Proof Obligations (POs).

Structure of This Paper. Next section presents the Event-B state-based method and theories used to formalise our models. Section 3 is devoted to an overview of the state of the art in handling domain knowledge in system models. Our approach is synthesised in Sect. 4. Then, Sect. 5 presents a generic theory encoding OWL-like ontologies. In Sect. 6, we address the problem of domain knowledge handling in system design through the case of Aircraft Critical Interactive Systems design. Section 7 provides an assessment of our approach and Sect. 8 concludes the paper.

2 Event-B: A Refinement and Proof-Based Formal Method

2.1 Core Event-B

First-order logic (FOL) and set theory underpin the Event-B [1] modelling language. The design process consists of a series of refinements[1] of an abstract model (specification) leading to a final concrete model. The core modeling components of the Event-B language are *Contexts*, *Machines* and *Theories*.

```
CONTEXT  ContextName
EXTENDS  context_i
SETS  s_i
CONSTANTS c_i
AXIOMS
  A
THEOREMS
  T_ctx
END
```

```
MACHINE  MachineName
REFINES  machine_i
VARIABLES  x
INVARIANTS  I(x)
VARIANTS  V(x)
EVENTS
  EVENT
    ANY a
    WHERE  G(x, α)
    THEN
      x :|  BAP(x, α, x')
END
```

```
THEORY  TheoryName
IMPORT  Theory_1, ...
TYPE PARAMETERS T_1, T_2, ...
DATATYPES
  Datatype1(T_1, ...)
    CONSTRUCTORS
      cstr1(p: T_1, ...)
OPERATORS
  operator1 <nature> (p_1 : T_1)
    well-definedness  WD(p_1, ...)
    direct definition  D
  ...
AXIOMATIC DEFINITIONS
  AxiomaticDefinitionsName_1
    Types AT_1
    Operators
      operator1 <nature> (p_1 : T_1)
        well-definedness  WD(p_1, ...)
    Axioms Axm_1, ...
THEOREMS Thm1, ...
END
```

Listing 1.1. Basic Event-B building blocks: context, machine and theory

Event-B Contexts. Contexts (see Listing 1.1) define the static part of a model. They introduce definitions, axioms and theorems describing the required con-

---

[1] As refinement is not necessary to understand our contribution, it has been skipped. More details can be found in [1].

cepts and their properties. *Carrier sets s* defining algebraically new types (possibly constrained in axioms or other extending contexts), *constants c, axioms A* and *theorems T_{ctx}* are introduced.

Event-B Machines. A *machine* (see Listing 1.1) describes the dynamic part of a model as a transition system. A set of possibly parameterised and/or guarded events (transitions) modifying a set of state variables (state) represents the core concepts of a machine. *Variables x, invariants $I(x)$, theorems $T_{mch}(x)$, variants $V(x)$* and *events evt* (possibly guarded by G and/or parameterised by α) are defined in a machine. *Invariants* and *theorems* formalise system safety while *variants* define convergence properties (reachability).

Before-After Predicates (BAP) express state variables changes using prime notation x' to record the new value of a variable x after a change. The *"becomes such that"* $:|$ substitution is used to define the next (transition or event) value of a state variable. We write $x :| BAP(x, x')$ to express that the next value of x (denoted by x') satisfies the predicate $BAP(x, x')$ defined on before and after values of variable x. When a parameter α is involved in a variable the BAP is expressed as $x :| BAP(\alpha, x, x')$.

Proof Obligations (PO) and Property Verification. To establish the correctness of an Event-B model (machine) the POs (automatically generated from the calculus of substitutions) need to be proved.

Table 1. Relevant Proof Obligations

PO designation	PO formal definition
(1) Ctx Theorems (THM)	$A \Rightarrow T_{ctx}$ (For contexts)
(2) Mch Theorems (THM)	$A \wedge I(x) \Rightarrow T_{mch}(x)$ (For machines)
(3) Initialisation (INIT)	$A \wedge G(\alpha) \wedge BAP(\alpha, x') \Rightarrow I(x')$
(4) Invariant preservation (INV)	$A \wedge I(x) \wedge G(x, \alpha) \wedge BAP(x, \alpha, x') \Rightarrow I(x')$

The main POs, relevant for this paper, are listed in Table 1. They require to demonstrate that both contexts (1) and machines (2) theorems hold, initialisation (3) and each event preserves invariants (induction (4)).

Core Well-definedness (WD). WD POs are associated to all Event-B built-in operators of the Event-B modelling language. For example a WD proof obligation for the division operator $WD(a \div b)$ is $WD(a) \wedge WD(b) \wedge b \neq 0$ and for conjunction $WD(P \wedge Q)$ is $WD(P) \wedge (P \implies WD(Q))$. These proof obligations are defined for every operator of the core Event-B language.

2.2 Event-B Extensions with Theories

To handle additional abstract concepts beyond set theory and first order logic, an Event-B extension supports externally defined mathematical objects, modelled as *theories* [2,17]. Close to other proof assistants (e.g. Isabelle/HOL [35],

PVS [36]), this capability is convenient when modelling, using data types, concepts not available in core Event-B.

Theories for Abstract Data Types. They define types (possibly inductive) carried by sets and operators. They introduce axioms and theorems, and use the Event-B sequent calculus as proof system to prove theorems. The concepts defined in theories can be imported by Event-B models and used in further developments.

Well-Definedness (WD) in Theories. An important feature provided by Event-B theories relates to the definition of *well-definedness* conditions. Each defined operator may be associated to a condition guaranteeing its correct definition. When the operator is used (either in the theory or in an Event-B machine or context), this well-definedness condition generates a proof obligation requiring to establish that this condition holds, i.e. the use of the operator is correct. The theory developer defines these WD conditions, which are then added to the native Event-B WD POs. We extensively use this feature for defining domain knowledge operators.

Theory description (see Listing 1.1). Theories define and make available new data types, operators and theorems. Data types (**DATATYPES** clause) are associated with *constructors* i.e. operators to build inhabitant of the defined type. They may be inductive. A theory may define various *operators* further used in Event-B expressions. They may be *predicates* built using classical first order logic or *expressions* producing actual values (<nature> tag). Operators applications (predicates or expressions) can be used in other Event-B theories, contexts and/or machines. They *enrich the modelling language* as they may occur in the definitions of axioms, theorems, invariants, guards, assignments, etc.

As mentioned above, an operator may be associated with *WD conditions* encoding specific requirements. It defines, as a PO, the condition under which the operator is used. Each time the operator is used, this PO must be proved.

Operators may be defined explicitly using an explicit ("direct") equivalent definition, in the **direct definition** clause, (e.g., in the case of a constructive definition), or defined axiomatically in the **AXIOMATIC DEFINITIONS** clause, (e.g. a set of axioms). At the definition level, operators application mode is characterised: infix or prefix, or if they are commutative and/or associative. Last, a theory defines a set of axioms, completing the definitions, and theorems. Theorems are proved from the definitions and axioms.

We mention that many theories have been defined for sequences, lists, groups, reals, differential equations, etc.

Associated Proof System. As mentioned in [17], soundness of theories is achieved through the definition of soundness proof obligations generated following the standard approach of Event-B and their proofs are carried out using the sequent calculus of Event-B encoded in the Rodin provers. They rely on a set-theoretic formalisation of operators. More details can be found in [2,17]. Theories are also tightly integrated in the proof process. Depending on their definition (direct or axiomatic), operators definitions are expanded either using their direct definition (if available) or by enriching the set of axioms (behaving as hypotheses in proof sequents) using their axiomatic definition. Theorems may be imported as hypotheses and, like other theorems, they may be used in the proof as any other one. They are accessible by the interactive and automatic provers, and SMT solvers of Rodin.

Event-B and its IDE Rodin. Rodin[2] is an open source, Eclipse-based Integrated Development Environment for modelling in Event-B. It offers resources for model editing, automatic PO generation, project management, refinement and proof, model checking, model animation and code generation. Event-B's theories extension is available under the form of a plug-in, developed for the Rodin platform. Many provers like predicate provers, SMT solvers, are plugged to Rodin.

Application of the B method. Event-B method has been successfully applied to design critical systems for applications, like control system for the Meteor line 14 in Paris or the VAL shuttle for Paris CDG airport [9], medical devices [39], autonomous systems [41], security protocols [10], control-command systems [22] and distributed protocols [33,47]. More information can be found in [16,38].

3   Related Works

The contribution presented in this article is at the intersection of three scientific themes studied by the scientific community for decades.

Ontologies and Domain Modelling. Ontologies, as explicit knowledge models [25], have been extensively studied in the literature and applied in several domains spanning semantic web, artificial intelligence, information systems, system engineering etc. Several approaches for describing, designing and formalising ontologies for these application domains have been proposed. Models, browsers like Protégé or PlibEditor, repositories like JENA-SDB, TripleStore, OntoDB or OntoHub query languages like RQL, SPARQL or OntoQL, reasoners like Pellet, RACER or KAON, annotators like CREAM, Terminae or SAWSDL and translators have been proposed to engineer ontologies. Many ontologies have been described for several engineering domains and annotation mechanisms were proposed to establish links to domain objects like texts, images, videos and engineering models. Most of mentioned approaches rely on XML-based formats and are applied to the semantic web. As they are grounded on descriptive logics, they pay lot of attention to the *decidability criterion* for automated reasoning and inference purposes (which may limit the scope of addressed knowledge models and logics). To the best of our knowledge, *formal annotation of formal design models* and their *analysis* have not been set up using the above mentioned approaches or tools.

---

[2] http://www.event-b.org/index.html.

Explicit Domain Models in Formal Methods. Formalisation of domain knowledge witnessed high interest in the formal methods community where many approaches and frameworks were proposed in Coq [11], Isabelle/HOL [35] with ISADof [14,15] Framework, PVS [36], Event-B with theories [2,17] (e.g. control theory for control-command systems [21,23]) and critical systems [4], DOL - Distributed Ontology Model and Specification Language based on CASL algebraic specification [34] integrated to the OntoHub ontology repository and RSL - RAISE Specification Language [13] for transportation, shipping, and logistic systems. In [20], the authors present a two-layered language ground on higher-order logic of Coq formal system as a lower layer, and ontology language as upper layer for expressing and specifying contexts. Indeed, the higher-order KDTL language [8,19] supports the definition of new contextual categories and facts on the basis of low-order context. The language provides means to support comparability of diverse and non-countable information as well as numeric data.

Although the approaches cited above tackle the problem of formalising domain knowledge and provide modular frameworks, they differ from the modelling level where they apply. Two kinds of modelling levels incorporating domain knowledge have been identified. On the one hand, the modelling level that offers domain-specific language constructs, in particular constructs for ontologies allowing the explicit definition of ontology components like classes, properties and instances. In general, such approaches adopt a deep modelling style by explicitly encoding both syntax and semantics of some ontology description language like OWL. On the other hand, the second modelling language level adopts a shallow modelling style. It encodes domain knowledge concepts directly in the hosting formal modelling language using its syntactic and semantic constructs. Knowledge domain concepts are not made explicit in the obtained models.

Domain Knowledge in System Design. In [29], the authors clearly state the challenge of linking domain knowledge and design models. A mathematical analysis of models and meta models, ontologies, modelling and meta-modelling languages is included. Design models annotation by domain-specific knowledge has been studied for state-based methods in [4] as well. More recently, the textbook [5] reviewed many cases of exploiting explicit models of domain knowledge by system models spanning medical systems, e-voting systems, distributed systems etc. Indeed, [40] presents a four steps modelling approach based on the methodology described in [4]. It relies on Event-B contexts as domain knowledge models for ontologies for verifying medical protocols.   An assessment of the proposed approach is given through a complex case study of a real-life reference protocol (electrocardiogram (ECG) interpretation) covering a wide variety of protocol characteristics related to different heart conditions. [30] showcases how Event-B theories may be used to capture domain-specific abstract data types (ADTs) and build dynamic systems using the developed structures. The authors adopt an incremental approach to model domain knowledge concepts in parallel with the refinement of the model. The approach uses Event-B theories so it benefits from the use of the operators endowed with well-definedness conditions. The case studies used to illustrate the approach also define inference rules for easing the proving process. The work of [45] describes a meta model for a domain modeling language built from OWL and PLIB which is part of the SysML/KAOS requirements engineering method that includes a goal modeling language. The formal semantics of SysML/KAOS models is specified, verified, and validated using the Event-B method. Goal models provide machines and events of the Event-B specification while domain models provide its structural part (sets and constants with their properties and variables with their invariant). The proposal is exemplified through a case study dealing with a localization component for an autonomous vehicle Last, focusing on Event-B, a proposal of simplified ontology description language was put forward and illustrated on case studies in [27,28]. The approach was based on context extension where the design models need to discharge proof obligation in form of theorems to validate the compliance of the formal design models to the formalised domain knowledge.

The approaches mentioned above illustrate interesting solutions to the formalisation and incorporation of domain knowledge in formal design models. However, several limitations are identified. They constitute part of the challenges we address in our proposal. First, some of these approaches lack a general framework such as ontologies for defining domain knowledge in standardised way. They require to formalise the domain properties and their proofs in Event-B contexts. They do not offer explicit mechanisms enforcing domain knowledge constraints on the design models. The designer has to handle these constraints while formalising systems models.

Last, they strongly focus on full automation for reasoning and inference and target decidable fragments of logic like descriptive logics which do not enable the expression of all properties encountered in engineering domain (e.g. expression of arithmetic properties).

The main purpose of this paper is to define a general proof-based framework addressing the limitations identified above. It relies on engineering ontologies in the view of [3] to model domain knowledge as Event-B theories—a collection of data types and operators with well-definedness conditions—and use typing to annotate system design models formalised in Event-B.

4 Domain Knowledge in State-Based Formal Methods: The Case of Event-B

Formal methods are equipped with constructs allowing to support formal system developments and reasoning. In general these methods separate the system specification from the properties expressing requirements. They do not offer built-in constructs to axiomatise domain knowledge. In our approach, we propose *to use the capability of formal methods to describe, import and (re-)use theories in the system design models.*

In the sequel, we use Event-B theories to model domain ontologies as a collection of data types, constructors and operators defined by specific axioms. Each operator is accompanied with WD (Well-Definedness) properties defining the conditions for correct use of each operator. When an operator is used (i.e. applied), a WD proof obligation, corresponding to this condition, needs to be proved (discharged). Indeed, once the theory formalising an ontology is designed, models import and use its data types and operators and the corresponding WD proof obligations require to be discharged. As a consequence, domain knowledge model is factorised once and for all in a single *reusable* and *shareable* theory and second it does not require, from the designer, to write domain knowledge invariants and properties required to guarantee correctness of the design models. Indeed, the use of operators brings, *for free*, WD conditions as proof obligations to be discharged. Each design model is annotated by domain knowledge through typing. Event-B theories offer services and capabilities to implement the notion of design models conforming to domain knowledge constraints expressed by theories. These theories provide data types and operators for expressiveness while requiring discharging of WD conditions ensuring conformance checking.

At this level, a *formal setting to write theories for domain knowledge modelling is missing. A domain knowledge modelling language shall be used for this purpose.*

Next sections describe an Event-B based development process allowing to handle domain knowledge as formal ontologies and annotate formal models using typing. A generic theory for ontologies is presented and a case study issued from aircraft cockpits engineering showcases the overall approach.

5   Ontologies as Event-B Theories

From Sect. 3, we conclude that ontologies, as descriptive knowledge models for domains, are powerful models for knowledge representation and reasoning, and from Sect. 4 we also conclude that Event-B, and more generally state-based formal methods, are suitable for enforcing design models to reference domain knowledge concepts and express their constraints as well-definedness conditions.

To define our ontologies, we rely on defined ontology modelling languages (OML) like OWL [6] or PLIB [37]. In our case, provided that it can be described using data-types based on set theory and first order logic, whatever is the ontology modelling language, it can be described by Event-B theories.

Our approach proposes a formal parameterised theory, acting as a meta-theory associated to the OML and each ontology is described as a theory instance of this meta-theory. More precisely, the ontologies we use are based on a theory inspired from OWL[3] where domain knowledge is formalised as collections of classes, properties and instances.

Listing 1.2 shows an extract of OntologiesTheory theory allowing the formalisation of OWL-based ontologies. It is parameterised by C, P, and I which stand for classes, properties and instances. The Ontology(C,P,I) data type is built using the consOntology constructor based on seven components: classes, properties, instances (i.e. set of classes, properties and instances respectively), classProperties for associating classes to properties, classInstances

---

[3] https://www.w3.org/TR/owl-features/.

for relating instances to classes, `classAssociations` defining a set of property-named binary associations and `instanceAssociations` for representing the associations between instances. Besides the ontology structure, operators are defined to manipulate, access and update an ontology.

In Listing 1.2, the `getInstanceAssociations`, `instanceHasPropertyVal uei`, `addValueOfAnInstanceProperty` and `removeValueOfAnInstanceProp erty` operators define access to properties of a class and instances of an association, check if a property is valued and add/remove a property value. The `isA` relationship encoding class subsumption is defined and the theorem `isATransitivityThm`, stating its transitivity, is proven.

```
THEORY  OntologiesTheory
TYPE PARAMETERS
  C, P, I
DATATYPES
  Ontology(C, P, I)
    CONSTRUCTORS
      consOntology(classes: ℙ(C), properties: ℙ(P), instances: ℙ(I),
        classProperties: ℙ(C × P), classInstances: ℙ(C × I),
        classAssociations: ℙ(C × P × C),
                              instanceAssociations: ℙ(I × P × I) )
OPERATORS
  isWDClassProperites <predicate> (o : Ontology(C, P, I))
    ...
  getClassProperties <expression> (o : Ontology(C, P, I)
    ...
  isWDInstancesAssociations <predicate> (o : Ontology(C, P, I))
    ...
  getInstanceAssociations <expression> (o : Ontology(C, P, I)
    ...
  isWDOntology <predicate> (o : Ontology(C, P, I))
    direct definition
      isWDClassInstances(o) ∧ isWDClassProperites(o) ∧
      isWDClassAssociations(o) ∧ isWDInstancesAssociations(o)
    ...
  isWDinstanceHasPropertyValuei <predicate>
    ...
  instanceHasPropertyValuei <predicate>
  (o : Ontology(C, P, I), ipv: ℙ I × P × I), i: I, p: P, v: I)
    well-definedness
      isWDinstanceHasPropertyValuei(o, ipv, i, p)
    direct definition
      v ∈ ipv[{i ↦ p}]

  getInstancesOfaClass <expression> (o : Ontology(C, P, I), c: C)
    well-definedness
      isWDOntology(o) ∧ ontologyContainsClasses(o, {c})
    direct definition
      getClassInstances(o)[{c}]
  addValueOfAnInstanceProperty <expression>
    ...
  removeValueOfAnInstanceProperty <expression>
    ...
  isA <predicate>
  (o : Ontology(C, P, I), c1: C, c2: C)
    well-definedness
      isWDOntology(o)
      ontologyContainsClasses(o, {c1, c2})
    direct definition
      getInstancesOfaClass(o, c1) ⊆ getInstancesOfaClass(o, c2)
THEOREMS
  isATransitivityThm: ∀o, c1, c2, c3 · o ∈ Ontology(C, P, I)∧
    c1 ∈ C ∧ c2 ∈ C ∧ c3 ∈ C∧
            ontologyContainsClasses(o, {c1, c2, c3})
      ⇒ (isA(o, c1, c2) ∧ isA(o, c2, c3) ⇒ isA(o, c1, c3))
```

Listing 1.2. Excerpt of ontologies theory OML

Thanks to its type system, Event-B theories support the description of other operators e.g. arithmetic or defined-types operators. These operators are associated to WD conditions (logical expressions) to ensure correct use and to preserve a valid ontology structure at instantiation. When an operator is applied, generated WD proof obligations need to be proved. Hence, depending on the chosen OML, Event-B theories permit the modelling of complex domain knowledge.

Important Note. The choice of the OML is driven by the needs and complexity of the domain knowledge of interest: system engineering. It requires other modelling capabilities like property derivation using arithmetic expressions or context dependent properties and associated proof rules (see [3,4] for more details). To handle engineering knowledge, we use first-order logic with arithmetic in our OML. This richer expressive power leads to semi-automatic proofs requiring interactive proof effort[4].

6   Application to the Design of Critical Interactive Systems

We highlight the importance of system design models annotation relying on explicit formalised domain knowledge via the development of a critical interactive system (CIS): TCAS - Traffic Collision Avoidance System.

In this section, We describe the development of a critical interactive system (CIS): the TCAS - It is critical to the safe flight of any aircraft, namely Traffic Collision Avoidance System. We show the importance of formalising domain information and its integration to the system design model.

The formal development of this case study relies on domain knowledge formalised as an instantiated theory (`Displayability Theory`) of the ontology model (see Listing 1.2). Then, the definition of the knowledge related to the specific case of *aircraft* objects *displayability* is obtained by instantiating of the latter ontology using an Event-B context (see Listing 1.4), where the seven components of the ontology are defined and used to build the `aircraftOntology` ontology.

6.1   The TCAS Case Study

TCAS is an airborne avionics system that acts as a last resort safety net to mitigate risks of midair collisions. TCAS tracks aircraft in the surrounding airspace exploiting position sent by their transponders to detect collision risks. If an impedent collision is detected, TCAS issues a Resolution Advisory (RA) to the flight crews of concerned aircrafts. These advisories ask them to climb or descend at a given vertical rate to prevent collision [24,43].

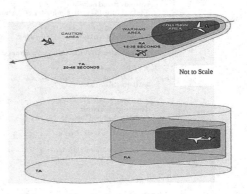

Fig. 1. Protection volume

---

[4] *Automatic* reasoners (decidable logics) like Pellet [42] or Racer [26] apply to *less rich* OML than the one offered by Event-B theories.

TCAS computes a virtual protected volume (Fig. 1) which includes the position of the aircrafts nearby. This volume depends on the aircraft speed and trajectory. It is permanently updated. Some of the information related to volume is displayed in a cockpit screen for flight crew usage. An example of such display can be found in [44]. Due to space constraints, we only focus on a single critical safety property: TCAS must display, on a PFD (Primary Flight Display) cockpit screen, the current status of all the aircrafts in the volume. Beyond, a *critical* aircraft (due to its proximity) must be *visible*.

6.2   A Domain Ontology for the Critical Interactive Systems

Two steps are required to build the domain ontology.

```
THEORY    DisplayabilityTheory
IMPORT    OntologiesTheory
AXIOMATIC DEFINITIONS
   IOOntology
   TYPES
      IOClasses ,    IOProperties ,    IOInstances
   OPERATORS
   isIOOntologyWD < predicate >
         (o : Ontology(IOClasses, IOProperties, IOInstances))
   visible < expression >: IOInstances
   hidden < expression >: IOInstances
   critical < expression >: IOInstances
   safe < expression >: IOInstances
   hasVisibility < expression >: IOProperties
   hasCriticality < expression >: IOProperties
   visibility < expression >: IOClases
   criticality < expression >: IOClases
   isVisibleWDi < predicate > ...
   isVisiblei < predicate >
         (o : Ontology(IOClasses, IOProperties, IOInstances),
          ipvs : ℙ(IOInstances × IOProperties × IOInstances),
          i : IOInstances)
   well-definedness
      isVisibleWDi(o, ipvs, i)
   setCriticaliWD < predicate > ...
   setCriticali < expression >
         (o : Ontology(IOClasses, IOProperties, IOInstances),
          ipv : ℙ(IOInstances × IOProperties × IOInstances),
          i : IOInstances)
   well-definedness
      setCriticaliWD(o, ipvs, i)
   AXIOMS
      axm1 : ∀o · o ∈ ... ⇒ (isIOOntologyWD(o) ⇔ isWDOntology(o))
      axm2 : partition(IOProperties, {hasVisibility}, {hasCriticality})
      axm3 : {visibility, criticality} ⊆ IOClasses
      axm4 : ∀o, ipv, i · o ∈ ... ⇒ (isVisibleWDi(o, ipv, i) ⇔
                                         i ⊂ dom(dom(ipv)))
      axm5 : ∀o, ipv, io ∈ ... ⇒ (isVisiblei(o, ipv, i) ⇔
                   instanceHasPropertyValuei(o, ipv, i, hasVisibility, visible)
      ...
      axm18 : ∀o, ipv, i · o ∈ ... ⇒ (setCriticaliWD(o, ipv, i) ⇔
                   i ∈ dom(dom(ipv)) ∧ isVisiblei(o, ipv, i))
      axm19 : ∀o, ipv1, ipv2, i · o ∈
              Ontology(IOClasses, IOProperties, IOInstances)∧
              ipv1 ∈ ℙ(IOInstances × IOProperties × IOInstances)∧
              ipv2 ∈ ℙ(IOInstances × IOProperties × IOInstances)∧
              i ∈ IOInstances ⇒ (ipv2 = setCriticali(o, ipv1, i) ⇔
              ipv2 = (ipv1 \ {i ↦ hasCriticality ↦ safe})∪
              {i ↦ hasCriticality ↦ critical})
```

Listing 1.3. Exerpt of Displayability theory

An Ontology of Interactive Objects. First, we define a generic domain knowledge model for interactive objects (IOs) by instantiating the ontology theory (see Listing 1.2) to get the `DisplayabilityTheory` Event-B theory (IO ontology - Listing 1.3). It axiomatises a collection of specific operators with WD conditions entailing *displayability* properties of critical IOs. Indeed, `IOClasses`, `IOProperties`, `IOInstances` types and two kinds of operators (predicates and expressions) are defined. Predicates check if a property holds in the system variable or introduce WD conditions required for other operators. Besides, we create constant operators like `visible`, `hidden`, `critical`, `safe` which are instances of `IOInstances` and `hasVisibility`, `hasCriticality` being elements of `IOProperties`.

The `instanceHasPropertyValuei` operator of `OntologiesTheory` is a predicate with five arguments: *ontology, system variable, instance, property* and *value*. The predicate is true when the 3-tuple *instance* $\mapsto$ *property* $\mapsto$ *value* is in *system variable*. For example, the operator `isVisiblei` uses it to state that an IO is visible if and only if its property `hasVisibility` relates the IO to *visible* and complies with the ontology schema (see `instanceHasPropertyValuei` in Listing 1.2). We adopted the same methodology for writing all operators.

For instance, we define the WD condition for `setCriticali` as a predicate `setCriticaliWD` encapsulating the conditions needed to use this operator: $i \in dom(dom(ipv))$ stating that i must be in the model variable and `isVisiblei(o,ipvs,i)` meaning that the IO i must be visible. Last, for domain coverage purposes, the domain knowledge model (theory) is self-contained, i.e. defined concepts and properties are manipulated using theory operators only (no other IO manipulation is allowed). Thus, proved theorems hold for all IOs.

Remark. From system engineering perspective, this assumption means that a designer shall **only** use the types and operators supplied by the theory encoding the domain knowledge ontology.

```
CONTEXT    InstantiationContext
CONSTANTS
    aircraftClass, aircraftInstances, ClassProperties, ClassInstances
    ClassAssociations, instanceAssociation, aircraftOntology,
    thingClass, thingInstances,
AXIOMS
    axm1 : partition(IOClasses, {thingClass}, {aircraftClass},
                     {visibility}, {criticality})
    axm2 : partition(IOInstances, {aircraftInstances},
                     {visible}, {hidden}, {safe}, {critical})
    axm3 : thingInstances = IOInstances
    axm4 : ClassProperties =
            {aircraftClass} × {hasVisibility, hasCriticality}
    axm5 : ClassInstances = (
                     {aircraftClass} × aircraftInstances)
                     ∪({visibility} × {visible, hidden})
                     ∪({criticality} × {critical, safe})
                     ∪(thingClass × thingInstances)
    axm6: ClassAssociations ∈ ℙ(IOClasses × IOProperties ×
                     IOClasses)
    axm7 : ClassAssociations =
            ({aircraftClass} × {hasVisibility} × {visibility})
            ∪({aircraftClass} × {hasCriticality} × {criticality})
    axm8 : instanceAssociation =
            (aircraftInstances × {hasVisibility} × {hidden})
            ∪(aircraftInstances × {hasCriticality} × {safe})
    axm9 : aircraftOntology = consOntology(IOClasses,
            IOProperties, IOInstances, ClassProperties,
            ClassInstances, ClassAssociations, instanceAssociation)
    ConformThm10 : isIOOntologyWD(aircraftOntology)
    isAthm11 : isA(aircraftOntology, aircraftClass, thingClass)
END
```

Listing 1.4. Context of instantiation

Instantiation for Aircraft Description IO (Listing 1.4**).** Displayability Theory is instantiated in the context OntologyInstantiation Context to define the specific IOs concepts and properties used in the TCAS models. For our development, three classes are introduced: aircraftClass (is a thing by isAthm11)), visibility and criticality. The latter two classes are borrowed from the DisplayabilityTheory theory. In addition, we introduce the aircraft Instances using an extensional axiom axm2 (Event-B partition operator asserts that the first argument is the disjoint union of the others). Afterwards, aircraftOntology is built in axm9. Last, note that ConformThm9 theorem is proved from the constituent of the ontology to ensure that this ontology is WD by isWDIOontology (Listings 1.3 and 1.2).

6.3   Ontology-Based Annotation of TCAS Design Model

The Event-B machine model TheoryOperatorsBasedModel (Listing 1.5) handles the *safety* requirement stating that *a critical aircraft must be visible* thanks to the annotation of the state variable system using isVariableOfOntology predicate operator in inv1 and to the use of setCriticali operator, borrowed from the DisplaybilityOntology, in the event CorrectAircraftStatusUpdate.

Indeed, isVariableOfOntology ensures that system variable fully complies with aircraftOntology rules. From the proof perspective, the guards of the event guarantee correct variable updating and invariant preservation. As a benefit, the two theories exempt the designer from writing domain-related properties, thus focusing only on the system-specific model. Listing 1.5 shows important parts of the TCAS model, noticebly the event CorrectAircraftStatusUpdate allows to update the aircraft i status so that it is visible (see its definition of setCriticali in Listing 1.3). The guards ensure that the operation is performed in a well-defined fashion through the use of the necessary WD operators.

```
MACHINE   TheoryOperatorsBasedModel
SEES   InstantiationContext
VARIABLES system
INVARIANTS
   inv1 : isVariableOfOntology(aircraftOntology, system)
INITIALISATION
   THEN
      act1 : system : |system' ⊆ instanceAssociation
EVENT CorrectAircraftStatusUpdate
   ANY    i
   WHERE
      grd1 : ontologyContainsInstances(aircraftOntology, {i})
      grd2 : isVisibleWDi(aircraftOntology, system, i)
      grd3 : isVisiblei(aircraftOntology, system, i)
      grd4 : isSafeWD(aircraftOntology, system, i)
      grd5 : isSafe(aircraftOntology, system, i)
      grd6 : isWDSetCriticali(aircraftOntology, system, i)
   THEN
      act1 : system := setCriticali(aircraftOntology, system, i)
   ...
```

Listing 1.5. Ontology theory based annotated model

7 Assessment

The complete Event-B development including all the theories and models may be downloaded from https://www.irit.fr/~Ismail.Mendil/recherches/

Previous Work. [31] proposed a correct-by-construction Event-B development of TCAS featuring many functionalities. However, domain knowledge formalisation is not explicit and domain-specific rules are hardcoded in the design models. Here, we improved our approach making domain knowledge explicit by annotating models with ontologies, using data types formalised as Event-B theories. Consequently, automatic domain oriented WD proof obligations are generated and proved in the annotated design models. It is worth noticing that *these theories are built and proved once and for all.*

Explicit Domain Knowledge and Reusability. The proposed ontology modelling language (an Event-B theory) makes it possible to design, systematically, a series of theories, composing and/or extending each other, to model various domain knowledge as instances of the generic theory of Listing 1.2. In addition, domain theories and system models are formalised (integrated) in the single setting of Event-B (Set theory and first order logic) avoiding semantic mismatch that may occur in case of heterogeneous modelling language semantics. Besides, Listing 1.2 generic theory of ontologies supports engineering standards formalisation. Confidence in the consistency of the standard rules is achieved by proving WD and theorems. Last, theorems of the theory are proved once and for all. Like domain knowledge types and operators, these theorems are reused in system models.

Reduction of Modelling Effort. When models are annotated by references to ontology (Listing 1.5) through typing in Event-B theories, guards are described by WD conditions (grd3 - grd5) systematically borrowed from the ontology when an operator is applied. They are mined, in a systematic way, from the well-definedness conditions of the used operator in act1. This model provides assistance to the designer as domain knowledge operators applications allow a designer to identify the operator WD conditions for its correct application.

Enhanced Safety of System Models. We presented an Event-B model (machine) defined for TCAS based on annotation of state variables through typing with domain theory defined types (Listing 1.5). This model based on WD and avoids the designer having to explicitly write invariants. This is a major strength of our approach as it assists the designer by *describing explicitly safety properties in the domain ontology* (Event-B theory of Listings 1.3 and 1.4) as axioms and theorems and by embedding these safety properties in the design model through the WD proof obligation. The designer uses *operators in the models that brings their WD proof obligations that ensure safety* when discharged (No need to write explicitly the invariants, this work is achieved on the ontology side).

Asynchronous Evolution. The neat separation of the general domain knowledge on which the system depends and the specific features of the system under study enforces the separation of concepts principle and promotes formal specification modularisation enabling the orthogonality principle i.e. both domain and system design models may evolve asynchronously with limited impact on previous developments. In case of evolution, solely the proof obligations generated due to this evolution are discharged again.

8   Conclusion and Future Work

The work presented in this paper takes advantage of foundations and methods of knowledge modeling and reasoning on the one hand and formal system engineering on the other hand. This work defines a uniform framework integrating both domain knowledge, system specification and safety requirements in a unique formal modelling setting and proof system offered by Event-B. It advocates the 1) *explicit* modelling of domain knowledge by ontologies as a well-accepted formal modelling framework and the 2) *separation* of domain and system models. The proposition yields three important advantages in formal modelling state-of-the-art. Indeed, it becomes possible to 1) refer to (annotation) domain models concepts (types, operators, etc.), 2) automatically bring, in the system model, checking of well-definedness proof obligations for robustness purposes, and 3) allow asynchronous evolution of both domain and system models thanks to the separation of concerns. However, this evolution does not prevent from checking new occurring proof obligations and/or old ones that may not be preserved.

The overall approach was showcased using a formalised an OWL-based domain modelling language as an Event-B theory where *data types, operators* and *Well-Definedness* play a central role. We used this formal ontology language to describe a domain theory for critical interactive systems (CIS) concepts and safety rules for displaying aircraft in TCAS. Moreover, the system engineering domain was exemplified to shed the light on the gain in robustness when using the *Well-Defined* operators of a domain theory. An assessment is provided to evaluate efficiency of knowledge formalisation and integration in our approach. Finally, the formalized theories developed in this paper were used to annotate design models as part of our approach for standard conformance in [32]. A large part of ARINC 661 [7] standard describing Cockpit Display Systems (CDS) interfaces used in all aircrafts has been formalised. This standard plays important role to minimise costs as well as to meet certification requirements.

Future Work. The current study opened a number of new research directions. From the foundational perspective, we intend to formalise knowledge models composition with theory composition operators (importation, extension and instantiation) in order to handle heterogeneity and multi-view problems of complex systems while maintaining consistency of obtained Event-B theories. Another significant perspective consists in addressing other engineering domains, specifically transportation systems.

References

1. Abrial, J.R.: Modeling in Event-B - System and Software Engineering. Cambridge University Press, Cambridge (2010)
2. Abrial, J.R., Butler, M., Hallerstede, S., Leuschel, M., Schmalz, M., Voisin, L.: Proposals for mathematical extensions for Event-B. Technical report (2009)
3. Aït Ameur, Y., Baron, M., Bellatreche, L., Jean, S., Sardet, E.: Ontologies in engineering: the OntoDB/OntoQL platform. Soft. Comput. **21**(2), 369–389 (2017)
4. Aït Ameur, Y., Méry, D.: Making explicit domain knowledge in formal system development. Sci. Comput. Program. **121**, 100–127 (2016)
5. Aït Ameur, Y., Nakajima, S., Méry, D.: Implicit and Explicit Semantics Integration in Proof-Based Developments of Discrete Systems. Springer, Heidelberg (2021). https://doi.org/10.1007/978-981-15-5054-6
6. Antoniou, G., van Harmelen, F.: Web ontology language: OWL. In: Staab, S., Studer, R. (eds.) Handbook on Ontologies. International Handbooks on Information Systems, pp. 67–92. Springer, Heidelberg (2004). https://doi.org/10.1007/978-3-540-24750-0_4
7. ARINC: ARINC 661 specification: Cockpit Display System Interfaces To User Systems. By AEEC, Published by SAE, 16701 Melford Blvd., Suite 120, Bowie, Maryland 20715 USA, June 2019
8. Barlatier, P., Dapoigny, R.: A type-theoretical approach for ontologies: the case of roles. Appl. Ontol. **7**, 311–356 (2012)
9. Behm, P., Benoit, P., Faivre, A., Meynadier, J.-M.: Météor: a successful application of b in a large project. In: Wing, J.M., Woodcock, J., Davies, J. (eds.) FM 1999. LNCS, vol. 1708, pp. 369–387. Springer, Heidelberg (1999). https://doi.org/10.1007/3-540-48119-2_22
10. Benaissa, N., Méry, D.: Cryptographic protocols analysis in event B. In: Pnueli, A., Virbitskaite, I., Voronkov, A. (eds.) PSI 2009. LNCS, vol. 5947, pp. 282–293. Springer, Heidelberg (2010). https://doi.org/10.1007/978-3-642-11486-1_24
11. Bertot, Y., Castran, P.: Interactive Theorem Proving and Program Development: Coq'Art The Calculus of Inductive Constructions, 1st edn. Springer, Heidelberg (2010). https://doi.org/10.1007/978-3-662-07964-5
12. Bjørner, D.: Software Engineering 3 - Domains, Requirements, and Software Design. Texts in Theoretical Computer Science. An EATCS Series, Springer, Heidelberg (2006). https://doi.org/10.1007/3-540-33653-2
13. Bjørner, D.: Domain analysis and description principles, techniques, and modelling languages. ACM Trans. Softw. Eng. Methodol. **28**(2), 8:1–8:67 (2019)
14. Brucker, A.D., Wolff, B.: Isabelle/DOF: design and implementation. In: Ölveczky, P.C., Salaün, G. (eds.) SEFM 2019. LNCS, vol. 11724, pp. 275–292. Springer, Cham (2019). https://doi.org/10.1007/978-3-030-30446-1_15
15. Brucker, A.D., Wolff, B.: Using ontologies in formal developments targeting certification. In: Ahrendt, W., Tapia Tarifa, S.L. (eds.) IFM 2019. LNCS, vol. 11918, pp. 65–82. Springer, Cham (2019). https://doi.org/10.1007/978-3-030-34968-4_4
16. Butler, M., et al.: The first twenty-five years of industrial use of the B-method. In: ter Beek, M.H., Ničković, D. (eds.) FMICS 2020. LNCS, vol. 12327, pp. 189–209. Springer, Cham (2020). https://doi.org/10.1007/978-3-030-58298-2_8
17. Butler, M., Maamria, I.: Practical theory extension in Event-B. In: Liu, Z., Woodcock, J., Zhu, H. (eds.) Theories of Programming and Formal Methods. LNCS, vol. 8051, pp. 67–81. Springer, Heidelberg (2013). https://doi.org/10.1007/978-3-642-39698-4_5

18. Calegari, D., Mossakowski, T., Szasz, N.: Heterogeneous verification in the context of model driven engineering. Sci. Comput. Program. **126**, 3–30 (2016)
19. Dapoigny, R., Barlatier, P.: Modeling ontological structures with type classes in Coq. In: Pfeiffer, H.D., Ignatov, D.I., Poelmans, J., Gadiraju, N. (eds.) ICCS-ConceptStruct 2013. LNCS (LNAI), vol. 7735, pp. 135–152. Springer, Heidelberg (2013). https://doi.org/10.1007/978-3-642-35786-2_11
20. Dapoigny, R., Barlatier, P.: Formalizing context for domain ontologies in Coq. In: Brézillon, P., Gonzalez, A.J. (eds.) Context in Computing, pp. 437–454. Springer, New York (2014). https://doi.org/10.1007/978-1-4939-1887-4_27
21. Dupont, G., Aït-Ameur, Y., Pantel, M., Singh, N.K.: Handling refinement of continuous behaviors: a refinement and proof based approach with Event-B. In: 13th International Symposium TASE, pp. 9–16. IEEE Computer Society Press (2019)
22. Dupont, G., Aït-Ameur, Y., Pantel, M., Singh, N.K.: Proof-based approach to hybrid systems development: dynamic logic and Event-B. In: Butler, M., Raschke, A., Hoang, T.S., Reichl, K. (eds.) ABZ 2018. LNCS, vol. 10817, pp. 155–170. Springer, Cham (2018). https://doi.org/10.1007/978-3-319-91271-4_11
23. Dupont, G., Aït-Ameur, Y., Pantel, M., Singh, N.K.: Formally verified architecture patterns of hybrid systems using proof and refinement with Event-B. In: Raschke, A., Méry, D., Houdek, F. (eds.) ABZ 2020. LNCS, vol. 12071, pp. 169–185. Springer, Cham (2020). https://doi.org/10.1007/978-3-030-48077-6_12
24. EUROCONTROL: Airborne collision avoidance system (ACAS) guide, December 2017
25. Gruber, T.R.: Towards principles for the design of ontologies used for knowledge sharing. In: Guarino, N., Poli, R. (eds.) Formal Ontology in Conceptual Analysis and Knowledge Representation. Kluwer Academic Publisher's (1993)
26. Haarslev, V., Möller, R.: Description of the RACER system and its applications, vol. 2083, January 2001
27. Hacid, K., Ait-Ameur, Y.: Strengthening MDE and formal design models by references to domain ontologies. a model annotation based approach. In: Margaria, T., Steffen, B. (eds.) ISoLA 2016. LNCS, vol. 9952, pp. 340–357. Springer, Cham (2016). https://doi.org/10.1007/978-3-319-47166-2_24
28. Hacid, K., Aït Ameur, Y.: Handling domain knowledge in design and analysis of engineering models. Electron. Commun. Eur. Assoc. Softw. Sci. Technol. **74**, 1–21 (2017)
29. Henderson-Sellers, B.: On the Mathematics of Modelling, Metamodelling. Springer Briefs in Computer Science, Ontologies and Modelling Languages. Springer, Heidelberg (2012). https://doi.org/10.1007/978-3-642-29825-7
30. Hoang, T.S., Voisin, L., Butler, M.: Domain-specific developments using rodin theories. In: Ait-Ameur, Y., Nakajima, S., Méry, D. (eds.) Implicit and Explicit Semantics Integration in Proof-Based Developments of Discrete Systems, pp. 19–37. Springer, Singapore (2021). https://doi.org/10.1007/978-981-15-5054-6_2
31. Mendil, I., Singh, N.K., Aït Ameur, Y., Méry, D., Palanque, P.A.: An integrated framework for the formal analysis of critical interactive systems. In: 27th Asia-Pacific Software Engineering Conference, APSEC 2020, Singapore, 1–4 December 2020, pp. 139–148. IEEE (2020)
32. Mendil, I., Aït-Ameur, Y., Singh, N.K., Méry, D., Palanque, P.: Standard conformance-by-construction with Event-B. In: Lluch Lafuente, A., Mavridou, A. (eds.) FMICS 2021. LNCS, vol. 12863, pp. 126–146. Springer, Cham (2021). https://doi.org/10.1007/978-3-030-85248-1_8

33. Méry, D., Singh, N.K.: Analysis of DSR protocol in Event-B. In: Défago, X., Petit, F., Villain, V. (eds.) SSS 2011. LNCS, vol. 6976, pp. 401–415. Springer, Heidelberg (2011). https://doi.org/10.1007/978-3-642-24550-3_30

34. Mossakowski, T.: The distributed ontology, model and specification language – DOL. In: James, P., Roggenbach, M. (eds.) WADT 2016. LNCS, vol. 10644, pp. 5–10. Springer, Cham (2017). https://doi.org/10.1007/978-3-319-72044-9_2

35. Nipkow, T., Wenzel, M., Paulson, L.C.: Isabelle/HOL: A Proof Assistant for Higher-order Logic. Springer, Heidelberg (2002). https://doi.org/10.1007/3-540-45949-9

36. Owre, S., Rushby, J.M., Shankar, N.: PVS: a prototype verification system. In: Kapur, D. (ed.) CADE 1992. LNCS, vol. 607, pp. 748–752. Springer, Heidelberg (1992). https://doi.org/10.1007/3-540-55602-8_217

37. Pierra, G.: The PLIB ontology-based approach to data integration. In: Jacquart, R. (ed.) Building the Information Society. IIFIP, vol. 156, pp. 13–18. Springer, Boston, MA (2004). https://doi.org/10.1007/978-1-4020-8157-6_2

38. Romanovsky, A.B., Thomas, M. (eds.): Industrial Deployment of System Engineering Methods. Springer, Heidelberg (2013). https://doi.org/10.1007/978-3-642-33170-1

39. Singh, N.K.: Using Event-B for Critical Device Software Systems. Springer, Heidelberg (2013). https://doi.org/10.1007/978-1-4471-5260-6

40. Singh, N.K., Ait-Ameur, Y., Méry, D.: Formal ontological analysis for medical protocols. In: Ait-Ameur, Y., Nakajima, S., Méry, D. (eds.) Implicit and Explicit Semantics Integration in Proof-Based Developments of Discrete Systems, pp. 83–107. Springer, Singapore (2021). https://doi.org/10.1007/978-981-15-5054-6_5

41. Singh, N.K., Aït Ameur, Y., Pantel, M., Dieumegard, A., Jenn, E.: Stepwise formal modeling and verification of self-adaptive systems with event-b. the automatic rover protection case study. In: 21st International Conference on Engineering of Complex Computer Systems, ICECCS, pp. 43–52 (2016)

42. Sirin, E., Parsia, B.: Pellet: an OWL DL reasoner. In: Description Logics, pp. 212–213 (2004)

43. ED 143 - Minimum Operational Performance Standards for Traffic Alert and Collision Avoidance System II (TCAS II) (2013)

44. U.S. Department of transportation, F.A.A.: Introduction to TCAS 2, version 7.1, February 2011

45. Tueno, S., Laleau, R., Mammar, A., Frappier, M.: Integrating domain modeling within a formal requirements engineering method. In: Ait-Ameur, Y., Nakajima, S., Méry, D. (eds.) Implicit and Explicit Semantics Integration in Proof-Based Developments of Discrete Systems, pp. 39–58. Springer, Singapore (2021). https://doi.org/10.1007/978-981-15-5054-6_3

46. Zave, P., Jackson, M.: Four dark corners of requirements engineering. ACM Trans. Softw. Eng. Methodol. **6**(1), 1–30 (1997)

47. Zoubeyr, F., Aït Ameur, Y., Ouederni, M., Tari, A.: A correct-by-construction model for asynchronously communicating systems. Int. J. Softw. Tools Technol. Transf. **19**(4), 465–485 (2017)

Program Analysis and Verifiation

Reasoning About Iteration and Recursion Uniformly Based on Big-Step Semantics

Ximeng Li[1,3(✉)], Qianying Zhang[2], Guohui Wang[2],
Zhiping Shi[1(✉)], Yong Guan[3(✉)]

[1] Beijing Key Laboratory of Electronic System Reliability and Prognostics,
Capital Normal University, Beijing, China
{lixm,shizp}@cnu.edu.cn
[2] Beijing Engineering Research Center of High Reliable Embedded System,
Capital Normal University, Beijing, China
[3] Beijing Advanced Innovation Center for Imaging Theory and Technology,
Capital Normal University, Beijing, China
guanyong@cnu.edu.cn

Abstract. A reliable technique for deductive program verification should be proven sound with respect to the semantics of the programming language. For each different language, the construction of a separate soundness proof is often a laborious undertaking. In language-independent program verification, common aspects of computer programs are addressed to enable sound reasoning for all languages. In this work, we propose a solution for the sound reasoning about iteration and recursion based on the big-step operational semantics of any programming language. We give inductive proofs on the soundness and relative completeness of our reasoning technique. We illustrate the technique at simplified programming languages of the imperative and functional paradigms, with diverse features. We also mechanize all formal results in the Coq proof assistant.

1 Introduction

It is commonly accepted that a reliable technique for deductive program verification should be designed with the formal semantics of the programming language as foundation. With the formal semantics used as axioms, a mathematical proof of a desired property for the target program can be constructed. Direct program proofs based on operational semantics are often cumbersome. Due to language constructs that may incur unbounded program behavior, inductive proofs along the structure of semantic derivations (e.g., [27]) are expected.

An established method for simplifying the verification is by devising a program logic (e.g., [18,34]) for the programming language. Program logics effectively reduce the burdens in dealing with many aspects of the verification, such as the reasoning about loops, recursive function calls, memory layout of objects, concurrency, etc. The effectiveness of program logics has been demonstrated by powerful tools (e.g., [6,9,10,20]) and significant projects (e.g., [30,37]).

A price to pay for enjoying the power of program logics, however, is the considerable amount of effort often needed in establishing their soundness and

© Springer Nature Switzerland AG 2021
S. Qin et al. (Eds.): SETTA 2021, LNCS 13071, pp. 61–80, 2021.
https://doi.org/10.1007/978-3-030-91265-9_4

completeness wrt. the baseline semantics – often an operational semantics. There have been a plethora of programming languages designed and implemented to meet the needs of different domains. The recent development of blockchain technology alone has led to the creation of multiple languages, such as Solidity [5], Yul [7], Scilla [36], Move [3], Michelson [2], EVM bytecode language [41], etc. Developing one program logic for each language that could be used in scenarios where correctness is of serious concern would require a huge amount of efforts.

To combat the cumbersomeness of direct program proofs based on operational semantics, while avoiding the full complexity in the development of program logics, one could seek to establish the infrastructure necessary for reasoning about specific kinds of language features, for any languages with those features. The results in [26] and [25] show how to deal with fundamental language features that may cause unbounded behavior, such as iteration and recursion, in a language-independent fashion. In [26], a technique is proposed to generate inductive invariants from annotated loop invariants. In [25], a method is presented to turn the semantics of a programming language into a program verifier by applying coinductive reasoning principles. Both developments are built on the small-step execution relation of programs.

Small-step semantics [31] is known to be a fine-grained approach to the definition of operational semantics. It supports a way to model concurrent execution. It also enables the differentiation of looping and abnormal termination. Big-step semantics (or natural semantics [15,21]), on the other hand, can be easier to formulate. For instance, the design of the semantic configurations need not track the intermediate control states. Big-step semantics can also be easier to use. It does not require the consideration of both derivation sequences and derivation trees at the same time, in performing proofs. There exist many formalizations of big-step semantics (e.g., [4,11,17,23,28,42]) with practical uses.

In this work, we propose a technique for reasoning about iteration and recursion in deductive program verification based on big-step operational semantics. For any programming language with a big-step semantics, once a generic predicate is defined to hold on the premises and corresponding conclusions for the semantic rules, a theorem becomes available – the theorem turns the verification of partial correctness results into symbolic execution of the target program with auxiliary information from the user specification. For loops and recursive function calls, this auxiliary information is provided in the same form via the specification, enabling the same pattern of reasoning. We illustrate our technique using verification tasks involving simplified imperative and functional languages. We mechanize the proofs of all formal results [8] in the Coq proof assistant [1].

The main technical contributions of this article are:

- a language-independent technique simplifying the deductive verification of iterative and recursive program structures based on big-step semantics,
- proofs for the soundness and relative completeness of the technique,
- illustration of the technique with the verification of example programs in simplified programming languages of different paradigms,
- mechanization of proofs and verification examples in the Coq proof assistant.

We provide an infrastructure that handles the routine part of the work in reasoning about programming constructs with potentially unbounded behavior, based on a common model of big-step execution in a proof assistant. This provides a basis for a language-independent deductive program verifier.

Structure. The remaining part of this article is structured as follows. In Sect. 2, we introduce the reasoning technique, and prove its soundness. In Sect. 3, we illustrate the technique with a toy example that is developed in detail. In Sect. 4, we present further verification examples targeting simplified imperative and functional languages. In Sect. 5, we discuss the completeness of the technique. In Sect. 6, we discuss related work. In Sect. 7, we discuss potential extensions of the current development. Finally, we conclude in Sect. 8.

2   The Technique

The proposed verification technique can be used to check that the potential execution results of a program satisfy pre-specified conditions. The potential execution results are estimated by a combination of concrete computation according to the big-step semantics of the programming language, and abstract inference according to the auxiliary information in the specification. The abstract inference helps realize what is usually accomplished with loop invariants in reasoning about loops, and with function contracts in reasoning about function calls.

2.1   Specifications

We capture the execution status of programs by *configurations*. We capture the results of program execution by *result configurations*. For imperative languages, a configuration can be a pair of a program and a state, and a result configuration can be a state. For functional languages, a configuration can be a functional expression, and a result configuration can be a canonical form.

Let C be the set of all possible configurations ranged over by c, for programs written in some language. Let R be the set of all possible result configurations ranged over by r, for programs in the same language. We do not rely on any assumptions about the structure of the elements in C or in R.

A *specification* is a function $\Phi \in C \to \mathcal{P}(R)$. For a configuration c, if c contains the complete program to be verified, then $\Phi(c)$ is the set of result configurations capturing the required range for the execution results of the program. Otherwise, $\Phi(c)$ is the expected set of potential results obtained by executing some statement within the overall program. This set provides auxiliary information for the verification.

2.2   Semantic Derivation and Correctness

We model the set of rules of a big-step operational semantics by a predicate $rule \in (C \times R)^* \to (C \times R) \to \{tt, ff\}$. Each semantic rule is captured as

$$rule\ [(c_1, r_1), \ldots, (c_n, r_n)]\ (c, r)$$

Here, the list $[(c_1, r_1), \ldots, (c_n, r_n)]$ models the list of premises of the rule, and (c, r) models the conclusion of the rule. Each premise or conclusion consists of a configuration in the set C and a corresponding result configuration in the set R. A side condition in a semantic rule can be captured by a condition on the parameters $c_1, \ldots, c_n, r_1, \ldots, r_n, c$, and r, in a concrete definition of *rule*.

A semantic derivation concluding that the configuration c can be evaluated to the result configuration r in the big-step semantics is captured by

$$deriv(c, r) := \exists k : \exists c_1, \ldots, c_k : \exists r_1, \ldots, r_k :$$
$$rule\ [(c_1, r_1), \ldots, (c_k, r_k)]\ (c, r) \wedge$$
$$\forall i \in \{1, \ldots, k\} : deriv(c_i, r_i)$$

Hence, the configuration c can be evaluated to the result configuration r, or (c, r) can be derived in the big-step semantics, if there is a semantic rule with (c, r) as conclusion, and each premise of the rule can itself be derived in the big-step semantics. Intuitively, if $deriv(c, r)$ can be established, then there is a finite derivation tree rooted at (c, r).

With the notion of semantic derivation defined above, we formalize the notion of partial correctness as the validity of specifications.

$$valid(\Phi) := \forall c, r : deriv(c, r) \Rightarrow r \in \Phi(c)$$

A specification Φ is valid, if for each configuration c, any result configurations semantically derivable from c is a member of $\Phi(c)$.

2.3   Specification-Aware Inference and Verification

We infer the potential execution results of a configuration under a given specification Φ according to the following definition.

$$infer^{\Phi}(c, r) := \exists k : \exists c_1, \ldots, c_k : \exists r_1, \ldots, r_k :$$
$$rule\ [(c_1, r_1), \ldots, (c_k, r_k)]\ (c, r) \wedge$$
$$\forall i \in \{1, \ldots, k\} : res^{\Phi}(c_i, r_i)$$
$$res^{\Phi}(c, r) := r \in \Phi(c) \wedge (\Phi(c) = R \Rightarrow infer^{\Phi}(c, r))$$

The result configuration r is infered from the configuration c with the help of the specification Φ, if there is a semantic rule with (c, r) as conclusion, and for each premise (c_i, r_i) of the semantic rule, r_i is a potential result for c_i according to Φ, as is captured by the auxiliary predicate res^{Φ}. The expression $res^{\Phi}(c_i, r_i)$ says that the possible candidates for r_i are constrained by the information contained in the specification about c_i. In addition, if Φ does not provide any useful information about c_i (i.e., $\Phi(c_i) = R$), then r_i should be inferable from c_i.

Intuitively, the application of the semantic rules in the inference corresponds to the symbolic execution of the target program. The information in the specification can be used to overcome the inability to symbolically execute the constructs with potentially unbounded behavior, such as iteration and recursion.

We formulate the condition to be verified on specifications Φ using the predicate *verif*. In other words, $verif(\Phi)$ is the syntactical correctness condition.

$$verif(\Phi) := \forall c, r : infer^{\Phi}(c, r) \Rightarrow r \in \Phi(c)$$

A specification Φ is verified, if for each configuration c, any result configurations that can be infered from c with the help of Φ are contained in $\Phi(c)$.

2.4 Soundness

We prove the implication from $verif(\Phi)$ to $valid(\Phi)$. The following lemma is a key component of this proof.

Lemma 1. *If $verif(\Phi)$ holds, and $deriv(c, r)$ holds, then $infer^{\Phi}(c, r)$ holds.*

Proof. According to the definition of $deriv(c, r)$, if this predicate holds, then there is a finite derivation tree generated by the following inference rule.

$$\frac{deriv(c_1, r_1) \quad \dots \quad deriv(c_m, r_m) \qquad rule \; [(c_1, r_1), \dots, (c_m, r_m)] \; (c, r)}{deriv(c, r)}$$

The proof is by induction on the derivation tree for $deriv(c, r)$.

From $deriv(c, r)$, we have $deriv(c_1, r_1)$, ..., $deriv(c_m, r_m)$, and

$$rule \; [(c_1, r_1), \dots, (c_m, r_m)] \; (c, r) \tag{1}$$

for some $m, c_1, \dots, c_m, r_1, \dots, r_m$.

For each $i \in \{1, \dots, m\}$, we have $infer^{\Phi}(c_i, r_i)$ from $deriv(c_i, r_i)$ and the induction hypothesis. We show that $res^{\Phi}(c_i, r_i)$ holds by distinguishing between the cases where $\Phi(c_i) = R$ and where $\Phi(c_i) \neq R$.

- Suppose $\Phi(c_i) = R$. Then, it holds that $r \in \Phi(c_i)$. Hence, we have $res^{\Phi}(c_i, r_i)$ because of $infer^{\Phi}(c_i, r_i)$, and the definition of res^{Φ}.
- Suppose $\Phi(c_i) \neq R$. From $infer^{\Phi}(c_i, r_i)$, and $verif(\Phi)$, we have $r_i \in \Phi(c_i)$. Hence, we have $res^{\Phi}(c_i, r_i)$ according to the definition of res^{Φ}.

Hence, for each $i \in \{1, \dots, m\}$, we have $res^{\Phi}(c_i, r_i)$. Thus, we can deduce $infer^{\Phi}(c, r)$ using (1) and the definition of $infer^{\Phi}$. This completes the proof. □

Using this lemma, the soundness theorem can be obtained directly.

Theorem 1 (Soundness). *If $verif(\Phi)$ can be established, then $valid(\Phi)$ holds.*

Proof. Assume $verif(\Phi)$ and $deriv(c, r)$. Then, we have $infer^{\Phi}(c, r)$ according to Lemma 1. Thus, we can deduce $r \in \Phi(c)$ using $verif(\Phi)$. □

The application of this theorem reliably turns the problem of establishing the validity of a specification Φ into the problem of proving $verif(\Phi)$, irrespective of the language used for the program that is specified in Φ. The examples in Sect. 3 and Sect. 4 show that the proof of $verif(\Phi)$ is free from induction for reasoning about iterative and recursive programming constructs, once auxiliary information summarizing the effects of these constructs is provided.

Remark 1. Lemma 1 suggests that an abstract form of computation is obtained leveraging verified user specification. This abstract computation over-approximates the concrete computation, which indicates a potential connection with abstract interpretation [16]. However, we do not attempt at a formal interpretation of our technique in the framework of abstract interpretation in this work.

3   Illustrative Example

In this section, we illustrate our technique using a toy example. In this example, a program computing the factorial of a natural number is written in the While language [27]. We show how the big-step semantics of the While language can be formulated with the *rule* predicate introduced in Sect. 2.2. We then show how the functional correctness of the factorial program can be specified and proven.

3.1   Big-Step Semantics of the While Language

The main syntactical categories of the While language are arithmetic expressions a, Boolean expressions b, and statements S. A statement can be skip that performs no operation, an assignment $x := a$, a sequential composition $S_1; S_2$, a branching statement if b then S_1 else S_2, or a loop while b do S. Let the set of all statements be *Stmt*.

For programs in the While language, the states σ are elements of $\Sigma := Var \rightarrow \mathbb{Z}$. Here, *Var* is the set of variables and $\mathbb{Z}$ is the set of integers. The evaluation of arithmetic expressions and Boolean expressions in states can be formalized by defining evaluation functions $\mathcal{A}$ and $\mathcal{B}$, respectively, as in [27].

For the semantics of the While language, the set C of configurations is *Stmt* $\times \Sigma$, and the set R of result configurations is Σ. We formulate the big-step semantics by defining the predicate *rule*, as in Fig. 1. In each line, a combination of the parameter values for which *rule* holds is given.

$rule\ []\ (\langle \text{skip}, \sigma \rangle, \sigma)$

$rule\ []\ (\langle x := a, \sigma \rangle, \sigma[x \mapsto \mathcal{A}[\![a]\!]\sigma])$

$rule\ [(\langle S_1, \sigma \rangle, \sigma''), (\langle S_2, \sigma'' \rangle, \sigma')]\ (\langle S_1; S_2, \sigma \rangle, \sigma')$

$rule\ [(\langle S_1, \sigma \rangle, \sigma')]\ (\langle \text{if } b \text{ then } S_1 \text{ else } S_2, \sigma \rangle, \sigma')\quad \text{if } \mathcal{B}[\![b]\!]\sigma = tt$

$rule\ [(\langle S_2, \sigma \rangle, \sigma')]\ (\langle \text{if } b \text{ then } S_1 \text{ else } S_2, \sigma \rangle, \sigma')\quad \text{if } \mathcal{B}[\![b]\!]\sigma = ff$

$rule\ [(\langle S, \sigma \rangle, \sigma''), (\langle \text{while } b \text{ do } S, \sigma'' \rangle, \sigma')]\ (\langle \text{while } b \text{ do } S, \sigma \rangle, \sigma')\ \text{if } \mathcal{B}[\![b]\!]\sigma = tt$

$rule\ []\ (\langle \text{while } b \text{ do } S, \sigma \rangle, \sigma)\ \text{if } \mathcal{B}[\![b]\!]\sigma = ff$

Fig. 1. The semantic rules for the statements of the While language

There is a direct correspondence between the formulation in Fig. 1 and a formulation using inference rules (e.g., [27]). For instance, the inference rule for the loop while b do S in the case where the conditional expression evaluates to true can be formulated as

$$\frac{\langle S, \sigma \rangle \to \sigma'' \quad \langle \text{while } b \text{ do } S, \sigma'' \rangle \to \sigma'}{\langle \text{while } b \text{ do } S, \sigma \rangle \to \sigma'} \quad \text{if } \mathcal{B}[\![b]\!]\sigma = tt$$

It is captured exactly by the second last line in the definition of *rule* in Fig. 1.

3.2   Factorial Program and Its Specification

Consider the program S_{fac} in the While language. The program computes the factorial $m!$ where m is the initial value of the program variable m.

$$S_{\text{fac}} := (\texttt{fac} := \texttt{m}; S_{\text{wh}})$$
$$S_{\text{wh}} := (\texttt{while } 1 < \texttt{m do } (\texttt{m} := \texttt{m} - 1; \texttt{fac} := \texttt{fac} * \texttt{m}))$$

Let P_m be the set of states where fac has the value $m!$. Let $P'_{m,fac}$ be the set of states where fac has the value $fac * (m-1)!$.

$$P_m := \{\sigma'[\texttt{fac} \mapsto m!] \mid \sigma' \in \Sigma\}$$
$$P'_{m,fac} := \{\sigma'[\texttt{fac} \mapsto fac * (m-1)!] \mid \sigma' \in \Sigma\}$$

We consider the following specification for the program.

$$\Phi_{\text{fac}}(\langle S_{\text{fac}}, \sigma \rangle) := P_m \quad \text{if } m = \sigma(\texttt{m}) \wedge m > 0 \wedge \sigma \in \Sigma$$
$$\Phi_{\text{fac}}(\langle S_{\text{wh}}, \sigma \rangle) := P'_{m,fac} \text{ if } m = \sigma(\texttt{m}) \wedge m > 0 \wedge fac = \sigma(\texttt{fac}) \wedge \sigma \in \Sigma$$
$$\Phi_{\text{fac}}(c) := \Sigma \quad \text{if } c \text{ is not of the above forms}$$

The specification says that when S_{fac} finishes execution started in a state where the value of m is $m > 0$, the value of fac will be $m!$. The specification also contains the auxiliary claim that when the loop S_{wh} finishes execution started in a state where fac has the value fac and m has the value $m > 0$, the value of fac will be equal to the product of fac and $(m-1)!$ (noting that $0! = 1$).

3.3   Proof of the Factorial Program

A direct proof of the factorial program S_{fac} based on the big-step operational semantics of the While language would require an induction on the shape of derivation trees (e.g., [27]) to establish a suitable invariant for the loop S_{wh}.

Using the technique of Sect. 2, we aim at establishing $valid(\Phi_{\text{fac}})$. With Theorem 1, it suffices to show $verif(\Phi_{\text{fac}})$ – for all c and r, assuming $infer^{\Phi_{\text{fac}}}(c, r)$, we attempt to show $r \in \Phi_{\text{fac}}(c)$.

1. Firstly, assume c is $\langle S_{\text{fac}}, \sigma \rangle$, where $\sigma(\texttt{m}) > 0$. Then, $\Phi_{\text{fac}}(c)$ is P_m, where $m = \sigma(\texttt{m})$. Using $infer^{\Phi_{\text{fac}}}(\langle S_{\text{fac}}, \sigma \rangle, r)$ and the semantics of the While language in Fig. 1, it is not difficult to obtain

$$rule\ [(\langle \texttt{fac} := \texttt{m}, \sigma \rangle, \sigma''), (\langle S_{\text{wh}}, \sigma'' \rangle, r)]\ (\langle S_{\text{fac}}, \sigma \rangle, r)$$

for some σ'' such that $res^{\Phi_{\text{fac}}}(\langle \texttt{fac} := \texttt{m}, \sigma \rangle, \sigma'')$ and $res^{\Phi_{\text{fac}}}(\langle S_{\text{wh}}, \sigma'' \rangle, r)$. Since $\Phi_{\text{fac}}(\langle \texttt{fac} := \texttt{m}, \sigma \rangle) = R$, we deduce $infer^{\Phi_{\text{fac}}}(\langle \texttt{fac} := \texttt{m}, \sigma \rangle, \sigma'')$ from

$res^{\Phi_{\text{fac}}}(\langle \texttt{fac} := \texttt{m}, \sigma \rangle, \sigma'')$. Hence, we deduce $\sigma'' = \sigma[\texttt{fac} \mapsto \sigma(\texttt{m})]$. Hence, we have $\sigma''(\texttt{m}) = \sigma(\texttt{m}) > 0$. Hence, we have $\Phi_{\text{fac}}(\langle S_{\text{wh}}, \sigma'' \rangle) = P'_{\sigma''(\texttt{m}), \sigma''(\texttt{fac})} = \{\sigma'[\texttt{fac} \mapsto \sigma''(\texttt{fac}) * (\sigma''(\texttt{m}) - 1)!] \mid \sigma' \in \Sigma\} = \{\sigma'[\texttt{fac} \mapsto \sigma(\texttt{m})!] \mid \sigma' \in \Sigma\} = P_m$. Moreover, from $res^{\Phi_{\text{fac}}}(\langle S_{\text{wh}}, \sigma'' \rangle, r)$ we have $r \in \Phi_{\text{fac}}(\langle S_{\text{wh}}, \sigma'' \rangle)$. Ultimately, we have $r \in P_m$.

2. Secondly, assume c is $\langle S_{\text{wh}}, \sigma \rangle$, where $\sigma(\texttt{m}) > 0$. Then, $\Phi_{\text{fac}}(c)$ is $P'_{m, fac}$, where $m = \sigma(\texttt{m})$, and $fac = \sigma(\texttt{fac})$. Using $infer^{\Phi_{\text{fac}}}(\langle S_{\text{wh}}, \sigma \rangle, r)$ and the semantics of the While language in Fig. 1, we have the following two cases.

   (a) We have $m \leq 1$, $rule \ [\ ] \ (\langle S_{\text{wh}}, \sigma \rangle, \sigma)$, and $r = \sigma$. Since $m > 0$ and $m \leq 1$, we have $m = 1$. Hence, it is not difficult to deduce $r \in P'_{m, fac}$.

   (b) We have $m > 1$, and

$$rule \ [(\langle \texttt{m} := \texttt{m} - 1; \texttt{fac} := \texttt{fac} * \texttt{m}, \sigma \rangle, \sigma''), (\langle S_{\text{wh}}, \sigma'' \rangle, r)] \ (\langle S_{\text{wh}}, \sigma \rangle, r)$$

   for some σ'' such that $res^{\Phi_{\text{fac}}}(\langle \texttt{m} := \texttt{m} - 1; \texttt{fac} := \texttt{fac} * \texttt{m}, \sigma \rangle, \sigma'')$ and $res^{\Phi_{\text{fac}}}(\langle S_{\text{wh}}, \sigma'' \rangle, r)$. From the former we have

$$infer^{\Phi_{\text{fac}}}(\langle \texttt{m} := \texttt{m} - 1; \texttt{fac} := \texttt{fac} * \texttt{m}, \sigma \rangle, \sigma'')$$

   The specification Φ_{fac} provides no information about the two assignments, $\texttt{m} := \texttt{m} - 1$ and $\texttt{fac} := \texttt{fac} * \texttt{m}$. Hence, $infer^{\Phi_{\text{fac}}}$ applies to these two individual assignments, and it can be deduced that $\sigma'' = \sigma[\texttt{m} \mapsto m - 1, \texttt{fac} \mapsto fac * (m - 1)]$. Hence, we have $\sigma''(\texttt{m}) = m - 1 > 0$. Hence, $\Phi_{\text{fac}}(\langle S_{\text{wh}}, \sigma'' \rangle) = P'_{\sigma''(\texttt{m}), \sigma''(\texttt{fac})} = \{\sigma'[\texttt{fac} \mapsto (fac * (m - 1)) * (m - 1 - 1)!] \mid \sigma' \in \Sigma\} = P'_{m, fac}$. Moreover, from $res^{\Phi_{\text{fac}}}(\langle S_{\text{wh}}, \sigma'' \rangle, r)$ we have $r \in P'_{\sigma''(\texttt{m}), \sigma''(\texttt{fac})}$. Ultimately, we have $r \in P'_{m, fac}$.

In the other cases, we have $\Phi_{\text{fac}}(c) = R$. Hence, it trivially holds that $r \in \Phi_{\text{fac}}(c)$ The proof is thus complete.   □

The above proof of the factorial program does not require the use of induction. Essentially, the induction required for the loop is already encapsulated in the proof of Theorem 1.

3.4   Comparison with Hoare-Style Program Verification

A Hoare-style specification of the factorial program would be $\{\texttt{m} = n \wedge n > 0\} \ S_{\text{fac}} \ \{\texttt{fac} = n!\}$ Here, n is a logical variable that is used to record the initial value of the program variable m. This specification corresponds to our definition of $\Phi_{\text{fac}}(\langle S_{\text{fac}}, \sigma \rangle)$ for $\sigma(\texttt{m}) > 0$. The latter is more verbose for its explicit reference to states. On the other hand, the use of the latter specification spares the efforts to define an assertion language for each specific programming language.

In Hoare logic, the verification of the program can be performed with the loop invariant $1 \leq \texttt{m} \leq n \wedge \texttt{fac} = n * (n - 1) * \cdots * \texttt{m}$. It captures the condition that is preserved under the effects of a single round of loop. In comparison, the specification Φ_{fac} features the loop variant $\Phi_{\text{fac}}(\langle S_{\text{wh}}, \sigma \rangle)$ (with $\sigma(\texttt{m}) > 0$). It captures the cumulative effects of the loop from the start of any round to the end of the last round. It can be seen that different ways of thinking are required in coming up with the two kinds of specifications. With the proposed technique, the same style as Φ_{fac} can be used for different programming languages, for both loops and recursive functions, as can be seen in Sect. 4.

In Hoare logic, the reasoning about programs is often performed in a backward fashion. For a statement that is neither a loop nor a function call, a precondition is derived from the post-condition based on the logical rule for the statement. For a loop or a function call, the pre-condition is inferred based on the invariant of the loop or the contract of the function. In our technique, the reasoning is performed in a forward fashion. If a specification provides no information about a configuration, a result configuration is derived directly using the semantics. For instance, the result configuration $\sigma[\mathtt{fac} \mapsto \sigma(\mathtt{m})]$ is derived from the configuration $\langle \mathtt{fac} := \mathtt{m}, \sigma \rangle$ using the semantics in the factorial example. Otherwise, the specification is used to infer the potential result configurations. For instance, the specification Φ_{fac} is used to infer the potential result configurations for the configuration $\langle S_{\mathrm{wh}}, \sigma[\mathtt{fac} \mapsto \sigma(\mathtt{m})] \rangle$ in the factorial example.

In Hoare-style program verification, a loop invariant is justified by assuming that it holds after a round of loop, and showing that it also holds before that round. In our technique, a loop variant is justified by executing one round of loop from each configuration satisfying the pre-condition of the loop variant, and showing that no more result configurations are possible according to the loop variant for each configuration reached after that round (e.g., $\langle S_{\mathrm{wh}}, \sigma[\mathtt{m} \mapsto m - 1, \mathtt{fac} \mapsto fac * (m - 1)] \rangle$ in the factorial example), than for the original configuration (e.g., $\langle S_{\mathrm{wh}}, \sigma \rangle$ in the factorial example) before that round.

4 Verification of Iterative and Recursive Programs

In this section, we evaluate our technique with two further examples. In the two examples, programming languages of the imperative and functional paradigms are used, respectively, to implement the functionality of merging two sorted lists of integers into a single sorted list of integers.

4.1 Extended While Language and Array-Merging Program

Extended While Language. The programming language of this section is an extension of the While language. This extension contains the extra features of one-dimensional arrays and functions.

We give the syntax for arithmetic expressions a, Boolean expressions b, and statements S. We then explain the constructs present in the extension only.

$$
\begin{aligned}
a &::= n \mid x \mid X \mid X[a] \mid a + a \mid a - a \mid a * a \mid a / a \\
b &::= \mathsf{true} \mid \mathsf{false} \mid a = a \mid a < a \mid b \,\&\&\, b \mid !b \\
S &::= \mathsf{var}\ x \mid \mathsf{arr}\ X[n] \mid x := a \mid X[a] := a \mid \mathsf{skip} \mid \\
&\quad\ \mathsf{if}\ b\ \mathsf{then}\ S\ \mathsf{else}\ S \mid \mathsf{while}\ b\ \mathsf{do}\ S \mid S; S \mid f(a, \ldots, a) \to [x, \ldots, x]
\end{aligned}
$$

$\rho_{\mathrm{mg}} := [\,\mathsf{merge} \mapsto ([\mathsf{S}, \mathsf{T}, \mathtt{i}, \mathtt{m}, \mathtt{n}], [\,], S_{\mathrm{mg}})\,]$

$S_{\mathrm{mg}} := \mathsf{var}\ \mathtt{j}; \mathsf{var}\ \mathtt{k};\ \mathtt{j} := \mathtt{m} + 1; \mathtt{k} := \mathtt{i};\ S_{\mathrm{wh}}; S_{\mathtt{i},\mathtt{m}}; S_{\mathtt{j},\mathtt{n}}$

$S_{\mathrm{wh}} := \mathsf{while}\ \mathtt{i} \leq \mathtt{m}\ \&\&\ \mathtt{j} \leq \mathtt{n}\ \mathsf{do}\ ($

           $(\mathsf{if}\ \mathsf{S}[\mathtt{i}] \leq \mathsf{S}[\mathtt{j}]\ \mathsf{then}\ \mathsf{T}[\mathtt{k}] := \mathsf{S}[\mathtt{i}]; \mathtt{i} := \mathtt{i} + 1\ \mathsf{else}\ \mathsf{T}[\mathtt{k}] := \mathsf{S}[\mathtt{j}]; \mathtt{j} := \mathtt{j} + 1);$

           $\mathtt{k} := \mathtt{k} + 1\,)$

$S_{\mathtt{i},\mathtt{m}} := \mathsf{while}\ \mathtt{i} \leq \mathtt{m}\ \mathsf{do}\ (\mathsf{T}[\mathtt{k}] := \mathsf{S}[\mathtt{i}]; \mathtt{i} := \mathtt{i} + 1; \mathtt{k} := \mathtt{k} + 1)$

$S_{\mathtt{j},\mathtt{n}} := \mathsf{while}\ \mathtt{j} \leq \mathtt{n}\ \mathsf{do}\ (\mathsf{T}[\mathtt{k}] := \mathsf{S}[\mathtt{j}]; \mathtt{j} := \mathtt{j} + 1; \mathtt{k} := \mathtt{k} + 1)$

Fig. 2. The program ρ_{mg} that merges sorted array fragments

Here, X is an array identifier, and $X[a]$ is the expression used to retrieve the element of the array X at the index a. In addition, var x is the declaration of the variable x, arr $X[n]$ is the declaration of the array with identifier X and size n, $X[a_1] := a_2$ is an assignment of the result of a_2 to the element of the array X indexed at a_1, and $f(a_1, \ldots, a_m) \to [x_1, \ldots, x_n]$ is a call to the function with identifier f with arguments $a_1, \ldots, a_m$ and return variables $x_1, \ldots, x_n$. If some argument a_i is an array, then it is passed by reference in the call. We denote the set of all statements of the extended While language by $Stmt_{\mathrm{ewh}}$.

A *program* in the extended While language is a mapping ρ from each function identifier f to a triple $([w_1, \ldots, w_m], [x_1, \ldots, x_n], S)$ or $\bot$. Here, each w_i ($i \in \{1, \ldots, m\}$) is a parameter of the function that is either a variable x or an array X. Each x_i ($i \in \{1, \ldots, n\}$) is a return variable of the function. The S is the statement of the function. If $\rho(f) = \bot$, then there is no function defined for the function identifier in the program.

For programs of the extended While language, a *state* σ is a pair (s, ι). Here, $s \in (Var \cup Arr \to \mathbb{Z}_\bot) \cup (\mathbb{Z} \to \mathbb{Z})$ is a *store* that maps each variable to an optional integer that is the value of the variable, maps each array name to an optional integer representing the starting location of the array, and maps each location to an integer that is the value stored at the location. In addition, $\iota \in \mathbb{Z}$ is the *next fresh location* that can be used as the starting location of an array. For $\sigma = (s, \iota)$, we write $\sigma(a)$ for $s(a)$. We denote the set of all states by Σ_{ewh}.

For the extended While language, the set C of configurations is $Stmt_{\mathrm{ewh}} \times \Sigma_{\mathrm{ewh}}$, and the set R of result configurations is Σ_{ewh}. For space reasons, we omit the definition of the *rule* predicate that captures the big-step semantics of the extended While language. This definition can be found in the extended version of this paper, as well as the formalization in the Coq proof assistant.

Array-Merging Program and Its Verification. The program ρ_{mg} as shown in Fig. 2 merges the elements in two sorted fragments of an array S into one sorted fragment in a different array T.

The only function in this program is merge. Formally, this function is the triple $([\mathsf{S}, \mathsf{T}, \mathtt{i}, \mathtt{m}, \mathtt{n}], [\,], S_{\mathrm{mg}})$. The parameters $\mathtt{i}$ and $\mathtt{m}$ represent the initial and final index, respectively, for the first fragment of the array S participating in the merger. The second fragment participating in the merger is from the index represented by $m + 1$ to the index represented by n in the same array S. The target array fragment of the merger is from the index represented by i to the index represented by n, in the array T.

For the specification of the program, we use a few pieces of auxiliary notation. We write X_l^h for a triple (X, l, h) that represents the fragment of the array X from the index l to the index h. We write $(\!|X_l^h|\!)_\sigma$ for the list $[\sigma(\ell + l), \dots, \sigma(\ell + h)]$ where $\ell = \sigma(X)$, i.e., the list of elements of the array X from the index l to the index h. We write $occ\,[z_1, \dots, z_n]$ for the function h mapping each integer z to the number of occurrences of z in the list $[z_1, \dots, z_n]$ of integers. For two such functions h_1 and h_2, we write $h_1 \oplus h_2$ for the function $\lambda z.h_1(z) + h_2(z)$. We write $sorted\,[z_1, \dots, z_n]$ to express that the list $[z_1, \dots, z_n]$ of integers is sorted in ascending order. We write $sep(X_{l_1}^{h_1}, Y_{l_2}^{h_2}, \sigma)$ to express that the elements of the array X from the index l_1 to the index h_1 occupy a separate memory area from that occupied by the elements of the array Y from the index l_2 to the index h_2, in the state σ. In addition, we write $[u_1, \dots, u_n]_\sigma^{\sigma'}$ to express for each $i \in \{1, \dots, n\}$, the value of each u_i is the same in the states σ and σ'. Here, u_i can be a variable x or an array fragment X_l^h. In the latter case, that the value of X_l^h is the same in the two states means $\forall i : l \leq i \leq h \Rightarrow \sigma(\sigma(X) + i) = \sigma'(\sigma'(X) + i)$.

For the program ρ_{mg}, we devise the specification Φ_{mga}. We denote the starting index for the first source array fragment in S as well as for the target array fragment in T by l. We use l as a global parameter in the specification.

We specify the function merge as

$$\Phi_{\mathrm{mga}}(\langle \mathrm{merge}(X, Y, a_{\mathrm{l}}, a_{\mathrm{m}}, a_{\mathrm{h}}) \to [], \sigma \rangle_{\rho_{\mathrm{ms}}}) :=$$

$$\{\sigma' \mid occ\,(\!|X_l^h|\!)_\sigma = occ\,(\!|Y_l^h|\!)_{\sigma'} \wedge sorted\,(\!|Y_l^h|\!)_{\sigma'}\}$$

$$\text{if } \mathcal{A}[\![a_{\mathrm{l}}]\!]\sigma = l \wedge 0 \leq l \leq m < h \wedge sorted\,(\!|X_l^m|\!)_\sigma \wedge sorted\,(\!|X_{m+1}^h|\!)_\sigma \wedge sep(X_l^h, Y_l^h, \sigma)$$

$$\text{where } m = \mathcal{A}[\![a_{\mathrm{m}}]\!]\sigma \wedge h = \mathcal{A}[\![a_{\mathrm{h}}]\!]\sigma$$

This specification says that if we call the function merge with two array identifiers X and Y, and expressions $a_{\mathrm{l}}, a_{\mathrm{m}}, a_{\mathrm{h}}$ that evaluate to l, m and h, such that

- $0 \leq l \leq m < h$ holds,
- the array fragments X_l^m and X_{m+1}^h are sorted in the pre-state,
- the array fragments X_l^m and X_{m+1}^h are separated in the pre-state,

then the number of occurrences of each integer in the target array fragment Y_l^h in the post-state is the same as its number of occurrences in the source array fragment X_l^h in the pre-state, and the target array fragment Y_l^h is sorted in ascending order in the post-state.

The core part of the function merge is the loop statement S_{wh} (see Fig. 2). We specify this loop as

$\Phi_{\mathrm{mga}}(\langle S_{\mathrm{wh}}, \sigma \rangle_{\rho_{\mathrm{ms}}}) :=$

$\quad \{\sigma' \mid (i \leq \sigma'(i) = m+1 \wedge j \leq \sigma'(j) \leq n \vee j \leq \sigma'(j) = n+1 \wedge i \leq \sigma'(i) \leq m) \wedge$

$\qquad \sigma'(k) = k + \sigma'(i) - i + \sigma'(j) - j \wedge [m, n, S, T, S_l^n, T_l^{k-1}]_\sigma^{\sigma'} \wedge$

$\qquad occ \, (\!|S_i^{\sigma'(i)-1}|\!)_\sigma \oplus occ \, (\!|S_j^{\sigma'(j)-1}|\!)_\sigma = occ \, (\!|T_k^{\sigma'(k)-1}|\!)_{\sigma'} \wedge sorted \, (\!|T_l^{\sigma'(k)-1}|\!)_{\sigma'} \wedge$

$\qquad (\sigma'(i) \leq m \wedge \sigma'(k) \geq l+1 \Rightarrow \mathcal{A}[\![S[i]]\!]\sigma' \geq \mathcal{A}[\![T[k-1]]\!]\sigma') \wedge$

$\qquad (\sigma'(j) \leq n \wedge \sigma'(k) \geq l+1 \Rightarrow \mathcal{A}[\![S[j]]\!]\sigma' \geq \mathcal{A}[\![T[k-1]]\!]\sigma')\}$

$\quad \text{if } 0 \leq l \leq i \leq m < j \leq n \wedge k = i + j - m - 1 \wedge$

$\qquad (k \geq l+1 \Rightarrow \mathcal{A}[\![S[i]]\!]\sigma \geq \mathcal{A}[\![T[k-1]]\!]\sigma \wedge \mathcal{A}[\![S[j]]\!]\sigma \geq \mathcal{A}[\![T[k-1]]\!]\sigma) \wedge$

$\qquad sorted \, (\!|S_i^m|\!)_\sigma \wedge sorted \, (\!|S_j^n|\!)_\sigma \wedge sorted \, (\!|T_l^{k-1}|\!)_\sigma \wedge sep(S_l^n, T_l^n, \sigma)$

$\quad \text{where } i = \sigma(i) \wedge j = \sigma(j) \wedge k = \sigma(k) \wedge m = \sigma(m) \wedge n = \sigma(n)$

In the specification, we are concerned with pre-states in which either the overall loop is yet to be executed, or some rounds of the loop have been completed and some further rounds are to be executed. We constrain these pre-states with a few further conditions. One of these conditions states that the elements with indexes i and j that are to be compared in the next round are both greater than or equal to the last element that has been set in the target array fragment. For each pre-state that satisfies all the conditions in the "if" part, several conditions are asserted for the potential post-state σ'. A key condition here says that the two fragments $S_i^{\sigma'(i)-1}$ and $S_j^{\sigma'(j)-1}$ in the source array that are scanned between the reaching of the pre-state and the post-state agree with the fragment $T_k^{\sigma'(k)-1}$ that is filled between the reaching of the pre-state and the post-state. Another key condition says that the fragment $T_l^{\sigma'(k)-1}$ of the target array that is already filled in the post-state for the loop is sorted in ascending order.

Without specification inference, the two remaining loops in the array-merging program also need to be explicitly specified. The specification of these two loops is much less involved than that for the first loop, and it is omitted here. With the technique of Sect. 2, the validity of Φ_{mga} can be established.

Theorem 2. *It holds that valid(Φ_{mga}).*

With the help of Theorem 1, the proof requires no induction for reasoning about the loops. This proof boils down to symbolic execution with the help of a series of auxiliary lemmas about the memory layout.

Remark 2. The global parameter l in the specification Φ_{mga} relates the auxiliary information about calls to merge and about the loops in this function. The role of l can be compared to that of a logical variable in a concrete program logic. Such global parameters are captured in the Coq formalization by an explicit argument in the specifications. The type of this argument can be instantiated according to the needs in verifying each specific program. The verification of a program is required to go through for all possible values of this argument.

4.2 Eager Functional Language and List-Merging Program

Eager Functional Language. The language considered in this section is a fragment of the eager functional language as discussed in [33].

$$
\begin{aligned}
e ::=\ & n \mid \text{true} \mid \text{false} \mid \\
& e + e \mid e - e \mid e * e \mid e/e \mid \\
& e = e \mid e < e \mid \neg e \mid e \wedge e \mid \\
& \text{if } e \text{ then } e \text{ else } e \mid \\
& \text{nil} \mid e :: e \mid \text{listcase } e \text{ of } (e, e) \mid \\
& x \mid e\,e \mid \lambda x.e \mid \text{letrec } x = \lambda x'.e \text{ in } e
\end{aligned}
\qquad
\begin{aligned}
cf ::=\ & icf \mid bcf \mid fcf \mid lcf \\
icf ::=\ & \ldots \mid -2 \mid -1 \mid 0 \mid 1 \mid 2 \mid \ldots \\
bcf ::=\ & \text{true} \mid \text{false} \\
fcf ::=\ & \lambda x.e \\
lcf ::=\ & \text{nil} \mid cf :: cf
\end{aligned}
$$

Fig. 3. The expressions and canonical forms of the eager functional language

A program of the eager functional language is an expression. The syntax for expressions is given in the left part of Fig. 3. Here, n is a numeral, x is a variable, $e\,e'$ is an application, $\lambda x.e$ is a lambda abstraction, nil is the empty list, and $e_1 :: e_2$ is the list obtained by prefixing the list e_2 with the element e_1. The expression listcase e of (e', e'') branches to e' or e'' depending on whether the result of e is the empty list nil. The expression letrec $x = \lambda x'.e'$ in e binds x to $\lambda x'.e'$ in e. This expression allows x to be used in e', thereby allowing recursion. We denote the set of all expressions by *Expr*.

The evaluation of expressions results in *canonical forms cf* as given in the right part of Fig. 3. A canonical form cf can be a canonical form icf for integers, a canonical form bcf for Boolean values, a canonical form fcf for functions, or a canonical form lcf for lists. We denote the set of all canonical forms by *Cf*.

For the eager functional language, the set C of configurations is *Expr*, and the set R of result configurations is *Cf*. For space reasons, we omit the definition of the *rule* predicate that captures the big-step semantics of the eager functional language. This definition can be found in the extended version of this paper, as well as the formalization in the Coq proof assistant.

List-Merging Program and Its Verification. The program $e_{\mathrm{mg}}(lcf_1, lcf_2)$ below merges two sorted lists, lcf_1 and lcf_2, into a single sorted list. More concretely, the variable merge is bound to the expression $\lambda \mathrm{x}.\lambda \mathrm{x}'.e_{\mathrm{lcase}}$ that destructs the lists that are bound to x and x', respectively. In case one of the lists is empty, the result of the merger is the other list. Otherwise, the result of the merger is obtained by prefixing the smaller head element of the two given lists over the merging result of the remaining parts of the lists.

$$
e_{\mathrm{mg}}(lcf_1, lcf_2) := \text{letrec } \mathrm{merge} = (\lambda \mathrm{x}.\lambda \mathrm{x}'.e_{\mathrm{lcase}}) \text{ in } \mathrm{merge}\ lcf_1\ lcf_2
$$
$$
e_{\mathrm{lcase}} := \text{listcase x of } (\mathrm{x}', \lambda \mathrm{i}.\lambda \mathrm{r}.\text{listcase x}' \text{ of } (\mathrm{x}, \lambda \mathrm{i}'.\lambda \mathrm{r}'.e_{\mathrm{if}}))
$$
$$
e_{\mathrm{if}} := \text{if i} \leq \mathrm{i}' \text{ then i} :: \mathrm{merge}\,\mathrm{r}\,\mathrm{x}' \text{ else i}' :: \mathrm{merge}\,\mathrm{x}\,\mathrm{r}'
$$

To develop a specification for the list-merging program, we define a piece of auxiliary notation. We write $\langle\!| lcf |\!\rangle$ for the mathematical list of integers represented by the canonical form lcf for lists. Formally, we define $\langle\!| nil |\!\rangle := [\,]$, $\langle\!| icf :: lcf |\!\rangle := icf :: zs$ if $zs = \langle\!| lcf |\!\rangle \wedge zs \in \mathbb{Z}^*$, and $\langle\!| lcf |\!\rangle := \bot$ otherwise.

We devise the a specification for the list-merging program, Φ_{mgl}. Using the function occ and the predicate $sorted$ introduced in Sect. 4.1, we specify the expression $e_{\mathrm{mg}}(lcf_1, lcf_2)$ as

$$\Phi_{\mathrm{mgl}}(e_{\mathrm{mg}}(lcf_1, lcf_2)) :=$$
$$\{ lcf \mid \exists zs \in \mathbb{Z}^* : zs = \langle\!| lcf |\!\rangle \wedge occ\, zs = occ\, zs_1 \oplus occ\, zs_2 \wedge sorted\, zs \}$$
$$\text{if } zs_1 \in \mathbb{Z}^* \wedge zs_2 \in \mathbb{Z}^* \wedge sorted\, zs_1 \wedge sorted\, zs_2$$
$$\text{where } zs_1 = \langle\!| lcf_1 |\!\rangle \wedge zs_2 = \langle\!| lcf_2 |\!\rangle$$

This specification says that given list canonical forms lcf_1 and lcf_2 that are both sorted in ascending order, the result of executing $e_{\mathrm{mg}}(lcf_1, lcf_2)$ is a list canonical form lcf. The list canonical form lcf contains the elements as contained in either lcf_1 or lcf_2. Furthermore, the list canonical form lcf is sorted in ascending order.

To support the verification of the specification for $e_{\mathrm{mg}}(lcf_1, lcf_2)$, we specify an unfolded form of this expression. The execution of this unfolded form either terminates directly, or gives the same form again.

$$\Phi_{\mathrm{mgl}}((\lambda\mathrm{x}.\mathsf{letrec\ merge} = \lambda\mathrm{x}.\lambda\mathrm{x}'.e_{\mathrm{lcase}} \text{ in } \lambda\mathrm{x}'.e_{\mathrm{lcase}})\, lcf_1\, lcf_2) :=$$
$$\{ lcf \mid \exists zs \in \mathbb{Z}^* : zs = \langle\!| lcf |\!\rangle \wedge occ\, zs = occ\, lcf_1 \oplus occ\, lcf_2 \wedge sorted\, zs \}$$
$$\text{if } zs_1 \in \mathbb{Z}^* \wedge zs_2 \in \mathbb{Z}^* \wedge sorted\, zs_1 \wedge sorted\, zs_2$$
$$\text{where } zs_1 = \langle\!| lcf_1 |\!\rangle \wedge zs_2 = \langle\!| lcf_2 |\!\rangle$$

This specification reflects that the unfolded expression $(\lambda\mathrm{x}.\mathsf{letrec\ merge} = \lambda\mathrm{x}.\lambda\mathrm{x}'.\, e_{\mathrm{lcase}} \text{ in } \lambda\mathrm{x}'.e_{\mathrm{lcase}})\, lcf_1\, lcf_2$ delivers analogous guarantees to those delivered by the original expression $e_{\mathrm{mg}}(lcf_1, lcf_2)$.

With the technique of Sect. 2, the validity of Φ_{mgl} can be established.

Theorem 3. *It holds that valid*(Φ_{mgl}).

With the help of Theorem 1, the proof requires no induction for reasoning about the recursive applications of the function bound to merge. This proof boils down to symbolic execution with the help of a few auxiliary lemmas about substitution and evaluation related to canonical forms.

Remark 3. It might appear that the auxiliary information needed for the verification of the list-merging program should be for expressions of the form merge _ _. However, these expressions cannot be evaluated, because information about the actual function bound to merge is missing. The form that recurs in the evaluation of $e_{\mathrm{mg}}(lcf_1, lcf_2)$ is actually $(\lambda\mathrm{x}.\mathsf{letrec\ merge} = \lambda\mathrm{x}.\lambda\mathrm{x}'.e_{\mathrm{lcase}} \text{ in } \lambda\mathrm{x}'.e_{\mathrm{lcase}})$ _ _.

5   On Completeness of the Technique

It is untrue that any valid specification can be verified. Intuitively, a specification Φ that is valid but missing the necessary auxiliary information such as loop variants might not be verifiable.

Consider the factorial example in Sect. 3, and the specification Φ'_{fac} that is the same as Φ_{fac} except that Φ'_{fac} maps $\langle S_{wh}, \sigma \rangle$ where $\sigma(\mathrm{m}) > 0$ to Σ. The specification Φ'_{fac} is valid as the specification Φ_{fac} is. This is because Φ'_{fac} is a loosened version of Φ_{fac}. However, Φ'_{fac} cannot be verified using our proposed technique. Due to missing auxiliary information, the verification procedure leads to a non-terminating symbolic execution of the factorial program.

In the following, we show that for a given specification that is valid, there is always a more informative specification Φ' than Φ that is verifiable. Formally, a specification Φ' is *at least as informative as* a specification Φ, as denoted by $\Phi \preceq \Phi'$, if for each configuration c, it holds that $\Phi(c) \supseteq \Phi'(c)$.

The lemma below says the specification mapping each configuration to the set of all the semantically derivable result configurations can be verified.

Lemma 2. *Let Φ_* be the specification satisfying $\Phi_*(c) = \{r \mid deriv(c, r)\}$ for all configurations c. Then, $verif(\Phi_*)$ can be established.*

Proof. We show that for all c and r, if $infer^{\Phi_*}(c, r)$, then $r \in \Phi_*(c)$. This boils down to showing if $infer^{\Phi_*}(c, r)$, then $deriv(c, r)$. Below, we give an inductive proof of this statement.

Assume $infer^{\Phi_*}(c, r)$. Then, there exist some $m, c_1, \ldots, c_m, r_1, \ldots, r_m$, such that $res^{\Phi_*}(c_1, r_1), \ldots, res^{\Phi_*}(c_m, r_m)$, and

$$rule \; [(c_1, r_1), \ldots, (c_m, r_m)] \; (c, r) \qquad (2)$$

For each i, we show that $deriv(c_i, r_i)$ holds by distinguishing between the cases where $\Phi_*(c_i) = R$ and $\Phi_*(c_i) \neq R$.

- Suppose $\Phi_*(c_i) = R$. Then we deduce $infer^{\Phi_*}(c_i, r_i)$ from $res^{\Phi_*}(c_i, r_i)$. Hence, we have $deriv(c_i, r_i)$ from the induction hypothesis.
- Suppose $\Phi_*(c_i) \neq R$. We have $r_i \in \Phi_*(c_i)$ using $res^{\Phi_*}(c_i, r_i)$. Hence, we have $deriv(c_i, r_i)$ using the definition of Φ_*.

Ultimately, we have $deriv(c_i, r_i)$ for each $i \in \{1, \ldots, m\}$, and we obtain $deriv(c, r)$ using (2). This completes the proof.   □

The following theorem says that for each valid specification Φ, there is a specification that is at least as informative as Φ, and that can be verified.

Theorem 4 (Relative Completeness). *For each valid specification Φ, there exists a specification Φ' such that $\Phi \preceq \Phi'$, and $verif(\Phi')$ can be established.*

Proof. We first show that the specification Φ_* in Lemma 2 is at least as informative as any valid specification. Let Φ be a specification satisfying $valid(\Phi)$.

Let c be an arbitrary configuration. Let r be any result configuration satisfying $r \in \Phi_\star(c)$. We have $deriv(c, r)$ from the definition of $\Phi_\star$. Hence, we have $r \in \Phi(c)$ because of $valid(\Phi)$. Hence, $\Phi_\star(c) \subseteq \Phi(c)$ holds. Hence, we have $\Phi \preceq \Phi_\star$. Moreover, we have $verif(\Phi_\star)$ using Lemma 2. This completes the proof.   □

If the program contained in a configuration exhibits only bounded behavior, then the corresponding result configuration can be obtained through symbolic execution. Hence, it is not necessary that a verifiable specification should cover these configurations. In an informal sense, this argument supports that for a specification to be verified, it is only necessary to provide auxiliary information about constructs such as loops and recursive function calls in the specification.

6 Related Work

Inductive invariants [24] are well-studied means to sound program verification directly based on operational execution models. An inductive invariant needs to be preserved by all the possible atomic steps that can be taken in the execution of the target program. This requirement often leads to difficulties in identifying the exact condition that qualifies as an inductive invariant, and that enables the verification of the target program.

In [26], a method is proposed to generate inductive invariants from inductive assertions. The method is based on a small-step execution relation. Minimal information about the syntactical structure of the programming language is required in the generation of the inductive invariants. In comparison, our technique targets big-step operational semantics, and its soundness does not rely on the reduction of the verification problem to the generation of inductive invariants.

In [25], a technique is proposed to generate sound program verifiers based on existing formalizations of small-step semantics in proof assistants. The soundness of the technique is established with a coinductive argument. In comparison, our technique targets big-step operational semantics, and is based on inductive reasoning. Nevertheless, we are inspired by this work in the style of language-independent program specifications and the form of completeness statements.

In [40], a language-independent verification technique based on reachability logics and semantics formulated in rewriting systems is introduced. In comparison, our technique can only be used for big-step semantics. However, our technique can be used with semantic definitions using inductive predicates in a proof assistant, and requires only the logical foundation of the proof assistant to function. Our technique also has a succinct, inductive argument for soundness.

Several developments provide means to systematically derive abstract semantics from concrete semantics such as big-step operational semantics and its variants [12,13,35]. Among these, [12] proposes a language-independent notion of skeletal semantics that can be instantiated to obtain concrete and abstract semantic interpretations. However, the emphasis of these developments is in obtaining automated static analyses of programs, rather than in exploiting user-provided specification in the deductive verification of deep correctness properties.

To some extent, language-independent program verification can also be supported by encoding the target languages or target programs in the same language (e.g., WhyML, Boogie, etc.) or calculus (e.g., CSP, the π-calculus, etc.) supporting verification. This encoding can be considerably more light-weight than the direct formalization of the syntax and semantics of the source language. However, when the features of the source language are sufficiently complicated, it can be highly non-trivial to justify the encoding.

In Unifying Theories of Programming [14,19,22,29,32,38], the semantics of programming constructs (e.g., assignment, conditional, sequential composition, parallel composition, etc.) involved in diverse languages is formulated in a relational calculus. The connection between different kinds of semantics – algebraic semantics, denotational semantics, and operational semantics – is investigated. In comparison, we study the verification of programs based on a common model of big-step opperational semantics. We do not look at concrete programming constructs, or investigate the connection between different types of semantics.

7 Future Directions

Reuse of Existing Formalization of Semantics. For the related language-independent verification techniques based on small-step operational semantics [25,26], it is not difficult to obtain a verification infrastructure by directly reusing an existing formalization of semantics. This is because a small-step semantics readily provides a step relation that can be used to interface with the verification framework. In comparison, we have only shown that our language-independent verification technique can be applied after the big-step semantics of the target language is formalized via a predicate that explicitly captures the premises and conclusions of the semantic rules. Although the big-step semantics formulated using this predicate closely resemble their classical formulation, it is desirable if a higher level of reusability can be enabled. A potential solution is to construct a program that automatically transforms a formalization of big-step semantics into a formulation with the *rule* predicate. Such transformation could be attempted using the MetaCoq framework [39] to achieve seamless integration with the Coq proof assistant.

Integration of Techniques for Other Aspects of Deductive Verification. The purpose of the present work is not to simplify the overall task of deductive program verification beyond achievable by existing techniques. Instead, the focus has been the ability to reason about different types of programming constructs that potentially cause unbounded behavior, in a uniform way. This ability helps simplify the reasoning about these programming constructs, relative to direct inductive proofs based on big-step operational semantics. To construct a full-fledged language-independent program verifier in a proof assistant, effective treatment of other aspects of deductive program verification (e.g., memory layout, mathematical reasoning in diverse problem domains, etc.) is required. In principle, it is desirable to deal with the language-generic and language specific aspects of program verification separately (as advocated in UTP [19]). Concretely, existing formalization of program logics and mathematical theories in proof assistants are expected to provide the essential technical ingredients for simplifying the remaining aspects of verification tasks.

8   Conclusion

To tackle the problem caused by the proliferation of programming languages in deductive program verification, we provide a language-independent verification technique that addresses the cross-cutting concern of reasoning about programming constructs potentially causing unbounded behavior. Typically, these constructs include loops and recursive functions in different forms. The proposed technique can be applied to any programming language with a big-step operational semantics. The user of this technique need not set up inductions for the loops and recursive calls in performing a program proof, but performs symbolic execution of the program based on the big-step semantics, and with the help of a specification containing auxiliary information about these constructs. The technique admits succinct, inductive arguments for soundness and relative completeness that are verified in the Coq proof assistant along with other formal claims [8]. It has been illustrated with verification examples targeting languages of different paradigms. It provides a basis for a language-independent program verifier based on big-step operational semantics in proof assistants.

Acknowledgments. This work was supported by the National Natural Science Foundation of China (61876111, 62002246).

References

1. The Coq proof assistant. https://coq.inria.fr/
2. Michelson - the language of Tezos. https://www.michelson.org/
3. The move language. https://developers.libra-china.org/docs/crates/move-language/index.html
4. A sequential imperative programming language - syntax, semantics, Hoare logics and verification environment. https://www.isa-afp.org/entries/Simpl.html
5. Solidity. https://docs.soliditylang.org/en/v0.8.0/
6. VCC: A verifier for concurrent C. https://www.microsoft.com/en-us/research/project/vcc-a-verifier-for-concurrent-c/
7. Yul. https://docs.soliditylang.org/en/v0.8.0/yul.html
8. Formalization of the verification technique in Coq (2021). https://github.com/lixm/ind-verify/tree/master
9. Ahrendt, W., Beckert, B., Bubel, R. (eds.): Deductive Software Verification - The KeY Book. From Theory to Practice. Lecture Notes in Computer Science, vol. 10001. Springer, Heidelberg (2016). https://doi.org/10.1007/978-3-319-49812-6
10. Appel, A.W.: Verified Software Toolchain - (invited talk). In: Barthe, G. (ed.) ESOP 2011. LNCS, vol. 6602, pp. 1–17. Springer, Heidelberg (2011). https://doi.org/10.1007/978-3-642-19718-5_1

11. Blazy, S., Leroy, X.: Mechanized semantics for the Clight subset of the C language. J. Autom. Reason. **43**(3), 263–288 (2009)
12. Bodin, M., Gardner, P., Jensen, T.P., Schmitt, A.: Skeletal semantics and their interpretations. Proc. ACM Program. Lang. **3**(POPL), 44:1–44:31 (2019)
13. Bodin, M., Jensen, T.P., Schmitt, A.: Certified abstract interpretation with pretty-big-step semantics. In: Proceedings of the 2015 Conference on Certified Programs and Proofs (CPP), pp. 29–40 (2015)
14. Cavalcanti, A., Wellings, A., Woodcock, J.: The safety-critical Java memory model: a formal account. In: Butler, M., Schulte, W. (eds.) FM 2011. LNCS, vol. 6664, pp. 246–261. Springer, Heidelberg (2011). https://doi.org/10.1007/978-3-642-21437-0_20
15. Clément, D., Despeyroux, J., Despeyroux, T., Kahn, G.: A simple applicative language: mini-ML. In: Proceedings of the 1986 ACM Conference on LISP and Functional Programming (LFP), pp. 13–27 (1986)
16. Cousot, P., Cousot, R.: Abstract interpretation: a unified lattice model for static analysis of programs by construction or approximation of fixpoints. In: Fourth ACM Symposium on Principles of Programming Languages (POPL), pp. 238–252 (1977)
17. Hirai, Y., et al.: Defining the ethereum virtual machine for interactive theorem provers. In: Brenner, M. (ed.) FC 2017. LNCS, vol. 10323, pp. 520–535. Springer, Cham (2017). https://doi.org/10.1007/978-3-319-70278-0_33
18. Hoare, C.A.R.: An axiomatic basis for computer programming. Commun. ACM **12**(10), 576–580 (1969)
19. Hoare, C.A.R., He, J.: Unifying Theories of Programming. Pearson College Div (1998)
20. Jung, R., Krebbers, R., Jourdan, J., et al.: Iris from the ground up: a modular foundation for higher-order concurrent separation logic. J. Funct. Program. **28**, e20 (2018)
21. Kahn, G.: Natural semantics. In: Brandenburg, F.J., Vidal-Naquet, G., Wirsing, M. (eds.) STACS 1987. LNCS, vol. 247, pp. 22–39. Springer, Heidelberg (1987). https://doi.org/10.1007/BFb0039592
22. Ke, W., Li, X., Liu, Z., Stolz, V.: rCOS: a formal model-driven engineering method for component-based software. Front. Comput. Sci. China **6**(1), 17–39 (2012)
23. Klein, G., Nipkow, T.: Jinja is not Java. Arch. Formal Proofs (2005)
24. McCarthy, J.: Towards a mathematical science of computation. In: Proceedings of the 2nd IFIP Congress on Information Processing, pp. 21–28 (1962)
25. Moore, B., Peña, L., Rosu, G.: Program verification by coinduction. In: Ahmed, A. (ed.) ESOP 2018. LNCS, vol. 10801, pp. 589–618. Springer, Cham (2018). https://doi.org/10.1007/978-3-319-89884-1_21
26. Moore, J.S.: Inductive assertions and operational semantics. In: Geist, D., Tronci, E. (eds.) CHARME 2003. LNCS, vol. 2860, pp. 289–303. Springer, Heidelberg (2003). https://doi.org/10.1007/978-3-540-39724-3_27
27. Nielson, H.R., Nielson, F.: Semantics with Applications: An Appetizer. Undergraduate Topics in Computer Science, Springer, Heidelberg (2007). https://doi.org/10.1007/978-1-84628-692-6
28. Nipkow, T., von Oheimb, D.: Java$_{light}$ is type-safe - definitely. In: Proceedings of the 25th ACM SIGPLAN-SIGACT Symposium on Principles of Programming Languages (POPL), pp. 161–170 (1998)
29. Oliveira, M., Cavalcanti, A., Woodcock, J.: A UTP semantics for Circus. Formal Aspects Comput. **21**(1–2), 3–32 (2009)

30. Pierce, B.C.: The science of deep specification (keynote). In: Visser, E. (ed.) Companion Proceedings of the 2016 ACM SIGPLAN International Conference on Systems, Programming, Languages and Applications: Software for Humanity (SPLASH), p. 1 (2016)

31. Plotkin, G.D.: A structural approach to operational semantics. Lecture notes, DAIMI FN-19 (1981)

32. Qin, S., Dong, J.S., Chin, W.-N.: A semantic foundation for TCOZ in unifying theories of programming. In: Araki, K., Gnesi, S., Mandrioli, D. (eds.) FME 2003. LNCS, vol. 2805, pp. 321–340. Springer, Heidelberg (2003). https://doi.org/10.1007/978-3-540-45236-2_19

33. Reynolds, J.C.: Theories of Programming Languages. Cambridge University Press, Cambridge (1998)

34. Reynolds, J.C.: Separation logic: a logic for shared mutable data structures. In: Proceeding of 17th IEEE Symposium on Logic in Computer Science (LICS), pp. 55–74 (2002)

35. Schmidt, D.A.: Natural-semantics-based abstract interpretation (preliminary version). In: Mycroft, A. (ed.) SAS 1995. LNCS, vol. 983, pp. 1–18. Springer, Heidelberg (1995). https://doi.org/10.1007/3-540-60360-3_28

36. Sergey, I., Nagaraj, V., Johannsen, J., et al.: Safer smart contract programming with Scilla. Proc. ACM Program. Lang. 3(OOPSLA), 185:1–185:30 (2019)

37. Sewell, T.A.L., Myreen, M.O., Klein, G.: Translation validation for a verified OS kernel. In: ACM SIGPLAN Conference on Programming Language Design and Implementation (PLDI), pp. 471–482 (2013)

38. Sheng, F., Zhu, H., He, J., et al.: Theoretical and practical approaches to the denotational semantics for MDESL based on UTP. Formal Aspects Comput. 32(2–3), 275–314 (2020)

39. Sozeau, M., Anand, A., Boulier, S., et al.: The MetaCoq project. J. Autom. Reason. 64(5), 947–999 (2020)

40. Stefanescu, A., Park, D., Yuwen, S., et al.: Semantics-based program verifiers for all languages. In: 2016 ACM SIGPLAN International Conference on Object-Oriented Programming, Systems, Languages, and Applications (OOPSLA), pp. 74–91 (2016)

41. Wood, G.: Ethereum: a secure decentralised generlised transaction ledger. https://gavwood.com/paper.pdf

42. Yang, Z., Lei, H.: Lolisa: formal syntax and semantics for a subset of the Solidity programming language. CoRR, abs/1803.09885 (2018)

Trace Semantics and Algebraic Laws
for MCA ARMv8 Architecture Based
on UTP

Lili Xiao and Huibiao Zhu[✉]

East China Normal University, Shanghai, China
hbzhu@sei.ecnu.edu.cn

Abstract. Hardware architectures like x86 and ARM provide relaxed
memory models for efficiency reasons. The revised ARMv8 architecture is multi-copy atomic (MCA), which brings relaxed-memory effects
through thread-local out-of-order, speculative execution and thread-local
buffering. In this paper, we investigate the trace semantics for the MCA
ARMv8 architecture, acting in the denotational semantics style based
on Unifying Theories of Programming (UTP). In order to present all
the valid execution results including reorderings of any program under
ARMv8, a trace expressed as a sequence of snapshots is introduced,
and it relies heavily on various dependencies. The snapshots record the
change of variables of different types of actions. We also study the algebraic laws for MCA ARMv8, including a set of sequential and parallel
expansion laws. The concept of head normal form is explored for each
program, and every program is described in the form of guarded choice
which can model the execution of a program with reorderings. Therefore,
the linearizability for ARMv8 is supported.

Keywords: Relaxed memory model · MCA ARMv8 architecture ·
Unifying Theories of Programming (UTP) · Trace semantics ·
Algebraic laws

1 Introduction

ARMv7 and early ARMv8 architectures defined a relaxed memory model used to
improve the performance of concurrent programs. This model is non multi-copy
atomic (non MCA). However, the complexity of implementation, verification and
reasoning produced by allowing non MCA behaviors does not bring in sufficient
performance benefits [1]. Then the revised ARMv8 architecture is shift to the
model under multi-copy atomic (MCA) semantics [2], which illustrates that when
a write is visible to some other thread, it becomes visible to all other threads.
Therefore, it simplifies the allowed behaviors of every program.

The MCA ARMv8 architecture maintains the buffer of each thread, throwing
away the redundant buffers in [3], shown in Fig. 1. Always, a memory write is
split into two steps, committing the write to buffer and propagating it to memory later. A read from location x demands to first check the private buffer to

© Springer Nature Switzerland AG 2021
S. Qin et al. (Eds.): SETTA 2021, LNCS 13071, pp. 81–101, 2021.
https://doi.org/10.1007/978-3-030-91265-9_5

see whether it contains such a write to the same location. If yes, the read operation terminates. Otherwise, the shared memory will be explored. TSO [4] and ARMv8 are both MCA models [5], and TSO only omits store-load constraint. However, ARMv8 releases store-store, store-load, load-store and load-load constraints, if a variety of dependencies (explained in the following section) do not exist. In addition, ARMv8 supports speculative execution, which describes that the instructions in a branch may execute before the evaluation of the branching condition has completed. The cfence instruction is used to prohibit it.

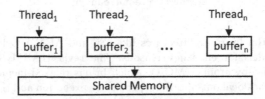

Fig. 1. The MCA ARMv8 architecture.

To demonstrate how ARMv8 exhibits reorderings, consider the parallel program $(x := 1; y := 1) \| (a := y; b := x)$. Since the statements $x := 1$ and $y := 1$ do not depend on each other, $x := 1$ and $y := 1$ can be reordered. If $y := 1$ is scheduled firstly and then the reads from y and x happen, the variables a and b can obtain 1 and 0 in the same execution.

Unifying Theories of Programming (UTP) [6] was developed by Hoare and He in 1998. It aims at proposing a convincing unified framework to combine and link operational semantics [7], denotational semantics [8] and algebraic semantics [9]. In this paper, we consider the denotational semantics of the MCA ARMv8 architecture, where our approach is based on UTP and the trace structure is applied. In our semantic model, a trace is in the form of the sequence of snapshots, and the snapshots record the changes on registers, buffers and memory contributed by different types of actions. With the dependencies among those actions, all the valid execution traces can be achieved. We also explore the algebraic laws for MCA ARMv8, including a set of sequential and parallel expansion laws. On the basis of the laws, we can see that every program can be converted into a guarded choice.

The operational and axiomatic models of MCA ARMv8 are introduced in [1,10], while our investigation for it can not only support the linearizability [11,12] of this architecture, but also support to deduce some interesting algebraic properties of programs.

The remainder of this paper is organized as follows. We investigate the trace semantics of the MCA ARMv8 architecture in Sect. 2. Section 3 presents a set of algebraic laws including sequential and parallel expansion laws. Section 4 concludes the paper and discusses the future work. We leave some technical definitions and analyses in the appendix.

2 Trace Semantics

2.1 The Syntax of ARMv8

In this section, we give the description of the programs under ARMv8 with a simple imperative language, which is adapted and extended from [13]. In the following syntax, e ranges over arithmetic expressions on real numbers, h over Boolean expressions and p over programs. Particularly, a Fence instruction is used to guarantee the absolute order of the memory accesses separated by it, while speculative execution can be prevented by the control fence (cfence) instructions. The program illustrated in the previous section is one quick example.

$$v ::= ..., -2, -1, 0, 1, 2, ...$$
$$e ::= v \mid x \mid e_1 + e_2 \mid e_1 * e_2 \mid ...$$
$$h ::= true \mid false \mid e_1 = e_2 \mid \neg h \mid h_1 \vee h_2 \mid h_1 \wedge h_2 \mid ...$$
$$p ::= x := e \mid \text{Fence} \mid \text{cfence} \mid p_1; p_2 \mid \text{if } h \text{ then } p_1 \text{ else } p_2 \mid \text{while } h \text{ do } p \mid p_1 \| p_2$$

2.2 The Semantic Model

This section investigates the denotational semantic model for the MCA ARMv8 architecture, with the application of the trace structure. We illustrate the behaviors of a process by a trace of snapshots, which records the sequence of actions.

A snapshot in a trace can be expressed as a triple $(cont, oflag, eflag)$, where:

1. Generally, $cont$ is composed of two elements var and val, denoting the data state of one variable at a given moment. However, it can also be illustrated as a branching condition h or Fence or cfence.
2. $oflag$ works on distinguishing different types of operations, and Table 1 gives a brief description of it.
   (a) If $cont$ is in the form of (var, val), $oflag$ can be divided into three categories. When var is a global variable, committing to the buffer leads to that $oflag$ is 1, and propagating to the whole memory results in that $oflag$ is 2. When writing to a local variable, $oflag$ is set to be 3.
   (b) Otherwise, the corresponding $oflag$ to a branching condition h or Fence or cfence is 0 or -1 or -2.

Table 1. Different types of operations divided by the parameter $oflag$.

$oflag$	Values					
	1	2	3	0	-1	-2
Types	Committing	Propagating	Register write	Branching condition	Fence	cfence

3. For a process, in order to include its environment's behaviors, we introduce the parameter $eflag$. Once the process does the action, $eflag$ is set to be 1. If the operation is performed by its environment, $eflag$ is equal to 0.

The projection function $\pi_i(i \in \{1,2,3\})$ is defined to get the i-th element of a snapshot, e.g., $\pi_3(cont, oflag, eflag) = eflag$. Then, if $cont$ is in the form of (var, val), we use the function $\pi_i(i \in \{1,2\})$ to obtain the relevant variable and value, i.e., $\pi_1(\pi_1(cont, oflag, eflag)) = var$, $\pi_2(\pi_1(cont, oflag, eflag)) = val$.

We use the notation $traces(P)$ to stand for all the valid execution results. Two simple examples are shown below to provide an intuitive illustration of it.

Example 1.1. Consider the program $a := 1; b := 1$, where a and b are both local. Because $a := 1$ and $b := 1$ do not have dependency, either $a := 1$ or $b := 1$ can be chosen to execute first. Then, two traces can be generated.

$$traces(a := 1; b := 1) = \left\{ \boxed{\langle((a,1),3,1),\ ((b,1),3,1)\rangle}, \boxed{\langle((b,1),3,1),\ ((a,1),3,1)\rangle} \right\}$$

Example 1.2. Given a program $P\|Q$, where $P =_{df} a := 1$, $Q =_{df} b := 1$, and a and b are local, $\langle((\boldsymbol{a}, \boldsymbol{1}), \boldsymbol{3}, \boldsymbol{1}),\ ((b,1),3,0)\rangle$ is one of $traces(P)$. Since the former and latter are contributed by P and P's environment (i.e., Q), the third elements are 1 and 0 respectively. Meanwhile, $\langle((a,1),3,0),\ ((\boldsymbol{b}, \boldsymbol{1}), \boldsymbol{3}, \boldsymbol{1})\rangle$ is one of $traces(Q)$. Hence, $P\|Q$ can produce one trace $\langle((\boldsymbol{a}, \boldsymbol{1}), \boldsymbol{3}, \boldsymbol{1}),\ ((\boldsymbol{b}, \boldsymbol{1}), \boldsymbol{3}, \boldsymbol{1})\rangle$, reflected in the trace semantics of parallel construct.   □

2.3   Trace Semantics

In the following, we present the trace semantics $traces(P)$ for each program P under the MCA ARMv8 architecture.

Local Assignment. Local variables are written to the private registers in every thread directly. Here, it is denoted by the second parameter 3 in the snapshot.

$$traces(a := e) =_{df} \{s \ ^\wedge \langle((a, r(e)), 3, 1)\rangle\} \text{ where, } \pi_3^*(s) \in 0^*$$

Here, the expression $\pi_3^*(s) \in 0^*$ informs that $eflag$ in every snapshot of the sequence s is 0, i.e., s is contributed by the environment. On the basis of the introduction to the projection function π_3, the notation $\pi_3^*(s)$ denotes the repeated execution of the function π_3 on each snapshot in the trace s. Then, with the application of this approach, a process can include its environment's behaviors. The notation $=_{df}$ refers to definitions, whereas $s^\wedge t$ stands for the concatenation of traces s and t. Further, $s^\wedge T =_{df} \{s^\wedge t \mid t \in T\}$ and $S^\wedge T =_{df} \{s^\wedge t \mid s \in S \wedge t \in T\}$.

In addition, we introduce a read function named r to get the concrete value of a variable, and the detailed definition of it is given in Appendix A (page 20). Note that $r(e)$ requires us to execute the read function of every variable which appears in the expression e. For instance, $r(x + y)$ is expressed as $r(x) + r(y)$. After getting the values of those variables, the value of the expression can be calculated.

The definitions for $traces(Fence)$ and $traces(cfence)$ are similar.

$$traces(Fence) =_{df} \{s \ ^\wedge \langle(Fence, -1, 1)\rangle\} \text{ where, } \pi_3^*(s) \in 0^*$$
$$traces(cfence) =_{df} \{s \ ^\wedge \langle(cfence, -2, 1)\rangle\} \text{ where, } \pi_3^*(s) \in 0^*$$

Global Assignment. We split the global assignment into two steps: (1) committing the write to the store buffer; (2) propagating it to the shared memory. The two steps cannot be swapped.

$$traces(x := e) =_{df} \{u^\wedge \langle ((x, r(e)), 1, 1) \rangle ^\wedge v^\wedge \langle ((x, r(e)), 2, 1) \rangle \}$$
$$\text{where, } \pi_3^*(u) \in 0^* \text{ and } \pi_3^*(v) \in 0^*$$

Similar to the explanation of local assignment, the environment can perform any number of operations before each step of global assignment. Thus, two sub-traces u and v are inserted, which are contributed by the environment. In the above trace, $(x, r(e))$ denotes that the value of x is changed to $r(e)$. The second parameter being 1 or 2 says that the effect of x's change has been brought to buffer or memory. The assignment is done by the thread itself, i.e., $eflag$ is 1.

Conditional and Iteration

Example 2. Consider the execution of conditional in P_1, where the variables x, y and z are global, and a and b are local.

```
if (x == 1) {        if (x == 1) {        if (x == 1) {
    a := y;              y := 1;              cfence;
} else {             }                        a := y;
    b := z;                                 }
}
        (P_1)                (P_2)                (P_3)
```

Now, we introduce the speculative execution [14] in conditional. Speculative execution is that the instructions in a branch can be executed before the branching condition is evaluated to increase performance. Because the speculative execution is allowed by the specification of the MCA ARMv8 architecture, the branching condition $x == 1$, $a := y$ in one branch and $b := z$ in another have the same possibility to be performed firstly. The middle layer in Fig. 2 depicts these three situations, and each framed part is done first.

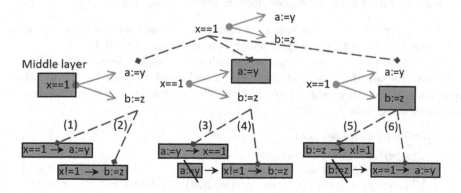

Fig. 2. The illustration of if structure.

- When the evaluation $x == 1$ is scheduled, the conditional will behave the same as $a := y$ if the judgment is true, otherwise behave as $b := z$, shown as the situations (1) and (2) in Fig. 2. The traces $\langle (x == 1, 0, 1), ((a, r(y)), 3, 1) \rangle$ and $\langle (x! = 1, 0, 1), ((b, r(z)), 3, 1) \rangle$ are related to these two situations.
- The conditional executes the load $a := y$ first, and then evaluates the branching condition $x == 1$. If true, the process terminates successfully and produces the trace $\langle ((a, r(x)), 3, 1), (x == 1, 0, 1) \rangle$. Otherwise, the result caused by $a := y$ is discarded. The conditional continues to carry out the instruction $b := z$, and then generates the trace $\langle (x! = 1, 0, 1), ((b, r(z)), 3, 1) \rangle$. They are described by the situations (3) and (4) in Fig. 2. The analysis of executing $b := z$ first is similar and presented in cases (5) and (6). □

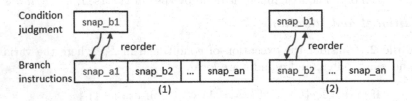

Fig. 3. The dependency in if structure.

Now, we study the trace semantics of conditional. Firstly, to judge whether a common statement can be speculatively executed, shown in Fig. 3(1), we introduce the function $NoDepd_1(snap\_b, snap\_a)$. It defines the requirements that $snap\_b$ and $snap\_a$ should achieve if there is no dependency between them:

(1) The assigned variable in $snap\_a$ is not global, because a thread cannot discard the result once it makes some changes in any location in the memory.
(2) $dom(\pi_1(snap\_b))$ records the set of all the variables in the branching condition. The written variable in $snap\_a$ cannot appear in the mentioned set.
(3) The variables read by $snap\_a$ and those read by $snap\_b$ do not contain the same global variables. The former ones are denoted by $dom(\pi_2(\pi_1(snap\_a)))$ and the latter ones are represented as $dom(\pi_1(snap\_b))$.

Here, $snap\_a$ is one snapshot of an assignment. The snapshot of a condition judgment h is denoted by $snap\_b$, which is in the form of $(h, 0, 1)$.

$NoDepd_1(snap\_b, snap\_a)$ can be formalized as below. Here, we use $Globals$ to denote the set of all the global variables, and $dom(\_)$ stands for the variables appearing in the argument. Note that the three formulas below correspond to the three items above.

$$NoDepd_1(snap\_b, snap\_a)$$
$$=_{df} \begin{pmatrix} (\pi_1(\pi_1(snap\_a)) \notin Globals) \wedge & ...(2.3.1) \\ (\pi_1(\pi_1(snap\_a)) \notin dom(\pi_1(snap\_b))) \wedge & ...(2.3.2) \\ ((dom(\pi_2(\pi_1(snap\_a))) \cap dom(\pi_1(snap\_b))) \cap Globals = \varnothing) & ...(2.3.3) \end{pmatrix}$$

Secondly, for nested conditional, in order to investigate whether two branching conditions can be reordered, which is illustrated in Fig. 3(2), we give the definition of the function $Nodepd_2(snap\_b_1, snap\_b_2)$. If two branching conditions do not depend on each other, the following condition that $snap\_b_1$ and $snap\_b_2$ may not refer to the same global variables should be satisfied, which is defined as $Nodepd_2(snap\_b_1, snap\_b_2)$.

$$Nodepd_2(snap\_b_1, snap\_b_2) =_{df} (dom(\pi_1(snap\_b_1)) \cap dom(\pi_1(snap\_b_2))) \cap Globals = \varnothing$$

For a condition judgment h, $traces(h) =_{df} \{s^\wedge \langle snap\_b \rangle\}$, where $\pi_3^*(s) \in 0^*$, and $snap\_b = (h, 0, 1)$. It means that the environment is allowed to do any number of operations before h, denoted by the sequence s.

Then, given a snapshot $snap\_b$ of branching condition h and a trace t of all the instructions in a branch, we interleave $s^\wedge \langle snap\_b \rangle$ and t which is formalized as $addCond(s^\wedge \langle snap\_b \rangle, t)$ to produce all the possible execution results.

$$addCond(s^\wedge \langle snap\_b \rangle, t)$$
$$=_{df} hd(s^\wedge \langle snap\_b \rangle)^\wedge addCond(tl(s^\wedge \langle snap\_b \rangle), t)$$
$$\cup \left(\begin{pmatrix} (hd(t)^\wedge addCond(s^\wedge \langle snap\_b \rangle, tl(t))) \\ \pi_3(hd(t)) = 0 \\ \lhd \ \vee(\pi_2(hd(t)) \in \{1,2,3\} \wedge NoDepd_1(snap\_b, hd(t))) \ \ ...(2.3.4) \ \rhd \\ \vee (\pi_2(hd(t)) = 0 \wedge NoDepd_2(snap\_b, hd(t))) \ \ ...(2.3.5) \\ \phi \end{pmatrix} \right)$$

where, $addCond(\langle \rangle, \langle \rangle) = \{\langle \rangle\}$

$addCond(s^\wedge \langle snap\_b \rangle, \langle \rangle) = \{s^\wedge \langle snap\_b \rangle\}, addCond(\langle \rangle, t) = \{t\},$

During the process of interleaving, we skip all the environment behaviors included in s and t. When meeting a snapshot in t which has dependency with $snap\_b$ (i.e., none of $NoDepd_1$ or $NoDepd_2$ can be satisfied shown as the formulas (2.3.4) and (2.3.5)), only the element in $s^\wedge \langle snap\_b \rangle$ can be scheduled. The calculation of t will be explained in the later paragraph.

The notation $hd(s)$ is used to denote the first snapshot of the trace s and $tail(s)$ stands for the result of removing the first snapshot in the trace s.

Therefore, we give the definition of conditional by applying $addCond$.

$$traces(\text{if } h \text{ then } P \text{ else } Q) =_{df} \bigcup_{c_1} addCond(s_1, t_1) \lhd h \rhd \bigcup_{c_2} addCond(s_2, t_2)$$

where, $c_1 = s_1 \in traces(h) \wedge t_1 \in traces(P)$, $c_2 = s_2 \in traces(\neg h) \wedge t_2 \in traces(Q)$

Example 2: Continuation. Now, we give different scenarios to help understand conditional better.

Case 1: As analyzed in Fig. 2, the traces of P_1 are produced as below.

$$traces(P_1) = \left\{ \begin{array}{l} \langle(x == 1, 0, 1), \ ((a, r(y)), 3, 1)\rangle, \ \langle((a, r(x)), 3, 1), \ (x == 1, 0, 1)\rangle, \\ \langle(x! = 1, 0, 1), \ ((b, r(z)), 3, 1)\rangle, \ \langle((b, r(z)), 3, 1), \ (x! = 1, 0, 1)\rangle \end{array} \right\}$$

Case 2: Assume x and y in P_2 are global variables. Then the instruction $y := 1$ cannot be executed before the branching condition $x == 1$.

$$traces(P_2) = \{ \langle(x == 1, 0, 1), \ ((y, 1), 1, 1), ((y, 1), 2, 1)\rangle, \ \langle(x! = 1, 0, 1)\rangle \}$$

Case 3: Consider the program P_3. Although a is a local variable, the load $a := y$ cannot be performed before $x == 1$ since the special instruction cfence exists.

$$traces(P_3) = \{\ \langle(x == 1, 0, 1),\ (\text{cfence}, -2, 1),\ ((a, r(y)), 3, 1)\rangle,\ \langle(x! = 1, 0, 1)\rangle\ \}\quad \square$$

The trace semantics of *Iteration* is discussed based on that of *Conditional* and least fixed point concept [15,16]. For while h do P, we consider it as if h then $(P; \text{while } h \text{ do } P)$ else II. Then, the trace semantics of it can be achieved.

$$traces(\text{while } h \text{ do } P) =_{df} \bigcup_{n=0}^{\infty} traces\{F^n(\text{STOP})\},$$

$$\text{where, } F(X) =_{df} \text{if } h \text{ then } (P; X) \text{ else } II,$$

$$F^0(X) =_{df} X,$$

$$F^{n+1}(X) =_{df} F(F^n(X))$$

$$= \underbrace{F(...(F(F(X)))...)}_{n \text{ times}}$$

$$traces(II) =_{df} \{\varepsilon\} \text{ and } traces(\text{STOP}) =_{df} \{\}$$

Sequential Composition. To facilitate making sequential composition between two traces s and t, we continue to introduce two more functions firstly.

If $x := e$ and $y := f$, which are represented by two snapshots $snap\_a_1$ and $snap\_a_2$ under the formal model, do not have dependency, four constraints should hold [17]. Here, x and y may be global or local, and e and f are expressions.

(1) The variables assigned in $snap\_a_1$ and $snap\_a_2$ are distinct, and they can be extracted from these snapshots through $\pi_1(\pi_1(snap\_a_1))$ and $\pi_1(\pi_1(snap\_a_2))$.
(2) y should not be referred to in e. In other words, the assigned variable in $snap\_a_2$ cannot be free in the variables read by $snap\_a_1$ represented as $dom(\pi_2(\pi_1(snap\_a_1)))$.
(3) The variables read by $snap\_a_2$ which we use $dom(\pi_2(\pi_1(snap\_a_2)))$ to denote should not contain the assigned variable in $snap\_a_1$.
(4) The variables read by $snap\_a_1$ and those by $snap\_a_2$ can have the same variables, but those variables must be local.

And we use the four lines below (i.e., (2.4.1), (2.4.2), (2.4.3) and (2.4.4)) in the function $NoDepd_3(snap\_a_1, snap\_a_2)$ to outline the mentioned four conditions.

$NoDepd_3(snap\_a_1, snap\_a_2)$

$$=_{df} \begin{pmatrix} \begin{pmatrix} (\pi_1(\pi_1(snap\_a_1)) \neq \pi_1(\pi_1(snap\_a_2)))\ \wedge & ...(2.4.1) \\ (\pi_1(\pi_1(snap\_a_2)) \notin dom(\pi_2(\pi_1(snap\_a_1))))\ \wedge & ...(2.4.2) \\ (\pi_1(\pi_1(snap\_a_1)) \notin dom(\pi_2(\pi_1(snap\_a_2))))\ \wedge & ...(2.4.3) \\ ((dom(\pi_2(\pi_1(snap\_a_1)))) \cap dom(\pi_2(\pi_1(snap\_a_2)))) \cap Globals = \varnothing)...(2.4.4) \end{pmatrix} \\ \vee \begin{pmatrix} (\pi_2(snap\_a_1) = 2 \wedge \pi_2(snap\_a_2)! = 2)\ \vee \\ (\pi_2(snap\_a_1) = \pi_2(snap\_a_2) = 2 \wedge \pi_1(\pi_1(snap\_a_1)) \neq \pi_1(\pi_1(snap\_a_2))) \end{pmatrix} \end{pmatrix}$$

In particular, the term *forwarding*, which has the equivalent effect with *bypassing* [18] under TSO memory model, is illustrated by the last two lines in the formula above. It says that the operation propagating to the shared memory does not depend on the load action later. However, if the load is also related to a write to one location, two propagation actions should follow the principle named modify order of the same location.

Example 3. Consider the sequential program $x := 1; a := x$, where a is local and x is global. As explained above, the sub-traces $\langle((x, 1), 2, 1),\ ((a, r(x)), 3, 1)\rangle$ and $\langle((a, r(x)), 3, 1),\ ((x, 1), 2, 1)\rangle$ are both valid.

$$traces(x := 1; a := x) = \left\{ \begin{array}{l} \langle((x, 1), 1, 1),\ ((x, 1), 2, 1),\ ((a, r(x)), 3, 1)\rangle, \\ \langle((x, 1), 1, 1),\ ((a, r(x)), 3, 1),\ ((x, 1), 2, 1)\rangle \end{array} \right\}$$

Here, the environment operations are not exhibited. We also ignore how to make composition of these snapshots, and the technique of it is given later. □

There is an assignment $x := e$ and a branching condition h, and they conform to program order. $snap\_a$ is one snapshot of $x := e$, while $snap\_b$ is the snapshot of h. If the snapshots can be reordered, two requirements should be met, defined by $NoDepd_4(snap\_a, snap\_b)$. One is that both of them cannot load the same global variables, modeled as the former conjunct in the formula (2.4.5). Informally, the other requirement is that x does not appear free in h. Hence, the variables which $snap\_b$ reads do not contain the variable which $snap\_a$ writes.

Specially, if $snap\_a$ is the snapshot of propagation, it and $snap\_b$ do not have dependency without any constraint according to *forwarding*, denoted by the last line in the formula.

$NoDepd_4(snap\_a, snap\_b)$

$$=_{df} \left(\begin{array}{l} \left(\begin{array}{l} \left(\left(dom(\pi_2(\pi_1(snap\_a))) \right) \cap dom(\pi_1(snap\_b)) \right) \cap Globals = \varnothing \right) \\ \wedge\ (\pi_1(\pi_1(snap\_a)) \notin dom(\pi_1(snap\_b))) \\ \vee\ \pi_2(snap\_a) = 2 \end{array} \right) \end{array} \quad ...(2.4.5) \right)$$

Then, we give a detailed introduction to the function $seqcom(s, t)$ whose target is to interleave two traces s and t. The result of interleaving two empty traces is still empty. If one of them is empty and the other is nonempty, the result follows the nonempty one.

$seqcom(s, t)$

$$=_{df} \left(\bigcup \left(\begin{array}{l} hd(s)^\wedge seqcom(tl(s), t) \\ \left(\begin{array}{l} (hd(t)^\wedge seqcom(s, tl(t))) \\ \vartriangleleft \pi_3(hd(t)) = 0 \vee \bigvee_{i \in \{1,2,3,4,5\}} case_i(s, t) \vartriangleright \end{array} \right) \\ \phi \end{array} \right) \right)$$

where, $seqcom(s, \langle\rangle) = \{s\}$, $seqcom(\langle\rangle, t) = \{t\}$, $seqcom(\langle\rangle, \langle\rangle) = \{\langle\rangle\}$

The first snapshot in s can always be scheduled. However, if the first in the next trace t wants to be triggered, it should satisfy the conditions that it is contributed by the environment, or it is done by the thread itself but meets one of the following five requirements. The requirements are expressed by $case_i$ where $i \in \{1, 2, 3, 4, 5\}$. Table 2 gives a brief introduction to $case_i$. It is worth noting that, the mentioned conditions lead to the difference between this interleaving introduced here and traditional interleaving [16].

Table 2. The description of $Case_i$.

Cases	Description
$case_1(s, t)$	If the first in the latter trace t is the snapshot of a Fence instruction, how to make it be the head of the interleaving of s and t
$case_2(s, t)$	The snapshot of a cfence instruction is at the head of t
$case_3(s, t)$	One snapshot of a global assignment takes the lead in t
$case_4(s, t)$	A local assignment's snapshot comes first in the trace t
$case_5(s, t)$	The branching condition is scheduled first in t

Now, we give the detailed formalization and illustration of those cases as below. $case_1$ is that the first in t is the snapshot of a Fence instruction, and it wants to become the head of the interleaving of s and t. Then all the snapshots in s, which are not done by the environment (The same applies to the following cases), should only be related with local assignments. And those assignments cannot read any global variables. The reason for these constraints is that for a Fence instruction, all the po-previous memory access instructions, conditional branch instructions and barriers are finished.

$$case_1(s, t)$$
$$=_{df} \left(\wedge \forall a' \in s \bullet \left(\pi_3(a') = 1 \rightarrow \left(\begin{array}{c} \pi_1(hd(t)) = \text{Fence} \wedge \pi_3(hd(t)) = 1 \\ \pi_2(a') = 3 \\ \wedge \forall x \in dom(\pi_2(\pi_1(a'))) \bullet x \notin Globals \end{array} \right) \right) \right)$$

The snapshot of a cfence instruction at the beginning of the next trace t would like to be scheduled first. It requires that any snapshot related to a barrier or a branching condition, does not occur in the trace s, which is formalized as $case_2$.

$$case_2(s, t) =_{df} \left(\wedge \forall a' \in s \bullet \left(\pi_3(a') = 1 \rightarrow \left(\begin{array}{c} \pi_1(hd(t)) = \text{cfence} \wedge \pi_3(hd(t)) = 1 \\ \pi_2(a')! = 0 \\ \wedge \pi_2(a')! = -1 \\ \wedge \pi_2(a')! = -2 \end{array} \right) \right) \right)$$

Provided that the first snapshot $hd(t)$ in t is resulted from committing or propagating a memory write, it is impossible for the trace s to include the snapshots of the Fence and cfence instructions, and branching conditions (Taking no account of any environment operation). In other words, s is the sequence of the snapshots of global and local assignments contributed by the thread itself, as well as some environment actions. Therefore, for each snapshot a' in s, once $eflag$ is 1, $NoDepd_3$ holds between the snapshots a' and $hd(t)$. This case is modeled as below.

$$case_3(s,t) =_{df} \left(\begin{array}{c} \pi_1(\pi_1(hd(t))) \in Globals \wedge \pi_3(hd(t)) = 1 \\ \wedge \forall a' \in s \bullet \left(\pi_3(a') = 1 \rightarrow \left(\begin{array}{c} \pi_2(a')! = -1 \wedge \pi_2(a')! = -2 \\ \wedge \pi_2(a')! = 0 \wedge NoDepd_3(a', hd(t)) \end{array} \right) \right) \end{array} \right)$$

If the head in t, which is the snapshot of a local assignment, wants to be executed first, there are mainly two cases. And $case_4$ modeled as $case_4(s,t) =_{df}$ $case_{4\_1}(s,t) \vee case_{4\_2}(s,t)$ presents the both cases.

Now, we define the case $case_{4\_1}$ that the register write reg_write is demanded to read some global variables. Then, all the instructions, which are po-previous to the write, may be branching conditions and assignments. If the previous is a condition judgment, $NoDepd_1$ is supposed to be satisfied between the snapshots of it and reg_write. Otherwise, $NoDepd_3$ should hold between the snapshots of reg_write and the po-previous assignment.

$$case_{4\_1}(s,t)$$
$$=_{df} \left(\begin{array}{c} \pi_1(\pi_1(hd(t))) \in Locals \wedge \pi_3(hd(t)) = 1 \\ \wedge \exists x \in domain(\pi_2(\pi_1(hd(t)))) \bullet x \in Globals \\ \wedge \forall a' \in s \bullet \left(\pi_3(a') = 1 \rightarrow \left(\begin{array}{c} (\pi_2(a') = 0 \wedge NoDepd_1(a', hd(t))) \vee \\ (\pi_2(a') - 1,2,3 \wedge NoDepd_3(a', hd(t))) \end{array} \right) \right) \end{array} \right)$$

Here, we use $Locals$ to denote the set of all the local variables.

We start to give a brief introduction to $case_{4\_2}$. The difference from $case_{4\_1}$ is that in this case, the trace s can have the snapshot of Fence.

$$case_{4\_2}(s,t)$$
$$=_{df} \left(\begin{array}{c} \pi_1(\pi_1(hd(t))) \in Locals \wedge \pi_3(hd(t)) = 1 \\ \wedge \forall x \in domain(\pi_2(\pi_1(hd(t)))) \bullet x \notin Globals \\ \wedge \forall a' \in s \bullet \left(\pi_3(a') = 1 \rightarrow \left(\begin{array}{c} \pi_2(a') = -1 \vee \\ (\pi_2(a') = 0 \wedge NoDepd_1(a', hd(t))) \vee \\ (\pi_2(a') = 1,2,3 \wedge NoDepd_3(a', hd(t))) \end{array} \right) \right) \end{array} \right)$$

The analysis of a branching condition and that of a local assignment are similar. Hence, we ignore the detailed definition, which is denoted by $case_5$.

Finally, we give the definition of sequential composition.

$$traces(P;Q) = \bigcup_c seqcom(s,t), \text{ where, } c = s \in traces(P) \wedge t \in traces(Q)$$

Example 4. Consider the example $P;Q$, where $P =_{df} x := 1$, $Q =_{df} y := 1$, x and y are global variables. $P;Q$ is activated with $x = y = 0$. Figure 4 gives a description of the trace of P (i.e., s) and Q (i.e., t) respectively. tr is one trace of $P;Q$, which is interleaved from P and Q.

For simplicity, we do not exhibit the environment operations. Although there are many executing cases for $P;Q$, we only analyze one scenario shown above.

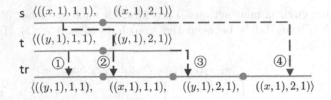

Fig. 4. The illustration of sequential composition.

1. The head $((y,1),1,1)$ in t has no dependency with every snapshot in s, in consequence, it can be fetched firstly.
2. As the first element in s, $((x,1),1,1)$ can be scheduled at any time, and here it is triggered in the second step.
3. We put the snapshot $((y,1),1,1)$ in the third position of the trace tr of $P;Q$. Then, $((x,1),2,1)$ can only be placed in the forth of tr.   □

Parallel Construct. In this section, we discuss the trace semantics of parallel construct, which is formed by the merging of contributed components' traces.

Example 5. We use the example $P||Q$, where $P =_{df} x := 1$ and $Q =_{df} a := 1; b := x$, to illustrate how the trace semantics of parallel composition can be constructed. Here, the variable a and b are local, and x is a global variable.

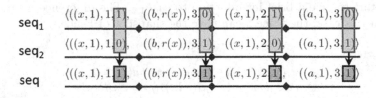

Fig. 5. The illustration of merging.

Here, we consider one scenario for the execution of $P||Q$. The operation committing the write to x is performed first. Then Q carries out the read from the location x. Finally, both processes complete their rest actions in proper order.

Then, the process P can produce the following sequence seq_1 shown in Fig. 5. The first and third snapshots are made by P itself, hence the last elements of them are both 1. The remaining snapshots in seq_1 with $eflag$ being 0 are contributed its environment Q. And Q yields the sequence seq_2 of snapshots.

Regardless of the fact that one action is done by the process P or Q, it is contributed by the parallel program $P||Q$. Hence, their merge gives a trace of $P||Q$ which is illustrated by seq in the above figure.

Note that, the thread Q carries out the read function $r(x)$ when the sequential composition just completes, because Q cannot classify the private and shared information if the parallel composition starts to execute. As a consequence, the value of $r(x)$ in Fig. 5 is 0.   □

The sequence seq_1 of process P and seq_2 of Q are said to be comparable, if

1. $\pi_i^*(seq_1) = \pi_i^*(seq_2)$, where $i = 1, 2$.
   The above formula when $i = 1$ indicates that they are built from the same sequence of states, when $i = 2$ stands for that two sequences of operation type are the same.
2. Any state contributed by a parallel process cannot be made by both of its components, i.e., $2 \notin \pi_3^*(seq_1) + \pi_3^*(seq_2)$.

Next, their merge is defined as below.

$$
Merge(seq, seq_1, seq_2) =_{df} \begin{pmatrix} (\pi_1^*(seq) = \pi_1^*(seq_1) = \pi_1^*(seq_2)) \wedge \\ (\pi_2^*(seq) = \pi_2^*(seq_1) = \pi_2^*(seq_2)) \wedge \\ (\pi_3^*(seq) = \pi_3^*(seq_1) + \pi_3^*(seq_2)) \wedge \\ (2 \notin \pi_3^*(seq_1) + \pi_3^*(seq_2)) \end{pmatrix}
$$

Then, we define the trace semantics of parallel composition. The purpose for concatenating the sequence s contributed by the environment of P is to facilitate merging, and it is the same for Q, i.e., $\pi_3^*(s) \in 0^*$, and $\pi_3^*(t) \in 0^*$.

$$
traces(P\|Q)
$$
$$
=_{df} \{tr|tr_1 \in traces(P) \wedge tr_2 \in traces(Q) \wedge (Merge(tr, tr_1^\frown s, tr_2) \vee Merge(tr, tr_1, tr_2^\frown t))\}
$$

3   Algebraic Properties

Program properties can be expressed as algebraic laws (equations usually). In this section, we investigate algebraic laws for the MCA ARMv8 architecture including a set of sequential and parallel expansion laws. They can facilitate producing all the valid in-order and out-of-order executions. In our approach, every program can be expressed as a head normal form of guarded choice. Therefore, the linearizability of MCA ARMv8 is supported.

3.1   Guarded Choice

The introduction to guarded choice is to support the sequential and parallel expansion laws. It has the ability to model the execution of a program including various reorderings under ARMv8. $h\&(action, tid, index)[q] \looparrowright P$ is a guarded component. Here, h is a Boolean condition, and others are defined below.

1. (a) If the element $action$ is the operation writing to the store buffer taking $\langle x = e \rangle$ for example, q is in the form of $h\&(action', tid, index')$, and $action'$ is propagating to the main memory $x = e$.
   (b) Furthermore, $action$ may be assigning to a local variable $a = e$ or special actions such as Fence and cfence. Then q is ε.
   (c) In particular, $h\&(action, tid, index)[q]$ where $action$ and q are both ε, indicates that the configuration is of a branching condition.

2. *tid* is the identity of the thread which performs the action.
3. We use the parameter *index* to denote the location of an action, and it is a pair shown as $(num, isMem)$. num indicates the sequence number of the action in the program order, and it starts from 1 for each single process. $isMem$ is to distinguish whether the action is propagation or not. If yes, it is 2, otherwise, it is 1. Example 6 below helps to illustrate the intuitive understanding of *index*.

Example 6. Consider the process $P =_{df} x := 1; a := x$, where x and a are global and local respectively. Since $x := 1$ is the first statement, two actions $\langle x = 1 \rangle$ and $x = 1$ split from it have the same num. The value of num is 1 and it is framed in Fig. 6. $\langle x = 1 \rangle$ and $x = 1$ target at the buffer and memory respectively. Then the values of $isMem$ are 1 and 2, and they are circled in Fig. 6. The action $a = x$ is extracted from the second statement $a := x$, thus its num is 2. Because it is not a memory action, its $isMem$ is 1. Hence the indices of the three actions $\langle x = 1 \rangle$, $x = 1$ and $a = x$ are $(1,1)$, $(1,2)$ and $(2,1)$.   □

We use Example 7 below to describe the intuitive understanding of *tid*.

Example 7. Consider the parallel process $(P\|Q)\|R$ shown in Fig. 7. The left edge is assigned a label whose value is 1. Otherwise, the label is 2.

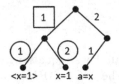
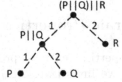

Fig. 6. The presentation of *index*.   **Fig. 7.** The structure of thread id.

We assume that every sequential process has the thread id λ. For parallel composition, the thread id of $P\|Q$ is $\langle 1 \rangle$, and that of R is $\langle 2 \rangle$. Lower down, the processes P and Q can be labeled by $\langle 1, 1 \rangle$ and $\langle 1, 2 \rangle$ respectively. From the point of view of the tree structure, P, Q and R are all leaf processes. Please note, for any thread id (i.e., *tid*), we have $tid^\wedge \lambda = tid$.   □

Now we introduce the concept of guarded choice, which is in the form of $\|_{i \in I}\{h_i \& (action_i, tid_i, index_i)[q_i] \looparrowright P_i'\}$, where $h_i \& (action_i, tid_i, index_i)[q_i] \looparrowright P_i$ is a guarded component. For the component $h \& (action, tid, index)[q] \looparrowright P$, if h is satisfied, the subsequent is $(action, tid, index)[q] \looparrowright P$.

Every program can be represented in the form of a guarded choice. And then for MCA ARMv8, the guarded choice can only have the following three types.

1. $\|_{i \in I}\{h_i \& (action_i, tid_i, index_i)[(action_i', tid_i, index_i')] \looparrowright P_i'\}$
2. $\|_{i \in I}\{h_i \& (action_i, tid_i, index_i) \looparrowright P_i'\}$
3. $\|_{i \in I}\{h_i \& (action_i, tid_i, index_i)[(action_i', tid_i, index_i')] \looparrowright P_i'\}\|$
   $\|_{j \in J}\{h_j \& (action_j, tid_j, index_j) \looparrowright Q_j'\}$

- The first type of guarded choice is only composed of a set of global assignment components. The operation committing any memory write can be scheduled to execute, provided that the corresponding Boolean condition is satisfied.
- The second type of guarded choice is made up of local assignment, or Fence, or cfence, or branching condition components.
- The third type can be obtained through combining the first and second types of guarded choice.

3.2 Head Normal Form

Now, we assign every program P a normal form, which is named *head normal form, HF(P)*. $HF(P)$ is in the form of guarded choice.

(1) For a global assignment, two actions committing to the write buffer and propagating to the whole memory are separated from it. Therefore, the two configurations corresponding to the above actions have the same *num*. However, the value of *isMem* of the former is 1, while that of the latter is 2. And we use the notation E to denote the empty process.

$$HF(x := e) =_{df} [\![\{\text{true}\&(\langle x = e \rangle, \lambda, (1,1))[(x = e, \lambda, (1,2))] \looparrowright E\}$$

(2) For a local assignment, after the first step expansion, there remains the empty process. The treatment of Fence and cfence instructions is similar.

$$HF(a := e) =_{df} [\![\{\text{true}\&(a = e, \lambda, (1,1)) \looparrowright E\} \quad ....HF(2\text{--}1)$$
$$HF(\text{Fence}) =_{df} [\![\{\text{true}\&(\text{Fence}, \lambda, (1,1)) \looparrowright E\} \quad ....HF(2\text{--}2)$$
$$HF(\text{cfence}) =_{df} [\![\{\text{true}\&(\text{cfence}, \lambda, (1,1)) \looparrowright E\} \quad ....HF(2\text{--}3)$$

(3) For conditional, $h\&(\varepsilon, \lambda, (1,1))$ and $\neg h\&(\varepsilon, \lambda, (1,1))$ are used to produce the head normal form. That *action* is ε says that the evaluation does not have an effect on the registers, buffers and the unique memory.

$$HF(\text{if } h \text{ then } P \text{ else } Q) =_{df} ([\![\{h\&(\varepsilon, \lambda, (1,1)) \looparrowright P, \neg h\&(\varepsilon, \lambda, (1,1)) \looparrowright Q\})$$

(4) With regard to iteration, the analysis of it is similar to that of conditional.

$$HF(\text{while } h \text{ do } P)$$
$$=_{df} ([\![\{h\&(\varepsilon, \lambda, (1,1)) \looparrowright (P; \text{while } h \text{ do } P), \quad \neg h\&(\varepsilon, \lambda, (1,1)) \looparrowright E\})$$

The definition of the head normal form for sequential and parallel composition can be achieved, with the application of corresponding expansion laws which are discussed in the following section.

3.3 Algebraic Laws

In this section, we study a set of sequential and parallel expansion laws. Based on these laws, every program can be converted to a guarded choice, which supports the linearizability of the MCA ARMv8 architecture.

Firstly, we focus on sequential expansion laws. Law $(guar\text{--}1)$ indicates that the sequential composition distributes leftward over guarded choice.

(guar–1) $[\!]_{i \in I}\{P_i\}; Q = [\!]_{i \in I}\{P_i; Q\}$

As a special case of the law $(guar\text{--}1)$, law $(seq\text{--}1)$ teaches us to transfer the program into configurations statement by statement. And the subsequent program Q is only attached to the tail of the selected P_i.

(seq–1) Let $P = [\!]_{i \in I}\{h_i \&(action_i, tid_i, index_i)[q_i] \looparrowright P_i'\}$
    Then $P; Q = [\!]_{i \in I}\{h_i \&(action_i, tid_i, index_i)[q_i] \looparrowright (P_i'; Q)\}$

After the transformation, we construct the relations among those configurations. Except for $h\&(action, tid, index)[q]$ fetched, the parameter num of every configuration left increases 1 to guarantee the program order. Law $(seq\text{--}2)$ describes this, and seq denotes the sequence of the remaining configurations.

(seq–2) $h\&(action, tid, index)[q] \looparrowright seq = (h\&(action, tid, index) \to q) \hookrightarrow (seq \uparrow 1)$

Table 3. The description of three operators.

Operator	Exhibiting configurations	Program order relation	Fixed executing order
$\looparrowright$	$\checkmark$	$\times$	$\times$
$\hookrightarrow$	$\checkmark$	$\checkmark$	$\times$
$\to$	$\checkmark$	$\checkmark$	$\checkmark$

Note that, the operator $\looparrowright$ is used to connect the configurations with original indices. Different from $\looparrowright$, the operator $\hookrightarrow$ links the configurations whose indices can reflect the program order (po) relation. The configurations connected by the two operators above can still be reordered, but those linked by the operator $\to$ cannot. Table 3 gives a brief and intuitive description of them.

Now, we give the definition of the function $seq \uparrow 1$. Only num in each configuration in seq adds 1, and other parameters remain unchanged. Here, '/' denotes the replacement operator.

$seq \uparrow 1 =_{df} \forall h\&(action, tid, index) \in seq\bullet$
$\qquad seq[h\&(action, tid, (num + 1, isMem))/h\&(action, tid, (num, isMem))]$

Example 8. Consider the sequential process $P; Q$, where $P =_{df} x := 1$, $Q =_{df} a := x$, and x and a are global and local respectively.

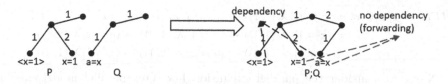

Fig. 8. The combination of configurations.

With the laws $(seq\text{-}1)$ and $(seq\text{-}2)$, we get the normal form of $P; Q$ formalized as below. The combination of configurations of P and Q are shown in Fig. 8. For simplicity, if the guard is true, it is ignored.

$$HF(x := 1; a := x) = (\langle x = 1 \rangle, \lambda, (1,1))[(x = 1, \lambda, (1,2))] \looparrowright (a = x, \lambda, \boxed{(1,1)})$$

$$= (((\langle x = 1 \rangle, \lambda, (1,1)) \rightarrow (x = 1, \lambda, (1,2))) \hookrightarrow (a = x, \lambda, \boxed{(2,1)}) \quad \square$$

Law $(seq\text{-}3)$ is used to obtain all the configuration sequences (including the results of reorderings) under MCA ARMv8. The first configuration with the least num, formalized as c_{11}, can always be scheduled. If we want to select the configuration after the operator $\hookrightarrow$ and its num is greater than that of c_{11}, modeled as c_{i1} where $i \neq 1$, the conditions covered by $cond_i$ should be satisfied.

(seq-3) $(c_{11} \rightarrow c_{12} \rightarrow ...c_{1n_1}) \hookrightarrow (c_{21} \rightarrow c_{22} \rightarrow ...c_{2n_2}) \hookrightarrow ...(c_{m1} \rightarrow c_{m2} \rightarrow ...c_{mn_m})$

$= c_{11} \rightarrow \boxed{(c_{12} \rightarrow ...c_{1n_1})} \hookrightarrow (c_{21} \rightarrow c_{22} \rightarrow ...c_{2n_2}) \hookrightarrow ...(c_{m1} \rightarrow c_{m2} \rightarrow ...c_{mn_m})$

$\| \; c_{21} \rightarrow (c_{11} \rightarrow c_{12} \rightarrow ...c_{1n_1}) \hookrightarrow \boxed{(c_{22} \rightarrow ...c_{2n_2})} \hookrightarrow ...(c_{m1} \rightarrow c_{m2} \rightarrow ...c_{mn_m})$ if $cond_2$

$\| \; ...$

$\| \; c_{m1} \rightarrow (c_{11} \rightarrow c_{12} \rightarrow ...c_{1n_1}) \hookrightarrow (c_{21} \rightarrow c_{22} \rightarrow ...c_{2n_2}) \hookrightarrow ... \boxed{(c_{m2} \rightarrow ...c_{mn_m})}$ if $cond_m$

$cond_i$ has a number of situations, and these situations are similar to $case_j$ under the trace model (page 10), where $j \in \{1, 2, 3, 4, 5\}$. For lack of space, we only give the description and formalization of the situation that is corresponding to $case_1$, combining the features of the algebraic model in the following.

If the action in c_{i1} is a Fence instruction, any configuration c whose num is less than that of c_{i1} can only have an action in the form of $a = e$. Furthermore, the expression e does not refer to global variables. In a consequence, c has nothing to do with any global variable, and we use dom to collect all the variables appearing in $a = e$. Then this situation is formalized as below.

$$\forall c \bullet \left(\begin{array}{l} (\pi_1(\pi_3(c)) < \pi_1(\pi_3(c_{i1}))) \rightarrow \\ (\pi_1(c) \text{ is in the form of part of HF(2-1)} \wedge \forall x \in dom(\pi_1(c)) \bullet x \notin Globals) \end{array} \right)$$

Example 8: Continuation

According to the dependencies in Fig. 8, with the first application of the law $(seq\text{-}3)$, only the configuration $(\langle x = 1 \rangle, \lambda, (1,1))$ can be the head. After removing it, we apply the law $(seq\text{-}3)$ for the second time, and both of the remaining configurations can be scheduled. The formalization is shown as below.

$$HF(x := 1; a := x) = ((\langle x = 1 \rangle, \lambda, (1, 1)) \to ((x = 1, \lambda, (1, 2)) \hookrightarrow (a = x, \lambda, (2, 1)))$$
$$= ((\langle x = 1 \rangle, \lambda, (1, 1)) \to (x = 1, \lambda, (1, 2)) \to (a = x, \lambda, (2, 1))$$
$$\|((\langle x = 1 \rangle, \lambda, (1, 1)) \to (a = x, \lambda, (2, 1)) \to (x = 1, \lambda, (1, 2)) \qquad \square$$

Next, we consider the parallel expansion law. Our parallel model can be explained as an interleaving model. The detail we pay attention to is that when the configuration in the left branch is selected, the prefix $\langle 1 \rangle$ should be added to the corresponding tid_i. The prefix $\langle 2 \rangle$ is attached to the corresponding tid_j with the configuration in the right being chosen.

(par–1) Let $P = \|_{i \in I} \{h_i \& (action_i, tid_i, index_i) \to P_i'\}$,
$$Q = \|_{j \in J} \{h_j \& (action_j, tid_j, index_j) \to Q_j'\}$$
Then $P \| Q = \|_{i \in I} \{h_i \& (action_i, \langle 1 \rangle^\wedge tid_i, index_i) \to (P_i' \| Q)\}$
$$\|_{j \in J} \{h_j \& (action_j, \langle 2 \rangle^\wedge tid_j, index_j) \to (P \| Q_j')\}$$

Example 9. Consider the parallel program $P \| Q$, where $P =_{df} x := 1$, $Q =_{df}$ $a := 1; b := x$, a and b are local variables, and x is a global variable.

$$HF(P \| Q) = HF(x := 1) \| HF(a := 1; b := x)$$
$$= (((\langle x = 1 \rangle, \lambda, (1, 1)) \to (x = 1, \lambda, (1, 2))) \| ((a = 1, \lambda, (1, 1)) \hookrightarrow (b = x, \lambda, (2, 1)))$$
$$= \left(((\langle x = 1 \rangle, \lambda, (1, 1)) \to (x = 1, \lambda, (1, 2))) \| \left(\begin{array}{c} (a = 1, \lambda, (1, 1)) \to (b = x, \lambda, (2, 1)) \\ \| \ (b = x, \lambda, (2, 1)) \to (a = 1, \lambda, (1, 1)) \end{array} \right) \right.$$

For lack of space, we only describe the generation of one sequence of $P \| Q$ shown in Fig. 9 here. $\square$

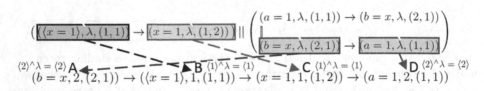

Fig. 9. One configuration sequence of $P \| Q$.

4   Conclusion and Future Work

The MCA ARMv8 architecture allows out of order execution through thread-local out-of-order, speculative execution and thread-local buffering. In this paper, we have studied the trace semantics for ARMv8, acting in the denotational semantics style. In addition, a set of algebraic laws including sequential and parallel expansion laws has been investigated with the concept of the guarded choice. Therefore, the linearizability of ARMv8 is supported in our model. Our semantics study for MCA ARMv8 is based on UTP approach.

In the future, we would like to continue our work on ARMv8. We plan to explore further relating theories for the ARMv8 architecture [19–21]. Using the theorem proof assistant Coq [22–24] to formalize the UTP-based semantics for ARMv8 is also in our plan.

Acknowledgements. This work was partly supported by National Natural Science Foundation of China (Grant Nos. 61872145 and 62032024) and Shanghai Collaborative Innovation Center of Trustworthy Software for Internet of Things (Grant No. ZF1213).

A   Read Function

Now, we present the read function r in detail. Above all, we need to judge if the variable read from is global. If true, we introduce the function g to complete the following operations. Otherwise, the function l is given. For simplicity, we only use $r(x)$ in the snapshots. Here, *Globals* is the set of all the global variables.

$$r(x, tr^\wedge \langle event \rangle) =_{df} g(x, tr^\wedge \langle event \rangle) \triangleleft x \in Globals \triangleright l(x, tr^\wedge \langle event \rangle)$$
$$r(x, \langle \rangle) =_{df} g(x, \langle \rangle) \triangleleft x \in Globals \triangleright l(x, \langle \rangle)$$

The read mechanism for global variables supported by this architecture is that when a thread performs a read, if its buffer cannot provide the concrete value, the shared memory will be explored.

$$g(x, tr^\wedge \langle event \rangle) =_{df} \left(\begin{array}{c} m(x, tr^\wedge \langle event \rangle) \\ \triangleleft \left(\begin{array}{c} w(x, tr^\wedge \langle event \rangle) = \text{null } \vee \\ cnt_1(x, tr^\wedge \langle event \rangle) = cnt_2(x, tr^\wedge \langle event \rangle) \quad ...(A.1) \end{array} \right) \triangleright \\ w(x, tr^\wedge \langle event \rangle) \end{array} \right)$$

$$g(x, \langle \rangle) =_{df} m(x, \langle \rangle)$$

It means that the execution of g will jump to that of m, if the values of x have not been committed to the buffer, or the writes to x have all been propagated to the memory. The latter situation is modeled as the formula (A.1) in the trace model. It illustrates that the number of the snapshots which contain x and target at the buffer, and that aiming at memory contributed by the same thread are identical. The numbers mentioned above can be calculated by the functions cnt_1 and cnt_2. We ignore the definition of cnt_2, because it is similar to that of cnt_1.

$$cnt_1(x, tr^\wedge \langle event \rangle) =_{df} \left(\begin{array}{c} cnt_1(x, tr) + 1 \\ \triangleleft \left(\begin{array}{c} \text{ASCII}(\pi_1(\pi_1(event))) - \text{ASCII}(x) \\ \wedge \pi_2(event) = 1 \wedge \pi_3(event) = 1 \end{array} \right) \triangleright \\ cnt_1(x, tr) \end{array} \right)$$

$$cnt_1(x, \langle \rangle) =_{df} 0$$

The function w is used to search the store buffer. Since we always want the most recent value, the trace (the sequence of snapshots) will be checked in reverse order, and the same is true for the functions as below. When executing w, for each snapshot, we first examine whether its $oflag$ and $eflag$ are both 1, because all threads can see their own buffers merely. If the conditions are satisfied, we have a look at the variable contained in $\pi_1(\pi_1(event))$ of the snapshot. Once it is identical to the one that we want to read, the corresponding value $\pi_2(\pi_1(event))$ is returned, and the process terminates. If we do not achieve anything until the trace becomes ε, null will be assigned to this function.

$$w(x, tr^{\wedge}\langle event \rangle)$$

$$=_{df} \begin{pmatrix} (\pi_2(\pi_1(event)) \vartriangleleft \text{ASCII}(\pi_1(\pi_1(event))) = \text{ASCII}(x) \vartriangleright w(x, tr)) \\ \vartriangleleft \pi_2(event) = 1 \wedge \pi_3(event) = 1 \vartriangleright \\ w(x, tr) \end{pmatrix}$$

$$w(x, \langle \rangle) =_{df} \text{null}$$

We know that ASCII is used to specify the binary numbers of common symbols.

We use the function m to seek the shared memory for the value of a specific variable. Due to the fact that the main memory is visible to all threads, we are only demanded to check whether $oflag$ of the snapshot we meet is 2 or not. The remainder is similar to that of w. However, the difference between them is that the return value of the function m is set to the initial value 0 if we cannot get the value from the trace.

$$m(x, tr^{\wedge}\langle event \rangle)$$

$$=_{df} \begin{pmatrix} (\pi_2(\pi_1(event)) \vartriangleleft \text{ASCII}(\pi_1(\pi_1(event))) = \text{ASCII}(x) \vartriangleright m(x, tr)) \\ \vartriangleleft \pi_2(event) = 2 \vartriangleright \\ m(x, tr) \end{pmatrix}$$

$$m(x, \langle \rangle) =_{df} 0$$

When reading a variable from the register, what we should do is to check whether $oflag$ is 3 and $eflag$ is 1, because the registers are all private.

$$l(x, tr^{\wedge}\langle event \rangle)$$

$$=_{df} \begin{pmatrix} (\pi_2(\pi_1(event)) \vartriangleleft \text{ASCII}(\pi_1(\pi_1(event))) = \text{ASCII}(x) \vartriangleright l(x, tr)) \\ \vartriangleleft \pi_2(event) = 3 \wedge \pi_3(event) = 1 \vartriangleright \\ l(x, tr) \end{pmatrix}$$

$$l(x, \langle \rangle) =_{df} 0$$

Based on the read function generated from the read mechanism of the MCA ARMv8 architecture, we can know that the private information will not be visible to other threads.

References

1. Pulte, C., Flur, S., Deacon, W., French, J., Sarkar, S., Sewell, P.: Simplifying ARM concurrency: multicopy-atomic axiomatic and operational models for ARMv8. Proc. ACM Program. Lang. **2**(POPL), 1–29 (2017)
2. Pulte, C.: The Semantics of Multicopy Atomic ARMv8 and RISC-V. University of Cambridge (2019)
3. Flur, S., et al.: Modelling the ARMv8 architecture, operationally: concurrency and ISA. In: Proceedings of the 43rd Annual ACM SIGPLAN-SIGACT Symposium on Principles of Programming Languages, pp. 608–621 (2016)
4. Owens, S., Sarkar, S., Sewell, P.: A better x86 memory model: x86-TSO. In: Berghofer, S., Nipkow, T., Urban, C., Wenzel, M. (eds.) TPHOLs 2009. LNCS, vol. 5674, pp. 391–407. Springer, Heidelberg (2009). https://doi.org/10.1007/978-3-642-03359-9_27

5. Colvin, R.J., Smith, G.: A wide-spectrum language for verification of programs on weak memory models. In: Havelund, K., Peleska, J., Roscoe, B., de Vink, E. (eds.) FM 2018. LNCS, vol. 10951, pp. 240–257. Springer, Cham (2018). https://doi.org/10.1007/978-3-319-95582-7_14

6. Hoare, C.A.R., He, J.: Unifying Theories of Programming. Prentice Hall, Englewood Cliffs (1998)

7. Plotkin, G.D.: A Structural Approach to Operational Semantics. Aarhus University (1981)

8. Stoy, J.E.: Denotational Semantics: The Scott-Strachey Approach to Programming Language Theory. MIT Press, Cambridge (1981)

9. Hoare, C.A.R., et al.: Laws of programming. Commun. ACM **30**(8), 672–686 (1987)

10. Winter, K., Smith, G., Derrick, J.: Modelling concurrent objects running on the TSO and ARMv8 memory models. Sci. Comput. Program. **184**, 102308 (2019)

11. Smith, G., Winter, K., Colvin, R.J.: Linearizability on hardware weak memory models. Formal Aspects Comput. **32**, 1–32 (2019)

12. Winter, K., Smith, G., Derrick, J.: Observational models for linearizability checking on weak memory models. In: International Symposium on Theoretical Aspects of Software Engineering (TASE), pp. 100–107. IEEE (2018)

13. Kavanagh, R., Brookes, S.: A denotational semantics for SPARC TSO. Electron. Notes Theor. Comput. Sci. **336**, 223–239 (2018)

14. Colvin, R.J., Smith, G.: A high-level operational semantics for hardware weak memory models, arXiv preprint arXiv:1812.00996 (2018)

15. Brookes, S.: Full abstraction for a shared-variable parallel language. Inf. Comput. **127**(2), 145–163 (1996)

16. Hoare, C.A.R.: Communicating Sequential Processes. Prentice-Hall, Hoboken (1985)

17. Smith, G., Coughlin, N., Murray, T.: Value-dependent information-flow security on weak memory models. In: ter Beek, M.H., McIver, A., Oliveira, J.N. (eds.) FM 2019. LNCS, vol. 11800, pp. 539–555. Springer, Cham (2019). https://doi.org/10.1007/978-3-030-30942-8_32

18. Sorin, D.J., Hill, M.D., Wood, D.A.: A primer on memory consistency and cache coherence. Synthesis Lect. Comput. Archit. **6**(3), 1–212 (2011)

19. Zhu, H., Yang, F., He, J., Bowen, J.P., Sanders, J.W., Qin, S.: Linking operational semantics and algebraic semantics for a probabilistic timed shared-variable language. J. Logic Algebraic Program. **81**(1), 2–25 (2012)

20. He, J., Hoare, C.A.R.: From algebra to operational semantics. Inf. Process. Lett. **45**(2), 75–80 (1993)

21. Hoare, C.A.R., He, J., Sampaio, A.: Algebraic derivation of an operational semantics. In: Proof, Language, and Interaction: Essays in Honour of Robin Milner, pp. 77–98 (2000)

22. Sheng, F., Zhu, H., He, J., Yang, Z., Bowen, J.P.: Theoretical and practical aspects of linking operational and algebraic semantics for MDESL. ACM Trans. Softw. Eng. Methodol. (TOSEM) **28**(3), 1–46 (2019)

23. Huet, G., Kahn, G., Paulin-Mohring, C.: The Coq Proof Assistant a Tutorial (2005)

24. Bertot, Y., Castéran, P.: Interactive Theorem Proving and Program Development: Coq'Art: The Calculus of Inductive Constructions. Springer, Heidelberg (2013)

Formal Analysis of 5G AKMA

Tengshun Yang[1,2], Shuling Wang[1,2], Bohua Zhan[1,2(✉)], Naijun Zhan[1,2],
Jinghui Li[3], Shuangqing Xiang[3], Zhan Xiang[3], and Bifei Mao[3]

[1] SKLCS, Institute of Software, CAS, Beijing, China
{yangts,wangsl,bzhan,znj}@ios.ac.cn
[2] University of Chinese Academy of Sciences, Beijing, China
[3] Trustworthiness Theory Research Center, Huawei Technologies Co., Ltd.,
Shenzhen, China
{jinghui.li,xiangshuangqing,xiangzhan1,maobifei}@huawei.com

Abstract. Security and privacy of users' information in mobile communication networks have drawn increasing attention. The development of 5G system has demanded new protocols to realize authentication and key management service. AKMA (Authentication and Key Management for Application) service aims at establishing authenticated communication between users and application functions. For this purpose, the 3GPP group has standardized 5G AKMA service in Technical Specifications defining the 5G AKMA security architecture and procedures. To ensure security of communication between users and applications, AKMA service should meet strong security properties. In this paper, we apply formal methods to model and analyze the AKMA service. We construct a formal model of AKMA in the Tamarin verification tool, and specify the security properties extracted from informal descriptions given in the Technical Specifications. We identify the security assumptions for each security property during the modeling process. We prove that some properties are not satisfied, and by analyzing the counterexamples constructed by Tamarin, put forward some potential attacks. Moreover, we propose some suggestions and fixes for the 5G AKMA service.

1 Introduction

With mobile communication networks widely used across the world, more and more people subscribe to their home networks and communicate with each other or use online services, such as phone calls, emails, and entertainment applications. Much of these communications occur through public channels, which can be intercepted or suffer from other kinds of attacks. In order to ensure security and privacy of subscribers and application providers communicating along insecure channels, 3GPP (3rd Generation Partnership Project) has been specifying the security architecture, i.e. security features and mechanisms, for the 5G System and the 5G Core, and the security procedures performed within the 5G System including 5G Core and 5G New Radio in the Technical Specification (TS) [7]. One of the main mechanisms is to support authentication and key management aspects for applications, that is mutual authentication between users and

© Springer Nature Switzerland AG 2021
S. Qin et al. (Eds.): SETTA 2021, LNCS 13071, pp. 102–121, 2021.
https://doi.org/10.1007/978-3-030-91265-9_6

application providers. Specifically, a major aim of this service is to allow application providers to authenticate users without knowing the users' identifier, with the home network of the user as an intermediary.

5G AKMA (Authentication and Key Management for Application) is a novel cellular-network-based delegated authentication service. This service, specified in 3GPP TS 33.535 [8], aims to provide a protocol to support authentication and key management aspects for applications based on subscription credentials. In AKMA, application provider, denoted by AKMA Application Function (AF), delegates the authentication of application user (UE) to the corresponding home network (HN) where the user subscribes. In this way, application provider could verify the identity of the user through home network without having chance to acquire knowledge and information of the user, especially, the real identifier of the user. The standardization of 5G AKMA service started with Release 16 in 2019 and the latest version was specified in Release 17. In this paper, according to the version 17.1.0 of Release 17 of the Technical Specification (TS) [8], we will provide the first formal model of 5G AKMA and also verify formally the security requirements using Tamarin.

Formal Methods. In this paper, we apply formal methods to analyze the AKMA service, using the Tamarin verification tool [31]. Tamarin specifies protocols as a set of rewrite rules acting on a multiset of facts, and properties as two-sorted first-order logic assertions. By writing appropriate actions in the rules and in the trace, it is possible to formulate various threat models, such as Dolev-Yao [20] and eCK [27], as well as various authentication specifications [29]. Using a backward-search style algorithm [33], Tamarin attempts to prove the properties or find a counterexample. The counterexamples help users find potential attacks of protocols.

Contribution. In this work, we formally specify the standard's security assumptions and requirements of 5G AKMA, and build the first formal model of 5G AKMA for a precise security analysis. First, we construct a formal model of 5G AKMA, as specified in TS 33.535 [8], as a set of rewrite rules in Tamarin. As we describe in Sect. 4, the model contains main features and functions in the protocol. During the modeling process, we identity the security assumptions about the protocol for guaranteeing the security properties, which are implicitly stated in the standard documents. Next, we model the classical properties (e.g. secrecy, weak agreement, non-injective agreement) and check them in Tamarin. During the verification, for some of these security properties, Tamarin returns a counterexample showing that the model does not satisfy the given property. We then analyze the attacks according to the counterexamples and put forward the potential security and privacy problems about AKMA protocol. Also, we give suggestions to fix these problems.

Related Work. In the earlier generations of mobile network, the corresponding services were also specified by 3GPP. GBA (Generic Bootstrapping Architecture) [5] and BEST (Battery Efficient Security for very low Throughput Machine Type Communication (MTC) devices) [4], served use cases similar to that of AKMA in the 3rd and 4th generation respectively. 5G AKMA inherits and evolves features of GBA and BEST, performs better in all kinds of requirements (refering to 3GPP TR33.835 [1]). In [23], Khan *et al.* analyzed potential AKMA requirements and compared AKMA with GBA and BEST. Beyond that, they put forward two new privacy requirements arose from AKMA applications, developed a privacy mode for fulfilling them and analyzed the security and privacy of their solution informally. In another work [24], they introduced designated authentication system and summarized recent work about AKMA.

There are lots of work on formal modeling and verification of security systems. For adversaries, the most important models are Dolev-Yao model [20], eCK model [27], and its extension SeCK model [32]. The adversaries are given different powers for each of them. Especially, the eCK model inherits the spirit of Bellare and Rogaway [14] and Canetti and Krawczyk [17,25] by an experiment in which the adversary is given many corruption powers for various key exchange sessions and must solve a challenge on a test session. Formal modeling languages and logics are used for modeling security protocols, and for capturing security properties, facilitating verification and debugging. These work include the process algebra CSP [21,29,34,35], BAN logic [16], applied π-calculus [9], Horn clauses [15], TLA [10,28], rewriting system [31] and so on. Some security protocol verification tools are developed based on these theories, such as Tamarin [31], Maude-NPA [18], ProVerif [15], and so on. Tamarin will be introduced in Sect. 3. The Maude-NPA tool [18] supports protocols specified as linear role-scripts and properties specified as symbolic states [22]. ProVerif [15] models a protocol as a set of Horn clauses, analyzes them using a two-phase resolution algorithm, and uses abstractions to obtain an efficient analysis method.

There are lots of work on verification of security protocols. Protocols with loops and non-monotonic mutable global states such as TESLA protocols, YubiKey and YubiHSM protocols were considered in [26,30]. In [11], ARPKI protocol with many messages and multiple parties was modeled and analyzed. The group protocols STR and GDH based on Diffie-Hellman were verified on security and privacy. TLS 1.3 and 5G AKA protocol were analyzed in [12,19], which are important for Internet security and also widely used to establish secure channels in a variety of contexts. Significantly, 3GPP [2] formally analyzes the 3G AKA protocol using TLA [28] on the absence of failure scenarios and uses BAN logic [16] on proving security goals respectively.

2   AKMA in 5G System

In this section, we give an informal introduction to the 5G AKMA service. We first describe the main entities of the service, and then present the steps of the protocol in detail. See the Technical Specification [8] for further information.

2.1   General Architecture

There are three main entities (roles) in the 5G AKMA service, as shown in Fig. 1.
We explain them below.

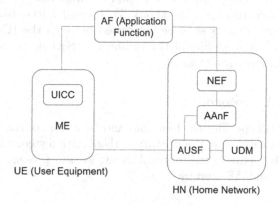

Fig. 1. AKMA architecture

1. User Equipment (UE): represents user of the service, consisting of two parts:
   Mobile Equipment (ME) and Universal Integrated Circuit Card (UICC).
2. Home Network (HN): represents the mobile network provider. HN has all of
   the information about its subscribers, and is always considered to be credible.
   Home network plays the role of authenticating users and helps application
   providers to reach an agreement with the users on session keys in the AKMA
   service. There are several functions located within the HN, as follows:

   - UDM (Unified Data Management): stores information about all sub-
     scribers of the home network.
   - AAnF (AKMA Anchor Function): manages temporary information about
     subscribers, and generates temporary session keys K_{AF} for the application
     functions.
   - AUSF (Authentication Server Function): connection between UDM and
     AAnF, obtains the 5G authentication vector from UDM and generates
     relative AKMA materials.
   - NEF (Network Exposure Function): when the target AF is located outside
     the HN, establishes connection between AAnF and AF.

   In general, there is also a Serving Network (SN) which the user connects to
   when roaming. In this paper, we consider only the case when the user is not
   roaming, that is, SN is part of the HN, so we do not consider SN separately.
3. Application Function (AF or AApF): also called application provider or service provider, represents the online services that the user may wish to use.
   The goal of AKMA is to help to establish a secure channel (exchange a secret
   key) between AF and UE, with authentication of UE delegated to its corresponding HN.

Every user in the cellular network subscribes to a home network and has a unique long-term identifier SUPI (Subscription Permanent Identifier) and a long-term key K. These are stored at both UE and HN.

It is worth noting that the mutual authentication between HN and AF is not part of the AKMA service. That is, it should be prepared before the execution of the protocol. According to TS 33.501 [7], mutual authentication based on client and server certificates shall be performed between the HN and AF using TLS protocol. In our modeling of the protocol in Sect. 4, we will model their communication in a private channel.

2.2 5G AKMA Protocol

5G AKMA protocol specifies the functions and behaviors of the AKMA service. We will begin by introducing the primary authentication step, which is a prerequisite but not a key part of the protocol. Next, we will present the interactions between UE, HN and AF step by step.

Primary Authentication. Before AKMA service can start, UE and HN must execute mutual authentication. This primary authentication step is known as 5G Authentication and Key Agreement (5G AKA [7]). Prior generations of cellular networks have different AKA protocols: 3G has UMTS AKA protocol [3]; 4G has LTE AKA protocol [6]; in 5G, besides AKA protocol, there exists EAP-AKA' [7]. Whether to use 5G AKA or EAP-AKA' is decided by HN.

As mentioned above, UE has its unique and permanent identifier SUPI and secret key K, which are also stored in HN. Roughly speaking, when 5G AKA protocol runs, HN sends a random number to UE. With the random number and information of the UE, both UE and AUSF in HN side would generate K_{AUSF}, which will be used for generating subsequent keys during AKMA.

Deriving AKMA Materials. The steps for deriving AKMA materials are shown in Fig. 2. After UE finishes primary authentication with HN, and before it initiates communication with an AKMA Application Function (AF), it generates the AKMA Anchor Key K_{AKMA} and A-KID from K_{AUSF} (Steps 3, 4). The A-KID (AKMA Key Identifier) consists of A-TID (AKMA Temporary UE Identifier) and HN-ID (identity of home network).

After receiving K_{AUSF} from UDM, AUSF stores this key and generates the AKMA Anchor Key K_{AKMA} and A-KID from K_{AUSF} (Steps 3, 4). Then AUSF sends the AKMA key materials (K_{AKMA}, A-KID) together with the SUPI of UE to AAnF (Step 5). AUSF does not need to store any AKMA key materials after sending them to AAnF.

When AAnF receives the AKMA key materials from AUSF, it first deletes the old materials with the same SUPI (if there exists any). This means, if re-authentication runs, AAnF only stores the latest materials from AUSF, and each UE only has one AKMA key material at any time in AAnF. Then AAnF would give a response back to AUSF (Step 6).

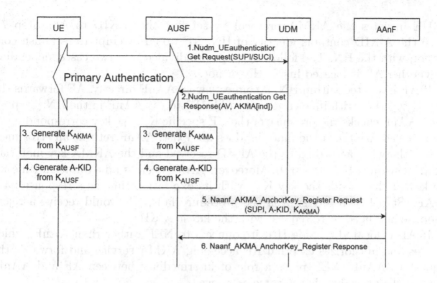

Fig. 2. Deriving AKMA materials (taken from [8])

Deriving AKMA Application Key for a Specific AF. The steps for deriving AKMA application key are shown in Fig. 3. If UE attempts to connect to AF without initiating AKMA protocol, AF would reject the request with an AKMA initiation message. Then UE would re-send the request in accordance to AKMA.

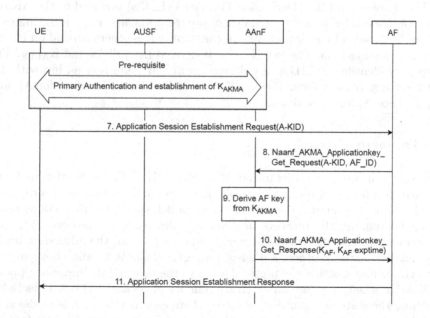

Fig. 3. Deriving AKMA application key for a specific AF (taken from [8])

UE initiates the AKMA protocol by sending the A-KID to AF (Step 7). Since the A-KID contains identity of HN, AF would attempt to establish connection with the HN. The following steps are divided into two cases, depending on whether AF is located inside HN or not.

If AF is located within HN, it connects with AAnF directly. AF forwards the A-KID together with its own identity (AF-ID) to the AAnF in the HN (Step 8). Then AAnF checks the presence of the UE specific K_{AKMA} key corresponding to the received A-KID. If the material does not exist, AAnF returns an error message. Otherwise, according to the AF-ID received and the AKMA key material, AAnF generates K_{AF} (Step 9). Moreover, AAnF decides an expiration time for the key. It then sends the key K_{AF} with its expiration time as a response back to AF (Step 10). If any step in the procedure fails, UE would receive a reject response and need to re-request with the latest A-KID.

If AF is located outside HN, it connects to NEF rather than AAnF, which enables and authorizes external AF accessing AKMA service and forwards the request to AAnF. NEF plays a role of intermediary between AF and AAnF. Most of the procedure is the same as above.

When AF receives the session key K_{AF} and K_{AF} expiration time, it responds to UE (Step 11). Since UE has all AKMA key materials, i.e. the latest K_{AKMA}, it can also generate K_{AF} by itself. Significantly, when the session key expires, AF ends the session with UE, but UE has a chance to refresh K_{AF}, depending on the protocol at the interface between AF and UE, i.e. the Ua* protocol. If this protocol supports refresh of K_{AF}, AF may refresh K_{AF} at any time using the Ua* protocol.

There are several Key Derivation Functions (KDFs) involved in the AKMA protocol. Each KDF accepts a number of input arguments. For generating each kind of key, some of the arguments are constant, while others depend on identifiers and existing keys. The key K_{AKMA} is derived from SUPI and K_{AUSF}. The temporary identifier A-TID is also derived from SUPI and K_{AUSF}, but with different settings of constants. The key K_{AF} is derived from identifiers for AF and K_{AKMA}. See [8] for more details.

3   Tamarin Prover

In this section, we give a brief introduction to the Tamarin verification tool [36]. Tamarin is a powerful tool for symbolic modeling and analysis of security protocols. It takes as input a security protocol model, specifying the actions taken by agents running the protocol in different roles (e.g., the protocol initiator, the responder, and the trusted server), a specification of the adversary, and a specification of the protocol's desired properties [36]. With the above inputs, Tamarin verifies whether the protocol satisfies the properties. Tamarin supports verification when there are an arbitrary number of sessions. This is reflected in modeling the state as a multiset of facts, where each new session is modeled by applying the corresponding initialization rule and adding new (linear) facts to the state. Hence, the state space is potentially infinite. Tamarin deals with the infinite state space using a backward-search style algorithm, starting from the violation of the property to be verified, and checking how the violation can result from applying the rules. The search does not always terminate as the verification problem can be shown to be undecidable. If the search terminates, Tamarin either proves that the property is satisfied, or finds a trace as counterexample against the property. The user interface shows the trace as a visual chart, which can be examined, to analyze for possible mistakes in the constructed model, the statement of properties, or the protocol itself. Since the verification problem is undecidable, to partially remedy the situation that does not terminate, Tamarin also provides an interactive mode where the user can guide the tool through the verification. We now introduce the usage of Tamarin from two aspects: modeling and property specification.

3.1   Modeling

In Tamarin, messages are described using *terms*, which are formed from variables, constants, and functions. For example, the theory of symmetric encryption is given by two functions *dec* and *enc*. The term $enc(m, k)$ denotes encryption of message m with key k, and the term $dec(m, k)$ denotes decryption. Moreover, a set of identities specify the equational theory. For example, symmetric encryption has the equation $dec(enc(m, k), k) = m$.

The protocol is specified using an expressive language based on multiset rewriting rules. These rules construct a labeled transition system whose states are multisets of facts, which give a symbolic representation of the current state of the protocol, messages on the network, and adversary knowledge. In Tamarin, the sort of a variable is expressed using the following prefixes: ~ for fresh variables, \$ for public variables, # for temporal variables, indicating the order of actions. There are three types of builtin fact symbols: Fr for generating a fresh value, In for receiving a message from the untrusted network, Out for sending a message to the untrusted network. As Tamarin assumes Dolev-Yao style attackers [20], the adversary can intercept any message that is output through Out, and insert any message as In. The adversary can construct new terms from existing knowledge (modulo rewriting rules), but cannot break the cryptography. For example, in the symmetric encryption theory above, the adversary cannot derive m if he knows only $enc(m, k)$, but will be able to do so if he additionally knows k, by constructing $dec(enc(m, k), k)$ and rewriting to m. In addition to the three builtin fact symbols, Tamarin allows defining any number of custom fact symbols. By default, a fact symbol is *linear*, meaning each fact with that symbol can be used only once. A fact symbol can be declared as *permanent* by prepending an exclamation sign (!).

Each rule consists of a list of premises, a list of conclusions, and a list of actions. A rule can be executed if each premise in the rule is present in the current multiset. The transition corresponding to executing this rule removes all premises from the multiset (except the permanent facts), and inserts conclusions into the multiset. The actions of the rule are appended together to form the trace of execution.

We illustrate these concepts with an example, in which agents A and B share a long-term key k, and A uses this key to send an encrypted message to B.

Example 1. In the protocol, A encrypts m with k and sends it to B.

```
rule Initial: [Fr(k)] --> [!Ltk($A, k), !Ltk($B, k)]
rule Send_A: [!Ltk($A, k), Fr(m)] --[Send_mes(A, m)]-> [Out(enc(m, k))]
rule Recv_B: [!Ltk($B, k), In(enc(m, k))] --[Recv_mes(B, m)]-> []
```

In the above code, each line specifies a rule of the protocol. If there are no actions in the rule, the premises and conclusions are joined by `-->`. Otherwise, the list of actions is written in the middle of the arrow. Terms preceded by the symbol $ are public terms (known to everyone including the adversary).

3.2 Property Specification

Security properties are defined over traces, formulated in terms of many-sorted first-order logic formulas over messages and timepoints, and checked against traces of the transition system. Using this logic, we can specify various secrecy and authentication properties.

Continuing Example 1, we show how to describe various levels of authentication specifications according to [29]. The following lemma specifies non-injective agreement between two agents A and B, meaning whenever B completes a run of the protocol, apparently with A, then A has been previously running the protocol, apparently with B, and they agree on the message m:

```
lemma Non_injective_agreement:
    "All m #i. Recv_mes(B, m) @ i ==> (EX #j. Send_mes(A, m) @ j & j < i)"
```

This property holds for the above example. The only way `Recv_mes(B,m)` can appear in the trace is for rule `Recv_B` to be executed. This can occur only if a term `enc(m,k)` is input. Since the adversary does not know `k`, there is no way for him to construct the message `enc(m,k)`. So the input can only come from rule `Send_A`, which creates the action `Send_mes(A,m)` at an earlier timepoint.

However, the following stronger property, injective agreement, does not hold:

```
lemma Injective_agreement:
    "All m #i. Recv_mes(B, m) @ i
      ==> (Ex #j. Send_mes(A, m) @ j & j < i
          & not (Ex #i2. Recv_mes(B, m) @ i2 & not (#i2 = #i)))
```

This is because the adversary can intercept the message `enc(m,k)` and resend it, resulting in another execution of the rule `Recv_B`. Clearly this protocol is too weak to guard against replay attacks.

4 Modeling and Specifying Properties of AKMA

In this section, we describe the detailed model of AKMA protocol and specify its properties of interest in Tamarin.

4.1 Threat Model

As we mentioned above, Tamarin assumes Dolev-Yao model for attackers. Adversary obeys the assumption of encryption, i.e., they can decrypt the secret messages only when having the corresponding key. In addition, we consider more advanced security properties corresponding to more powerful adversaries or compromised parties, following the eCK model [27]. In particular, we take into account the possibility of key reveal and the possibility that some of the entities have been compromised. In our protocol, the SUPI and K of a compromised UE could be revealed and the adversary would impersonate its identity to communicate with HN and AF. If HN is compromised, the information in UDM would be revealed and all information of the subscribers would be leaked, together with their asymmetric encryption key pairs, which play an important role in other protocols such as 5G AKA. Following [27], we define the concept of *clean session* as follows:

Definition 1 (Clean session). *We say a session is* clean *if neither of the following conditions holds:*

1. *One of the parties is an adversary-controlled party. This means in particular that adversary could reveal all private information known to the party, and perform all communications and computations on behalf of the compromised party;*
2. *Any of the long-term, temporary and session keys is revealed by adversary.*

Considering the following lemma:

```
All x #i. Secret(X) @i ==> not (Ex #j. K(x) @j)
```

it would be unsatisfiable when the agent is compromised. We call an agent is *Honest*(written as `Honest(X)`) if and only if the agent is not compromised. We indicate assumptions on honest agents by labeling the corresponding rule that the required action fact appears in with an `Honest(A)` action fact, where we assume A is honest. Intuitively, we explain the meaning of *Honest* by comparing the case where Honest is present in the properties and actions, and the case where it is not. If Honest is not present, then the meaning is that secrecy (or some other desired property) can be violated when any agent is compromised, whereas if Honest is present, then the meaning is that the desired property can be violated only when an agent participating in the protocol is compromised.

Therefore, following standard techniques of modeling using Tamarin [12,33], we model *Honest* participants and key reveals as follows. For each long-term, temporary, and session key that could be revealed, we add a rule which outputs the key (so it becomes known to the adversary), with an action of the form `Reveal(X,type)`, where X is the participant who owns the key, and `type` specifies the type of the key. Moreover, at steps of the protocol where `Running`, `Commit` and `Confirmation` actions are inserted (see the protocol rules in Sect. 4.2), we also insert actions of the form `Honest(X)`, which indicates that X should be an honest participant of the protocol, i.e., should not be compromised. Hence, `Ex X m #r. Reveal(X, m) @ r & Honest(X) @ i` means some participant of the protocol who is running (or finished) at time i has its secret key revealed (the session is not clean) at some time r. With this proposition, the considered lemma would be modified:

```
All x #i. Secret(X) @i ==> not (Ex #j. K(x) @j)
                    | (Ex X m #r. Reveal(X, m) @r & Honest(X)@i)
```

Propositions of this form will appear frequently in the properties stated below, which are usually of the form *either security conditions are satisfied, or the session is not clean.*

4.2   Modeling the AKMA Service in Tamarin

In this part, we analyze the functions and behaviors of AKMA service, including some of the underlying assumptions, then describe the model of the protocol in Tamarin.

Assumptions. As mentioned in Sect. 2, we make several reasonable assumptions about AKMA service:

1. Communication between UE and AF occurs along public channels. Hence it is subject to eavesdropping, interception and injection by the adversary. The protocol should remain secure under such attacks.
2. We assume that the communication inside HN is always clean and credible, as detailed in Sect. 4.1.
3. We only consider the case where AF can communicate directly with AAnF, without NEF as an intermediary. Hence, we do not include NEF in our model. Relaxing this assumption requires only changing the communication between AF and AAnF to taking two steps instead of only one step, which should not affect the security arguments about the protocol.
4. Mutual authentication between AAnF and AF occurs before running AKMA using the TLS protocol [7], which provides integrity, replay, and confidentiality protection of communication along a private channel. Following previous work [12,13], we abstract this to a secure channel between HN and AF. In Tamarin, the channel is modeled with four rules, representing four behaviors respectively: sending messages into the channels, receiving messages from the channel, eavesdropping messages from the channel, injecting messages into the channel (the latter two describe the behavior of the adversary).
5. Primary authentication using AKA is a prerequisite but not a proper part of AKMA service, and there are already a lot of work analyzing the 5G AKA protocol. Therefore, we assume the communication between HN and UE to be secure and private.

Significantly, we make some assumptions about permanent information: the subscriber credentials, i.e. SUPI, K of the UE, which are shared between UE and HN, should initially be secret, provided they are not compromised.

We also make some assumptions about compromised entities. In our model, there are no private and permanent information related to AFs. Therefore, we only need to consider compromised UE and HN. As we show in Sect. 5.1, the failure of non-injective agreement property is due to compromised HN. For compromised UEs, adversaries would know all secret information like SUPI and K. Likewise, adversaries could access SUPI and K of all subscribers from compromised HNs.

KDFs in the Protocol. Parameters of each key derivation function have been specified by 3GPP. These are abstracted for convenience of modeling. We define the KDF of K_{AUSF} with three parameters: identity of HN, K of UE and the random number HN sent to UE, while actually the parameters of K_{AUSF} derivative function contains $\langle CK, IK \rangle$ generated from K of UE, identity of HN and the random number; The A-KID and K_{AKMA} are generated from the same key K_{AUSF}, and the only difference is the setting of constants, so the parameters are SUPI of UE, K_{AUSF} and C_1 (or C_2); The parameters of the KDF of K_{AF} contain K_{AKMA} and identity of the AF.

Protocol Rules. We list some rules in the protocol and the corresponding Tamarin code below, in order to illustrate the modeling process.

– We model the process of redoing primary authentication. When AAnF receives a new AKMA key via fact AUSF_KEY, it deletes the old AKMA key materials by removing AAnF1 and only stores the latest message from AUSF by adding AAnF. The restriction in the action indicates that the rule would only trigger when K_AKMA_new does not equal K_AKMA and A_TID_new does not equal A_TID.

```
rule Re_pri_auth:
  [ AAnF1(~id_HN, ~SUPI, <A_TID, ~id_HN>, K_AKMA),
    AUSF_KEY(~SUPI, K_AUSF, ~id_HN, K_AKMA_new, <A_TID_new, ~id_HN>) ]
  --[_restrict(NotEqual(K_AKMA_new, K_AKMA)),
     _restrict(NotEqual(A_TID_new, A_TID)),
     K_AKMA_Re_Register(~id_HN)]->
  [ AAnF(~id_HN, ~SUPI, <A_TID_new, ~id_HN>, K_AKMA_new) ]
```

– Application Session Establishment Request: After UE and HN generated AKMA key materials, UE starts a session request to AF with its A-KID (containing the AKMA Temporary UE Identifier A-TID and HN-ID according to the TS [8]). Fact UE_KEY indicates that UE possesses all the information defined by the parameters. Fact UE_KEY1 is produced to indicate that these information does not disappear after this transition.

For two-party protocols, to analyze the desired authentication properties, we label the appropriate rules in the responder party B with an action fact

Commit(b, a, <'A', 'B', t>) and in the initiator party A with the corresponding action fact Running(a, b, <'A', 'B', t>). Likewise, Confirmation(a, b, <'A', 'B', t>) is added into the action fact in appropriate rules. We show the complete rule UE_send_request constructed in Tamarin as follows, but due to limited space, we will not list these actions in the remaining rules of this section.

```
rule UE_send_request:
  [ UE_KEY(~SUPI, K_AUSF, K_AKMA, <A_TID, ~id_HN>, K_AF, ~id_AF),
    !Sub(~SUPI, ~id_HN),
    !AF(~id_AF) ]
  --[UE_send_request(~SUPI),
    Secret(<'A_KID', <A_TID, ~id_HN>>, ~SUPI),
    Running(<A_TID, ~id_HN>, ~id_AF, <'UE', 'AF', <'A_KID', <A_TID, ~id_HN>>>),
    Running(~SUPI, ~id_HN, <'UE', 'HN', <'A_KID', <A_TID, ~id_HN>>>),
    Running(<A_TID, ~id_HN>, ~id_AF, <'UE', 'AF', <'K_AF', K_AF>>),
    Honest(<A_TID, ~id_HN>),
    Honest(~id_AF),
    Honest(~id_HN) ]->
  [ Out(<A_TID, ~id_HN>),
    UE_KEY1(~SUPI, K_AUSF, K_AKMA, <A_TID, ~id_HN>, K_AF, ~id_AF) ]
```

- Naanf AKMA ApplicationKey Get Request: AF forwards the request of UE with the identity of AF to HN, indicated by msg, via a secure channel cid.
- Naanf AKMA ApplicationKey Get Response: HN generates the session key K_{AF} and sends it through a message (indicated by session_msg) back to AF as a response.

```
rule AAnF_Send_K_AF:
  [ Fr(~exptime),
    AAnF_KEY(~id_HN, ~SUPI, <A_TID, ~id_HN>, K_AKMA, K_AF, ~id_AF),
    !AF(~id_AF),
    RcvS(~cid, ~id_AF, ~id_HN, < <A_TID, ~id_HN>, ~id_AF >) ]
  --[HN_Response(~id_HN, K_AF)]->
  [ SndS(~cid, ~id_HN, ~id_AF, < K_AF, ~exptime >) ]
```

- Application Session Establishment Response: After receiving the session key together with other information, AF would start an implicit authentication. In the specification [8], when AF receives a request from UE with its A-KID, AF would return a response without any parameters to UE. In order to let UE and AF confirm the session key, we add a key-confirmation round trip. When AF obtains the session key and the expiration time from AAnF, it would hash the session key with "AF" and send the hash value to UE. UE would confirm the hash value, then hash the session key with "UE" and send the hash value to AF. The implicit authentication is finished when UE and AF have both confirmed the hash values. We list the case for UE key confirmation.

```
rule UE_Key_Confirmation:
  [ In(f(K_AF, 'AF')),
    UE_KEY1(~SUPI, K_AUSF, K_AKMA, <A_TID, ~id_HN>, K_AF, ~id_AF),
    !AF(~id_AF) ]
  --[UE_Key_Confirmation(~SUPI, K_AF)]->
  [ Out(f(K_AF, 'UE')) ]
```

4.3   Specifying Properties

Now we introduce the properties of interest and describe them in the Tamarin prover. First, we introduce Lowe's taxonomy of authentication properties [29], which consists of four authentication levels from one party's view and many security properties are extended from these four basic properties. Considering the authentication of the given two parties A and B, from party A's point of view, the authentication levels are defined as follows:

1. **Aliveness:** Whenever A completes a run of the protocol, apparently with B, then B has previously been running the protocol (not necessarily with A);
2. **Weak agreement:** Whenever A completes a run of the protocol, apparently with B, then B has previously been running the protocol, apparently with A (but not necessary agreeing on the same messages);
3. **Non-injective agreement:** In addition to the condition for weak agreement, the parties A and B also agree on the same message;
4. **Injective agreement:** In addition to the conditions for non-injective agreement, there is a unique matching partner instance for each completed run of an agent, which effectively prevents replay attacks.

In Technical Specifications and Technical Requirements by 3GPP [1,7,8], we find that many security requirements are based on these four authentication properties, as well as confidentiality of some messages. Therefore, we will mainly characterize security of AKMA service in terms of these properties.

- Weak agreement between UE and AF is defined by the following lemma

```
lemma weakagreement_UE_AF:
  all-traces
    "All A B t #i. Commit(A, B, <'UE', 'AF', t>) @i
      ==> (Ex t2 #j. Running(B, A, t2) @j)
        | (Ex X m #r. Reveal(X, m) @r & Honest(X) @i)"
```

The weak agreement between AF and HN, HN and AF, UE and HN can be defined similarly.
- Non-injective agreement between UE and AF (agreeing on the target session key K_{AF}):

```
lemma Non_injective_agreement:
  all-traces
    "All A B t #i.
      Confirmation(<'AF', A>, <'UE', B>, <'UE', 'AF', <'K_AF', t>>) @i
      ==> (Ex #j. Running(B, A, <'UE', 'AF', <'K_AF', t>>) @j & j < i)
        | (Ex D m #l. Reveal(D, m) @l & Honest(D) @i)"
```

- Confidentiality of A-KID and K_{AF}. We find the leakage of A-KID will result in lots of security problems and we check its security. Meanwhile, The protocol must prevent the session key K_{AF} from being revealed, i.e., adversaries will never know the session key. We list the latter case.

```
lemma secure_K_AF:
  all-traces
    "All n A #i. Secret(<'K_AF', n>, A) @i
      ==> (not (Ex #j. K(n) @j))
        | (Ex X data #r. Reveal(X, data) @r & Honest(X) @i)"
```

Moreover, we describe the executability of the AKMA protocol, i.e., it is possible to complete the protocol and agree on a session key for the first time and more than once.

We specified our model and properties through Tamarin[1]. The total number of lines of code is approximately 500.

5   Results and Analysis

We verify the properties listed in Sect. 4.3 using Tamarin. Except that the verification time of non-injective agreement between UE and AF is close to 30 s and the verification time of confidentiality of K_{AF} is about 15 s, the verification time of resting properties is less than 6 s. We present the verification results, and for the properties that fail to hold, analyze the counterexamples returned by Tamarin. For each counterexample, we put forward some potential attacks and propose suggestions.

5.1   Verification Results and Analysis

First of all, the executability of the protocol, the weak agreement between AF and HN, HN and AF, UE and HN, and confidentiality of K_{AF} turn out to be correct. The protocol does protect the secrecy of the session key. The confidentiality of A-KID turns out to be incorrect, which is obvious because A-KID is transferred along public channels. Next we mainly discuss the main properties that do not hold for the service.

Weak Agreement Between UE and AF. For weak agreement between UE and AF, we construct two lemmas, one with implicit authentication, and one without. The first one turns out to be correct, but the second fails. For the second case, Tamarin returns the following counterexample: (1) UE starts a session request to an AF (denoted by AF_1) with A-KID of UE; (2) the leakage of A-KID occurs, then adversary M connects another AF (denoted by AF_2) with this A-KID; (3) AF_2 thinks that UE should have connected AF_2 before and asks HN for the session key K_{AF}, while UE only connects to AF_1 and generates K_{AF1}. Therefore M would not communicate with AF_2 and could not complete the protocol. In conclusion, if there is no implicit authentication to confirm the session key, weak agreement between UE and AF would not be satisfied, although nothing harmful would actually happen.

---

[1] The code is publicly available at https://github.com/TengshunYang/5G-AKMA.

We find that the main problem is the leakage of A-KID. In real life, adversaries would eavesdrop the A-KID, or a malicious AF would play the role of adversary and forward the received A-KID to another AF, i.e. linkability between AFs, which is mentioned as a privacy violation in [23,24]. Adversary could impersonate UE's identity and start a session with AF. Although the adversary has no way to obtain the session key except by stealing from the UE, it would result in waste of trust and materials. Here we describe the situation of *linkability between AFs* as follows: (1) UE starts a session with an AF (denoted by AF_1), and completes AKMA service with AF_1 successfully; (2) With the possession of A-KID, AF_1 would forward it to another AF (denoted by AF_2). Knowing the A-KID helps AF_2 distinguish the UEs, even without knowing the user's true identity. AFs in the collusion group would share all the information of users with the same A-KID with each other, which would result in leakage of users such as history, hobbies and habits, etc. After combining all the information, the user's true identity could be revealed.

Non-injective Agreement. Non-injective agreement property between UE and AF turns out to be incorrect, indicating that either weak-agreement between UE and AF does not hold, or UE and AF could not agree on the session key K_{AF}. Tamarin returns a counterexample: (1) UE starts a session request to the AF with A-KID$_1$; (2) AF forwards this message to HN and expects a session key as a response; (3) The interchange between HN and AF occurs. HN sends back to AF another A-KID$_2$ (actually consisting of A-TID and identifier of AF) together with identifier of HN. As a result, this A-KID$_2$ plays the role of K_{AF}, which could be computed by adversaries as a hash value for confirmation. Therefore, the confirmation in the protocol would execute successfully.

The reason for the above situation comes from the interchange between AF and HN and the leakage of A-KID. Considering the practical situation, the probability of HN being compromised is small and the AKMA service is assumed to trust HNs. Therefore, the interchange between HN and AF is not likely to happen. We conclude that the counterexample is unreasonable. However, to eliminate the counterexample, we make a simple fix to the rule AAnF_send_K_AF as follows: when AAnF sends the session key together with expiration time, AAnF also adds A-KID into the message.

```
rule AAnF_Send_K_AF:
  let
    session_msg = < K_AF, ~exptime, <A_TID, ~id_HN> >
    msg_In = < <A_TID, ~id_HN>, ~id_AF >
  in
  [ Fr(~exptime),
    AAnF_KEY(~id_HN, ~SUPI, <A_TID, ~id_HN>, K_AKMA, K_AF, ~id_AF),
    !AF(~id_AF),
    RcvS(~cid, ~id_AF, ~id_HN, msg_In) ]
  --[_restrict(Equal(fst(msg_In), <A_TID, ~id_HN>)),
    HN_Response(~id_HN, K_AF)]->
  [ SndS(~cid, ~id_HN, ~id_AF, session_msg) ]
```

With this fix, the property is satisfied. Significantly, this fix helps AF distinguish between K_{AF} for different users. Actually in the execution of the protocol, the message would contain the session id, which is a default setting in mobile network. In a word, we prove the importance and value of the session id.

5.2 Suggestions

According to the results of verification using Tamarin, several of the security properties that we expect to hold actually fail for the initial model we constructed for AKMA. We find that leakage of A-KID plays an important role in disturbing the protocol, such as, waste of materials and causing linkability between AFs, which is harmful to users' privacy. So we suggest adding protection for the communication of A-KID. For example, pre-construct a channel for UE and AF with asymmetric encryption, or use TLS protocol. Aiming at resolving the collusion among AFs, dynamic A-KID or increasing the frequency of primary authentication are worth considering.

Moreover, in the technical specification [8], the session key K_{AF} could still be used while UE restarts a primary authentication. We find that the leakage of K_{AF} would result in the situation where more than one dishonest UEs (impersonating the original UE) connect to one AF with the leaked K_{AF}, which would use the service from AF or even steal properties and private information, even though these dishonest UEs have never started primary authentication. We suggest that HN could inform the AF when the session key K_{AF} expires ahead of the time when UE starts a primary authentication. It would reduce the risk of leakage, at the price of only one message.

6 Conclusion

We have formalized for the first time the 5G AKMA service specified in TS 33.535 [8], using Tamarin verification tool. The formalization includes the formal model of the AKMA service, the security properties that are expected to hold, the verification, the potential attacks of the AKMA service and some suggestions for fixing the problems. During the modeling, we identify formally the assumptions for the security properties to hold. For the security properties that do not hold, we analyze the corresponding counterexamples and construct the potential attacks, and at the end, suggest some fixes for the model to resolve the attacks and weaknesses. For future work, we will follow the future development of the AKMA standard and update the formalization. We will also consider the privacy requirements of 5G AKMA and their formalization, e.g. the privacy caused by the linkability between AFs mentioned in this paper deserving consideration.

Acknowledgements. This work is supported in part by the NSFC under grants No. 61625206, 61972385, 62002351 and 61732001, and by the CAS Pioneer Hundred Talents Program under grant No. Y9RC585036.

References

1. 3GPP: TR33.835 v16.1.0 Study on authentication and key management for applications based on 3GPP credential in 5G. https://portal.3gpp.org/desktopmodules/Specifications/SpecificationDetails.aspx?specificationId=3483
2. 3GPP: TR33.902 v4.0.0 3g Security; Formal Analysis of the 3G Authentication Protocol. https://portal.3gpp.org/desktopmodules/Specifications/SpecificationDetails.aspx?specificationId=2337
3. 3GPP: TS33.102 v16.0.0 3G Security; Security architecture. https://portal.3gpp.org/desktopmodules/Specifications/SpecificationDetails.aspx?specificationId=2262
4. 3GPP: TS33.163 v16.2.0 Battery Efficient Security for very low throughput Machine Type Communication (MTC) devices (BEST). https://portal.3gpp.org/desktopmodules/Specifications/SpecificationDetails.aspx?specificationId=3128
5. 3GPP: TS33.220 v17.1.0 Generic Authentication Architecture (GAA); Generic Bootstrapping Architecture (GBA). https://portal.3gpp.org/desktopmodules/Specifications/SpecificationDetails.aspx?specificationId=2280
6. 3GPP: TS33.401 v16.3.0 3GPP System Architecture Evolution (SAE); Security architecture. https://portal.3gpp.org/desktopmodules/Specifications/SpecificationDetails.aspx?specificationId=2296
7. 3GPP: TS33.501 v17.1.0 Security architecture and procedures for 5G system (Release 17). https://portal.3gpp.org/desktopmodules/Specifications/SpecificationDetails.aspx?specificationId=3169
8. 3GPP: TS33.535 v17.1.0 Authentication and Key Management for Applications (AKMA) based on 3GPP credentials in the 5G System (5GS). https://portal.3gpp.org/desktopmodules/Specifications/SpecificationDetails.aspx?specificationId=3690
9. Abadi, M., Blanchet, B., Fournet, C.: The applied pi calculus: mobile values, new names, and secure communication. J. ACM **65**(1), 1:1–1:41 (2018)
10. Armando, A., et al.: The AVISPA tool for the automated validation of internet security protocols and applications. In: Etessami, K., Rajamani, S.K. (eds.) CAV 2005. LNCS, vol. 3576, pp. 281–285. Springer, Heidelberg (2005). https://doi.org/10.1007/11513988_27
11. Basin, D.A., Cremers, C., Kim, T.H., Perrig, A., Sasse, R., Szalachowski, P.: Design, analysis, and implementation of ARPKI: an attack-resilient public-key infrastructure. IEEE Trans. Dependable Secur. Comput. **15**(3), 393–408 (2018)
12. Basin, D.A., Dreier, J., Hirschi, L., Radomirovic, S., Sasse, R., Stettler, V.: A formal analysis of 5G authentication. In: Lie, D., Mannan, M., Backes, M., Wang, X. (eds.) Proceedings of the 2018 ACM SIGSAC Conference on Computer and Communications Security, CCS 2018, Toronto, ON, Canada, 15–19 October 2018, pp. 1383–1396. ACM (2018)
13. Basin, D.A., Radomirovic, S., Schmid, L.: Modeling human errors in security protocols. In: IEEE 29th Computer Security Foundations Symposium, CSF 2016, Lisbon, Portugal, 27 June–1 July 2016, pp. 325–340. IEEE Computer Society (2016)
14. Bellare, M., Rogaway, P.: Entity authentication and key distribution. In: Stinson, D.R. (ed.) CRYPTO 1993. LNCS, vol. 773, pp. 232–249. Springer, Heidelberg (1994). https://doi.org/10.1007/3-540-48329-2_21
15. Blanchet, B.: An efficient cryptographic protocol verifier based on prolog rules. In: 14th IEEE Computer Security Foundations Workshop (CSFW-14 2001), Cape Breton, Nova Scotia, Canada, 11–13 June 2001, pp. 82–96. IEEE Computer Society (2001)

16. Burrows, M., Abadi, M., Needham, R.M.: A logic of authentication. ACM Trans. Comput. Syst. **8**(1), 18–36 (1990)
17. Canetti, R., Krawczyk, H.: Analysis of key-exchange protocols and their use for building secure channels. In: Pfitzmann, B. (ed.) EUROCRYPT 2001. LNCS, vol. 2045, pp. 453–474. Springer, Heidelberg (2001). https://doi.org/10.1007/3-540-44987-6_28
18. Clavel, M., et al.: All About Maude - A High-Performance Logical Framework. LNCS, vol. 4350. Springer, Heidelberg (2007). https://doi.org/10.1007/978-3-540-71999-1
19. Cremers, C., Horvat, M., Hoyland, J., Scott, S., van der Merwe, T.: A comprehensive symbolic analysis of TLS 1.3. In: Thuraisingham, B.M., Evans, D., Malkin, T., Xu, D. (eds.) Proceedings of the 2017 ACM SIGSAC Conference on Computer and Communications Security, CCS 2017, Dallas, TX, USA, 30 October–03 November 2017, pp. 1773–1788. ACM (2017)
20. Dolev, D., Yao, A.C.: On the security of public key protocols. IEEE Trans. Inf. Theory **29**(2), 198–207 (1983)
21. Donovan, B., Norris, P., Lowe, G.: Analyzing a library of security protocols using Casper and FDR. In: In Workshop on Formal Methods and Security Protocols (1999)
22. Escobar, S., Meadows, C.A., Meseguer, J.: A rewriting-based inference system for the NRL protocol analyzer and its meta-logical properties. Theor. Comput. Sci. **367**(1–2), 162–202 (2006)
23. Khan, M., Ginzboorg, P., Niemi, V.: Privacy preserving AKMA in 5G. In: Mehrnezhad, M., van der Merwe, T., Hao, F. (eds.) Proceedings of the 5th ACM Workshop on Security Standardisation Research Workshop, London, UK, 11 November 2019, pp. 45–56. ACM (2019)
24. Khan, M., Ginzboorg, P., Niemi, V.: AKMA: Delegated Authentication System of 5G (2021). https://doi.org/10.13140/RG.2.2.28186.36804
25. Krawczyk, H.: HMQV: a high-performance secure Diffie-Hellman protocol. In: Shoup, V. (ed.) CRYPTO 2005. LNCS, vol. 3621, pp. 546–566. Springer, Heidelberg (2005). https://doi.org/10.1007/11535218_33
26. Künnemann, R., Steel, G.: YubiSecure? Formal security analysis results for the Yubikey and YubiHSM. In: Jøsang, A., Samarati, P., Petrocchi, M. (eds.) STM 2012. LNCS, vol. 7783, pp. 257–272. Springer, Heidelberg (2013). https://doi.org/10.1007/978-3-642-38004-4_17
27. LaMacchia, B., Lauter, K., Mityagin, A.: Stronger security of authenticated key exchange. In: Susilo, W., Liu, J.K., Mu, Y. (eds.) ProvSec 2007. LNCS, vol. 4784, pp. 1–16. Springer, Heidelberg (2007). https://doi.org/10.1007/978-3-540-75670-5_1
28. Lamport, L.: The temporal logic of actions. ACM Trans. Program. Lang. Syst. **16**(3), 872–923 (1994)
29. Lowe, G.: A hierarchy of authentication specification. In: 10th Computer Security Foundations Workshop (CSFW 1997), Rockport, Massachusetts, USA, 10–12 June 1997, pp. 31–44 (1997)
30. Meier, S.: Advancing automated security protocol verification. Ph.D. thesis, ETH (2013)
31. Meier, S., Schmidt, B., Cremers, C., Basin, D.: The TAMARIN prover for the symbolic analysis of security protocols. In: Sharygina, N., Veith, H. (eds.) CAV 2013. LNCS, vol. 8044, pp. 696–701. Springer, Heidelberg (2013). https://doi.org/10.1007/978-3-642-39799-8_48

32. Sarr, A.P., Elbaz-Vincent, P., Bajard, J.-C.: A new security model for authenticated key agreement. In: Garay, J.A., De Prisco, R. (eds.) SCN 2010. LNCS, vol. 6280, pp. 219–234. Springer, Heidelberg (2010). https://doi.org/10.1007/978-3-642-15317-4_15
33. Schmidt, B., Meier, S., Cremers, C.J.F., Basin, D.A.: Automated analysis of Diffie-Hellman protocols and advanced security properties. In: 25th IEEE Computer Security Foundations Symposium, CSF 2012, Cambridge, MA, USA, 25–27 June 2012, pp. 78–94 (2012)
34. Schneider, S., Holloway, R.: Using CSP for protocol analysis: the Needham-Schroeder public-key protocol. Technical report (1996)
35. Schneider, S.A.: Security properties and CSP. In: 1996 IEEE Symposium on Security and Privacy, Oakland, CA, USA, 6–8 May 1996, pp. 174–187. IEEE Computer Society (1996)
36. Tamarin Team: Tamarin-Prover Manual: Security Protocol Analysis in the Symbolic Model. https://tamarin-prover.github.io/manual/. Accessed 7 Jan 2021

Verifying the Correctness of Distributed Systems via Mergeable Parallelism

Teng Long[1]($\boxtimes$) (iD), Xingtao Ren[1], Qing Wang[1], and Chao Wang[2]

[1] School of Information Engineering, China University of Geosciences,
Beijing 100083, China
{longteng,xintao,qingw}@cugb.edu.cn

[2] Centre for Research and Innovation in Software Engineering, School of Computer
and Information Science, Southwest University, Chongqing, China
wangch1@swu.edu.cn

Abstract. Distributed systems are the most basic elements of establishing services that deal with a large number of terminals (including clients and servers). Message passing is one of the communication methods in distributed systems. Verification of asynchronous distributed systems is valuable and challenging because of unpredictable interleavings and possible network faults. Asynchronous mode has better performance than the synchronous one, but asynchronous completion makes the task of specifying correct behaviors more difficult. In this paper, we propose a simple procedure for verifying the safety properties of asynchronous programs that satisfies the assumption of mergeable parallelism. And we characterize inference rules to describe the sequence combination that satisfies the conditions of the receiving operations. The program's execution can be reduced to executions with sets of fixed order. A proof is provided to show its soundness. The correctness of the mergeable message passing programs could be verified by a state-of-the-art verification framework. It can be used in various message passing cases.

Keywords: Asynchronous · Distributed systems · Hoare triples · Mergeable parallelism · Message passing programs

1 Introduction

Distributed systems are essential for building services to support the growing number of clients. Safety properties guarantee that nothing bad happens, including the correctness of protocols, error states being unreachable, free of deadlock, etc. However, it is not easy to verify these properties of distributed programs. One reason is the highly asynchronous events in distributed execution. Due to the existence of asynchronous events, invariants become more complicated. Even worse, in some cases, the asynchronous invariants are related to the contents of

Supported by National Natural Science Foundation of China (No. 62002332, 62072443, 62002298, 61972364).

S. Qin et al. (Eds.): SETTA 2021, LNCS 13071, pp. 122–140, 2021.
https://doi.org/10.1007/978-3-030-91265-9_7

a number of unbounded message buffers. Many previous work proposed verification approaches, such as partial-order techniques [9], bounded analysis [3,4], synthesized technique [6]. However, they did not consider all the possible interleavings.

Asynchronous message passing programs are designed to be executed in parallel among different processes (i.e., servers and clients). To prove the correctness of an asynchronous message passing program, researchers tried to reduce the verification in an asynchronous system to the verification in a simpler system [1]. The above paper uses the method of removing the message buffer to get sequential programs, but the scope of application is limited. For example, in a program that includes rounds, it is still possible for the receiver to randomly receive messages from different rounds, and it cannot be converted into a sequential program in this way. In order to solve more practical problems, we found that mergeable parallelism and its corresponding reduction may be an ideal solution. Moreover, our method is simpler, with reduction, any given trace of a mergeable program can be regarded as the execution sequence on a single instance of the rewritten concurrent program.

In this paper, we propose a novel approach for the analysis and verification of asynchronous message passing programs. If an original program has mergeable parallelism (a limited form of non-determinism network), it can be rewritten to a new one which is featured by a set of explicitly paralleled processes with the same code with atomic parts. The approach provides a simple procedure for analyzing a sequence of operations in one instance of above paralleled processes. The matching send-receive operation pairs can be generated by the inference rule that describes the sequence combination that satisfies the conditions of the receiving operations. With these rules, executions with sets of fixed order can be obtained to prove the safety properties in asynchronous message passing programs.

Our key insight is that, a subclass (distributed consensus) of protocols fits the assumption of mergeable parallelism, as they usually only loop through a set of processes, meanwhile many of them in a limited type of network in which the receive operation's matching send operation is only in a single process or in a set of processes with the same code. We will explore remaining subclasses of protocols in the future.

The paper is organized as follows: First, we propose a simple example to show the overview of our method. And then the basic concepts of asynchronous message passing programs are introduced, followed by the formal definitions of mergeable parallelism. Then, we proposed inference rules, simplified reasoning and the soundness proof. A merging algorithm is given, where a control flow graph is constructed for one parallel instance. The evaluation illustrates the effectiveness of this method in various message passing cases. The paper is ended with related work and conclusions.

2 Overview

We will start by demonstrating our approach on a simple example.

$$P :: \begin{bmatrix} for(q : Q)\{ \\ m_1 : id \leftarrow receive(q); \\ m_2 : send(id, ack)\} \end{bmatrix} \parallel \sqcap Q(j) :: \begin{bmatrix} l_1 : send(P, j) \\ l_2 : v \leftarrow receive(P); \\ l_3 : \text{assert } (v = ack) \end{bmatrix}$$

Fig. 1. SimpleMP

SimpleMP is a program in which a set of processes Q (running the same code) exchange messages with a single process P in Fig. 1 (including send and receive operations). Process P executes a loop which iterates over all processes q in Q. For each process q in Q, it first sends its identifier j and subsequently waits for a reply from P. Each iteration, P first waits for a message from q and, upon receipt, sends an "ack" message to q. The goal is to verify that, for all the q, it may only ever receive "ack". The CFG for P and the CFG for some $Q(j)$ is in Fig. 2. The dotted lines in Fig. 2 represent the enabling conditions for receiving operations. $[B_P > 0]$ and $[B_j > 0]$ indicate that the buffers of process P and process $Q(j)$ are not empty, respectively.

Mergeable Parallelism. A program is mergeable if (i) each process only receives messages either from a single process or from the same statement in a set of processes (running the same code), and (ii) for each iteration, a single process can exchange messages with only one specific process. For such mergeable program, its asynchronous execution can be reduced to an equivalent synchronous one.

For each iteration, P communicates only with a certain $Q(id)$, and in addition, all receives in the program either come from a single process or from a set of processes that run the same code, so SimpleMP is mergeable. According

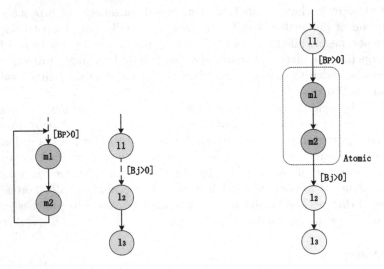

Fig. 2. SimpleMP: The CFGs of P and $Q(j)$

Fig. 3. SimpleMP: The CFG of $[P^I] \oplus Q(j)$

to the rewriting Algorithm 1, we get a set of static (but unbounded) groups of processes that constraints by a unique template $[P^I] \oplus Q(j)$ in Fig. 3, where symbol $\oplus$ means the communication between one iteration of P and some $Q(j)$.

Simplified Reasoning. A set of Hoare triples could be given by standard technology for the unique template. And then we use the inference rules: *Sequencing-C*, *Symmetry*, and *Conjunction*. The *Sequencing-C* rule is also necessary to consider both the combinatorial entailment relation [7] and the enabled conditions of the receive operations. The remaining two rules can only be used for the operations executed by Q.

Rule *Sequencing-C* composes two Hoare triples sequentially with enabled conditions, which can reflect the precedence order between the send and receive operations. Rule *Symmetry* permutes Q's identifiers. Rule *Conjunction* composes two Hoare triples by conjoining pre- and post-conditions.

In Fig. 3, the statements in the atomic part should be executed sequentially and atomically. While the conditional transitions (dotted line) could be executed sequentially. It shows that if the fetched message in the atomic block is legal (the message was indeed sent before being received by P), the corresponding sending operation can be combined through the rule *Symmetry* and *Sequencing-C*. The above renaming and combination transformations are the applications of Liption's mover theorem. The triples will result in false, which means that it is impossible for some $Q(id_e)$ to receive the messages without sending its id to P in advance.

3   Asynchronous Message Passing Programs

Asynchronous message passing programs (MPP) are featured with an explicit parallel composition and unbounded iteration. Its syntax is shown in Fig. 4:

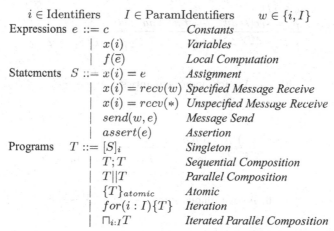

Fig. 4. Syntax of asynchronous message passing programs

- Expressions include constants c, variables indexed by its unique process identifier $x(i)$, and $f(\overrightarrow{e})$ the local computation without sending or receiving any messages. $x(i)$ refers to variable x in process i.

- Statements include assignment, message receive, message send and assertion. There are two cases for message receive: one is with a specified sender w, the other is with an unknown sender $*$. w can be either a process identifier i or a set of process identifiers I.
- Programs can be seen as singleton ones $[S]_i$, which represents process i executing statement S. Furthermore, it supports sequential composition. Atomic part is not proposed by the programmer, but is generated by the rewriting procedure. "Iteration" $for(i:I)\{T\}$ is used to show the sequential instantiations of T for i in the process identifiers set I. "Iterated Parallel Composition" $\sqcap_{i:I} T$ is used to show the parallel instantiations of T for i in the process identifiers set I. We regard the above two definitions as two types of templates. The program can be seen as a parallel composition of multiple templates of the above types.

We define a configuration $c = (\iota, B, \varphi)$, where ι is a vector of local statements, $\iota[\rho_p \leftarrow \rho]$ is a function that returns the same statements as ι except for the statement of process p where it returns ρ. B is a function from the process identifier to the values of the content of the buffer. $\varphi[x \leftarrow v]$ is a function that returns the same values as φ on all variables except for x where it returns v. The asynchronous semantics of send and receive operations in MPP are shown in Fig. 5 and Fig. 6, where $tgt()$ is the send/receive operations target statement and $src()$ is the send/receive statement.

- Semantics of *Send* Operations: The effect of a send operation is to enqueue a message to the buffer of the recipient.
- Semantics of *Receive* Operations: The effect of a receive operation is to dequeue a message from the non-empty local buffer.

$$\frac{q \in ID \qquad \rho_p = src(send), \rho' = tgt(send)}{\iota, B, \varphi \xrightarrow{send(q,v):p} \iota[\rho_p \leftarrow \rho'], B(q) \leftarrow B(q) \cdot v, \varphi}$$

Fig. 5. Asynchronous semantics of $c \xrightarrow{Send} c'$

$$\frac{B(q) = v \cdot b \qquad \rho_q = src(rec), \rho' = tgt(rec)}{\iota, B, \varphi \xrightarrow{x \leftarrow rec(*):q} \iota[\rho_q \leftarrow \rho'], B(q) \leftarrow b, \varphi[x(q) \leftarrow v]}$$

Fig. 6. Asynchronous semantics of $c \xrightarrow{Receive} c'$

4   Mergeable Message Passing Programs

We define a property of message passing programs called *mergeable* that satisfies the conditions in Definition 1.

To illustrate the matching between sending and receiving information, we denote sets $S_j = \{s_j : s \in S, j \in \mathcal{N}\}$ and $R_j = \{r_j : r \in R, j \in \mathcal{N}\}$, where S is a set of send operations, R is a set of receive operations, and $\mathcal{N}$ is the number of kinds of different send or receive operations. Given a send operation $s \in S_i$ and a receive operation $r \in R_i$, which are related to the same message, this pair is called a *matching* pair, otherwise it is called a *mismatched* pair.

$Proc(A), A \in S \cup R$ denote the set of processes that the operation A belongs to. $Com(A), A \in S \cup R$ denote the set of processes that the operation A communicates with.

Definition 1 (Mergeable Parallelism). *Let $\mathcal{M}$ is an MPP. Then $\mathcal{M}$ has mergeable parallelism if:*

– *for each receive operation set R_j $j \in \mathcal{N}$, its matching send operation $s \in S_j$ must satisfy the following conditions:*

• *$Proc(s) = \{p\}$ (p is an identifier variable) which means that s belongs to a single process p, or*
• *$Proc(s) = \{I\}$ (I is a paramidentifier variable) which means that s belongs to a set of processes running the same code.*

– *For operations a_1 and a_2 in a single process ($Proc(a_1) = p$ and $Proc(a_2) = p$), for each iteration there are no such different processes $i, j \in I$ that $Com(a_1) = i$ and $Com(a_2) = j$.*

5 Simplified Reasoning

We propose inference rules with additional pre/post-enabled conditions.

Definition 2 (Basic Hoare triple). *A basic Hoare triple is valid in the form $[C]\{\varphi\}\langle \sigma : i\rangle\{\psi\}[C']$ where*

– *σ can be seen as a send or receive statement. We will discuss these two statements next, and the processing of the remaining statements is similar to that of [7].*
– *$\langle \sigma : i\rangle$ shows the statement σ executed by process i.*
– *A trace $\tau = \langle \sigma : i\rangle\langle \sigma : j\rangle \dots \langle \sigma : k\rangle$ is a sequence of statements which are executed by process i, j, $\dots$, k, respectively.*
– *φ and ψ are formulas with variables in sequential instantiations and indexed variables parallel instantiations.*
– *The pre-enabled condition $[C]$ and the post-enabled condition $[C']$ indicate the status of buffer with an additional variable b. The process that appears in C is i, while the process that appears in C' is either i or $j \neq i$ with j must be in σ, where $\sigma \in S \cup R$ is a send/receive operation.*

Definition 3 (Rule: Sequencing-C). *Rule Sequencing-C shown in Fig. 7 is extended from rule Sequencing [7] with enabled conditions on the buffer status. It is composed of two Hoare triples where both the first triple's post-condition and post- enabled condition imply the second triple's pre-condition and pre- enabled condition.*

$$\frac{[C_1]\{\varphi_0\}\tau_0\{\varphi_1\}[C] \qquad \varphi_1 \Vdash \varphi_1', C \Vdash C' \qquad [C']\{\varphi_1'\}\tau_1\{\varphi_2\}[C_2]}{[C_1]\{\varphi_0\}\tau_0; \tau_1\{\varphi_2\}[C_2]}$$

Fig. 7. Rule: *Sequencing-C*

$$\frac{[C]\{\varphi\}\langle \sigma : i\rangle\{\psi\}[C']}{[C[\pi]]\{\varphi[\pi]\}\langle \sigma : \pi(i)\rangle\{\psi[\pi]\}[C'[\pi]]}$$

Fig. 8. Rule: *Symmetry*

Definition 4 (Rule: Symmetry [7]). *Rule* Symmetry *shown in Fig. 8 permutes process identifiers.* $\pi : \mathbb{N} \to \mathbb{N}$ *is a permutation.*

Definition 5 (Rule: Conjunction [7]). *Rule* Conjunction *shown in Fig. 9, consists of two Hoare triples by conjoining the pre-condition and post-condition.*

5.1   Analysis by Inference Rules

Given a *mergeable* message passing program $\mathcal{M}$ and the error situation (e.g. $assert(e)$, where e related to inconsistent message value), if a Hoare triple $\{true\}\tau\{false\}$ is derivable by using the above three inference rules, the trace τ is called infeasible.

We will construct a set of Hoare triples by using inference rules in $\mathcal{M}$.

- The analysis related to the enabled condition is shown by rule *Sequencing-C*. These conditions will finally be satisfied according to the order of statements in the code of a process, and the precedence order between send and their corresponding receive operations.
- *Symmetry* rule can only be used to permute the process identifiers between parallel instantiations.
- *Conjunction* rule can not be used for statements in sequential instantiations, as the execution of each statement in such an process is not concurrently.

The analysis by inference rules are shown as follows:

Sequencing-C. The composition operation by using rule *Sequencing-C* is symbolled as $\circ_c$. Symbol $p \oplus q_i$ denotes a program as an instance of communication between P and $\sqcap_{i \in I} Q$. Suppose the premises (related to a matching send-receive pair in instance $p \oplus q_1$) in its CFG $G_{p \oplus q_1}$ are as follows:

$$\frac{[C_0]\{\varphi_0\}\tau\{\psi_0\}[C_0'] \quad [C_1]\{\varphi_1\}\tau\{\psi_1\}[C_1']}{[C_0 \wedge C_1]\{\varphi_0 \wedge \varphi_1\} \ \tau \ \{\psi_0 \wedge \psi_1\}[C_0' \wedge C_1']}$$

Fig. 9. Rule: *Conjunction*

$$\rho_{p \oplus q_1, p} = src(send), \rho_{p \oplus q_1, q_1} = tgt(send)$$

$$\rho_{p \oplus q_1, q_1} = src(rec), \rho'_{p \oplus q_1, q_1} = tgt(rec)$$

The symbol $\rho_{p \oplus q_1, p}$ describes the statement of p in $G_{p \oplus q_1}$. $\rho_{p \oplus q_1, p} = src(send)$ and $\rho_{p \oplus q_1, q_1} = tgt(send)$ indicate that the send operation $\langle send(q_1, v) : p \rangle$ is from process p to process q_1.

We get Hoare triples (A) and (B) as follows:

$$(A) \qquad \{\varphi\} \langle send(q_1, v) : p \rangle \{\varphi\} [b_{q_1} > 0]$$

b_{q_1} is an additional variable that describes the status of process q_1's message buffer: $b_{q_1} > 0$ means nonempty. It is used to analyze whether the receive operation is enabled. We omit the pre/post enabled condition of $[true]$.

$$(B) \qquad [b_{q_1} > 0] \{\varphi\} \langle msg \leftarrow receive(p) : q_1 \rangle \{\varphi[msg(q_1) \leftarrow v]\}$$

The guard $[b_{q_1} > 0]$ here is the pre-enabled condition for receive operation in process q_1. The receive operation $\langle msg \leftarrow receive(v) : q_1 \rangle$ is blocked if $b_{q_1} > 0$ is not satisfied. Although the control position is not in the Hoare triple, all situations can be described by applying rule *Symmetry*.

We can get the following triple $(A \circ_c B)$ by applying rule *Sequencing-C*.

$$(A \circ_c B) \qquad \{\varphi\} \langle send(q_1, v) : p; msg \leftarrow receive(p) : q_1 \rangle \{\varphi[msg(q_1) \leftarrow v]\}$$

The matching send-receive pair in $p \oplus q_1$ can be seen in Fig. 10.

$$q_1 \in I$$
$$\frac{\rho_{p \oplus q_1, p} = src(send), \rho_{p \oplus q_1, q_1} = tgt(send), \rho_{p \oplus q_1, q_1} = src(rec), \rho_{p \oplus q_1, q'_1} = tgt(rec)}{\iota, B, \varphi \xrightarrow{\langle send(q_1, v) : p; msg \leftarrow rec(p) : q_1 \rangle} \iota[\rho_{p \oplus q_1, p} \leftarrow \rho'_{p \oplus q_1, q_1}], B, \varphi[msg(q_1) \leftarrow v]}$$

Fig. 10. Matching Send;Receive-Parallel

Sequencing-C:Blocked. Suppose the premises (related to a mismatched and blocked send-receive pair in different instances $p \oplus q_1$ and $p \oplus q_2$) are as follows:

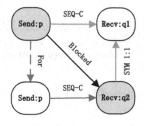

Fig. 11. Sequencing-C:Blocked (Color figure online)

$$\rho_{p\oplus q_1,p} = src(send), \rho_{p\oplus q_1,q_1} = tgt(send)$$

$$\rho_{p\oplus q_2,q_2} = src(rec), \rho'_{p\oplus q_2,q_2} = tgt(rec)$$

The mismatched send-receive operations in p and q_2 (the yellow nodes in Fig. 11) will be shown as Hoare triples (A) and (B'):

$$(B') \quad [b_{q_2} > 0]\{\varphi\}\langle msg \leftarrow receive(p) : q_2\rangle\{\varphi[msg(q_2) \leftarrow v]\}$$

The condition $[b_{q_2} > 0]$ will not be hold, so q_2 is blocked. The mismatched and blocked send-receive pair can be rewritten to two different matching pairs through the following two strategies in Fig. 11, respectively.

– Strategy 1 (red route): Waiting for the "For" loop of p program to execute to a certain iteration, which has a matching send (A'),

$$(A') \quad \{\varphi\}\langle send(q_2, v) : p\rangle\{\varphi\}[b_{q_2} > 0]$$

and then applying rule *Sequencing-C* directly to get $(A' \circ_c B')$ that shows the matching send-receive pair in $p \oplus q_2$.

$$(A' \circ_c B') \quad \{\varphi\}\langle send(q_2, v) : p; msg \leftarrow receive(v) : q_2\rangle\{\varphi[msg(q_2) \leftarrow v]\}$$

– Strategy 2 (blue route): We first apply rule $\text{SYM}_{(1:1)}$[1], get (B) from (B'), and then use rule *Sequencing-C* to get $(A \circ_c B)$ that mentioned above.

Sequencing-C:Enabled. Suppose the premises (related to a mismatched and enabled send-receive pair in instances $p \oplus q_1$ and $p \oplus q_2$) are as follows:

$$\rho_{p\oplus q_1,q_1} = src(send), \rho_{p\oplus q_1,p} = tgt(send)$$

$$\rho_{p\oplus q_2,p} = src(rec), \rho'_{p\oplus q_2,p} = tgt(rec)$$

The send operation is enabled, meanwhile, the receive operation in p is enabled, as the condition $[b_p > 0]$ is hold. However, it is possible to take $\langle msg \leftarrow receive(q_2) : p\rangle$. We may get mismatched but still enabled send-receive pair with additional buffer premise $b_p = w \cdot b$ in Fig. 12.

$$\frac{B(p) = v(q_2) \cdot b}{\rho, B, \varphi} \quad \frac{\rho_{p\oplus q_1,q_1} = src(send), \rho_{p\oplus q_1,p} = tgt(send), \rho_{p\oplus q_2,p} = src(receive), \rho_{p\oplus q_2,p'} = tgt(receive)}{\xrightarrow{\langle send(p,v):q_1;msg\leftarrow receive(q_2):p\rangle} \rho[\rho_{p\oplus q_1,q_1} \leftarrow \rho_{p\oplus q_1,p}, \rho_{p\oplus q_2,p} \leftarrow \rho'_{p\oplus q_2,p}],}$$
$$B(p) \leftarrow b \cdot v(q_1), \varphi[msg \leftarrow v(q_2)]$$

Fig. 12. Mismatched-Enabled Send;Receive-Parallel

---

[1] $\text{SYM}_{(1:1)}$ means that the reason for using rule *Symmetry* is because the send operation is unique for the recipient q_2.

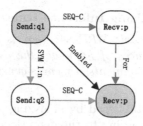

Fig. 13. Sequencing-C:Enabled (Color figure online)

$[b_p > 0]$ is presented in the Hoare triple as the pre-enabled condition, because $b_p = w \cdot b$ should be hold in the premises. We have Hoare triples (C) and (D) as follows:

$$(C) \qquad [b_p > 0]\{\varphi\}\langle send(p, v) : q_1 \rangle\{\varphi\}[b_p > 0]$$

$$(D) \qquad [b_p > 0]\{\varphi\}\langle msg \leftarrow receive(q_2) : p \rangle\{\varphi[msg \leftarrow v(q_2)]\}[b_p > 0]$$

We may get mismatched but still enabled send-receive pair (the yellow nodes in Fig. 13) with additional buffer premise $[b_p > 0]$ by the composition $(C \circ_c D)$.

$$(C \circ_c D) \qquad [b_p > 0]\{\varphi\}\langle send(p, v) : q_1; msg \leftarrow receive(q_2) : p \rangle\{\varphi[msg \leftarrow v(q_2)]\}[b_p > 0]$$

However, the mismatched but enabled send-receive pair is just the intermediate part of the execution of several matched send-receive pairs asynchronously. There are two strategies available in Fig. 13:

- Strategy 1 (red route): Waiting for the "For" loop of p program to execute to a certain iteration, which has a matching receive (D').

$$(D') \qquad [b_p > 0]\{\varphi\}\langle msg \leftarrow receive(q_1) : p \rangle\{\varphi[msg \leftarrow v(q_1)]\}[b_p > 0]$$

  and then applying rule *Sequencing-C* to get $(C \circ_c D')$.

$$(C \circ_c D') \qquad [b_p > 0]\{\varphi\}\langle send(p, v) : q_1; msg \leftarrow receive(q_1) : p \rangle\{\varphi[msg \leftarrow v(q_1)]\}[b_p > 0]$$

- Strategy 2 (blue route): We first apply rule $\text{SYM}_{(1:n)}{}^2$, get (C') from (C),

$$(C') \quad [b_p > 0]\{\varphi\}\langle send(p, v) : q_2 \rangle\{\varphi\}[b_p > 0]$$

  and then use rule *Sequencing-C* to get $(C' \circ_c D)$.

$$(C' \circ_c D) \quad [b_p > 0]\{\varphi\}\langle send(p, v) : q_2; msg \leftarrow receive(q_2) : p \rangle\{\varphi[msg \leftarrow v(q_2)]\}[b_p > 0]$$

Because the number of messages earlier than q_1 in the buffer is limited, we can apply the blue route several times to get the all the earlier messages in buffer b_p. And finally, with the red route to get message q_1.

---

[2] $\text{SYM}_{(1:n)}$ means that the reason for using rule *Symmetry* is because the send operations from a set of processes $q_j, j \in [1...n], j \neq i$ are symmetrical.

5.2   The Soundness of Using Inference Rules

Theorem 1. *Given a mergeable MPP $\mathcal{M}$, there is $Tr(\mathcal{M}) = inf\_ruleTr(\mathcal{M})$, where $Tr(\mathcal{M})$ is a set of traces of $\mathcal{M}$ under the asynchronous semantics and $inf\_ruleTr(\mathcal{M})$ is a set of statements sequences generated by using several inference rules.*

Proof. The correctness is established by analyzing pairs of send-receive operations in different traces. According to the definition, control flow graph for the rewritten program in $\mathcal{M}$ includes all matching send-receive pairs.

Therefore, for a send operation $s_1 \in S_i$, the execution of s_1 will enable the matching receive operation r_1 to be taken into the rewritten program.

- If the matching r_1 is the immediate successor of s_1 in $Tr(\mathcal{M})$, it must be the immediate successor in $inf\_ruleTr(\mathcal{M})$ as well, after using *Sequencing-C* rule directly.
- If the immediate successor is not the matching r_1 in $Tr(\mathcal{M})$,
  - if s_1 is the unique send operation, two strategies for $Sequencing - C$: *Blocked* can be used.
  - if s_1 is an indexed send operation, two strategies for $Sequencing - C$: *Enabled* can be used.

These operations could be executed as a combination by using *Sequencing-C* and *Symmetry* rules, s o r_1 can be the immediate successor to its matching s_1 in $inf\_ruleTr(\mathcal{M})$.

For a send operation $s_1 \in S_i$, if s_1 is blocked, the matching receive operation r_1 in the rewritten program will be blocked, too.

- If s_1 is blocked, the pre-enabled condition for its matching receive operation will not be hold. Because the receiving operation r_1 and its matching sending operation s_1 are both blocked in $inf\_ruleTr(\mathcal{M})$, no inference rule can be used, and r_1 will be blocked until its enabled condition is established.

It shows that any assertion checking problem for an MPP can be reduced to the Hoare triples that is closed by rule *Sequencing-C, Symmetry* and *Conjunction*. And the fixed order execution sequence that generated by analyzing Hoare triples with inference rules will simplified the reasoning.

6   Algorithm

Suppose that we have an MPP $P \| \sqcap_{j:N} Q$ with two kinds of processes P and Q. The merging procedure corresponds to three steps:

1. Firstly, we list all parts of loop in P, and check its mergeable parallelism, respectively. If it is valid, the procedure continues. Otherwise, it fails.
2. For each iteration of the loop part, we construct a CFG $[P^I] \oplus Q_j$ by redirecting edges that do not violate the inductiveness property of the original CFGs.
3. Finally, an iterated parallel composition $\sqcap_{j:N}[P^I] \oplus Q_j$ will be proposed. If there are several parts of loop in P, we combine them as a sequence of composition parallels.

Algorithm 1. Merging(G_P, G_{Q_j})

1: $Loop(G_P) = \{G_{P1}, G_{P2}, \ldots G_{PL}\}$
2: **for** each $\kappa \in [1..L]$ **do**
3:    $[P^I] = Iter(G_{P\kappa})$
4:    **if** $Valid([P^I])$ **then**
5:      **for** each stm in $[P^I]$ **do**
6:        $AtomicSet = AtomicBlock(stm)$
7:        $G_M = Link(stm, G_{Q_j})$
8:      **end for**
9:      $[P^I] \oplus Q_j = Create(AtomicSet, G_M)$
10:     $Connect([P^I] \oplus Q_j)$
11:    **end if**
12: **end for**

6.1   Algorithm_Merging

- The input to the Algorithm 1 includes CFGs G_P for P, and G_{Q_j} for an instance $Q(j)$, where $j \in N$.
- $Loop(G_P)$ is the list of all the parts of loop in G_P. The loop in P is split into L parts as $\{G_{P1}, G_{P2}, \ldots G_{PL}\}$.
- $[P^I]$ is one iteration of loop part $G_{P\kappa}$.
- $Valid([P^I])$ is the merging condition that all the communications in $[P^I]$ are related to the same $Q(j)$. Otherwise, the CFGs cannot be merged into one for $[P^I] \oplus Q(j)$, as P communicates with different processes $Q(j)s$ in one iteration. The issue is beyond the scope of this paper.
- $AtomicBlock$: The initial set of AtomicBlock is empty. All the statements in $[P^I]$ will be added. If the statement in $[P^I]$ is a send operation and not the last one, the matching receive operation in $[P^I] \oplus Q_j$ is added accordingly. If the statement in $[P^I]$ is a receive operation and not the first one, the matching send operation in $[P^I] \oplus Q_j$ is added accordingly.
- $Link(stm, G_{Q_j})$: If there are matching pairs such that $msg(stm) = msg(stm')$, $stm' \in G_{Q_j}$, we will redirect the direction of the edges according to $tgt(s) = src(r)$ where $tgt(s)$ is the send operation's target statement and $src(r)$ is the matching receive statement.
- $Connect([P^I] \oplus Q_j)$: If there is only one part of loop in P, there exists only one element: an iterated parallel composition $\sqcap_{j:N}[P^I] \oplus Q_j$. Otherwise, if there are several parts of loop in P, these parts can be connected as a sequence of each composition parallels with ";".

6.2   Validity of the Algorithm

The order of statements in the code of process $P \succ$ is preserved in $[P^I] \oplus Q(j)$ that is obtained by the algorithm. Suppose there is $\langle R_1 : P \rangle \succ \langle S_2 : P \rangle$ in P, there must be a part of atomic block in $[P^I] \oplus Q(j)$, such as $atomic\{\ldots; \langle R_1 : P \rangle; \ldots; \langle S_2 : P \rangle; \ldots\}$. As each parallel instance of $\sqcap_{j:N}[P^I] \oplus Q(j)$ just consider one iteration of P, $\langle R_1 : P \rangle \succ \langle S_2 : P \rangle$ is still hold in the atomic block for $[P^I] \oplus Q(j)$.

The order of statements in the code of process $Q(j) \succ$ is still preserved in $[P^I] \oplus Q(j)$. Suppose there is $\langle S_1 : j \rangle \succ \langle R_2 : j \rangle$ in $Q(j)$, there are $\langle S_1 : j \rangle \succ_{po} \langle R_1 : P \rangle$ and $\langle S_2 : P \rangle \succ_{po} \langle R_2 : j \rangle$ in $[P^I] \oplus Q(j)$, where $\succ_{po}$ is the precedence order between matching send-receive pairs. According to the definition of "mergeable parallelism", we have $\langle R_1 : P \rangle \succ_j \langle S_2 : P \rangle$ related to the specific j, where $\succ_j$ means the relation is based on the communication with the same j in some iteration. According to the transitivity, $\langle S_1 : j \rangle \succ_{po} \langle R_1 : P \rangle \succ_j \langle S_2 : P \rangle \succ_{po} \langle R_2 : j \rangle$ maintains the partial order in $Q(j)$.

7   Experimental Evaluation

7.1   Examples

We illustrate our approach with the following examples [1]. Simple examples (SimpleMP, SimpleAP) are related to an unbounded number of processes $Q(j), j \in Q$ and a single process P. These processes are symmetric. Process P executes a loop which iterates over all Q processes. The orders of send and receive operations are different in SimpleMP and SimpleAP. Complex examples include the examples with several parts of loops in a single process (CompMO), the examples with two sets of unbounded number of processes(CompMM) and Comp3Master which is related to the task distribution among a server, a master and several clients.

Example 2PC is the classic two-phase-commit protocol [16]. RoundNI [2] adds a round identifier $r \in R$, and each process $q \in Q$ uses a repeat statements to receive and send messages from multiple rounds.

The judgment of the indexed mapping variable requires the additional constraint of the round: according to the order of the round, messages received outside the current round will cause an error.

There are still some cases that our methods cannot deal with. The bad example EXBAD is not mergeable, as the sever process communicates with different clients in the same iteration.

7.2   Experimental Results

We implemented our rewriting algorithm in a prototype tool ASYSIM[3]. It takes asynchronous message passing protocols in the language from Fig. 4 as input. All experiments were run on a 2.50 GHz AMD A12-9700P RADEON R7,10 COMPUTE CORES 4C+6G CPU with 4 GB memory. We applied it to several distributed cases. Table 1 summarizes our results.

In Table 1, the column labeled **Temp** indicates the number of different templates. In the column labeled **RT**, we recorded the time to rewrite the mergeable parallelism examples. The rewriting procedure of EXBAD failed, and it took

---

[3] https://github.com/SmallBuffer/Asynchronous-simplification.

15 ms to get a reminder that it could not be merged. The transformation in [1] is limited by the form of the sequence program, so it is not applicable to some of our examples (2PC and RoundNI).

Table 1. Results

Examples	Temp	RT(ms)	Result
SimpleMP	2	24	*success*
SimpleAP	2	41	*success*
CompMO	2	32	*success*
CompMM	2	24	*success*
Comp3Master	3	50	*success*
2PC	2	68	*success*
RoundNI	2	36	*success*
EXBAD	2	15	*fail*

The rewritten programs are verified on top of the state-of-the-art tool Duet[4] [7]. Duet provides a procedure for unbounded parallelism. By adopting Duet's technology, the mergeable algorithm (Algorithm 1) can be regarded as the front end of the verification framework. We separately recorded the running time **PT** in Duet before and after rewriting each case. The results are visualized in line graphs from Figs. 14, 15, 16, 17, 18, 19, 20, 21, 22, 23, 24, 25, 26 and 27. This shows that with our method it performs better on these cases.

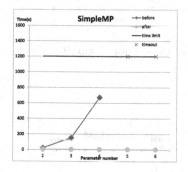

Fig. 14. PTs for SimpleMP (comparison)

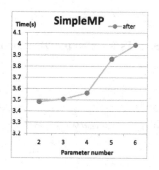

Fig. 15. PT for SimpleMP (after)

8   Related Work

The work in [1] transformed a message passing program to a canonical sequential program. If the transformation is successful, the program will avoid error or

---

[4] https://github.com/zkincaid/duet.

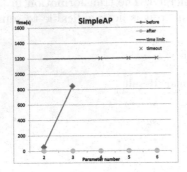

Fig. 16. PTs for SimpleAP (comparison)

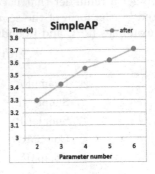

Fig. 17. PT for SimpleAP (after)

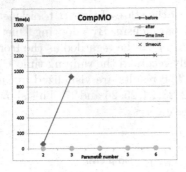

Fig. 18. PTs for CompMO (comparison)

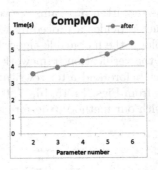

Fig. 19. PT for CompMO (after)

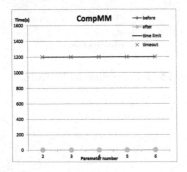

Fig. 20. PTs for CompMM (comparison)

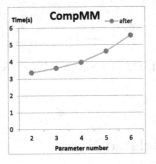

Fig. 21. PT for CompMM (after)

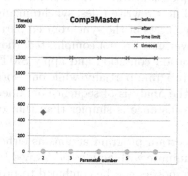

Fig. 22. PTs for 3Master (comparison)

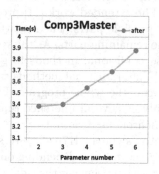

Fig. 23. PT for 3Master (after)

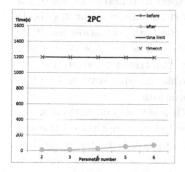

Fig. 24. PTs for 2PC (comparison)

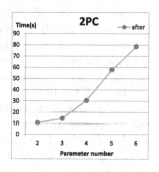

Fig. 25. PT for 2PC (after)

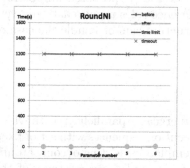

Fig. 26. PTs for RoundNI (comparison)

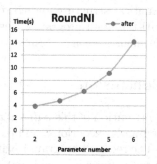

Fig. 27. PT for RounNI (after)

deadlock. Several cases had their canonical sequentialization, which is not sufficient. The extended work [11] proposed several new rewrite rules, synchronizing all the possible parts. The rewritten program consists of the synchronized parts and the remaining parts. As the synchronous invariants are not complicated, they can use traditional methods to get the verification condition and apply SMT-solver. The traditional methods transform the program partially, while our work transforms the whole program. Furthermore, the analysis of sequence obtained by applying several inference rules on a single instance is simpler than that of the synchronous invariants.

Lipton's theory [17] of movers designates certain program actions as either left or right movers, depending on how they commute with actions performed by concurrently executing threads. Left and right movers can be combined to produce a single action, resulting in a program with fewer possible interleavings of actions. The extended work in [5], proposed gated atomic actions to simplify the verification of assertions. Based on these prior work, [14, 15] considered the send action as calling a procedure, and the receive action as just the sub-procedure related to it. The concept of "atomic action" was used in different layers of the programs. However, the method can not be applied in consensus protocols. In [13], they propose a purely sequential program as the transformation result. In this paper, we use an atomic related concept to show how the operations in a rewritten singleton program is executed atomically. The transformation result in our method is a concurrent one, in which, it is possible to apply several inference rules to capture all the behaviors of the original program.

The k-synchronizability technique [3] dealt with a set of send actions and a set of receive actions. Instead of having unbounded size, it optimized the size of a message buffer to k. However, it is still not applicable to parameterized systems [8] such as the series of Paxos protocols [10, 18–20]. In this paper, we also handle a series of send and receive operations through simplified reasoning for programs who has mergeable parallelism.

The idea in [12] is to learn a proof by sampling error traces, proving them to be infeasible, and then assembling these proofs into an argument where every error trace is infeasible. As an extension, the article [7] proposed an abstract mathematical structure and corresponding inference rules to automatically verify multi-threaded programs. However, this structure cannot handle the case of asynchronous message passing.

9   Conclusion

The contribution of this paper is the notion of mergeable parallelism, with which the program's executions can be reduced to execution sequences with set of fixed order. The reduced program is with a unique template consisting of some atomic blocks with matching send and receive operations, and the correctness of the rewritten program can be verified by state-of-the-art analysis methods. In the future, we will consider the application and extension of this method in round interference scenarios with the additional well-founded expressions.

References

1. Bakst, A., von Gleissenthall, K., Kici, R.G., Jhala, R.: Verifying distributed programs via canonical sequentialization. PACMPL 1(OOPSLA), 110:1–110:27 (2017). https://doi.org/10.1145/3133934
2. Bernstein, A.J.: Analysis of programs for parallel processing. IEEE Trans. Electron. Comput. 15(5), 757–763 (1966). https://doi.org/10.1109/PGEC.1966.264565
3. Bouajjani, A., Enea, C., Ji, K., Qadeer, S.: On the completeness of verifying message passing programs under bounded asynchrony. In: Computer Aided Verification - 30th International Conference, CAV 2018, Held as Part of the Federated Logic Conference, FloC 2018, Oxford, UK, 14–17 July 2018, Proceedings, Part II, pp. 372–391 (2018). https://doi.org/10.1007/978-3-319-96142-2_23
4. Desai, A., Garg, P., Madhusudan, P.: Natural proofs for asynchronous programs using almost-synchronous reductions. In: Proceedings of the 2014 ACM International Conference on Object Oriented Programming Systems Languages & Applications, OOPSLA 2014, part of SPLASH 2014, Portland, OR, USA, 20–24 October 2014, pp. 709–725 (2014). https://doi.org/10.1145/2660193.2660211
5. Elmas, T., Qadeer, S., Tasiran, S.: A calculus of atomic actions. In: Proceedings of the 36th ACM SIGPLAN-SIGACT Symposium on Principles of Programming Languages, POPL 2009, Savannah, GA, USA, 21–23 January 2009, pp. 2–15 (2009). https://doi.org/10.1145/1480881.1480885
6. Esparza, J., Ganty, P., Majumdar, R.: Parameterized verification of asynchronous shared-memory systems. J. ACM 63(1), 10:1–10:48 (2016). https://doi.org/10.1145/2842603
7. Farzan, A., Kincaid, Z., Podelski, A.: Proof spaces for unbounded parallelism. In: Proceedings of the 42nd Annual ACM SIGPLAN-SIGACT Symposium on Principles of Programming Languages, POPL 2015, Mumbai, India, 15–17 January 2015, pp. 407–420 (2015). https://doi.org/10.1145/2676726.2677012
8. Farzan, A., Kincaid, Z., Podelski, A.: Proving liveness of parameterized programs. In: Proceedings of the 31st Annual ACM/IEEE Symposium on Logic in Computer Science, LICS 2016, New York, NY, USA, 5–8 July 2016, pp. 185–196 (2016). https://doi.org/10.1145/2933575.2935310
9. Flanagan, C., Godefroid, P.: Dynamic partial-order reduction for model checking software. In: Proceedings of the 32nd ACM SIGPLAN-SIGACT Symposium on Principles of Programming Languages, POPL 2005, Long Beach, California, USA, 12–14 January 2005, pp. 110–121 (2005). https://doi.org/10.1145/1040305.1040315
10. García-Pérez, Á., Gotsman, A., Meshman, Y., Sergey, I.: Paxos consensus, deconstructed and abstracted. In: Programming Languages and Systems - 27th European Symposium on Programming, ESOP 2018, Held as Part of the European Joint Conferences on Theory and Practice of Software, ETAPS 2018, Thessaloniki, Greece, 14–20 April 2018, Proceedings, pp. 912–939 (2018). https://doi.org/10.1007/978-3-319-89884-1_32
11. von Gleissenthall, K., Kici, R.G., Bakst, A., Stefan, D., Jhala, R.: Pretend synchrony: synchronous verification of asynchronous distributed programs. PACMPL 3(POPL), 59:1–59:30 (2019). https://doi.org/10.1145/3290372
12. Heizmann, M., Hoenicke, J., Podelski, A.: Refinement of trace abstraction. In: Static Analysis, 16th International Symposium, SAS 2009, Los Angeles, CA, USA, 9–11 August 2009. Proceedings, pp. 69–85 (2009). https://doi.org/10.1007/978-3-642-03237-0_7

13. Kragl, B., Enea, C., Henzinger, T.A., Mutluergil, S.O., Qadeer, S.: Inductive sequentialization of asynchronous programs. In: Donaldson, A.F., Torlak, E. (eds.) Proceedings of the 41st ACM SIGPLAN International Conference on Programming Language Design and Implementation, PLDI 2020, London, UK, 15–20 June 2020, pp. 227–242. ACM (2020). https://doi.org/10.1145/3385412.3385980

14. Kragl, B., Qadeer, S.: Layered concurrent programs. In: Computer Aided Verification - 30th International Conference, CAV 2018, Held as Part of the Federated Logic Conference, FloC 2018, Oxford, UK, 14–17 July 2018, Proceedings, Part I, pp. 79–102 (2018). https://doi.org/10.1007/978-3-319-96145-3_5

15. Kragl, B., Qadeer, S., Henzinger, T.A.: Synchronizing the asynchronous. In: 29th International Conference on Concurrency Theory, CONCUR 2018, 4–7 September 2018, Beijing, China, pp. 21:1–21:17 (2018). https://doi.org/10.4230/LIPIcs.CONCUR.2018.21

16. Lampson, B., Sturgis, H.E.: Crash recovery in a distributed data storage system. In: Technical report XEROX Palo Alto Research Center (1976)

17. Lipton, R.J.: Reduction: a new method of proving properties of systems of processes. In: Conference Record of the Second ACM Symposium on Principles of Programming Languages, Palo Alto, California, USA, January 1975, pp. 78–86 (1975). https://doi.org/10.1145/512976.512985

18. Padon, O., McMillan, K.L., Panda, A., Sagiv, M., Shoham, S.: Ivy: safety verification by interactive generalization. In: Proceedings of the 37th ACM SIGPLAN Conference on Programming Language Design and Implementation, PLDI 2016, Santa Barbara, CA, USA, 13–17 June 2016, pp. 614–630 (2016). https://doi.org/10.1145/2908080.2908118

19. Sergey, I., Wilcox, J.R., Tatlock, Z.: Programming and proving with distributed protocols. PACMPL 2(POPL), 28:1–28:30 (2018). https://doi.org/10.1145/3158116

20. Taube, M., et al.: Modularity for decidability of deductive verification with applications to distributed systems. In: Proceedings of the 39th ACM SIGPLAN Conference on Programming Language Design and Implementation, PLDI 2018, Philadelphia, PA, USA, 18–22 June 2018, pp. 662–677 (2018). https://doi.org/10.1145/3192366.3192414

Testing and Fault Detection

Mutation Testing of Reinforcement Learning Systems

Yuteng Lu, Weidi Sun, and Meng Sun(✉)

School of Mathematical Sciences, Peking University, Beijing 100871, China
{luyuteng,weidisun,sunm}@pku.edu.cn

Abstract. Reinforcement Learning (RL), one of the most active research areas in artificial intelligence, focuses on goal-directed learning from interaction with an uncertain environment. RL systems play an increasingly important role in many aspects of society. Therefore, its safety issues have received more and more attention. Testing has achieved great success in ensuring safety of the traditional software systems. However, current testing approaches hardly consider RL systems. To fill this gap, we propose the first Mutation Testing technique specialized for RL systems. We define a series of mutation operators simulating possible problems RL systems may encounter. Next, we design test environments that could reveal possible problems within the RL systems. The mutation score specialized for RL systems is proposed to analyze the extent of potential faults and evaluate the quality of test environments. Our evaluation in three popular environments, namely FrozenLake, CartPole, and MountainCar demonstrates the practicability of the proposed techniques.

Keywords: Mutation Testing · Reinforcement Learning · AI Safety

1 Introduction

Reinforcement Learning (RL) has achieved unprecedented progress in a diverse set of domains, including games [1], news recommendation [2] and safety-critical applications, such as self-driving cars [3], healthcare [4], robotics manipulation [5]. Such wide adoption of RL techniques, especially in safety-critical areas, puts forward new challenges to the security and robustness of RL systems.

Unfortunately, RL systems often produce unexpected or incorrect behaviors for different reasons. It is even more worrying that RL systems might be subject to adversarial attacks [6], resulting in disastrous consequences such as fatal accidents of self-driving cars.

Motivated by the great success of testing techniques in traditional software systems, more and more researches focus on testing Supervised Learning, in particular classification problems. However, current testing researches for artificial intelligence hardly consider RL systems. To fill this gap, we design, implement, and evaluate a Mutation Testing technique specialized for RL systems.

© Springer Nature Switzerland AG 2021
S. Qin et al. (Eds.): SETTA 2021, LNCS 13071, pp. 143–160, 2021.
https://doi.org/10.1007/978-3-030-91265-9_8

As one of the most important testing techniques for traditional software, Mutation Testing [7] can be applied at different levels. Based on mutation operators simulating potential errors of the software systems, Mutation Testing creates faulty programs called mutants. The quality of test data could be examined by its ability to detect differences in behaviors between mutants and the corresponding original software.

Even if testing for artificial intelligence systems is still at an early stage, it is comforting that there has been pioneering work to design Mutation Testing techniques specialized for DL systems [8]. However, [8] only investigates Supervised Learning and does not take RL systems into account. RL is different from Supervised Learning and Unsupervised Learning. RL agent with explicit goals learns how to interact with an uncertain environment so as to achieve its goals. Supervised Learning learns from training data with labels to obtain a function that maps input data to corresponding output labels. Thus, we design the Mutation Testing technique, including mutation operators and mutation scores, specialized for RL systems to fill this gap.

A RL system contains an agent, seeking to achieve a goal, and its environment. The agent interacts with its environment and the agent's action a could affect the future state s of the environment, thereby affects the options available to the agent at later times. Simultaneously, the agent always tries to maximize the amount of reward r, send by its environment after corresponding action a affects environment, over the long run. States, rewards, and actions are the main elements of the RL system.

Based on the features of RL systems, it is reasonable to design mutation operators by injecting potential faults at the state level and the reward level. For original agents trained by original RL system, after injecting potential faults into original RL system to obtain mutated RL system, we could get mutated agents. Intuitively, there should be behavior differences between original agents and mutated agents in the environment. To measure the differences and the test environment quality quantitatively, we propose the Mutation Testing metrics (mutation score) for RL systems. Furthermore, the same agent is supposed to behave differently in different environments. By modifying the original environment, we can get different test environments. Similar to Mutation Testing for traditional software, the quality of the test environment could be evaluated by mutation scores. Besides, we also design agent-level mutation operators, directly mutating RL agents. Eventually, we design a set of test environments that could find possible faults within RL systems.

In the evaluation phase, we apply the two most classic algorithms, namely Q-Learning [9] and DQN [10]. Our main contributions are summarized as follows:

(1) We design element-level and agent-level mutation operators for RL systems to introduce diverse potential faults as comprehensively as possible.
(2) We propose the mutation testing metrics (mutation score) specific for RL systems.
(3) We design a set of test environments that could find possible faults within RL systems based on mutation score changes.

The rest of the paper is organized as follows. We begin with backgrounds on Reinforcement Learning and Mutation Testing in Sect. 2. Section 3 proposes element-level and agent-level Mutation Testing techniques for RL systems. And then, we propose mutation scores for RL systems in Sect. 4. How to design test environments is presented in Sect. 5. Experimental results are shown in Sect. 6. We discuss related work in Sect. 7. Finally, Sect. 8 concludes and outlines future work.

2 Background

2.1 Reinforcement Learning

Reinforcement Learning, different from Supervised Learning and Unsupervised Learning, focuses on goal-directed learning from interaction with an environment in order to achieve the long-term goal of the RL agent. RL agent can sense states of its environment, choose actions to influence the environment and will obtain corresponding rewards after each action. In general, RL agents learn how to interact with their environment through trial-and-error so as to maximize the total amount of rewards obtained throughout the long run. Thus, RL is different from Supervised Learning, learning from a labeled training set, and Unsupervised Learning, finding the structure hidden in unlabeled data.

The learning process of RL agents can be referred to as the finite Markov Decision Process (finite MDP). A particular finite MDP always contains state sets, action sets and the one-step dynamics of the environment. Formally, the finite MDP can be formulated as (S, A, P, r, γ). Specifically, S is the finite state space, A is the finite action space, the one-step dynamics of the environment is transition probability $P : S \times A \times S \to [0, 1]$, $r : S \times A \to \mathbb{R}$ is the reward function and $\gamma \in [0, 1)$ is the discount-rate parameter. At each time step t, the agent observes a state s_t and takes action $a_t \sim \pi(s_t)$ according to its policy π. Then, the agent will receive the immediate reward $r_t = r(s_t, a_t)$ of a_t at state s_t. The better the selected action, the higher the corresponding reward, which defines what are the good and bad events for an agent. Immediately afterward, the agent will observe next state s_{t+1} at time step $t+1$. The goal of RL agent is to learn the optimal policy π^*, which maximizes the cumulative reward $R_0 = \sum_{i=0...\infty} r_i$. The RL framework shown in Fig. 1 presents the interaction between a learning agent and its environment.

2.2 Mutation Testing

Mutation Testing is a fault-based testing technique. Mutation operators are designed to simulate various faults that original program $\mathbf{P}$ may be suffered. Based on mutation operators, a set of faulty programs $\mathbf{P}'$, called mutants, are constructed by injecting faults into the corresponding original program $\mathbf{P}$. Intuitively, there should be behavior differences between original program $\mathbf{P}$ and mutants $\mathbf{P}'$. Thus, these mutants $\mathbf{P}'$ could be used to execute against a given

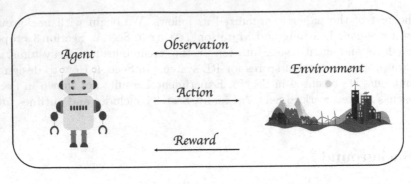

RL System

Fig. 1. The framework of Reinforcement Learning

test set **T** to assess the quality of the test set **T**. If the test result for a mutant $\mathbf{p}' \in \mathbf{P}'$ is different from the result of running the original program **P** for a test data $\mathbf{t} \in \mathbf{T}$, then $\mathbf{p}'$ is killed and the fault injected by the corresponding mutant operator is detected. Otherwise, $\mathbf{p}'$ is survived. The general process is shown in Fig. 2.

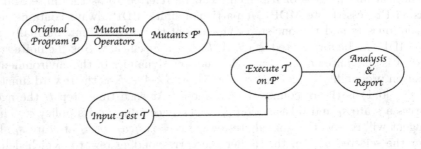

Fig. 2. The process of Mutation Testing

In traditional software testing, mutation score is used for indicating the quality of test set and providing further feedback for the test enhancements. The mutation score is the ratio of the number of killed mutants over the total number of generated mutants. Different from traditional mutation score, DeepMutation [8] proposes the mutation score specific to Supervised Learning, focusing on classification problems. Due to RL's characteristics and natural behavior differences of original agents and mutated agents, using above scores is prone to lose the precision of evaluating the environment's quality. Thus, the above scores are not applicable to RL systems. In this paper, we design and propose the mutation score specific to RL systems. The practicability of proposed scores is convinced by experiments.

3   Mutation Testing Specific to RL Systems

Traditional Mutation Testing introduces potential faults into software systems by modifying the program. Different from traditional software systems, which is the implementation of control flows directly specified by developers, agents of RL systems interact with and influence corresponding environments.

As described above, the learning process of RL agent can be referred to as the finite MDP (S, A, P, r, γ). States, rewards and actions are the main elements of the RL system. Therefore, we should specifically and pointedly introduce potential defects into these critical elements instead of simply modifying the source code. In this section, we propose Mutation Testing techniques for RL systems. Specifically, we propose a set of mutation operators, containing element-level mutation operators and agent-level mutation operators. Furthermore, we design and implement a universal Mutation Testing framework for RL systems.

3.1   Element-Level Mutation Operators

RL systems may encounter various risks. We design two types of element-level mutation operators, namely state-level mutation operators and reward-level mutation operators, which simulate potential risks to inject faults into RL systems.

Formally, the interaction between a learning agent and its environment can be defined in terms of three main elements, namely states, actions, and rewards. At time step t, the learning agent observes the environment's state s_t, and on that basis, selects action a_t. As a consequence of its action a_t, the agent receives corresponding numerical reward r_t and finds itself in a new state s_{t+1} at next time step. Proposed element-level mutation operators are designed based on the potential risks that agents could suffer during observing the environment's states and receiving numerical rewards. Note that potential risks may be due to mechanical faults[1], hacker attacks [11] or source code errors introduced by the developers.

Reward-Level Mutation Operators. As we mention above, hacker attacks [11] and source code errors could introduce potential risks into RL systems. Specifically, abnormal rewards could be introduced by attacks and source code errors. Considering the characteristics of RL training process (i.e., the objective of agents is to maximize the expected total reward over a time period), abnormal rewards will lead learning agents to go in the wrong direction. Based on this fact, we design the following reward-level operators.

* **Reward Reduction**: The reward, defining what is good or bad for the agent, is the primary basis for altering the policy. Using humans as an analogy, rewards are somewhat like happiness (if high) or pain (if low). The *Reward*

---

[1] Many learning agents in the RL system have a large number of sensors to observe the environment.

Reduction operator modifies part of the rewards to reduce the original higher rewards. Intuitively, *Reward Reduction* will make the agent run in the opposite direction.

* **Reward Increase**: Contrary to the *Reward Reduction* operator, the *Reward Increase* operator modifies part of the rewards to increase the original smaller rewards.

State-Level Mutation Operators. These proposed mutation operators simulate the practical potential risk. RL systems are widely deployed in domains such as autonomous driving. The learning agents in autonomous driving scenarios use sensors to observe the environment. However, sensors could suffer mechanical faults during the process of observing the environment. Our state-level mutation operators are designed based on the potential existence of mechanical faults.

* **State Loss**: Normally, the learning agent should observe the environment's state s_{t_0}, and on that basis, select action a_{t_0} at time step t_0. Because the sensors possibly suffer from robustness issues, it is not uncommon that some state-action pairs (s_t, a_t) can be lost[2]. The *State Loss* operator hides some of the state-action pairs to simulate such kind of faults.

* **State Delay**: At each time step t, the state-action pair (s_t, a_t) and corresponding reward r_t are supposed to be recorded in time. Based on correct and timely records, RL system is able to get the learning agent as expected. If the sensors delay the transmission of observation, state-action pairs and corresponding rewards will be recorded inaccurately. For example, state s_{t_i} may be incorrectly associated with action a_{t_j}, where $i > j$, when such fault happens. Thus, the *State Delay* operator introduces this risk by associating s_{t_i} with a_{t_j} selectively.

* **State Repetition**: To better understand this operator, we use autonomous driving cars as an example. When the vehicle is moving forward, but the sensors fail to update the new observations, new action will be repeatedly associated with the last observation. We call this situation *State Repetition*. Corresponding operator associates a fixed state with a series of continuous actions.

* **State Error**: The *State Error* operator constructs wrong connections between states and actions. Although it is possible to associate each state with a wrong action, merely constructing a few wrong associations is enough to inject such potential risk and cause huge damage.

3.2 Agent-Level Mutation Operators

Now, we have proposed the element-level Mutation Testing operators for RL systems. In order to cover more possible faults, we propose and implement a set of agent-level mutation operators. Training an agent to complete a task within

---

[2] Corresponding rewards are also considered as lost too.

an uncertain environment is the goal of RL system. The trained agent contains a policy to guide it to select action. Typically, the policy can be a Q-table [9] or a Neural Network [10]. Thus, we could directly mutate the trained agents to cover more potential risks. Actually, agent-level mutation operators are achieved by directly mutating agent's policy (i.e., corresponding Q-table or Neural Network).

* **Q-Table Fuzzing (QF)**: Q-table stores the maximum expected future rewards for corresponding state-action pairs. A natural and efficient way to mutate the Q-table is to fuzz its stored rewards. Obviously, the mutated Q-table will possibly change the agent's choice of action at each state. The *QF* operator follows the distribution selected in advance, such as the Gaussian distribution, to mutant stored rewards in Q-table.

* **Input-Layer Neuron Removal (INR)**: The Neural Networks in RL take the states of the environment as input and output a vector containing Q-values for each possible action. The *INR* operator removes some neurons in the input layer, which will cause the trained agent to ignore part of the environmental information.

* **Output-Layer Neuron Disappearance (OND)**: The *OND* operator tries to simulate the situation where agent cannot complete some actions. It can be achieved by removing chosen neurons in the output layer.

* **Output-Layer Neuron Addition (ONA)**: Different from *OND* operator, the *ONA* operator simulates the opposite situation where agent will do some unexpected behaviors. The way to achieve it is adding chosen neurons in the output layer.

The rationality of these operators stems from potential mistakes programmers may make. We should note that the main source of such mistakes is the natural complexity[3] of environments in RL system.

3.3 Mutation Testing Framework for RL Systems

At each time steps, the learning agent makes an observation of the environment state $s \in S$, selects an action $a \in A$. And the action a is applied back to the environment in time, modifying its state and getting corresponding reward r. Based on the correct results of these interactions, a RL agent $\mathfrak{A}$ is obtained. Now, we follow the proposed framework to start element-level Mutation Testing process. First, we apply mutation operators to RL systems, the record of interaction will be mutated, which means that some actions will be uncorrelated with states. For example, some state-action pairs could be discarded, which corresponds to the *State Loss* mutation operator. And then, the mutated interaction will be considered in the training process to produce a mutated RL agent $\mathfrak{A}'$. In the third step, the generated agent should be executed in the environment for evaluating its quality based on mutation score, which will be defined in the next section.

---

[3] The numbers of states that the agent should observe in different environments are with huge difference.

A higher-quality environment could be used to find out more potential risks contained in RL systems. The specific flow of proposed framework is shown in Fig. 3.

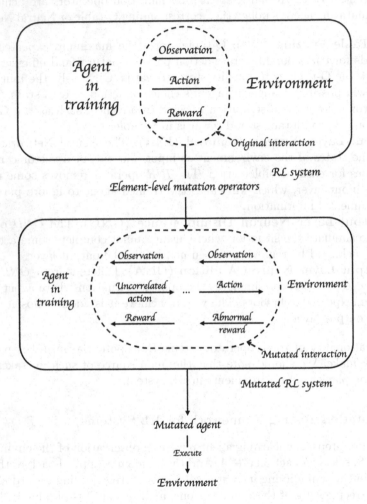

Fig. 3. Element-level Mutation Testing Framework

In contrast to the element-level technique, agent-level technique directly mutates agent $\mathfrak{A}$ to obtain mutated agent $\mathfrak{A}'$. Using the agent-level mutation technique to generate mutated agent is more efficient because such technique will reduce time consumption of the training process.

The detailed flow is demonstrated in Fig. 4. In the first step, we should obtain a RL agent $\mathfrak{A}$ based on correct records of interactions. And then, we mutate agent $\mathfrak{A}$ by the agent-level mutation operators to generate agent $\mathfrak{A}'$. Finally, same as element-level Mutation Testing technique, $\mathfrak{A}'$ will be executed in the test environment to evaluate environment's quality based on the same mutation score defined in Sect. 4.

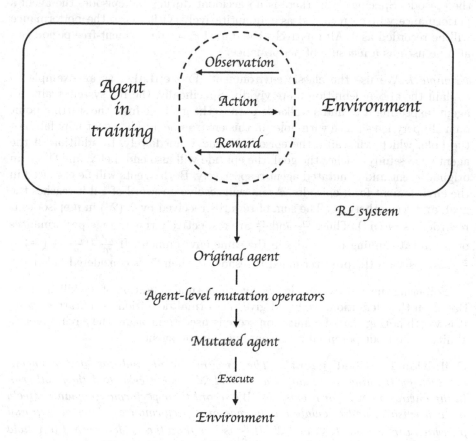

Fig. 4. Agent-level Mutation Testing Framework

4 Mutation Scores Specific to RL Systems

We design the mutation scores specific to RL systems to evaluate the quality of the test environment quantitatively. The mutation score is the ratio of the number of killed mutants over the total number of generated mutants. What we should emphasize is that for an input, the corresponding output of traditional software is deterministic. However, due to the inherent randomness of environment, every time the agent runs in the same environment, the result may be different. Apparently, we must define what means the mutated agent is killed first.

What needs to be underlined here is that for different tasks, the standards for measuring the performance of the agent are different. Actually, different standards depend on the goals of the corresponding tasks. We take self-driving cars as an example. If the goal of the car is to drive safely, the standard for measuring its performance can be whether there will be no accidents within the episode. Specifically, if there is no accident during the episode, the agent's performance will be recorded as 1 quantitatively. Otherwise, the performance will be recorded as 0. Alternatively, the duration of the accident-free period can also be used as a measure of performance.

Example 1. We use the classic environment, **FrozenLake**, as an example to explain the above definition more vividly. Specifically, the RL system trains an agent, expecting it to find a walkable path to the goal tile from the starting point on a slippery ice surface with holes in this environment. The agent may fall into the hole, which will cause the episode to end immediately. In addition, if the agent successfully reaches the goal, the episode will also end. Let $\mathfrak{A}$ and $\mathfrak{A}'$ be an original agent and a mutated agent respectively. Both agents will be executed in the environment for n episodes. Agent will receive a reward of 1 if it reaches the goal, and zero otherwise. The sum of rewards received by $\mathfrak{A}$ ($\mathfrak{A}'$) in n episodes is recorded as m (m'). Thus, $\frac{m'}{n}$ and $\frac{m}{n}$ are respectively the average performances of $\mathfrak{A}'$ and $\mathfrak{A}$ running n episodes in the same environment. If $\frac{m'}{m}$ $((\frac{m'}{n}) \div (\frac{m}{n}) = \frac{m'}{m})$ is less than the predetermined threshold θ, then $\mathfrak{A}'$ is considered killed.

Following the above example, we give the formal definition of the killed agent. Based on this definition, we could give the formal definition of mutation score. It is worth noting that the mutation score is used to measure the environment's ability to find out potential risks contained in the agent.

Definition 1 (Killed agent). *The original agent and the mutant agent obtained by training are denoted as $\mathfrak{A}$ and $\mathfrak{A}'$ respectively, and they both run in the environment E for n episodes. We record their performance quantitatively in each episode, and calculate the average of n performances, denoted as p and p', which corresponds to $\mathfrak{A}$ and $\mathfrak{A}'$. If $\frac{p'}{p}$ is less than the predetermined threshold θ, then $\mathfrak{A}'$ is considered killed.*

Definition 2 (Mutation score). *We denote a set of generated mutated agents, which contains N mutants, and environment as $\bar{\mathfrak{A}}'$ and E respectively. After all the mutants in $\bar{\mathfrak{A}}'$ have been executed in E, we could get the total number of killed mutants, denoted as N'. Mutation score corresponding to E is defined as $\frac{N'}{N}$.*

5 Design of Test Environments

Reinforcement Learning has been widely deployed in various safety-critical scenarios, such as autonomous vehicles, healthcare, and robotics manipulation. Intelligent agents trained by RL systems with potential errors may put human life and property at great risk. However, the hidden risks and errors in RL systems are not easy to be accurately located. Thus, test environments able to discover hidden risks in the RL system are urgently needed. Based on our mutation test framework, we put forward the idea of how to design a test environment that can locate potential problems in the RL system. Generally speaking, we want to use the designed test environment to find out what specific risks are injected in the RL system. We must note that the environment for agent training and executing is the same, which is different from the difference between training data and test data in Supervised Learning.

The test environment should be designed according to different characteristics of the risks introduced by operators. For example, reward-level mutation will cause the mutated agent to have a wrong perception of what is happiness or pain. If the agent mistakes happiness as pain, corresponding to *Reward Reduction*, in the latter part of the training process, it will be difficult to achieve original goals successfully. *So in practice, when the RL system encounters such a reward-level issue, making the trained agent produce poor performance, what should we do?*

First, we design a new environment (i.e., the test environment) to offset the risks within the RL system. Specifically, we can obtain the test environment by modifying the original environment so that *the agent can obtain positive rewards or the goal can be achieved at an earlier stage.* Then, based on the test environment, we use the original RL system and the mutated RL system to train the corresponding agents respectively. Intuitively, due to the characteristics of injected mutation, the system can train the agent normally at the earlier stage. Therefore, the trained mutated agent will have the ability to complete tasks in the new environment. In this way, the mutated agents are expected to produce better performance and even comparable to the original agent's performance.

So, we finally execute mutated agents and original agent in the test environment and calculate respective mutation scores of the test environment. Through the change of mutation scores, we could detect potential errors in the RL system.

Example 2. We again take **FrozenLake** as an example. For a mutated RL system injected with *Reward Reduction* operator, corresponding mutated agents trained in the environment E (shown in Fig. 5(a)) given by Gym always have poor performance, which means E will have a high mutation score. However, the designed test environment E^T, shown in Fig. 5(b), has lower mutation score for the certain potential error (i.e., the *Reward Reduction* issue) contained in the system, while still has high scores or even higher scores for other errors. In fact, E^T is designed with the idea of offsetting the *Reward Reduction* risk. Thus, with the help of the above **mutation score changes**, we can identify the problem contained in the system. This example is guaranteed by experiment.

In conclusion, by designing a test environment to offset the characteristics of possible errors, following our framework and observing changes in mutation scores, potential errors contained in the system may be accurately located. The test environment that causes the more drastic changes in scores, the more capable it is to find out more potential errors. The following experiments prove the validity and feasibility of the proposed idea. We hope that it can be the beginning of designing test environments for RL system.

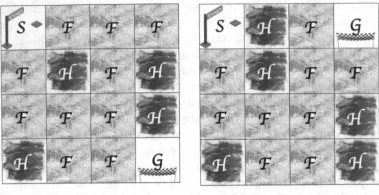

(a) Original Environment   (b) Test Environment

Fig. 5. Environments

6 Evaluation

We have evaluated and implemented the proposed Mutation Testing framework for two successful RL systems, Q-Learning and DQN, in three popular environments, namely FrozenLake, CartPole, and MountainCar. The technique's usefulness has been demonstrated through experiments. The implementation is based on Keras 2.2.2, Gym 0.17.3 and TensorFlow 1.10.0 backend. All our experiments were run on a server running CentOS 7.6 with 2 Xeon Gold 5118 2.30 GHz CPUs, 120 GB system memory and 8 NVIDIA Titan XP GPU.

RL algorithm is the core of the RL system. Q-learning introduced by Watkins [9] is one of the most widely used RL algorithms and uses the Bellman optimality equation. DQN [1,10] combines Q-learning with Deep Neural Networks to learn policies over large state spaces efficiently. We select three popular publicly available environments FrozenLake, CartPole, and MountainCar as the evaluation environments.

- FrozenLake: An agent stands on a frozen lake, which is a slippery ice surface with holes. The agent's goal is to walk from the start point to the goal without falling into the holes.
- Cartpole: There is an unstable pole attached to a cart. The cart moves along a frictionless track by applying forces to it. The goal is to keep the unstable pole balanced (i.e., the pole remains upright) by applying appropriate forces. We can better understand the environment through this video. The condition for the end of episode is that the pole is over 15° from vertical or the cart moves more than 2.4 units from the center.
- MountainCar: A vehicle is located at the bottom of the valley between a lower hill and a higher hill. The vehicle's goal is to hit the flag by climbing up the higher hill. However, the vehicle cannot directly climb the higher hill due to its weak engine. So, the only way to hit the flag is to drive back and forth until enough momentum is built for climbing.

Based on the idea of offsetting the characteristics of potential risks, we have designed corresponding test environments for these three environments. For example, when the RL system training in environment FrozenLake suffers a potential risk at the reward-level, we can use the test environment shown in Fig. 5(b) to locate the risk. If the RL system in environment MountainCar suffers from reward-level attacks, we could get the test environment by changing the position of the flag. Specifically, we could move the flag from the mountaintop of the higher hill to the hillside of the higher hill to lower its position. Besides, for the same reward-level issues in environment CartPole, we could reduce the length of frictionless track to create the test environment. In fact, by reducing the length, the condition for the end of episode can be changed to moving less than 2.4 units from the center, which means that the episode is easier to end. For state-level risks, we take environment FrozenLake as an example. In the situation where the RL system suffers from risks simulated by *State Loss* operator, we could obtain the test environment by modifying the ice surface around the starting point.

In the original environments (i.e., FrozenLake, CartPole, or MountainCar), we train the original agents and the mutated agents based on the RL system and the mutated RL system respectively. Then, let the obtained agents execute in the original environment to get their performance. Based on the results, we could find out the killed mutants and calculate the mutation score corresponding to the original environment. Analogously, we could calculate the mutation score corresponding to the test environment.

Through experiments, we have seen that when different mutation operators are injected into the RL system, even for the same group of original environment and test environment, the relationship between their mutation scores could have a huge difference. As shown in Fig. 6, we use the environments in Fig. 5(a) and Fig. 5(b) as a group. The two bars on the left corresponds to the case where the RL system is injected by *Reward Reduction* operator. We can see that the mutation score of E much higher than the mutation score of E^T. However, when we inject state-level operators into the RL system, corresponding to the bar on the right, there is no significant difference between the mutation score of E and the mutation score of E^T. *Such change in quantitative relationships can guide us in locating potential errors, which shows that the designed test environment does have the ability to looking for errors.* When we inject more similar errors into the RL system and train to get more mutants. Following the above process, we could find out errors contained in the system based on the designed environment. The bars on the right correspond to the case of injecting Q-Table Fuzzing operator. This experimental result inspires us to explore the connections between element-level operators and agent-level operators in the future.

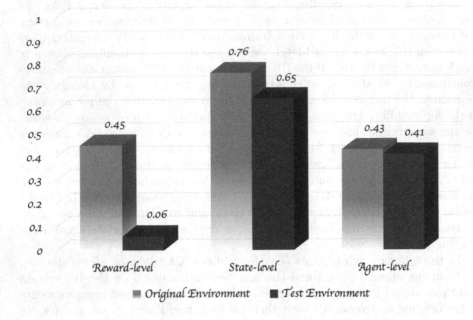

Fig. 6. Comparison of Mutation Scores

Threats To Validity. The inherent randomness of environment could be a threat to validity. Specifically, randomness may lead to different results when the agent does the same action in the same environment. To counter such issue, we let the agent run multiple times in the same environment to eliminate randomness as much as possible.

Besides, agents trained by the same RL system will also have differences in their ability to solve problems. This issue could be another threat to validity. To counter this problem, we train to obtain multiple agents and consider their average performances as a measurement for RL system capabilities to eliminate differences in the performance of different agents as much as possible.. The selection of the predetermined threshold θ could be the third threat to validity. In the above experiment, we use $\theta = 0.8$.

7   Related Work

In this section, we summarize the most relevant work about Mutation Testing, Reinforcement Learning and security of AI systems.

7.1   Mutation Testing

In late 1970s, three pioneering works [12–14] gave birth to Mutation Testing. It has made great achievements in the traditional software field, and been successful in assessing the effectiveness of test data. Over the past decades, traditional

Mutation Testing techniques are widely studied and applied to many domains, such as programming languages, integration testing, network-based protocols and Android apps. [15] proposes a mutation-based criterion, named Interface Mutation, suitable for integration testing. [16] introduces mutants to give developers an insight into the signatures used by network-based intrusion detection systems. [17] presents an automated Mutation Testing framework for Android apps. 38 mutation operators have been proposed and over 8,000 mutants have been generated by injecting these operators into more than 50 apps.

Nowadays, as AI systems are widely deployed in safety-critical applications, some pioneering works [8,18,19] began to apply Mutation Testing to AI systems. DeepMutation [8] proposes a Mutation Testing framework specialized for Supervised Learning (e.g., classification problems) and achieves great success. DeepMutation++ [18] supports Mutation Testing for both feed-forward neural networks and stateful recurrent neural networks. Wang et al. [19] propose an approach able to detect adversarial examples for DNNs at runtime based on Mutation Testing. As we know, our work is first Mutation Testing framework specialized for RL systems.

7.2   Reinforcement Learning

The DQN [10], combining Q-learning [9] and DNN, achieve shocking performance on classic Atari 2600 games. Its performance is comparable to that of a professional human player across 49 games of Atari 2600. After that, more and more work is devoted to improving the RL algorithm. For example, [20] studies diverse independent improvements to the DQN and combines them to provide state-of-the-art performance. [21] explores how to solve Atari games with fewer interactions. With such development, more and more RL systems have been applied to our lives. Since safety is the most basic requirement, RL algorithms considering safety have been proposed. [22] proposes a safe RL algorithm, called Parallel Constrained Policy Optimization (PCPO), for autonomous vehicles. Based on PCPO, potential risks can be taken into account during training. We believe that there will be more work to ensure the safety of the RL systems in the future.

7.3   AI Safety

Adversarial attacks [23,24] have raised more and more concerns about safety of artificial intelligence. [25] proposes a novel verification algorithm for solving queries on DNN with ReLU activation functions. DeepXplore [26] is the first white-box testing framework for Supervised Learning. Ma et al. [27] present a set of multi-granularity coverage criteria for testing DNNs. [28] presents Deep-Importance, a systematic testing framework containing an Importance- Driven test adequacy criterion. [29] focuses on testing for RL systems. And [30] introduces on two efficient, exact and over-approximate reachability algorithms for NN-based control systems with a RL controller.

8   Conclusion and Future Work

In this paper, we have designed, implemented, and evaluated Mutation Testing techniques for RL systems. We hope that this work could initiate the journey of exploring Mutation Testing for RL systems. A set of mutation operators, including element-level operators and agent-level operators, are designed to inject potential risks that could be introduced by mechanical faults, attacks or developers. We also propose corresponding Mutation Testing frameworks. Moreover, the proposed mutation scores can be used to measure the quality of environments and guide the design of test environments. Our experiments show that Mutation Testing provides a promising avenue for evaluating environments and building robust RL systems. In the future, we would perform more in-depth investigation on the design of more test environments. And we will explore the relations between these mutation operators and human faults.

Acknowledgement. This research was supported by the Guangdong Science and Technology Department (Grant No. 2018B010107004) and the National Natural Science Foundation of China under Grant No. 62172019, 61772038, 61532019.

References

1. Silver, D., et al.: Mastering the game of go with deep neural networks and tree search. Nature **529**(7587), 484–489 (2016)
2. Zheng, G., et al.: DRN: a deep reinforcement learning framework for news recommendation. In: Proceedings of the 2018 World Wide Web Conference on World Wide Web, WWW 2018, Lyon, France, 23–27 April 2018, pp. 167–176. ACM (2018)
3. El Sallab, A., Abdou, M., Perot, E., Yogamani, S.K.: Deep reinforcement learning framework for autonomous driving. Electron. Imaging **2017**(19), 70–76 (2017)
4. Yu, C., Liu, J., Nemati, S.: Reinforcement learning in healthcare: a survey. CoRR, abs/1908.08796 (2019)
5. Kober, J., Peters, J.: Reinforcement learning in robotics: a survey. In: Wiering, M., van Otterlo, M. (eds.) Reinforcement Learning. Adaptation, Learning, and Optimization, vol. 12, pp. 579–610. Springer, Heidelberg (2012). https://doi.org/10.1007/978-3-642-27645-3_18
6. Sun, J., et al.: Stealthy and efficient adversarial attacks against deep reinforcement learning. In: The Thirty-Fourth AAAI Conference on Artificial Intelligence, AAAI 2020, The Thirty-Second Innovative Applications of Artificial Intelligence Conference, IAAI 2020, The Tenth AAAI Symposium on Educational Advances in Artificial Intelligence, EAAI 2020, New York, NY, USA, 7–12 February 2020, pp. 5883–5891. AAAI Press (2020)
7. Jia, Y., Harman, M.: An analysis and survey of the development of mutation testing. IEEE Trans. Software Eng. **37**(5), 649–678 (2011)
8. Ma, L., et al.: DeepMutation: mutation testing of deep learning systems. In: 29th IEEE International Symposium on Software Reliability Engineering, ISSRE 2018, Memphis, TN, USA, 15–18 October 2018, pp. 100–111. IEEE Computer Society (2018)
9. Watkins, C.J.C.H., Dayan, P.: Q-learning. Mach. Learn. **8**, 279–292 (1992)

10. Mnih, V., et al.: Human-level control through deep reinforcement learning. Nature **518**(7540), 529–533 (2015)
11. Nguyen, T.T., Reddi, V.J.: Deep reinforcement learning for cyber security. CoRR (2019)
12. Lipton, R.: Fault diagnosis of computer programs. Ph.D. thesis, Carnegie Mellon University (1971)
13. DeMillo, R.A., Lipton, R.J., Sayward, F.G.: Hints on test data selection: help for the practicing programmer. Computer **11**(4), 34–41 (1978)
14. Hamlet, R.G.: Testing programs with the aid of a compiler. IEEE Trans. Software Eng. **3**(4), 279–290 (1977)
15. Delamaro, M.E., Maldonado, J.C., Mathur, A.P.: Interface mutation: an approach for integration testing. IEEE Trans. Software Eng. **27**(3), 228–247 (2001)
16. Vigna, G., Robertson, W.K., Balzarotti, D.: Testing network-based intrusion detection signatures using mutant exploits. In: Atluri, V., Pfitzmann, B., McDaniel, P.D. (eds.) Proceedings of the 11th ACM Conference on Computer and Communications Security, CCS 2004, Washington, DC, USA, 25–29 October 2004, pp. 21–30. ACM (2004)
17. Moran, K., et al.: MDroid+: a mutation testing framework for android. In: Chaudron, M., Crnkovic, I., Chechik, M., Harman, M. (eds.) Proceedings of the 40th International Conference on Software Engineering: Companion Proceeedings, ICSE 2018, Gothenburg, Sweden, 27 May–03 June 2018, pp. 33–36. ACM (2018)
18. Hu, Q., Ma, L., Xie, X., Yu, B., Liu, Y., Zhao, J.: DeepMutation++: a mutation testing framework for deep learning systems. In: 34th IEEE/ACM International Conference on Automated Software Engineering, ASE 2019, San Diego, CA, USA, 11–15 November 2019, pp. 1158–1161. IEEE (2019)
19. Wang, J., Dong, G., Sun, J., Wang, X., Zhang, P.: Adversarial sample detection for deep neural network through model mutation testing. In: Atlee, J.M., Bultan, T., Whittle, J. (eds.) Proceedings of the 41st International Conference on Software Engineering, ICSE 2019, Montreal, QC, Canada, 25–31 May 2019, pp. 1245–1256. IEEE/ACM (2019)
20. Hessel, M., et al.: Rainbow: combining improvements in deep reinforcement learning. In: McIlraith, S.A., Weinberger, K.Q. (eds.) Proceedings of the Thirty-Second AAAI Conference on Artificial Intelligence, (AAAI-18), the 30th Innovative Applications of Artificial Intelligence (IAAI-18), and the 8th AAAI Symposium on Educational Advances in Artificial Intelligence (EAAI-18), New Orleans, Louisiana, USA, 2–7 February 2018, pp. 3215–3222. AAAI Press (2018)
21. Kaiser, L., et al.: Model based reinforcement learning for atari. In: 8th International Conference on Learning Representations, ICLR 2020, Addis Ababa, Ethiopia, 26–30 April 2020 (2020)
22. Wen, L., Duan, J., Li, S.E., Xu, S., Peng, H.: Safe reinforcement learning for autonomous vehicles through parallel constrained policy optimization. CoRR, abs/2003.01303 (2020)
23. Szegedy, C., et al.: Intriguing properties of neural networks. In: Bengio, Y., LeCun, Y. (eds.) 2nd International Conference on Learning Representations, ICLR 2014, Banff, AB, Canada, 14–16 April 2014, Conference Track Proceedings (2014)
24. Goodfellow, I.J., Shlens, J., Szegedy, C.: Explaining and harnessing adversarial examples. In: Bengio, Y., LeCun, Y. (eds.) 3rd International Conference on Learning Representations, ICLR 2015, San Diego, CA, USA, 7–9 May 2015, Conference Track Proceedings (2015)

25. Katz, G., Barrett, C., Dill, D.L., Julian, K., Kochenderfer, M.J.: Reluplex: an efficient SMT solver for verifying deep neural networks. In: Majumdar, R., Kunčak, V. (eds.) CAV 2017. LNCS, vol. 10426, pp. 97–117. Springer, Cham (2017). https://doi.org/10.1007/978-3-319-63387-9_5
26. Pei, K., Cao, Y., Yang, J., Jana, S.: DeepXplore: automated whitebox testing of deep learning systems. In: Proceedings of the 26th Symposium on Operating Systems Principles, Shanghai, China, 28–31 October 2017, pp. 1–18. ACM (2017)
27. Ma, L., et al.: DeepGauge: multi-granularity testing criteria for deep learning systems. In: Huchard, M., Kästner, C., Fraser, G. (eds.) Proceedings of the 33rd ACM/IEEE International Conference on Automated Software Engineering, ASE 2018, Montpellier, France, 3–7 September 2018, pp. 120–131. ACM (2018)
28. Gerasimou, S., Eniser, H.F., Sen, A., Cakan, A.: Importance-driven deep learning system testing. In: ICSE 2020: 42nd International Conference on Software Engineering, Seoul, South Korea, June 27–19 July 2020, pp. 702–713. ACM (2020)
29. Uesato, J., et al.: Rigorous agent evaluation: an adversarial approach to uncover catastrophic failures. In: 7th International Conference on Learning Representations, ICLR 2019, New Orleans, LA, USA, 6–9 May 2019 (2019)
30. Tran, H.-D., Cai, F., Lopez, D.M., Musau, P., Johnson, T.T., Koutsoukos, X.D.: Safety verification of cyber-physical systems with reinforcement learning control. ACM Trans. Embed. Comput. Syst. 18(5s), 105:1–105:22 (2019)

AIdetectorX: A Vulnerability Detector Based on TCN and Self-attention Mechanism

Jinfu Chen(✉), Bo Liu, Saihua Cai(✉), Weijia Wang, and Shengran Wang

Jiangsu University, Zhenjiang 212013, China
{jinfuchen,caisaih}@ujs.edu.cn, boliu@stmail.ujs.edu.cn

Abstract. A vulnerability detector should have both excellent detection capabilities (such as high accuracy, low false positive rate, low false negative rate, etc.) and little time overhead. However, existing vulnerability detection methods often rely on manual intervention by human experts or result in high false positives and high false negatives. Additionally, the development of deep learning techniques has prompted many scholars to conduct research in the field of vulnerability detection. Since Temporal Convolutional Networks (TCN) have causal relationships between their convolutional layers and can process information in parallel, while self-attention mechanism can attach more attention to the information related to vulnerabilities. Therefore, in this paper, we combine TCN and self-attention mechanism for vulnerability detection. This leads to the design and implementation of an improved deep learning-based vulnerability detector, called AIdetectorX. We conduct experiments on publicly available and widely used datasets for evaluating the effectiveness of AIdetectorX. Evaluation results suggest that AIdetectorX is effective for vulnerability detection and that combining TCN and self-attention mechanism can lead to higher detection capabilities and decrease time overhead.

Keywords: Deep learning · Software security · Vulnerability detection · Temporal convolutional network · Self-attention mechanism

1 Introduction

Software vulnerabilities are still a very thorny issue, despite many efforts that we have made in pursuit of the software quality and security. Since vulnerabilities cannot be prevented, an efficient strategy is to detect the vulnerabilities that may be exploited by attackers, so as to avoid irreparable losses. Current vulnerability detection methods can be divided into three categories: code similarity-based vulnerability detection [1, 2], rule-based vulnerability detection [3, 4], and machine learning-based vulnerability detection [5, 6]. The core idea of code similarity-based vulnerability detection is that the same vulnerabilities is likely to be contained in the similar program code. However, it is difficult to detect the vulnerabilities that are not caused by code duplication, which results in the high false negative rate. For the rule-based vulnerability detection methods, they usually have high false positive rate and false negative rate because the vulnerability rules defined by the human experts are subjective and a few cases are difficult to be

© Springer Nature Switzerland AG 2021
S. Qin et al. (Eds.): SETTA 2021, LNCS 13071, pp. 161–177, 2021.
https://doi.org/10.1007/978-3-030-91265-9_9

fully considered in the vulnerability rules. For the machine learning-based vulnerability detection methods, they define the features by the human experts to characterize vulnerabilities and use machine learning to automatically detect vulnerabilities rather than relying on the vulnerability rules manually defined by the human experts.

With the popularity of deep learning, it has been widely used in many areas, such as anomaly detection, software language modeling, and code clone detection. However, deep learning in vulnerability detection is much less used. As the first deep learning-based vulnerability detection system dubbed VulDeePecker [7], which uses the Bidirectional Long Short-Term Memory (BLSTM) network to detect vulnerabilities at slice-level. VulDeePecker applies deep learning to the field of vulnerability detection, while freeing the human experts from the tedious task on manually defining features and effectively reducing the false positive rate and false negative rate. Although it is a successful detector for vulnerability detection, there are still some shortcomings, such as excessive time overhead and insufficient detection capabilities.

Among numerous neural networks, Recurrent Neural Network and its variants (i.e., LSTM and GRU), or simply RNNs for short, can sequentially process temporal data and are gradually becoming the dominant trend in various temporal tasks, but the time overhead is excessive when dealing with large-scale data. Compared to RNNs, Temporal Convolutional Networks (TCN) [8, 9] can process information in parallel, which compensates for the excessive time overhead caused by processing data sequentially in RNNs. Additionally, even if LSTM is designed to include a forget gate, it cannot fully remember all historical information, which will be gradually forgotten when a piece of information is invalid. However, TCN is a type of Convolutional Neural Networks (CNNs) in which the convolutional layers are correlated, which ensures that historical and future information is not lost. Currently, TCN has been used for URL classification, intrusion detection, etc. [10]. In this paper, we initiate the study of using TCN instead of RNNs for vulnerability detection and conduct a series of experiments to compare TCN and RNNs in terms of detection capabilities and time overhead. The experimental results show that the vulnerability detector using TCN can achieve higher accuracy while reducing false positive rate and false negative rate without incurring excessive time overhead.

Since neural networks require input equal-length vectors, we transform programs into vector representations that can be fed to TCN for training the model. In the process of vulnerability detection, vulnerabilities only appear in certain statements. It is not necessary to pay much attention to some statements that are not related to vulnerabilities. Therefore, we remove non-ASCII characters and comments, and then treat some variables and function declarations in programs that are not related to vulnerabilities with uniform naming. Furthermore, most neural network models use dense layers to generalize the detection capabilities of the model. However, too many dense layers do not significantly improve the detection capabilities, but rather waste time and increase computational overhead. Therefore, we attempt to introduce self-attention mechanism [11] on TCN to pay much attention to the major statements and effectively ignore the influence of the minor statements, thereby further improving the detection capabilities. Self-attention mechanism is similar to a scoring function, as it gives more weight to important statements and less weight to irrelevant statements. Currently, the self-attention mechanism has been used for defect prediction, malware classification, malicious URL detection, etc. [12, 13]. In this paper, we introduce the self-attention mechanism on TCN to further improve the improve the accuracy, precision, and F1-measure and to reduce the false positive rate and false negative rate in vulnerability detection.

The major contributions of this paper can be summarized as follows.

First, we use TCN as an alternative to RNNs for vulnerability detection, which leads to higher detection capabilities and less time overhead.

Second, we introduce self-attention mechanism to further improve the detection capabilities of the vulnerability detector proposed in this paper.

Third, we design and implement three vulnerability detectors to verify TCN and self-attention mechanism for vulnerability detection.

The remainder of this paper can be organized as follows. Section 2 presents the design of AIdetectorX. Section 3 introduces the experimental design. Section 4 describes the experimental results. Section 5 discusses threats to validity. Section 6 concludes the present paper and future work.

2   Design of AIdetectorX

Our objective is to design a vulnerability detector that can better detect vulnerabilities while reducing time overhead. Since TCN is thought to outperform RNNs in many tasks and self-attention mechanism has been shown to significantly enhance RNNs in other fields, we initiate the study of using TCN and self-attention mechanism for vulnerability detection. In this section, we first introduce how to transform programs into vector representation that can be fed to TCN. And then, we describe how to use TCN to train the model and how to use self-attention mechanism to improve detection capabilities. Finally, we present the design of AIdetectorX proposed in this paper.

2.1   Program Representation

Since neural networks require equal-length vectors as input and programs cannot be directly transformed to feature vectors, we need to consider how to transform programs into input for the neural networks. This section introduces how to pre-process the program, and the operation of transforming the programs into vectors can be concluded as the following four steps.

First, we extract library/API function calls from the programs and divide them into two categories: forward calls and backward calls. Forward calls are function calls that take one or more inputs directly from external inputs, such as command lines, programs, sockets, or files. For forward calls, statements that are affected by input arguments are critical, because they may be vulnerable to inappropriate argument values. Backward calls are function calls that do not take any external input directly from the environment in which the program is running. For backward calls, statements that affect argument values are critical, because they may make library/API function calls vulnerable. And then, we generate program slices corresponding to the arguments of the library/API function calls extracted from the training program and define two types of slices (i.e., forward and backward slices), where forward slices correspond to statements that are affected by the relevant argument, and backward slices correspond to statements that can affect the relevant argument. For each argument in a forward library/API function call, one or more forward slices are generated. In case of multiple forward slices, the forward slices of the argument will branch after the function call. For each argument in a backward library/API function call, one or more backward slices will be generated. In case of multiple backward slices, the backward slices of the argument will be merged before the function call. Figure 1 illustrates an example of the transformation from program to a code gadget.

```
1   void test(char *str)
2   {
3       int MAXSIZE = 40;
4       char buf[MAXSIZE];
5       strcpy(buf, str);
6       printf("result: %s\n", buf);
7   }
8   int main(int argc, char **argv)
9   {
10      char *userstr;
11      if(argc > 1){
12          userstr = argv[1];
13          test(userstr);
14      }
15      return 0;
16  }
```

```
8   int main(int argc, char **argv)
10  char *userstr;
11  if(argc > 1)
12  userstr = argv[1];
13  test(userstr);
1   void test(char *str)
3   int MAXSIZE = 40;
4   char buf[MAXSIZE];
5   strcpy(buf, str);
```

Fig. 1. Illustrating the generation of code gadgets.

Second, we assemble the programs into code gadgets according to data and control dependency, and label their ground truth. Given a library/API function call and the corresponding program fragment, we group statements into a single fragment for code segments belonging to the same user-defined function, in the order in which they appear in the user-defined function. If any statement is duplicated, we eliminate the duplicate statement and keep only one. Additionally, each code gadget needs to be marked with ground truth (e.g., "1" for vulnerable and "0" for non-vulnerable). If the code gadget corresponds to a known vulnerability in the training dataset, it is marked with a "1"; otherwise, it is marked with a "0".

Third, to eliminate the impact of irrelevant information as much as possible, we need to map user-defined variables and functions to symbolic names (e.g., "var_1" and "fun_1") and remove non-ASCII characters and comments (because they are irrelevant to vulnerabilities). This avoids the impact of irrelevant information on the neural network. Figure 2 shows an example of unified renaming of function and variable names. For example, in the generation of the code gadget in Fig. 2, the user defines a variable userstr on line 4, we rename it to var_1 and rename it wherever userstr is used in the rest of the code. Notably, the renaming operation is done automatically using regularization techniques.

Finally, we use the word2vec tool to encode the code gadgets into equal-length vectors. Since the coded vectors vary in length, we need to consider two cases for

```
8    int main(int argc, char **argv)        8    int main(int argc, char **argv)
10   char *userstr;                          10   char *var_1;
11   if(argc > 1){                           11   if(argc > 1){
12   userstr = argv[1];                      12   var_1 = argv[1];
13   test(userstr);                     ⇨   13   fun_1(var_1);
1    void test(char *str)                    1    void fun_1(char *var_2)
3    int MAXSIZE = 40;                       3    int var_3 = 40;
4    char buf[MAXSIZE];                      4    char var_4[var_3];
5    strcat(buf, str);                       5    fun_2(var_4, var_2);
```

Fig. 2. Illustrating the generation of code gadgets.

formatting the vectors. For a forward slice, if the vector length is greater than τ (i.e., the pre-given vector length), we truncate the front part; otherwise, we pad zeros at the end of the vector. For a backward slice, if the vector length is greater than τ, we truncate the back part; otherwise, we pad zeros at the beginning of the vector. In this paper, we set the vector length τ to 100.

2.2   TCN Layer

The structure of TCN includes causal convolution, dilated convolution, and residual connection, which can directly exploits the powerful features of convolution to extract features across time steps.

Causal Convolution. The value of current layer at time t only depends on the value of previous layer at time t and before. The difference from traditional CNNs is that causal convolution cannot anticipate future data. Its structure is unidirectional, but not bidirectional. This means that only causes can have the consequences, thus it is a strict time constraint model, which is why it is called the causal convolution. If the variable x from long ago is to be considered, then the number of convolutional layers must be increased. The increase of the number of convolutional layers can bring about the problems of disappearance of gradients, complex training, and poor fitting effect.

Dilated Convolution. Causal convolution still has the problem that exists in traditional CNNs, that is, the modeling time is limited by the size of convolution kernel. If we want to capture longer dependency, it is necessary to linearly stack many layers. To solve this problem, dilated convolution was proposed in recent years. Different from traditional convolution, dilated convolution allows interval sampling of the input during convolution, and the sampling rate is controlled by d. The $d = 1$ in the bottom layer means that every point is sampled during the input, and middle layer $d = 2$ means that every 2 points are sampled as input during the input. Generally, the higher of level, the larger size of d. In this way, convolutional network can use fewer layers to obtain a large receptive field.

Residual Connection. Residual connection has been proved to be an effective method for training deep networks, which allows the network to transmit information in a cross-layer manner.

Since RNNs need to process information sequentially, which results in a high time overhead. However, the computational process of TCN does not depend on previous information, and each computation is independent (i.e., parallel processing information), which can improve data processing speed. Additionally, TCN can better control the length of information remembered by the model through stacking more convolutional layers, using larger dilation coefficients and increasing the filter size. There is a cause-and-effect relationship between the layers of convolutional network, which means that no historical information or future data is missing. And even if the LSTM has memory gates, it cannot remember all historical information (especially if it is useless and is gradually forgotten). Since the back propagation of TCN and the temporal direction of sequence are different, which avoids the problem of vanishing gradient or exploding gradient that often occurs in RNNs. Training the model using TCN requires less memory, especially for long input sequences [9], thus, we use TCN (i.e., Conv layers) instead of traditional RNNs to detect vulnerability.

2.3 Self-attention Layer

The attention mechanism can be divided into three steps: obtaining query vectors (q) and key vectors (k) based on input vectors, calculating the correlation $\alpha_{i,j}$ (i.e., attention score) between each query vector (q_i) and each key vector (k_j), and extracting the important information according to attention score $\alpha_{i,j}$. Given N sets of input information $X = [x_1, ..., x_N]$, where each vector x_i ($i \in [1, N]$) represents an input information. Each input vector x_i in X is multiplied by W^q and W^k to obtain q_i and k_i, respectively. And then, the correlation α_{ij} between each two input information x_i and x_j is calculated separately, where the correlation between each two input information is calculated using the scaled dot product [11], as shown in (1). Notice that each input vector x_i also calculates the correlation with itself.

$$\alpha_{i,j} = \frac{q^i \cdot k^j}{\sqrt{d_k}} \tag{1}$$

Each attention score calculated in (1) needs to be normalized by softmax to obtain α', whose formula is shown in (2).

$$\alpha'_{i,j} = \frac{exp(\alpha_{i,j})}{\sum_{k=1}^{n} exp(\alpha_{i,k})} \tag{2}$$

According to $\alpha'_{i,j}$, we can obtain the degree of association between the current input vector x_i and each input vector x_j. Each input vector x_i in X is multiplied by W^v to obtain the value vector (v). Then it is multiplied with the corresponding attention fraction in turn and accumulated to obtain the output vector b_i, as shown in (3). Self-attention mechanism can be accelerated using a matrix where each output vector b_i is computed in parallel, $Q = W_q \cdot X$, $K = W_k \cdot X$, and $V = W_v \cdot X$. Using Q and K, A' is computed and multiplied by V to obtain the output vector. The formula of self-attention mechanism is shown in (4).

$$b^i = \sum_{j=1}^{n} \alpha'_{i,j} v^j \qquad (3)$$

$$Attention(Q, K, V) = softmax(\frac{QK^{\mathrm{T}}}{\sqrt{d_k}})V \qquad (4)$$

The purpose of self-attention mechanism is to focus on some details based on our goals, rather than analyzing the global situation. Therefore, the core task is how to identify the part we want to focus on based on our goals, and how to further analyze it after finding that part of the details. For example, the vulnerabilities occur in library/API function calls without much attention to other statements (e.g., declaring variables and initialization). Self-attention mechanism is equivalent to scoring each piece of information in the sequence individually (i.e., the more critical the information, the higher the score). Through continuous training, the model can achieve the optimal information weight, so as to obtain more accurate vulnerability detection. Therefore, we present the vulnerability detector that introduces self-attention mechanism (VulDeePecker+) and plot its structure.

2.4 Overview of AIdetectorX

Since the superior time overhead and generalization capabilities of TCN over RNNs, we apply it to vulnerability detection. In the process of training the model, we need to pre-process programs into vector representations for inputting TCN layers. Additionally, self-attention mechanism can set a higher weight on the information that needs more attention in the temporal data, thus highlighting important information. We can introduce self-attention mechanism to further improve the detection capabilities of the detector. Figure 3 depicts the structure of the vulnerability detector based on TCN and self-attention mechanism. The process for detecting vulnerabilities using AIdetectorX is as follows.

(1) Transforming training programs into the equal-length vector representation.
(2) Inputting the transformed vector representations into TCN for training the model.
(3) Improving vulnerability detection capabilities using self-attention mechanism.
(4) Transforming testing programs into the equal-length vector representation.
(5) Detecting vulnerabilities using the trained model.

Since programs cannot be directly fed to the neural network, we need to transform the programs into vector representation. Section 2.1 describes how to transform the programs into the equal-length vectors in detail. Second, we input the vectors into TCN (*kernel size* is 3, *filters* are 128, 128, and 64, and *dilation rates* are 1, 2, and 4, respectively). This differs from previous deep learning-based vulnerability detection methods. TCN is a CNN structure that was devised in 2016 to handle temporal data, which has the advantage of accommodating more information and effectively reduce time overhead.

In this paper, we initially transform programs into vector representation that can be input the neural network, and use TCN instead of traditional RNNs for training the model. Then, we introduce self-attention mechanism to replace dense layers [14] for improving vulnerability detection capabilities. The more complex the model, the better the detection, but this undoubtedly increases the complexity and time overhead of the model. The time overhead is a very important factor, and excessive training time is inappropriate. The introduction of self-attention mechanism addresses this issue effectively, and self-attention mechanism will focus on the information that is more important. It is equivalent to set a higher weight to some important information, and adjusting the corresponding parameters during the next back propagation. After continuous optimization, we can obtain a model with excellent vulnerability detection capabilities. Additionally, to avoid the errors caused by a bad random selection of the training set, we use 10-fold cross-validation to select the best parameter values and save it for vulnerability detection during the testing phase to validate the model.

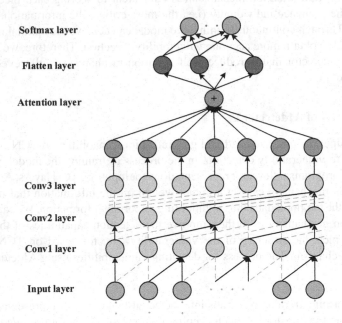

Fig. 3. AIdetectorX: A brief structure that combines TCN and self-attention mechanism.

3   Experimental Design

3.1   Evaluation Metrics

The effectiveness of vulnerability detection methods can be evaluated by the following five widely-used metrics [15]: accuracy (A), false positive rate (FPR), false negative rate (FNR), precision (P), and F1-measure (F1). In these metrics, the A measures the correctness of all detected programs; the FPR measures the proportion of false positive programs to the entire population of programs that are not vulnerable; the FNR measures the proportion of false negative programs to the entire population of programs that are vulnerable; the P measures the correctness of detected vulnerable programs; the F1 is the overall effectiveness considering both precision and FNR. Let TP denotes the number of vulnerable samples that are correctly judged as the vulnerable programs by the model, FP denotes the number of non-vulnerable samples that are incorrectly judged as the vulnerable programs by the model, TN denotes the number of non-vulnerable samples that are correctly judged as the non-vulnerable programs by the model, and FN denotes the number of vulnerable samples that are incorrectly judged as the non-vulnerable programs by the model. Then, the above four variables (i.e., *TP, FP, TN, FN*) can be used to calculate the evaluation metrics, and it is shown in Table 1.

Table 1. Evaluation metrics

Metric	Formula
Accuracy	$A = \frac{TP+TN}{TP+TN+FP+FN}$
False positive rate	$FPR = \frac{FP}{FP+TN}$
False negative rate	$FNR = \frac{FN}{TP+FN}$
Precision	$P = \frac{TP}{TP+FP}$
F1-measure	$F1 = \frac{2 \cdot P \cdot (1-FNR)}{P+(1-FNR)}$

3.2 Comparative Vulnerability Detector

The comparative vulnerability detector, VulDeePecker, is a deep learning-based system. The structure of VulDeePecker consists of a BLSTM layer (i.e., multiple bidirectional LSTM layers), two dense layers, and a softmax layer. In the experiments, the parameters of VulDeePecker are set as follows: (1) The number of neurons in the neural network is set to 300; (2) The dropout is set to 0.5; (3) The batch size is set to 64; (4) The number of epochs is set to 10; (5) The length of the input vector is set to 100. Additionally, the Adamax is chosen as the optimizer with the learning rate of 0.002, and the loss function is chosen as binary cross entropy. It is worth noting that in original design of VulDeePecker, the size of epochs is 4 and the length of the input vector is 50. However, this results in a lot of important information being lost due to the small vector length setting, and the network does not converge sufficiently when the number of epochs is 4.

In contrast, the structure of AIdetectorX consists of an input layer, a TCN layer (i.e., multiple convolutional layers), an attention layer, a flatten layer, and a softmax layer. The parameters of AIdetectorX are similar to those of VulDeePecker. In the design of TCN layer, we set the size of *filters* to 128, the number of *kernel size* to 3, and the size of *dilation rate* to 1, 2, and 4, respectively.

3.3 Evaluation Datasets

To evaluate the efficiency of the proposed vulnerability detector in this paper, we conduct extensive experiments on the publicly available and widely used datasets, which is available at https://github.com/CGCL-codes/VulDeePecker. The datasets are used to evaluate VulDeePecker, so as to avoid the errors caused by different datasets. The used dataset contains two categories (i.e., buffer errors and resource management errors), where 17,725 samples are vulnerable programs and 43,913 samples are non-vulnerable programs. Among the 17,725 vulnerable programs, 10,440 programs are related to buffer error vulnerabilities (recorded as BE-ALL) and the rest 7,285 vulnerable programs are related to resource management error vulnerabilities (recorded as RM-ALL), while the programs that contain both buffer error vulnerabilities and resource management error vulnerabilities are recorded as HY-ALL. Table 2 summarizes some specific information of the used datasets.

Table 2. Evaluation datasets

Dataset	Code gadgets	Vulnerable code gadgets	Not vulnerable code gadgets
BE-ALL	39,753	10,440	29,313
RM-ALL	21,885	7,285	14,600
HY-ALL	61,638	17,725	43,913

3.4 Experimental Produce

TCN and self-attention mechanism are implemented in Python3 using the Keras, and the experiments are running on a NVIDIA GeForce GTX 1050 Ti GPU with 6.1 computational capabilities and Intel Core i5-8400 CPU operating at 3.50 GHz. Additionally, we apply 10-fold cross-validation to train the neural network model and choose the optimal parameter values.

First, we propose the idea of using TCN instead of RNNs for vulnerability detection. We design and implement a TCN-based vulnerability detector (i.e., TCNDetector) and conduct a comparative experiment with VulDeePecker. The advantages of TCN are not only in its detection capabilities, but also in its time overhead. To validate its time complexity, we compare the training and detection times of TCNDetector and VulDeePecker. Additionally, we also verify the detection capabilities of TCN with other RNNs, we design the third experiment for comparing it with LSTM, GRU, and BGRU. Tables 3, 4 and 5 summarize the results of these three experiments.

Second, to verify whether self-attention mechanism can be introduced into the field of vulnerability detection to improve detection capabilities, we implement a vulnerability detector based on BLSTM and self-attention mechanism (i.e., VulDeePecker+). We compare VulDeePecker+ with the deep learning-based vulnerability detection system without self-attention mechanism (i.e., VulDeePecker). To verify whether the success of self-attention mechanism can be combined with TCNDetector to further improve detection capabilities, we implement a vulnerability detector based on TCN and self-attention mechanism (i.e., AIdetectorX) and compare it with TCNDetector. The experimental results are shown in Table 6.

4 Results and Discussions

Our experiments focus on answering the following three research questions (RQs):

- RQ1: Can TCN replace RNNs for better vulnerability detection capabilities and less time overhead?
- RQ2: Can self-attention mechanism further improve vulnerability detection capabilities?

4.1 Experiments for Answering RQ1

When given a piece of data, RNNs often suffer from the vanishing gradient problem and exploding gradient problem because of sharing the parameters over different time periods. However, TCN can process data in parallel rather than sequentially, thus, TCN is less likely to suffer from the above two problems. Additionally, RNNs need to save the information for each step when they are used, it can consume a lot of memory. In contrast, TCN shares the convolution kernels in each layer, which results in lower memory usage. To investigate which neural network is more suitable for vulnerability detection, we conduct comparative experiments on VulDeePecker (based on BLSTM) and TCNDetector (based on TCN) to answer RQ1, and the experimental results are shown in Table 3.

Table 3. Effectiveness of TCNDetector

System	Dataset	A (%)	FPR (%)	FNR (%)	P (%)	F1 (%)
VulDeePecker	BE-ALL	91.18	10.05	7.56	90.18	91.29
	RM-ALL	94.81	6.17	4.18	93.94	94.86
	HY-ALL	91.83	8.71	7.61	91.37	91.87
TCNDetector	BE-ALL	92.76	7.37	7.08	92.64	92.77
	RM-ALL	95.61	5.62	3.15	94.51	95.65
	HY-ALL	93.54	6.27	5.64	92.83	93.59

We can observe from Table 3 that the vulnerability detector using TCN (i.e., TCNDetector) outperforms the vulnerability detector using BLSTM (i.e., VulDeePecker) in terms of vulnerability detection because there is a causal relationship between the layers of the convolutional network in TCN. We conclude that the neural network has the best detection on the RM-ALL dataset because there are only 16 library/API function calls related to resource management errors and 124 function library/API calls related to buffer overflow errors. Neural networks can process faster and get better detection for simple data. This is because more complex data requires deeper neural networks. Too many neural network layers increase the time overhead and may lead to unsatisfactory detection due to overfitting. On BE-ALL and RM-ALL datasets, TCNDetector outperforms VulDeePecker in detection, while on HY-ALL dataset, the accuracy of TCNDetector is 93.54%, an improvement of 1.71% compared to VulDeePecker's 91.83%. The FPR and FNR are 6.27%. and 5.64% lower than VulDeePecker by 2.44% and 1.97%, respectively. TCNDetector is better than VulDeePecker for precision and F1-measure (i.e., 92.83% and 93.59% for TCNDetector vs. 91.37% and 91.87% for VulDeePecker).

The positive and negative examples in the original paper are not processed, so their false negative rate is relatively high, which is due to the large proportion of normal samples, and the neural network cannot learn the vulnerability features effectively. In this paper, we use undersampling to equalize the sample and sacrifice a certain false positive rate for a more reasonable false negative rate.

Additionally, time overhead is an issue to consider in deep learning, and the advantages of TCN are not only in its detection capabilities, but also in its time overhead. Table 4 summarizes the time complexity of VulDeePecker and TCNDetector, including training time and detection time. The training time refers to the time consumed in transforming the training programs to the input of the neural network and the time consumed in training the model. The detection time refers to the time consumed in transforming the testing programs to the input of the neural network and the time consumed in detecting whether the program contains some vulnerabilities.

Table 4. Effectiveness of TCNDetector

System	Dataset	Training time (s)	Detection time (s)
VulDeePecker	BE-ALL	1776.87	27.99
	RM-ALL	1244.06	17.14
	HY-ALL	3039.05	53.12
TCNDetector	BE-ALL	152.64	15.37
	RM-ALL	105.92	8.12
	HY-ALL	162.03	33.71

The experimental results in Table 4 demonstrate that the usage of TCN significantly reduces the time overhead compared to BLSTM. That is, TCN is more suitable for vulnerability detection than BLSTM. There are 39,753 programs on the BE-ALL dataset. We observe that the training and detection times of VulDeePecker are 1776.87 s and 27.99 s, respectively, while the training and detection times of TCNDetector are 152.64 s and 15.37 s, respectively.

Furthermore, there are 21,885 programs on the RM-ALL dataset. We observe that the training and detection times of VulDeePecker are 1244.06 s and 17.14 s, respectively, and the training and detection times of TCNDetector are 105.92 s and 8.12 s, respectively. The training time and detection time increase with the number of programs. VulDeePecker requires 3039.05 s to train on the HY-ALL dataset, which is more than the combined training time required to run on the BE-ALL and RM-ALL datasets, while TCNDetector takes 162.03 s to train the model, only 9.39 s more than the time required to train on the BE-ALL dataset. However, TCN is not necessarily superior to other neural networks in vulnerability detection. To further evaluate the efficiency of TCN, we implement three vulnerability detectors based on LSTM, GRU and BGRU, respectively. And then, we compare these three vulnerability detectors with BLSTM-based and TCN-based vulnerability detectors on the entire dataset, and the compared results are shown in Table 5.

Experimental results in Table 5 show that TCN performs better than other neural networks, (B)LSTM perform better than (B)GRU, and bidirectional neural networks are more effective than unidirectional neural networks, which provides some guidance for later scholars in vulnerability detection. And then, we set up different *epochs* to verify TCN and RNNs, where the accuracy, FPR, F1-measure, and training time are used to measure the detection capabilities of these neural networks. Experimental results on these metrics are as recorded in Fig. 4, where the X-axis indicates the *epochs* and the Y-axis represents accuracy, FPR, F1-measure, and time overhead, respectively. Since F1-measure integrates FNR and precision, we do not plot the variation curves of the FNR and precision.

Table 5. Effectiveness of TCNDetector

Neural network	A (%)	FPR (%)	FNR (%)	P (%)	F1 (%)
GRU	91.24	9.13	8.37	90.92	91.27
LSTM	91.62	8.81	7.95	91.27	91.65
BGRU	91.25	8.92	8.06	90.71	91.31
BLSTM	91.83	8.71	7.61	91.37	91.87
TCN	93.54	6.27	5.64	92.83	93.59

It can be observed from Fig. 4 that with the increase of the *epochs*, the neural network models become much better. When the number of *epochs* is equal to 10, the model has been trained very well and it not be further improved when the training is continued, but it will result in the waste of the computational capabilities and time overhead. When the number of *epochs* is less than 6, the differences between the different neural networks are very significant. When the number of *epochs* is equal to 3, the accuracy and F1-measure reach 91.76% and 91.88%, respectively, while the time cost on training the model is only 85.31 s. In contrast, under the same good results (that is, the accuracy and F1-measure of LSTM are 91.62% and 91.65% when the epoch is equal to 10, respectively), the time cost of other networks is at least 694.59 s. When the number of iterations equals 10, the time overhead of TCN is only 162.03 s and its detection capability is significantly better than other neural networks, and the time overhead of TCN does not increase exponentially.

From an overall perspective, as *epochs* increase, accuracy and F1-measure continue to increase and then level off, and FPR continues to decrease and then level off, but time overhead continues to increase. Furthermore, the bidirectional neural network is better than the unidirectional neural network in terms of detection performance, but its time overhead is larger. In contrast, the TCN used in this paper not only achieves higher detection performance but also does not have a significant increase in time overhead as *epochs* increase.

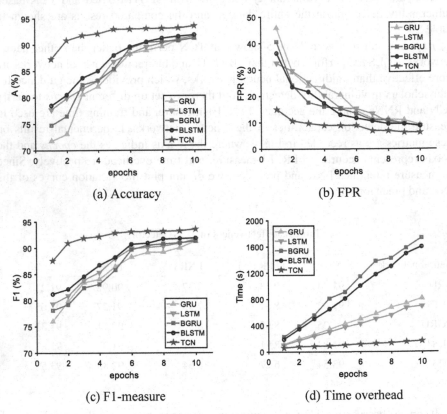

(a) Accuracy   (b) FPR

(c) F1-measure   (d) Time overhead

Fig. 4. Evaluation metrics for different epochs of five neural networks.

4.2 Experiments for Answering RQ2

Although RNNs are good enough for vulnerability detection, but there are some limitations. The RNN model would be more complex when a lot of information need to be remembered. Additionally, the computational capabilities are still a bottleneck that would limit the development of neural networks. Although some optimization operations (such as local connections, weight sharing, and pooling) can make the neural networks simpler, thus alleviating the conflict between the model complexity and the expressiveness, but the long-range dependency problem in RNNs is not sufficiently memorable for the information. Self-attention mechanism can dynamically generate weights to solve the long-range dependency problem and focus on more important information.

To verify whether self-attention mechanism can improve effectiveness in vulnerability detection, we introduce self-attention mechanism on VulDeePecker (i.e., VulDeePecker+) and compare it with VulDeePecker under the same conditions. We set all the parameters of the model to be the same as the default parameters of VulDeePecker, and experimental results are described in Table 6.

As described in Table 6, the vulnerability detector that introduces self-attention mechanism (i.e., VulDeePecker+) can effectively improve vulnerability detection capabilities. This is because VulDeePecker+ can better focus on the statements related to vulnerabilities and not so much on statements that are not relevant to vulnerabilities. This greatly avoids the influence of invalid information on the neural network and thus improve detection capabilities.

The above experimental results demonstrate that TCN is better suitable for detecting vulnerabilities than BLSTM, and the results also validate the effectiveness of self-attention mechanism for improving detection capabilities. In this experiment, we further introduce self-attention mechanism to improve TCNDetector, namely AIdetectorX. We conduct a comparative experiment to compare AIdetectorX with TCNDetector for verifying whether self-attention mechanism can be used in TCN to further improve detection capabilities. Experimental results are shown in Table 6.

In general, this paper proposes a TCN-based vulnerability detector (i.e., TCNDetector) and compares it with other RNNs-based vulnerability detectors that. The experimental results show that TCN not only outperforms RNNs in terms of detection capabilities, but also requires very little time overhead. Additionally, this paper introduces

Table 6. Effectiveness of TCNDetector

System	Dataset	A (%)	FPR (%)	FNR (%)	P (%)	F1 (%)
VulDeePecker	BE-ALL	91.18	10.05	7.56	90.18	91.29
	RM-ALL	94.81	6.17	4.18	93.94	94.86
	HY-ALL	91.83	8.71	7.61	91.37	91.87
VulDeePecker+	BE-ALL	92.24	9.38	6.13	90.89	92.36
	RM-ALL	95.47	5.21	3.84	94.85	95.51
	HY-ALL	92.71	7.94	5.96	92.34	93.18
TCNDetector	BE-ALL	92.76	7.37	7.08	92.64	92.77
	RM-ALL	95.61	5.62	3.15	94.51	95.65
	HY-ALL	93.54	6.27	5.64	92.83	93.59
AIdetectorX	BE-ALL	93.67	7.26	5.17	92.69	93.75
	RM-ALL	97.32	3.73	1.64	96.36	97.34
	HY-ALL	95.26	4.79	4.68	95.21	95.26

self-attention mechanism on VulDeePecker (i.e., VulDeePecker+) to verify whether self-attention mechanism can enhance the detection capabilities of the detector, and the experimental results demonstrate that self-attention mechanism can effectively improve detection capabilities. As a final experiment, we introduce self-attention mechanism to TCNDetector (i.e., AIdetectorX) and compare it with the current state-of-the-art vulnerability detection system (i.e., VulDeePecker), the AIdetectorX proposed in this paper can enhance the accuracy, precision and F1-measure while reducing the FPR and FNR.

5   Threats to Validity

A threat to external validity is that results are derived from only three datasets and may not hold on other datasets. To reduce this threat, we use publicly available and widely used datasets on GitHub, a well-known open-source community. The public dataset contains 61,638 programs (i.e., HY-ALL dataset). We further mitigate this threat with 10-fold cross-validation.

   Another threat to external validity is that conclusions are directed at programs written in C/C++, which may not apply to programs written in other programming languages. However, the approach presented in this paper is a generic solution and it would be interesting in future to detect vulnerabilities in other languages (e.g., Java).

   A threat to construct validity is that neural network structure and model parameters may affect detection performance. To reduce this threat, we carefully design the neural network architecture and select TCN and self-attention mechanism as the hidden layers. Furthermore, we set the parameters to default values or values that are widely used in the deep learning community.

   A threat to internal validity is that detection capabilities may be strongly dependent on vector representation. To reduce this threat, we remove comments and non-ASCII characters and uniformly name functions and variables. Additionally, we pad zeros or perform delete operations on each vector to obtain equal-length vectors for input to the neural network.

6   Conclusions

In this paper, we combine the advantages of TCN and self-attention mechanism and have presented AIdetectorX, which is a vulnerability detector that applies TCN to vulnerability detection and introduces self-attention mechanism to further improve detection capabilities. To validate the effectiveness of TCN and self-attention mechanism in vulnerability detection, we conduct extensive experiments on publicly available and widely used datasets, where the data are real and available to avoid bias in the experimental results caused by different datasets. Experimental results suggest that TCN is a superior neural network to RNNs in terms of detection capabilities and time overhead, and self-attention mechanism can effectively improve the detection capabilities of the vulnerability detector. AIdetectorX is not a flawless vulnerability detector yet. The limitations of the present study discussed below are interesting open problems for future research.

   Since deep learning requires input fixed-length vectors, which undoubtedly loses some information (possibly some critical information), we will consider how to better represent programs to accommodate more information in the future research. In future work, we will consider whether there are neural networks that are more suitable for vulnerability detection that can further improve the performance on vulnerability detection methods. Additionally, the present experiments are limited to buffer error vulnerabilities and resource management error vulnerabilities. We will perform a series of experiments on other available types of vulnerabilities.

References

1. Kim, S., Woo, S., Lee, H., Oh, H.: VUDDY: a scalable approach for vulnerable code clone discovery. In: 38th IEEE Symposium on Security and Privacy, San Jose, CA, USA, pp. 595–614. IEEE (2017)
2. Li, Z., Zou, D., Xu, S., Jin, H., Qi, H., Hu, J.: Vulpecker: an automated vulnerability detection system based on code similarity analysis. In: 32nd Annual Conference on Computer Security Applications, Los Angeles, California, USA, pp. 201–213. ACM (2016)
3. Flawfinder. https://dwheeler.com/flawfinder. Accessed 18 June 2021
4. Checkmarx. https://www.checkmarx.com. Accessed 18 June 2021
5. Walden, J., Stuckman, J., Scandariato, R.: Predicting vulnerable components: software metrics vs text mining. In: 25th International Symposium on Software Reliability Engineering, Naples, Italy, pp. 23–33. IEEE (2014)
6. Yamaguchi, F., Maier, A., Gascon, H., Rieck, K.: Automatic inference of search patterns for taint-style vulnerabilities. In: 36th IEEE Symposium on Security and Privacy, San Josc, CA, USA, pp. 797–812. IEEE (2015)
7. Li, Z., et al.: VulDeePecker: a deep learning-based system for vulnerability detection. In: 25th Annual Network and Distributed System Security Symposium, San Diego, California, USA, pp. 1–15. ISOC (2018)
8. Lea, C., Vidal, R., Reiter, A., Hager, G.D.: Temporal convolutional networks: a unified approach to action segmentation. In: Hua, G., Jégou, H. (eds.) ECCV 2016. LNCS, vol. 9915, pp. 47–54. Springer, Cham (2016). https://doi.org/10.1007/978-3-319-49409-8_7
9. Bai, S., Kolter, J.Z., Koltun, V.: An empirical evaluation of generic convolutional and recurrent networks for sequence modeling. arXiv preprint arXiv:1803.01271 (2018)
10. Li, Z., Qin, Z., Shen, P., Jiang, L.: Intrusion detection using temporal convolutional networks. In: Gedeon, T., Wong, K.W., Lee, M. (eds.) ICONIP 2019. CCIS, vol. 1142, pp. 168–178. Springer, Cham (2019). https://doi.org/10.1007/978-3-030-36808-1_19
11. Vaswani, A., et al.: Attention is all you need. In: 31st International Conference on Neural Information Processing Systems, Long Beach, CA, USA, pp. 6000–6010. ACM (2017)
12. Zhang, B., Xiao, W., Xiao, X., Sangaiah, A.K., Zhang, W., Zhang, J.: Ransomware classification using patch-based CNN and self-attention network on embedded N-grams of opcodes. Futur. Gener. Comput. Syst. **110**, 708–720 (2020)
13. Xiao, X., Zhang, D., Hu, G., Jiang, Y., Xia, S.: CNN–MHSA: a convolutional neural network and multi-head self-attention combined approach for detecting phishing websites. Neural Netw. **125**, 303–312 (2020)
14. Tan, Z., Wang, M., Xie, J., Chen, Y., Shi, X.: Deep semantic role labeling with self-attention. In: 32nd AAAI Conference on Artificial Intelligence, New Orleans, Louisiana, USA, pp. 4929–4936. AAAI Press (2018)
15. Pendleton, M., Garcia-Lebron, R., Cho, J.H., Xu, S.: A survey on systems security metrics. ACM Comput. Surv. **49**(4), 1–35 (2016)

MC/DC Test Cases Generation Based on BDDs

Faustin Ahishakiye[1](✉), José Ignacio Requeno Jarabo[1,2],
Lars Michael Kristensen[1], and Volker Stolz[1]

[1] Western Norway University of Applied Sciences, Bergen, Norway
{fahi,jirj,lmkr,vsto}@hvl.no
[2] Complutense University of Madrid, Madrid, Spain
jrequeno@ucm.es

Abstract. We present a greedy approach to test-cases selection for single decisions to achieve MC/DC-coverage of their Boolean conditions. Our heuristics take into account "don't care" inputs through three-valued truth values that we obtain through a compact representation via reduced-ordered binary decision diagrams (roBDDs). In contrast to an exhaustive, resource-consuming search for an optimal solution, our approach quickly gives frequently either optimal results, or otherwise produces "good enough" results (close to the optimal size) with little complexity. Users obtain different—possibly better—solutions by permuting the order of conditions when constructing the BDD, allowing them to identify the best solutions within a given time budget. We compare variations on metrics that guide the heuristics.

1 Introduction

Software testing techniques that achieve coverage effectiveness and provide test cases are cost intensive [31]. Certification standards for safety assurance such as DO-178C [28] in the domain of avionic software systems require software with the highest safety level (Level A) to show modified condition decision coverage (MC/DC) [10]. One of the advantages of MC/DC is that for a decision with n conditions, it may be satisfied with less test cases: between a lower-bound of $n + 1$ and upper-bound of $2n$ test cases, compared to multiple condition coverage (MCC) which requires 2^n test cases. MC/DC requires that each condition in a decision shows an independent effect on that decision's outcome by (1) varying just that condition while holding fixed all other possible conditions (**UC-MC/DC**), or (2) varying just that condition while holding fixed all other

This work was supported by the Spanish Ministry of Science and Innovation under project FAME (grant nr. RTI2018-093608-B-C31), the Comunidad de Madrid under project FORTE-CM (grant nr. S2018/TCS-4314) co-funded by EIE Funds of the European Union, the SFI Smart Ocean NFR Project 309612/F40, and the NFR Project COEMS Training Network 309527.

S. Qin et al. (Eds.): SETTA 2021, LNCS 13071, pp. 178–197, 2021.
https://doi.org/10.1007/978-3-030-91265-9_10

possible conditions that could affect the outcome. This criterion of showing independence effect for conditions is unique for MC/DC compared to other structure coverage criteria.

While trying all possible combinations is exhaustive and requires tremendous resources [18], as well as becoming impracticable for a high number of conditions [19,23], finding a test set equal or closer to $n + 1$ with MC/DC assurance is also a non-trivial task [15,24]. Therefore, it is important to investigate new strategies for generating good test suites both in terms of number of test cases [10] and coverage adequacy [14,34] with little complexity and with reasonable resources.

In this paper, we present a novel and alternative approach to test case generation satisfying MC/DC based on reduced-ordered binary decision diagrams (roBDDs) which are a concise representation of Boolean expressions. roBDDs are widely used in different areas such as computer aided design (CAD) tasks [26], symbolic model checking [11,26], and verification of combinational logic [20,29]. Due to their reduced form compared to other Boolean expressions representations such as disjunctive or conjunctive normal form, truth tables and formula equivalence [35]; roBDDs offer a unique normal form and were also already used in test cases generation [17,22] for different coverage criteria other than MC/DC.

We present an algorithm that takes as input the roBDD representing a Boolean expression and constructs a set of MC/DC pairs. For a decision of n conditions, we generate n pairs that contain between $n + 1$ to $2n$ test cases altogether. We select paths based on their length in roBDDs and reuse factor $(\alpha())$. The reuse factor refers to the number of pairs that use a given path.

We propose and compare heuristics with different preferences with respect to three-valued truth-values (1, 0 and ?) and the length of paths in the roBDD. All of them maximize the reuse factor $(\alpha())$ together with a second criteria, namely: the longest paths in BDD ($\mathcal{H}_{LPN}$, $\mathcal{H}_{LPB}$), the longest paths which may merge ($\mathcal{H}_{LMMN}$, $\mathcal{H}_{LMMB}$), and the longest paths with better size ($\mathcal{H}_{LPBS}$). Each type of heuristic implements two different flavors which sort the BDD paths depending on the interpretation of the reuse factor as a natural number ($\mathcal{H}_{LPN}$, $\mathcal{H}_{LMMN}$) or as a boolean value ($\mathcal{H}_{LPB}$, $\mathcal{H}_{LMMB}$) (e.g., $\alpha(p, \psi) < \alpha(q, \psi)$). Our algorithm is implemented in Python and the PyEDA library [13]. We test our algorithm on the Traffic Alert and Collision Avoidance System (TCAS II) benchmarks [33] which are widely used in the literature [17,19,21,22,37].

BDDs are sensitive to conditions ordering, such that different orders yield different BDDs and their size in the worst case grows to 2^{2^n} nodes [27]. As the number of nodes increases there are many paths to select MC/DC pairs from. We present evidence that to find an optimal or "good enough" solutions, instead of a search with backtracking, it is sufficient to try a few different permutations.

The rest of this paper is organized as follows: in Sect. 2 we present our terminology, notations and a background on MC/DC and BDDs. Section 3 describes our approaches and algorithm for generating test cases satisfying MC/DC based on BDDs. Section 4 explains the implementation of our algorithm and discuss the results. In Sect. 5 we provide the state of the art of the existing related work. Finally, we present the concluding remarks and future work in Sect. 6.

2   Background

In this section, we provide the background on MC/DC and BDDs. We present several basic definitions and terminology which are used throughout this paper. Conditionals in source code, as well as logical expressions in software specifications can be formalized as Boolean expressions. Both BDDs and MC/DC deal with Boolean expressions.

Definition 1 (Boolean expression). *A Boolean expression is defined as an expression that can be evaluated to either* true *(T) or* false *(F) and can contain connectives: NOT, AND, OR, XOR (exclusive-or), denoted by $\neg$, $\wedge$, $\vee$, and $\oplus$ respectively.*

There has been some confusion on what is a condition and decision in the context of source code and the Certification Authorities Software Team (CAST) provided suitable definitions [7]: each occurrence of a condition is considered as a distinct condition, whereas we treat multiple occurrences of a variable as one condition, where c and $\neg c$ are strongly coupled conditions.

Definition 2 (Condition). *A condition denotes a logical indivisible (atomic) expression containing no Boolean operators except for the unary operator $(\neg)$. It contains a Boolean variable represented by a, b, c,..., defined over "0" or "1".*

Definition 3 (Decision). *A decision is a Boolean expression composed of conditions and zero or more Boolean operators. It is denoted by $D = c_1 \square c_2 \square c_3 \cdots \square c_i \square \cdots \square c_n$, where c_i, $(1 \leq i \leq n)$ are Boolean conditions and $\square$ stands for a binary Boolean operator. A decision is also known as a Boolean function.*

Definition 4 (Two/Three-valued test case). *Given a decision D, a test case is a truth vector $tc = (I_1, I_2, I_3, \cdots, I_n)$ where $I_i \in \{0,1\}$ (respectively, $\{0,1,?\}$) are the inputs assigned to each conditions. ? is known as "don't care" meaning that a condition does not need to be evaluated due to short-circuiting. A set of test cases for a given decision is called a* test suite. *We denote the projection onto the truth-value at the position corresponding to some condition c in the test case tc as $tc[c]$.*

2.1   Modified Condition Decision Coverage (MC/DC) Criterion

We first give the well-known definitions for two-valued truth values, and will later extend the definitions into the three-valued setting. MC/DC subsumes the existing logical coverage criteria such as condition coverage (CC): each condition is tested once true and false, decision coverage (DC): a decision is evaluated once true and once false, and multiple condition coverage (MCC): an exhaustive testing that requires all possible combination of inputs. For MC/DC each condition has to independently affect the decision's outcome. According to DO-178C [28] and CAST-10 [7] the following definition has been provided for MC/DC:

Definition 5 (MC/DC [30]). *A decision is said to be MC/DC covered iff: (i) Every point of entry and exit in the program has been invoked at least once, (ii) every condition in a decision in the program has taken all possible outcomes at least once, (iii) every decision in the program has taken all possible outcomes at least once, (iv) each condition in a decision has shown to independently affect that decision's outcome by: (1) varying just that condition while holding fixed all other possible conditions(**UC-MC/DC**), or (2) varying just that condition while holding fixed all other possible conditions that could affect the outcome (**Masking MC/DC**).*

The coverage of program entry and exit in the Definition 5 is not directly connected with the main point of MC/DC [32], as we only consider expressions, not programs. The most interesting part of the MC/DC definition is showing the independent effect, which demonstrates that each condition of the decision has a defined purpose. The item (1) in the definition defines the unique cause MC/DC which is the original MC/DC [9]. The item (2) has been introduced in DO-178C to clarify that so-called *Masked MC/DC* is allowed [6,28]. Masked MC/DC means that it is sufficient to show the independence effect of a condition by holding fixed only those conditions that could actually influence the outcome. In our analysis, we are interested in generating MC/DC test cases that show an independence effect of each condition in the decision with acceptable size.

Definition 6 (Independence effect of a condition, independence pair, $\oplus_c$). *Given two test cases tc, tc' for a decision D, we call tc independent from tc' on condition c, iff i) $D(tc) = \neg D(tc')$ (they evaluate to opposite truth values), and ii) $tc \oplus_c tc'$, where $\oplus_c$ means they differ exactly only in the input position corresponding to condition c. We then say that "tc and tc' form an independence pair" (for some condition c), written $uc(tc, tc')$.*

We will later see that in our three-valued interpretation, a test case cannot form an independence pair if it does not contain enough concrete input to evaluate to either true or false. We now reformulate the general definition of MC/DC from Definition 5 for our purposes:

Definition 7 (MC/DC-cover). *Given a decision D and set of test cases ψ, we say that ψ MC/DC-covers D, iff $\forall c \in D, \exists tc, tc' \in \psi : tc \oplus_c tc' \wedge uc(tc, tc')$ (tc is independent from tc' for every condition c).*

In other words, a set is an MC/DC-cover for a decision D, if for every condition, there exists a pair of test cases in that set which shows the independence effect of that condition by evaluating to opposing truth values.

Example 1. Consider a decision $D = (a \wedge b) \vee c$. The truth table representing MCC and all possible MC/DC pairs is given in Table 1(a). Each pair is showing the independence effect for a condition. The advantage of MC/DC over MCC can be seen from Table 1(a). MCC requires eight test cases whereas all possible MC/DC pairs contain seven test cases. Indeed, only the four test cases shown in Table 1(b) are required to achieve MC/DC [9,10]. However, choosing a set equal or closer to minimal number of test cases is non-trivial for testers, especially

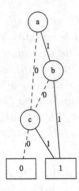

Table 1. MCC & MC/DC pairs for $D = (a \wedge b) \vee c$

tc	a	b	c	D	MC/DC pairs
1	0	0	0	0	
2	0	0	1	1	c(1, 2)
3	0	1	0	0	
4	0	1	1	1	c(3, 4)
5	1	0	0	0	
6	1	0	1	1	c(5, 6)
7	1	1	0	1	a(3, 7), b(5, 7)
8	1	1	1	1	

(a) MCC & All MC/DC pairs

π	a	b	c	D	MC/DC pairs
1	0	?	0	0	
2	1	1	?	1	a(1, 2)
3	1	0	0	0	b(2, 3)
4	1	0	1	1	c(3, 4)

(b) MC/DC set of paths

tc	a	b	c	D	MC/DC pairs
1	0	1	0	0	
2	1	1	0	1	a(1, 2)
3	1	0	0	0	b(2, 3)
4	1	0	1	1	c(3, 4)

(c) MC/DC set of test cases

Fig. 1. roBDD: $D = (a \wedge b) \vee c$

when there is more than one MC/DC pair for a certain condition, for example, condition c can be covered by either of three pairs (indicated in parentheses), as shown in Table 1(a).

Chilenski et al. [9,10] investigated that for a decision D with n conditions, UC-MC/DC can be achieved with a minimal number of $n+1$ tests while Masking MC/DC be achieved with a minimal number of $\lceil 2*(\sqrt{n}) \rceil$ tests. This is achieved by choosing MC/DC pairs that overlap where every condition past the first one (which requires two test cases), only adds a single test case to the existing set.

Lemma 1 (Minimal MC/DC-Covers [1,9]). *If a coverage set exists for a decision D with n conditions, then there also exists a smaller set (possibly with different test cases) thereof with exactly $n + 1$ test cases such that it MC/DC-covers D for UC MC/DC.*

2.2   Overview on Binary Decision Diagrams (BDDs)

BDDs are canonical representations of Boolean functions compared to other Boolean expressions representations such as disjunctive normal form (DNF), conjunctive normal form (CNF), truth tables and formula equivalence [35]. To reduce BDDs, conditions in a decision need to be ordered and duplicated terminals and isomorphic sub-trees have to be merged. The resulting graph is known as reduced ordered BDD (roBDD) and is shown in Fig. 1 for the Example 1.

BDDs represent formulas *compact* in the sense that it takes little memory to store the representation, the number of nodes in a roBDD is reduced and there is exactly one optimal and unique graph for each Boolean expression [35].

Definition 8 (Path through an roBDD, $\pi, \pi[x]$). *Given an roBDD for some decision D over Boolean variables $x_0, \ldots, x_1$. We denote a path from the root of the BDD to a terminal with π, and write $\pi[x] = 1$ if the path takes the true-branch in the node labelled with condition x (0/false respectively), and $\pi[x] =?$ if the path does not pass through a node labelled with condition x. That is, although paths through the roBDD can be of different lengths, for uniformity we always represent them as a vector with n elements.*

We also extend the evaluation of a decision wrt. some inputs $(D(0\ldots0))$ to BDDs and use $D(\pi)$ to denote the three-valued truth-value that the path represents. The obvious correspondence between a test case and a path through the roBDD is that a test case may provide more truth-values as inputs than are strictly necessary on this path. For example, an MC/DC pair of paths for condition a is $\{(0?0),(11?)\}$ as shown in row 1 & 2 of Table 1(b). The fully instantiated test cases for this pair are $\{(010),(110)\}$ (row 1 & 2, Table 1(c)).

3   Approaches and Algorithm for Test Cases Generation

Our approach and heuristics for test cases generation are based on roBDDs that guide our search for test case selection. We start with a set of roBDDs paths from the root and construct sets satisfying MC/DC for all conditions, where each set contains n MC/DC pairs.

BDDs are sensitive to variable ordering: to deal with the ordering effect, we collect solutions for a number of permutations on the variable ordering. As the number of conditions in a decision increases, the number of permutations ($n!$ for n conditions) increases over-exponentially. Since generating the set of solutions for all permutation would be infeasible in those cases, we show that for few permutations we generate some test suites of minimal size, based on the selection methods defined in Subsect. 3.2. In the following, we assume that all BDDs that occur are roBDDs.

3.1   Theorems and Definitions for MC/DC in Terms of BDDs

The core of our contribution is as follows: our algorithm produces a set of three-valued test cases, which we can instantiate to fulfill the original definition of MC/DC. We first extend general results from the standard two-valued Boolean logic to a three-valued logic.

Definition 9 (Three-valued independence pair, $\oplus_c^3$). *Given two three-valued test cases tc, tc' for a decision D, we write $uc3(tc, tc')$ iff i) $D(tc) = \neg D(tc')$ (they evaluate to opposite concrete truth values), and ii) $tc \oplus_c^3 tc'$, where $\oplus_c^3$ means at least one of the inputs for some condition c is a concrete truth value, and for every other condition the three-valued inputs coincide or one of them is "?".*

Example 2. Let $D(X, Y, Z) = X \wedge ((\neg Y \wedge \neg Z) \vee (Y \vee Z))$. Consider $tc = (0??)$ with $D(tc) = 0$ and $tc' = (11?)$ with $D(tc') = 1$ respectively, hence $uc3(tc, tc')$. Observe that hence also e.g. $uc3(011, 11?)$ and $uc(011, 111)$.

We next show that each three-valued independence pair can be instantiated to some two-valued independence pair by suitable substitution of unknown values. In the following, for readability, we describe functions from our implementation through their properties instead of operationally. The first function combines two compatible test cases into a single one. We need this later in our algorithm to refine existing test cases such that we keep only one test case when two cases overlap.

Definition 10 (*merge*(tc, tc')). *Given test cases tc, tc', we obtain σ = merge (tc, tc'), where $\forall c \in C, (\sigma[c] = tc[c] \wedge tc'[c] = ?) \vee (\sigma[c] = tc'[c] \wedge tc[c] = ?)$.*

In other words, *merge* substitutes some ? in a pair of paths, such that all conditions have equal values. The result is undefined if they disagree in one position where one has true and the other false. This can be understood as unifying both test cases with each other, taking ? as free variables.

Note that we ignore the actual outcome when merging wrt. a decision, but only ever consider the inputs. As we will also consider test cases that differ in *exactly one* position, we define the following variation:

Definition 11 (*merge$_x$*(tc, tc')). *Given test cases tc, tc', we obtain σ = merge$_x$(tc, tc'), where $\forall c \in C \backslash \{x\}, (\sigma[c] = tc[c] \wedge tc'[c] = ?) \vee (\sigma[c] = tc'[c] \wedge tc[c] = ?) \wedge \sigma[\mathbf{x}] = \mathbf{tc}[\mathbf{x}]$ (emphasis added).*

Note that this definition is biased to reproduce the truth-value in the designated position x from the first input, and we will consequently later see it applied *twice*, once from left to right argument, and also from right to left argument.

Example 3. We have $merge_{c_2}((1?0), (11?)) = (110)$, but $merge_{c_2}((11?), (1?0)) = (11?)$, with c_2 the condition that is placed in the last position.

Definition 12 (Specialization $\leqq$). *Given three-valued test cases p, q, we say that $p \leqq q$ iff $\exists p' : p = merge(p', q)$ ("p specializes q").*

Due to the same format for a test case and for a roBDD path (see Definition 8), both concepts are interchangeable and $\leqq$ can specialize any of them. The relation $\leqq$ is a partial order (straightforward).

Theorem 1 (Usefulness of three-valued MC/DC). *Given a decision D and set φ of three-valued test-cases that is a three-valued MC/DC cover for D, i.e., $\forall c \in D : \exists tc, tc' \in \varphi, tc \oplus_c^3 tc' \wedge uc3(tc, tc')$. Then there exists a two-valued set of test cases $\psi \subseteq 2^{B^{|D|}}$, such that:*

(1) $\forall tc, tc' \in \varphi : uc3(tc, tc') \Rightarrow \exists u, u' \in \psi : u \oplus_c u' \wedge u \leqq tc \wedge u' \leqq tc'$
    (each test case pair in φ has been specialised)
(2) $\forall u, u' \in \psi : D(u) = \neg D(u') \wedge u \oplus_c u' \Rightarrow \exists tc, tc' \in \varphi : uc3(tc, tc')$
    $\wedge u \leqq tc \wedge u' \leqq tc'$($\psi$ is the smallest set that specialises φ).

It follows that ψ is an MC/DC-cover for D.

Proof. (1) Because of $uc3(tc, tc')$, tc or tc' have a concrete value in c and coincide for the rest of conditions c_i, except for those positions c_i where one of the test cases is ?. Hence, $u = merge_{c_i}(tc, tc')$ returns a new test case where $u \leqq tc$ as the ? are instantiated (symmetrically, $u' = merge_{c_i}(tc', tc)$), excluding condition c. MC/DC imposes that $u[c] = \neg u'[c]$, so the selection of tc and tc' satisfies that either a) $tc[c] = \neg tc'[c]$, or b) $tc[c] =?$ or $tc'[c] =?$. In b), $u[c] = tc[c]$ and $u'[c] = tc'[c]$: if any of these values is a ?, then they are properly instantiated so that $u \oplus_c u'$.

(2) As $u \oplus_c u'$, u and u' are equal except for condition c. Then, tc and tc' are constructed by replacing a finite number of positions in u (similarly, u') with ? such that they keep $uc3(tc, tc')$. Because tc and tc' are abstractions of u and u', $u \leqq tc \wedge u' \leqq tc'$.

Due to the specialization relation, multiple sets of two-valued test cases can be constructed that satisfy the above property: φ may contain a test case tc with "don't care" for some condition c, and also "don't care" for every other partner tc' in the pairs it is participating in. Then, this input c can be instantiated to either truth value. Our Algorithm 1, which uses the roBDD to populate φ, guarantees that there will exist at least a pair tc, tc' such that $tc[c] = \neg tc'[c]$ for every condition c, if the decision can be MC/DC-covered.

Next, we define the function that identifies suitable test cases that we might want to add our set ψ. Based on the following criteria, for every uncovered condition the algorithm adds a new test case together with a complementary one such that the pair shows the independence effect of the condition.

Definition 13 (Reuse factor $\alpha(\pi, \psi)$, $\alpha_{=3}(\pi, \psi)$). *Given the set of MC/DC pairs of paths $(\pi^{\perp}, \pi^{\top}) \in \psi$ with $D(\pi^{\perp}) = 0$ and $D(\pi^{\top}) = 1$, the reuse factor $\alpha(\pi, \psi)$ represents the number of pairs in ψ that use π. It is calculated as*
$$\alpha(\pi, \psi) := |\{(\pi, (\pi^{\perp}, \pi^{\top})) \mid \pi = \pi^{\perp} \vee \pi = \pi^{\top}, (\pi^{\perp}, \pi^{\top}) \in \psi\}|.$$

Relation to BDDs. A pair (tc, tc') of test cases showing the independence of some condition c_i has a vivid graphical interpretation on the BDD. It corresponds to a pair of paths $(\pi^{\perp}, \pi^{\top})$ such that:

1. the tests evaluate the opposite truth values (i.e., $D(tc) = \neg D(tc')$);
2. $tc \leqq \pi^{\perp}, tc' \leqq \pi^{\top}$ (order wlog., the test cases may contain more input than strictly necessary).
3. both reach some node v_{c_i} using the same path through BDD(D) (i.e., $\pi^{\perp}[j] = \pi^{\top}[j]$ for $0 \leq j < i$);
4. their paths from v_{c_i} exit on either edge (i.e., $\pi^{\perp}[i] = \neg \pi^{\top}[i]$);
5. after v_{c_i}, both test cases take compatible choices along the paths for the remaining conditions, so that the independence property holds (i.e., $\pi^{\perp}[j] =_3 \pi^{\top}[j]$ for $i < j < n$).

This means especially that the two paths cannot cross (after the condition-node v_{c_i}), since this would immediately indicate an incompatible choice.

Figure 2 represents the overview on the selection of MC/DC pairs from the roBDD. The roBDD contains the root node labeled by R, non-terminal nodes labeled with conditions and two terminal nodes (0 and 1). The nodes are connected by solid and dashed edges representing assignments of 1 and 0 to each condition respectively. Every condition c may be represented multiple times on the BDD (nodes v_c). There may exist multiple paths to such a node. For every path reaching a (non-terminal) node, we attempt to extend it to construct pairs that show the independence effect of that condition. It is not guaranteed that

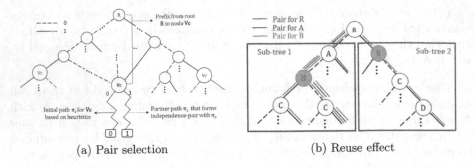

(a) Pair selection   (b) Reuse effect

Fig. 2. Overview on MC/DC pairs selection path from BDD and reuse effect

the two complementary paths lead to opposite terminal nodes and our algorithm must explicitly check it step-by-step (modulo "don't care"-steps). The figure shows a representative of such pairs, $(\pi^{\perp}, \pi^{\top})$: they share the same prefix for all ordered conditions up to v_c. They then proceed in lock-step through the two branches to the terminals.

Figure 2(b) illustrates some of the effects that we aim to achieve: as we search for pairs in the order of the roBDD, we will obtain some pair (shown in blue) from the heuristics (e.g. based on "longest path") which differs directly in the condition R for the root node. The next condition A in the order exists only in the left subtree, and we prefer a pair for it that reuses one of the previous path. Here, this can only be the left path for R, and hence we check if for the path that condition A shares with condition R we can construct a compatible path to the opposite terminal after leaving the node for A through the opposite edge (red pair). For condition B, we attempt to construct a pair by reusing the right branch for condition R (blue), and another one that uses the path that we used before both for R and A. We either take the only pair that fulfils our criteria, or again have the heuristics break a potential tie, here resulting in the green pair for condition B.

Due to the structure of roBDD, the derived test cases correspond to *MC/DC + short circuit* [5,6] where a test case can be composed with a three-valued assignment (*0: false, 1:true, and ?:not evaluated(a condition does not appear along the path)*). Therefore, to find the test cases that satisfy Unique Cause MC/DC [9], the "don't care" assignments will be replaced by either 0 or 1 pairwise (by the corresponding value at the same position in the partner path).

3.2   Algorithm and Heuristics for Test Cases Generation

Our approach for MC/DC test case generation for a decision D is based on the three-valued paths that are extracted from the equivalent roBDD. The MC/DC coverage criteria requires a pair of test cases that shows the independence effect for every condition. The presence of "don't care" values in a BDD path gives us some flexibility when instantiating it to a test case and finding the complementary test case that leads to the opposite Boolean evaluation. As the wildcards may specialize to any Boolean value, we propose a greedy algorithm that tries to minimize the overall number of test case pairs for a decision D with n conditions from $2n$ to a value as close as possible to $n + 1$.

To this end, our method is divided in two stages: during the first phase, it initializes the MC/DC test suite with paths that are extracted from the BDD through any of our predefined heuristics, which intend to maximize the reuse factor in order to reduce the differences among test cases. Secondly, the selected BDD paths are specialized so that the wildcards take a concrete value while preserving the independence effect. We lift this property to sets of pairs of test cases with the definition of *instantiate* which computes the smallest set such that it guarantees that all members have been merged if possible:

$\forall(s, s') \in instantiate(S):$
$\quad \exists(p, p') \in S : uc3(p, p') \land s \leq p \land s' \leq p'$ $\qquad$ (instantiated from S)
$\quad \land \ \forall(p, p') \ \forall(q, q') \in S : s \leq p \land p \leq q \land p \leq q' \Rightarrow s = p \land s' = p'$ (least upper bound)
$\quad \land \ \exists c : merge_c(s, s') = s \land merge_c(s', s) = s'$ $\qquad$ (fully merged).

This approach takes $n = |C|$ iterations, and each iteration adds a pair consisting of at most two new paths to the set. If S is empty, we can abort as this means there does not exist any pair showing the independence effect of that condition, and hence the decision D cannot be covered with the MC/DC-property. Correspondingly, unless we abort, the final set will contain n pairs, consisting of at most $2n$ individual paths. By construction, these pairs will provide three-valued MC/DC-coverage of the decision.

This leaves us two points to address: i) can we avoid constructing the set of *all* pairs for a condition, but instead only use a relevant, smaller subset as input to the heuristics, and ii) can we present evidence that our heuristics have a high likelihood of picking pairs that not only reuse a path from the already selected pairs (if possible), but also contributes a fresh path that will be reused

---

Algorithm 1: MC/DC Test case generation

Input: An $roBDD$ over conditions C with root r for a formula φ
Output: Set ψ of pairs of test cases that MC/DC-cover φ with
$\qquad |C| + 1 \leq |\bigcup\{\{tc, tc'\}|(tc, tc') \in \psi\}| \leq 2|C|.$

1 $\psi = \emptyset;$
2 **forall** $c \in C$ **do**
3 $\quad$ Let $S := \{(\pi_{v_c}^\top, \pi_{v_c}^\perp) \mid$ where $\pi_{v_c}^\top, \pi_{v_c}^\perp$ are paths from the root r via some v_c
$\qquad$ to $\top$ and $\perp$ respectively, such that $[\pi_{v_c}^\top] \oplus_c [\pi_{v_c}^\perp]\}.$
4 $\quad$ Abort if $S = \emptyset$: no MC/DC cover of φ possible.
5 $\quad$ Let $(p, q) := \mathcal{H}(\psi, S)$ be the result of applying a given heuristics $\mathcal{H}$, such
$\qquad$ that $\exists(p', q') \in S : p = merge_c(p', q'), q = merge_c(q', p').$
6 $\quad$ $\psi = instantiate(\psi \cup \{p, q\})$
7 **end**

in the future. We address the first point through algorithmic construction, and evaluate the second through a series of experiments using the TCAS case study.

Algorithmic Description. Any approach to a potentially optimal solution must reuse a test case that has already been selected as a partner in a pair for some other condition when selecting a pair for some other condition. It is hence clear that not all pairs for a condition may have to be constructed and evaluated. Rather, we first attempt to directly derive a pair from the existing set of test cases (by flipping only the corresponding condition), and only revert to deriving a new pair of completely fresh paths if such a derived path does not exist. Depending on the heuristics, identifying a completely fresh pair may entail a complete enumeration of pairs: it may be looking for the longest path with most reuse-potential (least number of "don't care"), which could ultimately be the last pair a given traversal of the BDD yields.

The representation as a BDD gives us an advantage in building fresh pairs: by exploring the tree from the root, the ordered labels tell us when we can preempt a search because the condition of interest does not exist in the remaining subtree, and we can continue our search in a sibling. Compared to an exploration of the corresponding truth-table, this effectively allows us to skip over irrelevant rows. We next formalize the notion of path-length in the roBDD.

Definition 14 (Length of a path/test case, $|\sigma|/|tc|$). *Given a path σ in the roBDD for a decision D from the root to a terminal, we denote the length of the path with $|\sigma|$. The length of a test case $|tc|$ is that of the underlying path.*

Note that since a test case can have more concrete inputs than are necessary for the path we have in the BDD, the length of a test case may be lower than the number of concrete inputs in that test case.

We propose five selection methods for test cases generation. All of them maximize the reuse factor ($\alpha()$) together with a second criteria, namely: the longest paths in BDD ($\mathcal{H}_{LPN}$, $\mathcal{H}_{LPB}$), the longest paths which may merge ($\mathcal{H}_{LMMN}$, $\mathcal{H}_{LMMB}$), and the longest paths with better size ($\mathcal{H}_{LPBS}$). Each type of heuristic implements two different flavors which sort the BDD paths depending on the interpretation of the reuse factor as a natural number ($\mathcal{H}_{LPN}$, $\mathcal{H}_{LMMN}$) or as a boolean value ($\mathcal{H}_{LPB}$, $\mathcal{H}_{LMMB}$) (e.g., $\alpha(p, \psi) < \alpha(q, \psi)$). We compare them with the *random reuser* ($\mathcal{H}_{RR}$) method as a baseline, which takes the first new path that forms a new pair with an existing test.

$\mathcal{H}_{LPN}/\mathcal{H}_{LMMN}$: This method chooses pairs of paths satisfying MC/DC based on the longest paths in BDDs with the highest reused factor. In case multiple pairs have equal reuse, we choose one where additionally the sum of the lengths is longest. The longest path or higher reuse factor may be better since it can be reused by many conditions that appear along the path.

$$\mathcal{H}_{LPN}(\psi, S) := (merge_c(p, q), merge_c(q, p)) \text{ where } (p, q) \in S$$

such that either (in order):

1. $\alpha(p,\psi) > 0 \wedge \alpha(q,\psi) > 0 \wedge \forall(p',q') \in S : \alpha(p',\psi) > 0 \wedge \alpha(q',\psi) > 0$
$$\Rightarrow |p| + |q| \geq |p'| + |q'|$$
(both test cases were already in the set)
2. $\forall(p',q') \in S : \alpha(p,\psi) + \alpha(q,\psi) \geq \alpha(p',\psi) + \alpha(q',\psi)$ (highest reuse)
$\wedge (\alpha(p,\psi) + \alpha(q,\psi) = \alpha(p',\psi) + \alpha(q',\psi) \Rightarrow |p| + |q| \geq |p'| + |q'|)$
(longest path).

$\mathcal{H}_{LPB}/\mathcal{H}_{LMMB}$: The previous heuristic $\mathcal{H}_{LPN}$ looks at the reuse of the paths in a pair: the existing path may have reuse > 0, and may occur in multiple pairs in the existing set. Its partner path may also be derived from another existing pair. Since it is not clear that past performance ("high reuse = used in multiple pairs by someone before") is an indication for future performance ("does it have more likelihood to be useful in future pairs?"), we also evaluate a variant that only prefers that there is *some* reuse, but not *how much*:

$\mathcal{H}_{LPB}(\psi, S) := (merge_c(p,q), merge_c(q,p))$ where $(p,q) \in S$:
$\alpha(p,\psi) + \alpha(q,\psi) > 0$ (has some reuse)
$\wedge \forall(p',q') \in S : \alpha(p',\psi) + \alpha(q',\psi) > 0 \Rightarrow |p| + |q| \geq |p'| + |q'|$(longest path).

The difference between this method and the previous one is that here we consider the reuse factor as Boolean. That is, we choose a pair with the longest paths in BDDs and we check if one of the paths is already reused as a part of an earlier pairs or not. This may give rise to greater non-determinism since more potential partners are considered equivalent.

Longest Paths Best Size ($\mathcal{H}_{LPBS}$): selects MC/DC pairs where the paths have together the highest reuse and the sum of the lengths is strictly the longest.

4   Implementation of MC/DC Test Cases Selection

In this section we describe how we evaluate our approach for the heuristics proposed in Sect. 3. For each heuristic, one run of Algorithm 1 derives a set of test cases for a decision with MC/DC-coverage if it exists. Our heuristics are sensitive to exactly one parameter: the ordering of conditions when constructing the BDD. Furthermore, there is some inherent non-determinism: a heuristic picks randomly among equally best-ranked pairs. It is quite common to observe equivalent pairs with identical reuse and identical path-length. Secondary sources of non-determinism include e.g. iteration over unordered structures like sets which are implementation-specific to a given Python platform.

To give a proper evaluation, we control these in the following way: every heuristic is applied for a number of permutations of the order of the conditions for each decision. For decisions with a low number of conditions, we can hence even exhaustively evaluate the outcome of the heuristics for all permutations. In addition, we repeat a run on a given permutation, exploring different random choices within the equivalent best pairs.

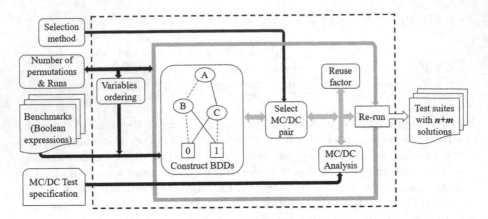

Fig. 3. Test cases generation framework

Our framework is based on the PyEDA library [13] and implemented in Python. We test our algorithm on the Traffic Alert and Collision Avoidance System (TCAS II) benchmark [25, 33] which has been frequently used in literature [17, 19, 21, 22, 37]. The benchmark refers to specifications written as Boolean expressions (decisions) which are logically evaluated to true or false depending on the truth values assigned to the contained conditions.

Below, we present detailed results for a well-known set of TCAS II decisions that can be reproduced with the code in our open source repository[1]. We do not report execution times for our experiment, as our implementation is not optimized in any way beyond obvious algorithmic constructions to minimize BDD-traversal.

4.1   Experimental Setup

Figure 3 shows our test cases generation framework. Our setup takes as input the roBDD for a given decision, the number of permutations, and the number of runs that we perform for each process of test cases generation. The selection method refers to the different heuristics proposed in Sect. 3: $\mathcal{H}_{LPN}$, $\mathcal{H}_{LPB}$, $\mathcal{H}_{LMMN}$, $\mathcal{H}_{LMMB}$, $\mathcal{H}_{LPBS}$ and $\mathcal{H}_{RR}$. The benchmarks refer to the specifications written as Boolean expressions (decisions) which are logically evaluated to true or false depending on the truth values assigned to the contained conditions. MC/DC test specifications are the meaning of what is MC/DC in the context of roBDDs and three values logic (cfr. Theorem 1 and Definition 9). We consider the reuse factor in our MC/DC analysis to reuse as much as possible the existing selected TCs and finally, we produce n MC/DC pairs as output for each decision with the size of n+m solutions. Our results show that we produce mostly $n + 1$ solutions and the rest of solutions are less than $2n$ with 100% MC/DC.

---

[1] https://github.com/selabhvl/py-mcdc/.

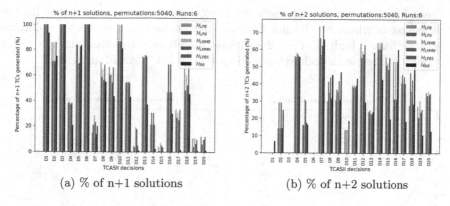

(a) % of n+1 solutions   (b) % of n+2 solutions

Fig. 4. Comparison of % for n + 1 and n + 2 solutions for different heuristics

4.2 Experimental Results

Figure 4(a) and (b) present our results as the percentage of generated solutions of sizes $n + 1$ and $n + 2$ for TCAS II based on our heuristics and the baseline RR heuristic. We consider 5040 different orders at most for each decisions (this exhaustively covers all orders for decisions with up to seven conditions). This sample size already yields evidence that repeated application of the algorithm to different orders will discover a (close to) optimal solution reasonably quickly.

For each heuristic we collect all possible sets of MC/DC covering test cases. MC/DC coverage is calculated as the percentage of the number of covered conditions to the total number of conditions in a decision. In case the MC/DC coverage percentage is less than 100%, it means that MC/DC is not fulfilled for that decision. We present results for solutions of size $n+1$ (optimal) and $n+2$ for our heuristics as shown in Fig. 4. The charts for the heuristics can be reproduced from our open repository. From the TCAS II benchmark results in Fig. 4 and 5, we highlight the following:

1. Our heuristics find the test suite sets of $n + 1$ solutions for each decision, whereas $\mathcal{H}_{RR}$ failed to find any minimal solution for D15. Our heuristics perform better compared to $\mathcal{H}_{RR}$ for 18 out of 20 decisions and have equal results for two decisions in terms of which heuristic has frequently the highest of $n + 1$ solutions with 100% MC/DC. This shows that the approach of permuting order is a viable strategy to eventually obtain an optimal results.
2. $\mathcal{H}_{LPB}$ and $\mathcal{H}_{LMMB}$ out-perform all others with 10 cases (50%) having the highest % of n+1 solutions.
3. Comparing the $\mathcal{H}_{LPB}$ to $\mathcal{H}_{LMMB}, \mathcal{H}_{LPB}$ is 2 cases (10%) higher than $\mathcal{H}_{LMMB}$.
4. We observed that $\mathcal{H}_{LMMN}$ is 2 cases (10%) higher than $\mathcal{H}_{LPN}$.
5. $\mathcal{H}_{LPBS}$ has better results in some decisions than $\mathcal{H}_{LMMN}$ and $\mathcal{H}_{LPN}$.
6. In three decisions (D2, D5 and D7), $\mathcal{H}_{RR}$ has better results than some of our our heuristics. We attribute this outcome to random chance.

7. From Fig. 4(b) which represents the n + 2 solutions, we can see that for the decisions in which we did not find the highest percentage of n + 1 solutions now we have a high % of n + 2 solutions, which indicates that our test suites generated are closer to lower bound (n + 1) of MC/DC minimal set.

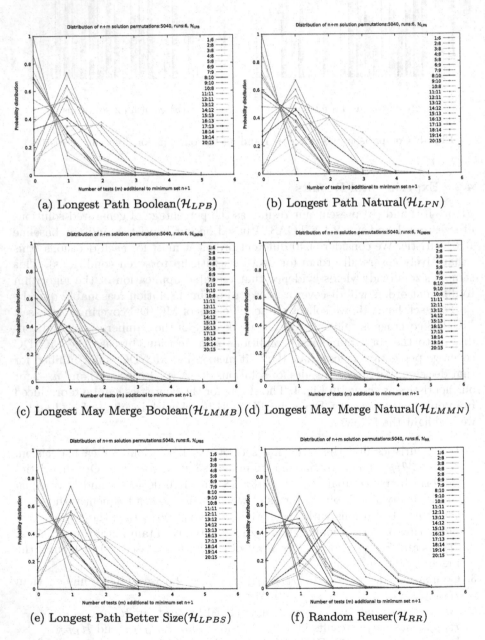

(a) Longest Path Boolean($\mathcal{H}_{LPB}$)

(b) Longest Path Natural($\mathcal{H}_{LPN}$)

(c) Longest May Merge Boolean($\mathcal{H}_{LMMB}$) (d) Longest May Merge Natural($\mathcal{H}_{LMMN}$)

(e) Longest Path Better Size($\mathcal{H}_{LPBS}$)

(f) Random Reuser($\mathcal{H}_{RR}$)

Fig. 5. Probability distribution of n + m solutions for 5040 permutations, 6 runs

In summary, our results show that we produce mostly $n+1$ solutions and the rest of solutions are less than $2n$ with 100% MC/DC adequacy. Figures 5(a)–(f) show the probability distribution of $n+m$ TCs generated for 5040 permutations, 6 runs for different heuristics. The x-axis shows the number of test cases (m) *additional* to the minimal solution $(n+1)$. The labels show the decision number and the contained conditions as presented in [25]. All the solutions are have less than $2n$ test cases, as the maximum observed for m is 6 while the range of number of conditions is 6 to 14. Figures 5 shows that most solutions are much closer to the minimal size (to the left) than to the worst case.

Another challenge which is not directly related to our approach but to MC/DC is the coupled and masked conditions where it is difficult to get a full MC/DC coverage with masked condition. For example the decision D10 in the TCAS II benchmark has two conditions (b and h) which are masked. Out of the nine conditions, hence only seven are retained in the roBDD and we compute our minimal solution accordingly.

For the complex example D15 in the 20 TCAS II decisions, our algorithm takes on average 0.7 s (incl. time for constructing the BDD) for a single run on an Intel(R) Core(TM) i7-7700 CPU @3.60 GHz Linux machine with 64 GB RAM. From the proposed heuristics, we recommend the longest paths with reuse as Boolean number($\mathcal{H}_{LPB}$) as it shows high performance both in terms of high percentage of $n+1$ solutions and short time to compute the solutions compared to the rest of the heuristics.

5   Related Work

Automatic test data generation approaches were proposed in [4,16,36] and are based on greedy or meta-heuristic search strategy. They use search algorithms to extract test paths from the control flow graph of a program, then invoke an SMT solver to generate test data [16] and afterwards reduce the test-suite with a greedy algorithm. The drawback for this approach is that often infeasible paths are selected, resulting in significant wasted computational effort. We did not investigate test *data* generation here, only boolean inputs to a single decision.

Kitamura et al. [25] and Yang et al. [37] use a SAT solver to construct minimal MC/DC test suites. That is, the MC/DC criterion is encoded in a single query, and the solver produces a suitable assignment for test case inputs if it exists, or times out. In contrast to the exhaustive nature of SAT queries which may lead to timeouts, our approach delivers a single answer in much less time, but may require repetition to find an optimal solution.

Some of their results do not satisfy UC-MC/DC in some cases, and generate test cases only for Masking MC/DC. There are also some conditions which are reported as infeasible, while the MC/DC pairs for those conditions can be found. For example in [25], decisions 6 and 8 of the TCAS II benchmarks have test suites with 3 and 4 test cases for 8 and 9 conditions respectively which cannot satisfy MC/DC.

A study of enhanced MC/DC coverage criterion for software testing based on n-cube graphs and gray code is presented in [8]. It is an exhaustive approach that takes input as a Boolean expression, builds the n-cube graph, and deduces test cases from all vertices of the graph. Their test cases selection is based on the weight of each test case in a similar way that we calculate the reuse factor of a path. The main difference is that they have to construct the n-cube graph which have the same effect as exhaustive traversal of a truth table and the resulting size of the test suite is not minimal.

Gay et al. [14,15], developed a technique to automatically generate test cases using model checkers for masking MC/DC. Using the JKind model checker, they produce a list of all test inputs and then select the desired test cases while preserving the coverage effectiveness. Their test suite reduction algorithm used to reduced the original test-suite does not guarantee to find the smallest set. They tested their approaches on different real-world avionics systems where they achieved an average MC/DC coverage of 67.67%.

Comar et al. [12] discussed MC/DC coverage in terms of BDD coverage. They examine the set of distinct paths through the BDD that have been taken based on the control flow graph. Based on BDDs they investigated the formalization and comparison of MC/DC to object branch coverage, but the test cases selection is out of their scope. We extend the formalization and definitions of MC/DC in terms of BDDs in the context of test cases selection.

The roBDDs have been used in [17,22] for test cases generation, and highlight the properties and benefits of roBDDs, however, MC/DC was not considered as coverage criterion. Like our approach, their greedy approach incrementally selects a pair of paths where only one condition changes for every condition.

6   Conclusion and Future Works

We presented a heuristics-based approach for generating test cases for a Boolean decision (given as roBDD) that satisfy the MC/DC criterion. We evaluate our approach on the TCAS II Benchmark and results shows that we frequently find solutions which are equal or close to the minimal number of test cases without expensive back-tracking.

Our approach is sensitive to variable ordering in the BDD as each order yields a different roBDD. We obtained MC/DC solutions of size $n + 1$ by performing few permutations of conditions in a decision for all tested decisions. We present also the other possible solutions which show full MC/DC coverage. In general, our solutions have a size ranging from $n + 1$ to $2n$, with a high percentage of size $n + 1$ or $n + 2$ solutions, where even the latter, although not optimal, may be acceptable to a user. We proposed different heuristics and compared their properties. All our heuristics perform better than $\mathcal{H}_{RR}$. $\mathcal{H}_{LPB}$ and $\mathcal{H}_{LMMB}$ out-perform all other heuristics with 10 times (50%) having highest percentage of $n + 1$ solutions. We recommend $\mathcal{H}_{LPB}$ since it is 10% better than $\mathcal{H}_{LMMB}$.

For the future work we plan to extend our algorithm so that we support data input coverage where conditions are not abstracted, which requires taking constraints into consideration. We will also attempt to integrate our test case generation algorithm into our MC/DC measurement tool and model [2,3].

Although the experimental data shows that we always find an optimal solution, it remains open if this is a general property of our approach.

References

1. Adacore. Technical report on OBC/MCDC properties. Technical report, Couverture project (2010)
2. Ahishakiye, F., Jakšić, S., Stolz, V., Lange, F.D., Schmitz, M., Thoma, D.: Nonintrusive MC/DC measurement based on traces. In: International Symposium on Theoretical Aspects of Software Engineering (TASE), pp. 86–92. IEEE (2019)
3. Ahishakiye, F., Requeno Jarabo, J.I., Kristensen, L.M., Stolz, V.: Coverage analysis of net inscriptions in coloured Petri net models. In: Ben Hedia, B., Chen, Y.-F., Liu, G., Yu, Z. (eds.) VECoS 2020. LNCS, vol. 12519, pp. 68–83. Springer, Cham (2020). https://doi.org/10.1007/978-3-030-65955-4_6
4. Awedikian, Z., Ayari, K., Antoniol, G.: MC/DC automatic test input data generation. In: Annual Conference on Genetic and Evolutionary Computation Conference (GECCO), pp. 1657–1664. ACM (2009)
5. Bordin, M., Comar, C., Gingold, T., Guitton, J., Hainque, O., Quinot, T.: Object and source coverage for critical applications with the COUVERTURE open analysis framework. In: European Congress Embedded Real Time Software and Systems (ERTS), pp. 1–9 (2010)
6. Certification Authorities Software Team (CAST). Rationale for accepting masking MC/DC in certification projects. Technical Report: Position Paper CAST-6 (2001)
7. Certification Authorities Software Team (CAST). What is a "Decision" in application of Modified Condition/Decision Coverage (MC/DC) and Decision Coverage (DC)? Technical Report: Position Paper CAST-10 (2002)
8. Chang, J.-R., Huang, C.-Y.: A study of enhanced MC/DC coverage criterion for software testing. In: Annual International Computer Software and Applications Conference (COMPSAC), pp. 457–464 (2007)
9. Chilenski, J.J.: An investigation of three forms of the modified condition decision coverage (MC/DC) criterion. Technical report, Office of Aviation Research (2001)
10. Chilenski, J.J., Miller, S.P.: Applicability of modified condition/decision coverage to software testing. Softw. Eng. J. 9(5), 193–200 (1994)
11. Clarke, E.M., Jr., Grumberg, O., Peled, D.A.: Model Checking. MIT Press, Cambridge (1999)
12. Comar, C., Guitton, J., Hainque, O., Quinot, T.: Formalization and comparison of MC/DC and object branch coverage criteria. In: European Congress Embedded Real Time Software and Systems (ERTS), pp. 1–10 (2011)
13. Drake, C.R.: PyEDA: data structures and algorithms for electronic design automation. In: Python in Science Conference (SciPy) (2015)
14. Gay, G., Rajan, A., Staats, M., Whalen, M., Heimdahl, M.P.E.: The effect of program and model structure on the effectiveness of MC/DC test adequacy coverage. ACM Trans. Softw. Eng. Methodol. 25(3), 1–34 (2016)
15. Gay, G., Staats, M., Whalen, M., Heimdahl, M.P.E.: The risks of coverage-directed test case generation. IEEE Trans. Softw. Eng. 41(8), 803–819 (2015)
16. Ghani, K., Clark, J.A.: Automatic test data generation for multiple condition and MC/DC coverage. In: International Conference on Software Engineering Advances (ICSEA), pp. 152–157 (2009)

17. Gong, H., Li, J., Li, R.: CTFTP: a test case generation strategy for general Boolean expressions based on ordered binary label-driven Petri nets. IEEE Access **8**, 174516–174529 (2020)
18. Halin, A., Nuttinck, A., Acher, M., Devroey, X., Perrouin, G., Baudry, B.: Test them all, is it worth it? Assessing configuration sampling on the JHipster Web development stack. Empir. Softw. Eng. **24**(2), 674–717 (2019)
19. Hallé, S., La Chance, E., Gaboury, S.: Graph methods for generating test cases with universal and existential constraints. In: El-Fakih, K., Barlas, G., Yevtushenko, N. (eds.) ICTSS 2015. LNCS, vol. 9447, pp. 55–70. Springer, Cham (2015). https://doi.org/10.1007/978-3-319-25945-1_4
20. Hu, A.J.: Formal hardware verification with BDDs: an introduction. In: IEEE Pacific Rim Conference on Communications, Computers and Signal Processing (PACRIM), vol. 2, pp. 677–682. IEEE (1997)
21. Jones, J.A., Harrold, M.J.: Test-suite reduction and prioritization for modified condition/decision coverage. IEEE Trans. Softw. Eng. **29**(3), 195–209 (2003)
22. Kalaee, A., Rafe, V.: An optimal solution for test case generation using ROBDD graph and PSO algorithm. Qual. Reliab. Eng. Int. **32**(7), 2263–2279 (2016)
23. Kandl, S., Chandrashekar, S.: Reasonability of MC/DC for safety-relevant software implemented in programming languages with short-circuit evaluation. Computing **97**(3), 261–279 (2014). https://doi.org/10.1007/s00607-014-0418-5
24. Kangoye, S., Todoskoff, A., Barreau, M.: Practical methods for automatic MC/DC test case generation of Boolean expressions. In: IEEE AUTOTESTCON, pp. 203–212. IEEE (2015)
25. Kitamura, T., Maissonneuve, Q., Choi, E.-H., Artho, C., Gargantini, A.: Optimal test suite generation for modified condition decision coverage using SAT solving. In: Gallina, B., Skavhaug, A., Bitsch, F. (eds.) SAFECOMP 2018. LNCS, vol. 11093, pp. 123–138. Springer, Cham (2018). https://doi.org/10.1007/978-3-319-99130-6_9
26. Meinel, C., Theobald, T.: Algorithms and Data Structures in VLSI Design, 1st edn. Springer, Heidelberg (1998). https://doi.org/10.1007/978-3-642-58940-9
27. Newton, J., Verna, D.: A theoretical and numerical analysis of the worst-case size of reduced ordered binary decision diagrams. ACM Trans. Comput. Log. **20**(1), 1–36 (2019)
28. Pothon, F.: DO-178C/ED-12C versus DO-178B/ED-12B: changes and improvements. Technical report, AdaCore (2012). https://www.adacore.com/books/do-178c-vs-do-178b
29. Reda, S., Salem, A.M.: Combinational equivalence checking using Boolean satisfiability and binary decision diagrams. In: Design, Automation and Test in Europe. Conference and Exhibition (DATE), pp. 122–126. IEEE (2001)
30. Rierson, L.: Developing Safety-Critical Software: A Practical Guide for Aviation Software and DO-178C Compliance. CRC Press (2013)
31. Tassey, G.: The economic impacts of inadequate infrastructure for software testing (2002)
32. Vilkomir, S.A., Bowen, J.P.: Reinforced condition/decision coverage (RC/DC): a new criterion for software testing. In: Bert, D., Bowen, J.P., Henson, M.C., Robinson, K. (eds.) ZB 2002. LNCS, vol. 2272, pp. 291–308. Springer, Heidelberg (2002). https://doi.org/10.1007/3-540-45648-1_15
33. Weyuker, E., Goradia, T., Singh, A.: Automatically generating test data from a Boolean specification. IEEE Trans. Softw. Eng. **20**(5), 353–363 (1994)
34. Weyuker, E.J., Weiss, S.N., Hamlet, D.: Comparison of program testing strategies. In: Symposium on Testing, Analysis, and Verification (TAV), pp. 1–10. ACM (1991)

35. Worrell, J.: Logic and proofs-binary decision diagrams. https://www.cs.ox.ac.uk/people/james.worrell/lec5-2015.pdf
36. Wu, T., Yan, J., Zhang, J.: Automatic test data generation for unit testing to achieve MC/DC criterion. In: International Conference on Software Security and Reliability (SERE), pp. 118–126. IEEE Computer Society (2014)
37. Yang, L., Yan, J., Zhang, J.: Generating minimal test set satisfying MC/DC criterion via SAT based approach. In: Annual ACM Symposium on Applied Computing (SAC), pp. 1899–1906. ACM (2018)

Software Quality

Predicting and Monitoring Bug-Proneness at the Feature Level

Shaozhi Wei, Ran Mo^(✉), Pu Xiong, Siyuan Zhang, Yang Zhao, and Zengyang Li

School of Computer, Central China Normal University, Wuhan, China
wsz@mails.ccnu.edu.cn, moran@mail.ccnu.edu.cn, zengyangli@ccnu.edu.cn

Abstract. Enabling quick feature modification and delivery is important for a project's success. Obtaining early estimates of software features' bug-proneness is helpful for effectively allocating resources to the bug-prone features requiring further fixes. Researchers have proposed various studies on bug prediction at different granularity levels, such as class level, package level, method level, etc. However, there exists little work building predictive models at the feature level. In this paper, we investigated how to predict bug-prone features and monitor their evolution. More specifically, we first identified a project's features and their involved files. Next, we collected a suite of code metrics and selected a relevant set of metrics as attributes to be used for six machine learning algorithms to predict bug-prone features. Through our evaluation, we have presented that using the machine learning algorithms with an appropriate set of code metrics, we can build effective models of bug prediction at the feature level. Furthermore, we build regression models to monitor growth trends of bug-prone features, which shows how these features accumulate bug-proneness over time.

Keywords: Code metrics · Machine learning · Feature bug prediction

1 Introduction

Bug prediction has been an active research area for decades, numerous studies have been proposed to predict the most bug-prone software units at different granularity levels [5,14,15,18,24,30,33,36], such as class level, package level, method level, module level, etc. For example, Giger et al. [14] developed bug prediction models at method level. Gyimothy et al. [15] predicted the failure-proneness at class level. Schroter et al. [36] and Nagappan et al. [33] have proposed to predict defects at package and module levels respectively.

However, there has been little work that investigates to build bug prediction models at feature level. A recent work by Wan et al. [42] has presented that defect prediction at the feature level is the most preferred level of granularity by practitioners, such bug predictions could help practitioners gain an insight into software quality at the feature level. Being able to rapidly delivery and modify

© Springer Nature Switzerland AG 2021
S. Qin et al. (Eds.): SETTA 2021, LNCS 13071, pp. 201–218, 2021.
https://doi.org/10.1007/978-3-030-91265-9_11

features is important for a project's success [11,31], it is helpful to obtain early estimates on the bug-proneness of features. Such estimates could identify bug-prone features requiring further modifications, which helps developers effectively and efficiently allocate resources to the bug-prone features to assist in quick fixings.

In this paper, we focused our investigations on developing bug prediction models at the feature level and monitoring how bug-prone features accumulate bug-proneness over time. To proceed our study, we first leveraged a feature detection method in [31] to identify all features in a project. For each identified feature, we calculated its code metrics and labeled it either as *bug-prone* or *not bug-prone* based on this feature's bug-proneness calculated from a project's bug data. Next, to address the difficulty caused by noisy or redundant independent variables in each dataset, we leveraged CFS method [17] to select an appropriate set of code metrics for each dataset. Using the selected code metrics as the input attributes, we applied six machine learning algorithms to develop bug prediction models at the feature level. Furthermore, we monitor the evolution of each bug-prone feature. The accurate prediction could help developers identify which features are likely to be bug-pone, and monitoring their evolution could help developers further to understand how each feature has been accumulating bug-proneness over time.

Based on our evaluation analyses on six open source projects, we have found that, by using machine learning techniques and an appropriate set of code metrics, we can build predictive models which accurately predict bug-prone features. However, different projects may need different sets of code metrics as input attributes. Besides, we analyzed how a bug-prone feature evolves over time with respect to its bug-proneness. We have found that 47.8%, 18.9%, and 33.2% of all bug-prone features could fit into linear, exponential and logarithmic regression models respectively, indicating these features have been accumulating bug-proneness steadily, drastically or slowly.

This work extends the state of the art as follows:

- To the best of our knowledge, our work is the first empirical study on predicting bug-proneness at feature level. This work reports how to systematically build feature-level bug prediction models by using code metrics and machine learning techniques.
- We investigate whether a single set of code metrics are generalized to all projects on predicting bug-proneness at the feature level.
- Instead of just building predictive models, we extend to build regression models which could help analyze and monitor how a project's bug-prone features accumulate bug-proneness over time.

2   Background and Related Work

Bug prediction has been extensively studied in the past decades. Researchers have proposed numerous predictive models at different granularity levels, such as method level, class level, file level, package level, module level etc.

2.1   Bug Prediction at Class or File Level

Numerous studies have been proposed to predict bug-prone classes or files in a software project. Gyimothy et al. [15] calculated the code metrics from the source code of Mozilla, then based on these metrics, they leveraged two statistical methods and two machine learning techniques to predict the failure-proneness of each class. In the study of Ostrand et al. [34], the authors developed a negative binomial regression model using file size and file change information, and demonstrated the model could effectively predict the expected number of faults in each file in the next release of a software project. Cataldo et al.'s work [5] reported a strong correlation between density of change coupling and failure proneness of a file. Yan et al.'s study [43] used both supervised and unsupervised models to predict defects at file level and compared the effectiveness of two types of prediction models.

2.2   Bug Prediction at Method Level

Researchers have also studied various bug prediction models at method level. For example, Kim et al. [24] proposed a model which could accurately predict future faults at method level by using cached histories. Giger et al.'s study [14] investigated to build bug prediction models at method level. The authors presented that their models based on method-level code metrics and change metrics could be used to accurately predict bug-prone methods. They also showed that change metrics outperformed source code metrics on bug prediction, and presented that their models are robust with respect to different distributions of samples. Hata et al. [18] extracted method-level histories and developed bug prediction model at method level by using the extracted histories. Their results presented that method-level bug prediction consumed less effort to find bugs than both package-level and file-level predictions. Yang et al.'s research [44] analyzed the relationship between dependency clusters and fault proneness at function (method) level. They demonstrated that their function-level prediction model could significantly increase the performance of fault-proneness prediction, and the inter-dependent functions are often more fault-prone than the other functions.

2.3   Bug Prediction at Coarse-Grained Level

Defect prediction at a coarse granularity has also been widely studied to facilitate understanding the bug-proneness of software systems. For example, Schroter et al. [36] leveraged failure history at different levels and the usage relationships between components to predict fault-prone components, and demonstrated that the prediction model using package-level defect history could have a better performance. Mishra et al. [30] proposed an approach of Support Vector based Fuzzy Classification System (SVFCS), which combined the advantages of SVM, FIS and Genetic algorithms to effectively predict defects at package level. Menzies et al. [29] applied Naive Bayes learner on a set of complexity metrics to predict module-level defects. They presented that the static code metrics should be treated as probabilistic, not categorical indicators, and these code metrics could be used to accurately predict defects at module level. Nagappan et al. [33] found that fault-prone software modules are statistically correlated with code complexity measures. The authors investigated various complexity metrics and demonstrated that these metrics were useful and successful for defect prediction. They also demonstrated there was no single set of metrics could be the best predictors in all projects.

2.4   Bug Prediction at Other Granularity Levels

Considering a software system could be structured as many interacting software entities at multiple granularity perspectives, such as component level, subsystem level, file level, etc. Zimmermann et al.'s work [46] explored the effective predictors for cross-project bug prediction. Mockus and Weiss [32] investigated change-level defect prediction, that is, examining the probability that a change to software will cause a failure. They used the properties of a change to be the predictors, such as added or deleted LOC in a change, the number of files and modules affected by a change, the type of a change. Their results showed that their approach was useful for predicting new failures. Kamei et al. [23] proposed an effort-aware linear regression (EALR) model for the defect prediction at change level. Yang et al. [45] also proposed a LT model for just-in-time change-level defect prediction, and compared the performance of unsupervised and supervised approaches.

As we have shown in the above studies, bug prediction at different granularity levels has been widely studied. Our study complementarily contributes to this field by investigating bug prediction at the feature level using code metrics and machine learning algorithms. Moreover, we provide regression models to represent how the bug-prone features evolve over time.

3   Study Design

3.1   Feature Identification

The objective of this work is to come up with bug prediction models at the feature level. For this purpose, we first need to identify features of software projects. Mo et al. [31] recently proposed an approach to identify features by examining a project's revision history and issue tracking system. They also demonstrated that features identified by their approach could form a maintenance unit that should be maintained and developed separately. Our work treats each feature as a software unit separately, predicts and monitors the bug-proneness of each unit at the feature level. Therefore, following the technique in [31], we identified each feature by matching a *new feature* ticket within a commit.

For example, Fig. 1 shows a Git commit from one of our studied projects. Based on the message of this commit, we can observe that 1) this commit is made to implement the issue, AMQ-5123, which is labeled as a *new feature* in this project's JIRA[1] issue tracking system; 2) Five java files were changed for this commit. Thus, we could extract a feature, which consists of all these java files. If there exists multiple commits in revision history for the same feature (i.e. multiple commits labeled with the same *new feature* ID), we then consider the feature contains the union of all involved files. After examining a project's revision history and issue tacking records, we can identify all features in this project, and for each feature, we can know its involved files.

```
commit 5da7ab3c0ee027a29c328e48614ffe1a69401577
Author: Hiram Chirino <hiram@hiramchirino.com>
Date:   2014-03-27 13:10:28 -0400

    Implements AMQ-5123: Optionally support encrypted passwords in ActiveMQ users.properties file.

activemq-console/src/main/java/org/apache/activemq/console/command/DecryptCommand.java
activemq-console/src/main/java/org/apache/activemq/console/command/EncryptCommand.java
activemq-console/src/main/java/org/apache/activemq/console/command/ShellCommand.java
activemq-jaas/src/main/java/org/apache/activemq/jaas/EncryptionSupport.java
activemq-jaas/src/main/java/org/apache/activemq/jaas/PrincipalProperties.java
```

Fig. 1. An example commit for feature identification

3.2 Attributes: Code Metrics

In this paper, we leveraged ten code metrics to build our bug prediction models at the feature level. These metrics could represent a software project's characteristics, and all of them have been widely used for bug prediction at different granularity levels [5,14,25,29,30,33,41]. In this paper, we presented how these metrics could be used for building predictive models at feature level. Next, we briefly described each of the code metrics as follows:

– *Cyclomatic complexity.* McCabe [28] proposed *cyclomatic complexity* to measure the code complexity by calculating the number of linearly independent paths through a program's source code. The higher of the metric value, the more complex the source code is.
– *CK metrics suite.* Chidamber and Kemerer [6] proposed six metrics which focus on measuring the characteristics of Object-oriented programs. We briefly introduced these metrics as follows: 1) WMC: the number of local methods in a class; 2) DIT: the maximum depth of the inheritance tree in a class; 3) NOC: the number of immediate subclassess of a class; 4) CBO: the number of other classes that are coupled to this class; 5) RFC: the sum of number of methods called within the class's bodies and the number of class's methods; and 6) LCOM: the number of methods in a class that are not related through the sharing of some of the class's fields.

---

[1] https://www.atlassian.com/software/jira.

– **Fan-in and Fan-out.** Fan-in is calculated as the number of calling subprograms and the number of global variables read by a class; Fan-out is calculated as the number of called subprograms and the number of global variables set by a class.
– **Lines of Code (LOC).** LOC is the number of lines of code in a file. This size metric has been widely accepted among the software engineering community. Various studies [25,41] have demonstrated that LOC could be used as an effective indicator for bug prediction.

Given a project's source code as input, we calculated these code metrics by using a static analysis tool, Understand[2]. In order to have all metrics apply to features, we summarized the metrics across each feature. For each metric X, we computed the total number per feature. As an example, considering the WMC metric, which counts the number of local methods per class, we calculated the sum of WMC of all files[3] involved in a feature to be the WMC of this feature.

3.3   Labeled Classes: Bug-Prone and Not Bug-Prone Feature

In this work, the developed prediction models are used to predict the outcome labels for each upcoming feature, that is, to classify an upcoming feature as *bug-prone* or *not bug-prone*.

Bug Data. To quantify the bug-proneness of a *feature*. We first proposed a history measure, Bug Rate (BR), which represents the bug-proneness of a *file*. To calculate a file's bug rate, we mined a project's revision history and bug reports by using the pattern matching method in [38]: if a bug ticket ID recorded in the bug tracking reports was identified in a commit's message, then we thought this commit was made for a bug fix, and each file in this commit were considered to be changed once for a bug fix. After analyzing all these bug-fixing commits, we could calculate each file's bug rate, which indicates how many times a file has been changed for bug fixes. To have this bug rate measure apply to features, we then calculated the sum of bug rates of all files involved in a feature to be the bug rate of this feature. A feature with a higher value of bug rate will be considered as more bug-prone.

Labeling. Our study trains and validates the prediction models at feature level with the binary target classes. Therefore, we labeled each feature in our dataset either as bug-prone or not bug-prone as follows:

$$Feature = \begin{cases} \text{bug-prone,} & \text{if } BR \geq P_t \\ \text{not bug-prone,} & otherwise \end{cases} \qquad (1)$$

where P_t represents the value at a particular percentile rank following the distribution of all features' bug rates per project. A feature will be terms as bug-prone if its bug rate ranks above the particular percentile. In this work,

---

[2] https://scitools.com/.
[3] In this paper, a file means a source file which contains one or more classes. A feature often contains multiple files.

we studied two levels of bug-proneness, denoted to $BR_{80_{th}}$ and $BR_{65_{th}}$. Using $BR_{80_{th}}$ as an example, if a feature's bug rate ranks over 80_{th} percentile in a project, meaning that this feature's bug rate is large than 80% of all features in the project, we then labeled this feature as *bug-prone*. Otherwise we labeled this feature as *not bug-prone*. To substantiate our analysis, we also studied the bug-proneness level of $BR_{65_{th}}$, where the bug rates of features that termed as *bug-prone* rank above 65_{th} percentile, meaning that these features are more bug-prone than 65% of all features in a project in terms of the bug rate measure.

3.4 Machine Learning Algorithms

We leveraged six supervised machine learning algorithms to build models for feature-level bug prediction. We conducted the predictions by using the default setting of Weka[4] tool, which contains a collection of machine learning algorithms for data mining tasks. Next, we briefly described various machine learning techniques used in our study.

- *Decision Tree (DT)* classifies data or predicts values by using a tree representation where each leaf node indicates a class label and the internal nodes of this tree represent the attributes of the data.
- *Naive Bayes (NB)* is one of the simple probabilistic classifiers [26]. Naive Bayes algorithm leverages Bayes Theorem to calculate the conditional probability of all classes from the training data, and assumes the attributes to be independent.
- *K-Nearest Neighbors (KNN)* is a non-parametric, lazy learning algorithm, which could be used to classify new samples based on a similarity measure [9].
- *Random Forest (RF)* is an ensemble of decision trees, which could build predictive models for classification [4]. It outputs the class by using the average results from its included decision trees to improve the predictive accuracy and control over-fitting of the decision trees.
- *Multilayer Perceptron (MLP)* is a class of feedforward artificial neural network. A MLP contains at least three layers that simulate the biological neurons [19]: an input layer for receiving data; an output layer for making a decision; and one or more hidden layers acting as computational engines.
- *Support Vector Machine (SVM)* is a discriminative classifier formally defined by a separating hyper-plane [8]. Given a set of labeled training samples, an SVM training algorithm could build a model to output an optimal hyper-plan which could differentiate new samples into one category or the other.

3.5 Researched Projects

To conduct our evaluation, we analyzed six open source projects with different size and in different domains: ActiveMQ[5] is a multi-protocol, Java-based mes-

---

[4] https://www.cs.waikato.ac.nz/~ml/weka/.
[5] http://activemq.apache.org/.

saging server; Camel[6] is an Integration framework; Cassandra[7] is a distributed NoSQL database management system; Hibernate ORM[8] is an object-relational mapping framework for java environments; Hive[9] is a data warehouse software infrastructure; Wicket[10] is a component-based web application framework.

For each project, we selected its latest release as our subject, Table 1 shows the basic facts for each studied project. Column "Rel." indicates the selected release of each project. Column "#Files" shows the number of files in the selected release of a project. For each project, our analysis just focuses on its source files, so all test or example files have been filtered out. Column "#Com." shows the number of commits extracted from the studied revision history of each project. Column "#Ft" shows the number of identified features from each project. Column "#Bugs" presents the number of bug issues calculated by examining a project's bug reports and revision history. Column "History" shows the number of months of each project's revision history we studied, from its beginning to the selected release date.

Table 1. Researched projects

	Rel	#Files	#Com.	#Ft	#Bugs	History
ActiveMQ	5.15.9	2,526	6,091	205	1,695	159
Camel	2.21.5	8,697	21,1260	968	2,776	142
Cassandra	3.11.4	1,744	14,701	270	2,914	119
Hibernate	5.4.1	4,073	5,686	141	1,506	138
Hive	2.3.4	4,203	7,785	403	4,921	122
Wicket	8.3.0	2,558	12,255	110	1,701	172

4 Evaluation

4.1 Research Questions

We proceeded our empirical study by investigating the following research questions:

RQ1: Is there a single set of metrics that predicts bug-prone features over all projects?

RQ2: Can we build effective bug prediction models at the feature level?

RQ3: Is it possible to monitor the bug-proneness of bug-prone features?

---

[6] http://camel.apache.org/.
[7] http://cassandra.apache.org/.
[8] http://hibernate.org/.
[9] https://hive.apache.org/.
[10] https://wicket.apache.org/.

Using a set of code metrics as attributes often encounters the issue of Multi-collinearity due to the existence of inter-correlations among the metrics. Thus, we first analyzed whether there exists a single set of code metrics which is generalized to all projects (RQ1).

Then we investigated how to build bug prediction models at the feature level, and whether the developed models could effectively predict a feature as *bug-prone* or *not bug-prone* (RQ2); Accurate prediction would identify the features that are likely to be bug-pone, which helps developers efficiently allocate resources for quick fixings.

Furthermore, we explored to model and monitor growth trends of the bug-prone features (RQ3). Positive answer to RQ3 would help developers understand how each bug-prone feature evolve over time in terms of bug-proneness, and even guide future modifications.

4.2 Prediction Model Development

To develop bug prediction models with code metrics and machine learning techniques, we used the ten-fold cross validation technique [40]. In ten-fold cross-validation, the original dataset will be randomly divided into 10 subsets with equal size. Next, the technique will iteratively performs 10 times where nine subsets will be used for training and the other one will be used for validation. During each iteration, a subset will be used exactly once as the validation data. The results from 10 folds would then be summarized to present a single estimation. The advantage of this technique is that all observations are used for both training and validation, thus could reduce validation bias [10,35].

4.3 Evaluation Method

In order to evaluate the performance of our bug prediction models at the feature level, we selected three widely used performance metrics: *Accuracy, F-measure* and *AUC*.

We first selected a traditional metric, *Accuracy*, which indicates the ratio of the number of correct predictions to the total number of input samples. However, accuracy may not work very well when prediction models are applied on imbalanced data (i.e., the number of samples belonging to each class is different) [13,20]. *F-measure* takes both precision and recall into consideration, it is the *Harmonic Mean* between precision and recall which assesses how precise and how robust a classifier is [7,39]. Besides, various studies [20,37,39] proposed ROC analysis and demonstrated that Area Under ROC Curve (AUC) could effectively reflect the performance of prediction models built on imbalanced data, which just likes our dataset where the distributions of two classes (bug-prone or not bug-prone) are imbalanced. AUC could effectively deal with the skewness from class distributions.

4.4   Results

RQ1: Is there a single set of metrics that predicts bug-prone features over all projects?

One difficulty from using a set of metrics as attributes is the issue of multi-collinearity among metrics, since there often exists inter-correlations among the code metrics, which causes noisy and redundant independent variables from each dataset [12,17]. Thus, the initial step in building prediction models is often to select the relevant set of attributes to be used in a ML algorithm. Attribute selection methods [3,12,17] have been widely studied for reducing the dimensionality of attribute space and removing redundant or noisy attributes. In our paper, we leveraged the Correlation-based Feature Selection (CFS) method to select an appropriate set of attributes for building prediction models. Hall's work [17] has shown that the CFS method could identify the attributes that have high individual predictive ability on the class, but are not correlated between each other. Moreover, numerous existing studies [2,10,27] have used the CFS method and demonstrated its effectiveness in attribute selection for developing prediction models.

We conducted attribute selections for both bug-proneness levels. For each project, we applied CFS method on its two datasets, and the attributes selected from each dataset are shown in Table 2. According to this table, the first straight-forward observation to make is that:

all the ten code metrics have been selected more than once for building feature-level prediction models, but there isn't a single set of metrics that has been selected for predicting bug-prone features over all projects. Even for the same project, if we choose different bug-proneness level for labeling, the selected attributes could be different. This result is consistent to the other work at different granularity levels [14,33].

> **Answer:** There is no single set of code metrics is suitable for the feature-level bug prediction over all projects.

RQ2: Is it possible to build effective bug prediction models at the feature level?

To answer this question, we used the selected attributes (discussed in RQ1) in the six machine learning algorithms to build prediction models for each dataset (each project has two datasets derived from both two bug-proneness levels). Table 3 shows the effectiveness of our predictive models reflected by the performance metrics. Column 3–5 show the *Accuracy, F-measure* and *AUC* values with respect to $BR_{80_{th}}$ bug-proneness level. Similarly, column 6–8 show values of the three performance metrics with respect to $BR_{65_{th}}$.

Using column 3–5 at the first row in Table 3 as an example, where the bug-proneness level of $BR_{80_{th}}$ was adopted to label *bug-prone* or *not bug-prone* features. We applied Decision Tree (DT) algorithm with the selected code metrics: *WMC, NOC, CBO, DIT, LCOM, Fan-out* (discussed in Table 2) to develop a

Table 2. Selected code metrics after applying CFS method

	Bug-proneness level: $BR_{80_{th}}$
ActiveMQ	WMC, NOC, CBO, DIT, LCOM, Fan-out
Camel	NOC, CBO, Cyclomatic, Fan-in
Cassandra	WMC, CBO
Hibernate	WMC, CBO, RFC, Fan-in, LOC
Hive	Fan-in, LOC
Wicket	WMC, NOC, RFC, Fan-in
	Bug-proneness level: $BR_{65_{th}}$
ActiveMQ	NOC, CBO, RFC, LCOM, Fan-out
Camel	NOC, CBO, Cyclomatic, Fan-in, LOC
Cassandra	CBO, DIT, Cyclomatic, Fan-out, LOC
Hibernate	CBO, LCOM, Cyclomatic, Fan-out, LOC
Hive	Fan-in, LOC
Wicket	WMC, NOC, Cyclomatic, Fan-in

bug prediction model. The results show that the developed prediction model achieves a very good performance: *Accuracy* is 93.2%, *F-measure* is 0.929 and *AUC* is 0.838. According to the whole Table 3, we can observe that, for all the values of the three performance metrics, most of them (79% of all metric values) are higher than 0.8, and many of them (35% of all metric values) are even higher than 0.9. As a result, we believe that we are able to effectively build bug prediction model at the feature level by leveraging ML algorithms with an appropriate set of code metrics.

Answer: Using an appropriate set of code metrics for each dataset, we could apply machine learning techniques to build feature-level bug prediction models achieving high *Accuracy*, *F-measure* and *AUC*.

RQ3: Is it possible to monitor the bug-proneness of features?

So far we could use the developed prediction models to accurately classify a feature as bug-prone or not bug-prone. In this way, we can help development teams efficiently allocate resources to the bug-prone features for quick fixings. Besides, *could we monitor how each bug-prone feature accumulate bugs-proneness over time?* If so, development teams would be able to model the growth trends of each feature's bug-proneness, and guide possible future modifications. Using this kind of information, development teams could assess the severity of each bug-prone feature, rank even prioritize each feature's possible fixes. For example, if $feature_i$'s bug-proneness increases exponentially, and $feature_j$'s bug-proneness increases smoothly, we may rank $feature_i$ with a higher priority for future modifications.

Table 3. Results of prediction models using different ML techniques

Project	ML	$BR_{80_{th}}$			$BR_{65_{th}}$		
		ACC	F-m	AUC	ACC	F-m	AUC
ActiveMQ	DT	0.932	0.929	0.838	0.854	0.855	0.883
	NB	0.898	0.896	0.935	0.834	0.824	0.865
	KNN	0.888	0.888	0.855	0.878	0.878	0.866
	RF	0.922	0.92	0.94	0.868	0.868	0.949
	MLP	0.907	0.905	0.943	0.849	0.841	0.907
	SVM	0.868	0.842	0.679	0.746	0.695	0.639
Camel	DT	0.90	0.896	0.902	0.831	0.830	0.864
	NB	0.885	0.881	0.892	0.79	0.771	0.844
	KNN	0.887	0.888	0.84	0.853	0.854	0.841
	RF	0.913	0.911	0.958	0.88	0.880	0.932
	MLP	0.888	0.882	0.888	0.813	0.810	0.862
	SVM	0.866	0.851	0.709	0.767	0.730	0.671
Cassandra	DT	0.863	0.865	0.866	0.881	0.881	0.893
	NB	0.774	0.744	0.697	0.644	0.566	0.685
	KNN	0.907	0.909	0.886	0.896	0.895	0.879
	RF	0.893	0.891	0.947	0.867	0.867	0.948
	MLP	0.874	0.869	0.921	0.837	0.836	0.911
	SVM	0.789	0.702	0.495	0.637	0.544	0.508
Hibernate	DT	0.922	0.922	0.909	0.823	0.826	0.786
	NB	0.901	0.896	0.918	0.78	0.757	0.880
	KNN	0.943	0.941	0.871	0.844	0.842	0.824
	RF	0.929	0.929	0.966	0.837	0.839	0.921
	MLP	0.922	0.921	0.925	0.801	0.796	0.904
	SVM	0.809	0.735	0.534	0.667	0.563	0.565
Hive	DT	0.916	0.919	0.912	0.913	0.914	0.926
	NB	0.806	0.766	0.855	0.677	0.598	0.814
	KNN	0.921	0.921	0.897	0.906	0.906	0.890
	RF	0.923	0.924	0.967	0.931	0.931	0.965
	MLP	0.916	0.919	0.950	0.898	0.899	0.950
	SVM	0.806	0.766	0.574	0.675	0.594	0.576
Wicket	DT	0.964	0.964	0.962	0.809	0.811	0.862
	NB	0.955	0.954	0.988	0.873	0.866	0.898
	KNN	0.955	0.954	0.904	0.909	0.910	0.909
	RF	0.936	0.936	0.968	0.873	0.873	0.946
	MLP	0.964	0.962	0.905	0.773	0.762	0.838
	SVM	0.809	0.739	0.543	0.673	0.566	0.538

At this step, we investigated how each of the bug-prone features accumulate bug-proneness during software evolution. To make a larger scope of investigation, we analyzed all the bug-prone features labeled at the bug-proneness level of $Bug_{65_{th}}$, since the set of bug-prone features at $Bug_{80_{th}}$ level is just a subset of it. To proceed this investigation, we first constructed an evolution sequence for each feature in terms of its bug rate: for each bug-prone feature, we back-forwardly calculated its bug rates based on different periods of revision history. For example, if $feature_i$ is one of the bug-prone features in project A, which was released in 2018-08, and the feature started to accumulate bugs (i.e. its bug rate became larger than 0, and started to increase) in 2016-10. For this $feature_i$, we back-forwardly decreased its history period by a 6-month history interval to calculate a series of values of the bug rate. In this way, we would calculate the bug rate sequence of $feature_i$ by using four history periods: 2016-10 - 2017-02, 2016-10 - 2017-08, 2016-10 - 2018-02, and 2016-10 - 2018-08. For all bug-prone features in our studied projects, we repeated the calculations to obtain all bug rate sequences.

Secondly, we selected three widely used regression models to simulate the growth trend of each feature's bug-proneness. The three models reflect three types of growth trends in practice:

- Linear Model. It indicates a feature's bug rate increases linearly, meaning that this feature has been accumulating bug-proneness steadily.
- Exponential Model. It indicates a feature's bug rate increases exponentially, meaning that this feature has been accumulating bug-proneness dramatically, and the speed becomes faster and faster;
- Logarithmic Model. It indicates a feature's bug rate increases slower and slower, meaning that this feature accumulated bug-proneness quickly at the beginning, but it is accumulating bug-proneness very slow now.

Given a sequence of bug rates of a feature, we modeled the feature's growth trend to one of the three models: linear, exponential and logarithmic regression models, which indicated the feature was accumulating bugs in different trends. For each feature, the regression model with highest R^2 would be selected to be the best fit for it. Besides, the P-value of each fitting model should be less than 0.05, which guarantees that the derived model is significant.

In this work, we categorized the regression models by following the guidelines in [16, 22], where the authors described $R^2 = 0.75$, 0.5 and 0.25 as substantial, moderate and weak models, respectively. We summarized all the fitting results in Table 4. Column "#Features" shows the total number of bug-prone features we analyzed for each project. Columns "Lin", "Exp" and "Log" present the number of features whose growth trends fit into linear, exponential or logarithmic models respectively. The following "P." columns show the corresponding ratios to the total number of bug-prone features. In the column of "$0.5 <= R^2 < 0.75$", we only used "Num" and "P." columns to show the number and percentage of the features fitted into a moderate model, that is, the R^2 ranges from 0.5 to 0.75.

Using "Camel" in Table 4 as an example, we can observe that 339 features were labeled as bug-prone at the bug-proneness level of $Bug_{65_{th}}$, and 99.7% of these features could be substantially modeled by the regression models

Table 4. Distribution of bug-prone features' regression models in terms of bug rate

Project	#Features	$R^2 >= 0.75$								$0.5 <= R^2 < 0.75$	
		Lin	P.	Exp	P.	Log	P.	Total	P.	Num	P.
ActiveMQ	72	72	100.0%	–	–	–	–	71	100.0%	–	–
Camel	339	122	36.0%	6	1.8%	210	61.9%	338	99.7%	1	0.3%
Cassandra	95	81	85%	–	–	14	15%	95	100%	–	–
Hibernate	50	44	88%	6	12%	–	–	50	100%	–	–
Hive	142	15	10.6%	127	89.4%	0	0%	142	100%	–	–
Wicket	39	18	46%	–	–	21	54%	39	100%	–	–
Total	737	352	47.8%	139	18.9%	245	33.2%	736	99.9%	1	0.1%

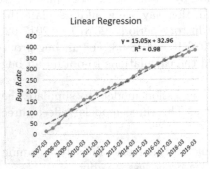

(a) An Example of Linear Regression

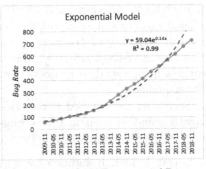

(b) An Example of Exponential Regression

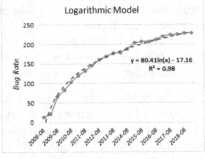

(c) An Example of Logarithmic Regression

Fig. 2. Example features fitting into different regression models

($R^2 >= 0.75$). 36.0% of all these features could fit into a linear model, meaning that these features has accumulated bug-proneness steadily. 1.8% and 61.9% of all these features could fit into the exponential and logarithmic models respectively. Only 1 feature, 0.3% of all the studied features, couldn't fit into a substantial, but fitted into a moderate regression model.

The last row of Table 4 presents that, considering all the studied features over all projects together, almost all of them (99.9%) could fit into a substantial regression model. 47.8% of them could be modeled by linear models. For both exponential and logarithmic models, there are 18.9%, 33.2% of all the studied features that follow a substantial fitting respectively.

Figure 2 shows the examples for all types of regression models derived from our studied features. Using Fig. 2a as an example to illustrate the results, we can observe that the selected release date of this project is "2019-03", and files in this feature started to accumulate bugs before 2007-03. The growth trend of this feature's bug rates is fitted into a linear model, which has a $R^2 = 0.98$, with a formula as: $y = 15.05x + 32.96$. Figure 2b and 2c show the cases where growth trends of these two features' bug-proneness fit into an exponential and a logarithmic regression model respectively.

Answer: In terms of the bug rate measure, almost all of the bug-prone features (99.9% of all bug-prone features) can substantially fit into a regression model, wherein 47.8%, 18.9% and 33.2% of all these features could fit into the linear, exponential and logarithmic models respectively. Thus, we can effectively monitor the bug-proneness of each bug-prone feature and present how this feature accumulates bugs over time.

---

5   Threats to Validity

First, to calculate the bug rate, we use the pattern matching method in [38] to identify a bug-fixing commit if its change message contains a bug ticket ID. A file's bug rate will be the number of times a files involved in bug-fixing commits. However, we cannot guarantee that the bug data extracted from revision history are not biased. Prior studies [1,21] have shown that: 1) a file changed in a bug-fixing commit doesn't necessarily implies this file is changed for a bug fix; 2) and there is sometimes no explicit link which could be used for targeting the bug-fixing commits in revision history. Thus findings with respect to the research questions could be impacted by the accuracy of available data. We acknowledge this is a threat to internal validity and requires more investigation.

Second, the selection of bug-proneness level may rise a threat to internal validity. We labeled each feature based on the bug rate measure. Different bug-proneness levels could lead to different distributions of labeled classes, which may have an influence on building the bug prediction models. To weaken the interference of noise in data result, we used both bug-proneness levels of $Bug_{65_{th}}$ and $Bug_{80_{th}}$. Our results have presented that, for both levels, our approach could develop accurate bug prediction models at the feature level. Besides, project practitioners could select bug-proneness level of the input dataset based on their own interests.

Third, a threat to external validity is in our data set. We only analyzed six open-source projects. To partially address this problem, we selected the projects having different sizes and in different domains.

Forth, we only analyzed the projects that use Git for version control and use JIRA for issue tracking, hence we can not claim that our results are generalizable to other projects managed by other version control or issue tracking systems. We are planning to repeat our experiments to a broader set of projects.

6   Conclusion

In this paper, we have studied how to develop bug prediction models at the feature level. More specifically, for each dataset, we selected an appropriate set of static code metrics as the attributes to be used for six machine learning algorithms, and developed a feature-level bug prediction model.

From our analyses on six open source projects, we have demonstrated that: based on an appropriate set of code metrics, we can apply machine learning algorithms to build feature-level bug prediction models achieving good performance in terms of *Accuracy*, *F-Measure* and *AUC* metrics. But there isn't a common set of code metrics applied to all studied projects; For all the bug-prone features, we can effectively model the growth trends of their bug-proneness, so that we can monitor how these bug-prone features accumulate bugs during software evolution.

Acknowledgments. This work is supported by the National Natural Science Foundation of China under the grant No. 62002129, the Hubei Provincial Natural Science Foundation of China under the grant No. 2020CFB473, and the Fundamental Research Funds for the Central Universities under the grant No. CCNU19TD003.

References

1. Antoniol, G., Ayari, K., Penta, M.D., Khomh, F., Gueheneuc, Y.-G.: Is it a bug or an enhancement?: a text-based approach to classify change requests. In: Proceedings of the 2008 Conference of the Center for Advanced Studies on Collaborative Research: Meeting of Minds, pp. 23:304–23:318 (2008)
2. Arisholm, E., Briand, L.C., Johannessen, E.B.: A systematic and comprehensive investigation of methods to build and evaluate fault prediction models. J. Syst. Softw. **83**(1), 2–17 (2010)
3. Blum, A.L., Langley, P.: Selection of relevant features and examples in machine learning. Artif. Intell. **97**(1–2), 245–271 (1997)
4. Breiman, L.: Random forests. Mach. Learn. **45**(1), 5–32 (2001)
5. Cataldo, M., Mockus, A., Roberts, J.A., Herbsleb, J.D.: Software dependencies, work dependencies, and their impact on failures. IEEE Trans. Softw. Eng. **35**(6), 864–878 (2009)
6. Chidamber, S.R., Kemerer, C.F.: A metrics suite for object oriented design. IEEE Trans. Softw. Eng. **20**(6), 476–493 (1994)
7. Chinchor, N.: MUC-4 evaluation metrics. In: Proceedings of the 4th Conference on Message Understanding, pp. 22–29 (1992)
8. Cortes, C., Vapnik, V.: Support-vector networks. Mach. Learn. **20**(3), 273–297 (1995)

9. Cover, T., Hart, P.: Nearest neighbor pattern classification. IEEE Trans. Inf. Theor. **13**(1), 21–27 (2006)
10. de Carvalho, A.B., Pozo, A., Vergilio, S.R.: A symbolic fault-prediction model based on multiobjective particle swarm optimization. J. Syst. Softw. **83**(5), 868–882 (2010)
11. Dit, B., Revelle, M., Gethers, M., Poshyvanyk, D.: Feature location in source code: a taxonomy and survey. J. Softw. Maint. Evol.: Res. Pract. **25**, 53–95 (2011)
12. Forman, G.: An extensive empirical study of feature selection metrics for text classification. J. Mach. Learn. Res. **3**, 1289–1305 (2003)
13. Gao, K., Khoshgoftaar, T.M., Napolitano, A.: Combining feature subset selection and data sampling for coping with highly imbalanced software data. Int. J. Softw. Eng. Knowl. Eng. 115–146 (2015)
14. Giger, E., D'Ambros, M., Pinzger, M., Gall, H.C.: Method-level bug prediction. In: Proceedings of the ACM-IEEE International Symposium on Empirical Software Engineering and Measurement, ESEM 2012, pp. 171–180 (2012)
15. Gyimothy, T., Ferenc, R., Siket, I.: Empirical validation of object-oriented metrics on open source software for fault prediction. IEEE Trans. Softw. Eng. **31**(10), 897–910 (2005)
16. Hair, J.F., Ringle, C.M., Sarstedt, M.: PLS-SEM: indeed a silver bullet. J. Mark. Theory Pract. **19**(2), 139–151 (2011)
17. Hall, M.A.: Correlation-based feature selection for discrete and numeric class machine learning. In: Proceedings of the Seventeenth International Conference on Machine Learning, pp. 359–366 (2000)
18. Hata, H., Mizuno, O., Kikuno, T.: Bug prediction based on fine-grained module histories. In: Proceedings of the 34th International Conference on Software Engineering, pp. 200–210 (2012)
19. Haykin, S.: Neural Networks: A Comprehensive Foundation. 2nd edn. (2004)
20. He, H., Garcia, E.A.: Learning from imbalanced data. IEEE Trans. Knowl. Data Eng. **21**(9), 1263–1284 (2009)
21. Herzig, K., Just, S., Zeller, A.: It's not a bug, it's a feature: how misclassification impacts bug prediction. In: Proceedings of the 2013 International Conference on Software Engineering, pp. 392–401 (2013)
22. Joseph, J., Hair, F., Hult, G.T.M., Ringle, C., Sarstedt, M.: A Primer on Partial Least Squares Structural Equation Modeling (PLS-SEM). Sage, Thousand Oak (2013)
23. Kamei, Y., et al.: A large-scale empirical study of just-in-time quality assurance. IEEE Trans. Softw. Eng. **39**(6), 757–773 (2013)
24. Kim, S., Zimmermann, T., James Whitehead, J.E., Zeller, A.: Predicting faults from cached history. In: Proceedings of 29thInternational Conference on Software Engineering, pp. 489–498 (2007)
25. Koru, A.G., Zhang, D., Emam, K.E., Liu, H.: An investigation into the functional form of the size-defect relationship for software modules. IEEE Trans. Softw. Eng. **35**(2), 293–304 (2009)
26. Lewis, D.D.: Naive (bayes) at forty: the independence assumption in information retrieval. In: Nédellec, C., Rouveirol, C. (eds.) ECML 1998. LNCS, vol. 1398, pp. 4–15. Springer, Heidelberg (1998). https://doi.org/10.1007/BFb0026666
27. Malhotra, R., Khanna, M.: An empirical study for software change prediction using imbalanced data. Empir. Softw. Eng. **22**(6), 2806–2851 (2017). https://doi.org/10.1007/s10664-016-9488-7
28. McCabe, T.J.: A complexity measure. IEEE Trans. Softw. Eng. **2**(4), 308–320 (1976)

29. Menzies, T., Greenwald, J., Frank, A.: Data mining static code attributes to learn defect predictors. IEEE Trans. Softw. Eng. **33**(1), 2–13 (2007)
30. Mishra, B., Engg, C., Shukla, K.: Defect prediction for object oriented software using support vector based fuzzy classification model. Int. J. Comput. Appl. (2012)
31. Mo, R., Cai, Y., Kazman, R., Feng, Q.: Assessing an architecture's ability to support feature evolution. In: Proceedings of the 26th Conference on Program Comprehension, pp. 297–307 (2018)
32. Mockus, A., Weiss, D.M.: Predicting risk of software changes. Bell Labs Tech. J. **5**(2), 169–180 (2000)
33. Nagappan, N., Ball, T., Zeller, A.: Mining metrics to predict component failures. In: Proceedings of 28th International Conference on Software Engineering, pp. 452–461 (2006)
34. Ostrand, T.J., Weyuker, E.J., Bell, R.M.: Predicting the location and number of faults in large software systems. IEEE Trans. Softw. Eng. **31**(4), 340–355 (2005)
35. Pai, G.J., Dugan, J.B.: Empirical analysis of software fault content and fault proneness using Bayesian methods. IEEE Trans. Softw. Eng. **33**(10), 675–686 (2007)
36. Schröter, A., Zimmermann, T., Zeller, A.: Predicting component failures at design time. In: Proceedings of the 2006 ACM/IEEE International Symposium on Empirical Software Engineering, ISESE 2006, pp. 18–27 (2006)
37. Shatnawi, R.: Improving software fault-prediction for imbalanced data. In: 2012 International Conference on Innovations in Information Technology (IIT), pp. 54–59 (2012)
38. Sliwerski, J., Zimmermann, T., Zeller, A.: When do changes induce fixes? In: Proceedings of the 2005 International Workshop on Mining Software Repositories, pp. 1–5 (2005)
39. Sokolova, M., Lapalme, G.: A systematic analysis of performance measures for classification tasks. Inf. Process. Manage. **45**(4), 427–437 (2009)
40. Stone, M.: Cross-validation choice and assessment of statistical predictions. J. Roy. Stat. Soc. **36**, 111–133 (1974)
41. Syer, M.D., Nagappan, M., Adams, B., Hassan, A.E.: Replicating and re-evaluating the theory of relative defect-proneness. IEEE Trans. Softw. Eng. **41**(2), 176–197 (2015)
42. Wan, Z., Xia, X., Hassan, A.E., Lo, D., Yin, J., Yang, X.: Perceptions, expectations, and challenges in defect prediction. IEEE Trans. Softw. Eng. **46**, 1241–1266 (2018)
43. Yan, M., Fang, Y., Lo, D., Xia, X., Zhang, X.: File-level defect prediction: unsupervised vs. supervised models. In: 2017 ACM/IEEE International Symposium on Empirical Software Engineering and Measurement (ESEM), pp. 344–353 (2017)
44. Yang, Y., et al.: An empirical study on dependence clusters for effort-aware fault-proneness prediction. In: Proceedings of the 31st IEEE/ACM International Conference on Automated Software Engineering, ASE 2016, pp. 296–307 (2016)
45. Yang, Y., et al.: Effort-aware just-in-time defect prediction: simple unsupervised models could be better than supervised models. In: Proceedings of the 2016 24th ACM SIGSOFT International Symposium on Foundations of Software Engineering, pp. 157–168 (2016)
46. Zimmermann, T., Nagappan, N., Gall, H., Giger, E., Murphy, B.: Cross-project defect prediction: a large scale experiment on data vs. domain vs. process. In: Proceedings of the the the 7th Joint Meeting of the European Software Engineering Conference and the ACM SIGSOFT Symposium on The Foundations of Software Engineering, ESEC/FSE 2009, pp. 91–100 (2009)

CSFL: Fault Localization on Real Software Bugs Based on the Combination of Context and Spectrum

Yue Yan[1,2], Shujuan Jiang[1,2(✉)], Shenggang Zhang[1,2], and Ying Huang[1,2]

[1] Engineering Research Center of Mine Digitalization, China University of Mining and Technology, Ministry of Education, Xuzhou 221116, China
shjjiang@cumt.edu.cn
[2] School of Computer Science and Technology, China University of Mining and Technology, Xuzhou 221116, China

Abstract. Spectrum-based fault localization has been intensively studied recently. Previous studies have shown that the traditional spectrum-based fault localization applies statistical analysis on the coverage information about failed or passed tests to calculate the suspiciousness of program elements by specific formula. However, the traditional spectrum-based fault localization does not consider the propagation of faults, it only counts whether a single program element is covered by failed or passed tests. In this work, we propose an approach of Context and Spectrum based Fault Localization (CSFL), which combines program context analysis with spectrum for fault localization. Program context can not only improve the effectiveness of fault localization, but also provides help for developers. CSFL has been studied on 414 real bugs from the widely used Defects4J benchmark. The experimental results show that CSFL outperforms the SBFL techniques (e.g., localizing 61 more faults within Top-1). Furthermore, we also investigate the time cost of CSFL.

Keywords: Software fault localization · Spectrum-based · Context analysis · Real software bugs

1 Introduction

Software testing is the most time-consuming and labor-intensive key step in the software life cycle. Accurately locating the faults is both the highest priority and the most significant for software testing. Early fault localization is mostly set by developers artificially or relying on coding experience and personal intuition. Manual method of fault localization is costly in terms of time and labor. At present, many semi-automatic methods for fault localization have been proposed, such as spectrum-based fault localization (SBFL) [1], mutation-based fault localization [2], machine learning-based fault localization [3], etc. Recently, the most widely used method in the field of fault localization is the spectrum-based fault localization. The program spectrum can describe the execution information, such as the execution information of conditional branches or loop paths, which can be

© Springer Nature Switzerland AG 2021
S. Qin et al. (Eds.): SETTA 2021, LNCS 13071, pp. 219–238, 2021.
https://doi.org/10.1007/978-3-030-91265-9_12

used to track the behavior of program elements [4]. With the information of the program spectrum, it is possible to determine which elements are related to the program failure and narrow the search range for faults.

Among the existing fault localization methods, SBFL has been extensively studied because of its lightness and effectiveness. SBFL is based on a certain granularity of the program spectrum for fault localization. SBFL has many formulas, such as *Tarantula* [5], *Ochiai* [6], *DStar* [7], *Jaccard* [8], *Kulczynski2* [9] and so on, which simply apply statistical analysis to the coverage data of failed or passed tests to calculate the suspiciousness of code elements. The basic assumption is that the code executed by more failed tests is more likely to be the fault. Despite widely studied, SBFL has a limitation in design, that is, SBFL only pays attention to the individual elements of the program, and does not consider the connections among the elements. In some cases, many potential faults are not located or only the statements that trigger the fault can be found, and it is hard to find the root statements that caused the fault by SBFL.

Program context [10] refers to the control flow or data flow information of the program. In fact, some researchers have proposed using context information for error location [11–13]. However, the previous works are mainly conducted on Siemens suite from SIR [9] for experimental evaluation, the bugs are artificial bugs instead of real bugs. Pearson et al. [14] had found that the fault localization technology of artificial bugs is not very effective on real bugs. Therefore, fault localization approaches need to be evaluated on real bugs.

To bridge the gap, we propose an approach of Context and Spectrum based Fault Localization (CSFL), which combines the context analysis of programs with SBFL for locating real software bugs. The time cost of the previous works [10, 11] that applied context analysis of program for fault localization was high. In order to reduce the time complexity, CSFL limits the scope when performing the context analysis.

In order to evaluate our CSFL, we conduct experiments on the Defects4J benchmark (v2.0.0) [15]. Experimental results show that the effectiveness of CSFL for fault localization is better than the technologies that pure based on spectrum, such as *Ochiai*, *Dstar2*, *Jaccard* and *Tarantula*. For example, CSFL can find 96 faults within Top-1, which is 61 faults more than *Ochiai*.

The main contributions of this work are summarized in the following two aspects:

(1) We propose an approach that combines program context analysis with SBFL for fault localization.
(2) We conduct experimental evaluation on real software bugs. The experimental results have shown that our approach has improved the effectiveness of fault localization compared with traditional SBFL technologies. In addition, we explore the time cost of CSFL.

The rest of this article is organized as follows. We introduce the background of SBFL and context analysis in Sect. 2, and describes the basic framework of our approach in Sect. 3. The research questions and evaluation are elaborated in Sect. 4. The experimental results and analysis are described in Sect. 5. We present the related work in Sect. 6. Finally, we conclude our work in Sect. 7.

2 Background

We mainly describe the research background of CSFL by introducing spectrum-based fault localization and context-based fault localization.

2.1 Spectrum-Based Fault Localization

As early as 1987, in order to find program elements related to time, the idea of using program spectra to achieve fault localization was first proposed in a study on the millennium bug problem [16]. Since then, SBFL has attracted extensive attention and research from scholars [17]. It has gradually matured in the field of software fault localization and has become the mainstream method.

The general form of spectrum matrix as shown in Table 1. The set of program elements is expressed as $E = \{e_1, e_2, \cdots, e_M\}$, the set of test cases of the program is indi- cated as $T = \{t_1, t_2, \cdots, t_N\}$. The table represents test cases of the program (column 1), the program elements (column 2), and the execution results of tests (column 3). Where P or F describes that the test result is passed or failed. The table indicates the element is covered or not covered through the test by 1 or 0 respectively (rows 3–7).

Table 1. Spectrum matrix.

T	e_1	e_2	e_3	$\cdots$	e_M
t_1	n_{11}	n_{01}	n_{11}	$\cdots$	n_{11}
t_2	n_{10}	n_{10}	n_{00}	$\cdots$	n_{10}
t_3	n_{10}	n_{00}	n_{10}	$\cdots$	n_{10}
$\cdots$	$\cdots$	$\cdots$	$\cdots$	$\cdots$	$\cdots$
t_N	n_{11}	n_{01}	n_{01}	$\cdots$	n_{11}

SBFL collects code coverage information during the execution of a test case firstly, and then calculates the suspicious value of the program element by a predefined formula. One of the assumptions of SBFL is that the statement covered by the failed test is more likely to be a fault than the statement covered by the passed test. The granularity of elements varies with requirements. Common granularities include statements,

functions, and methods. Different spectrum-based fault localization techniques follow the same paradigm, but use different formulas to calculate the suspicious score.

After obtaining the spectra and matrix file of the program, calculating the suspicious value of elements according to the specific formula of SBFL technique. Then, we output the suspicious value in descending order to the rank list. We define the commonly used symbols in the SBFL formulas as shown in Table 2 [18].

Table 2. Common symbols in SBFL.

Notation	Meaning
P	A program
N_{CF}	Number of failed test cases that cover a statement
N_{UF}	Number of failed test cases that do not cover a statement
N_{CS}	Number of successful test cases that cover a statement
N_{US}	Number of successful test cases that do not cover a statement
N_C	Total number of test cases that cover a statement
N_U	Total number of test cases that do not cover a statement
N_S	Total number of successful test cases
N_F	Total number of failed test cases
t_i	The ith test case

Recent studies [7, 19] often discuss the comparison among the SBFL formulas. Xie et al. [20] divided the formula into 6 groups and evaluated the performance of different SBFL formulas. We pick four formulas with better performance to study: *Ochiai* [6], *Tarantula* [5], *DStar2* [21] and *Jaccard* [22]. Their definitions are shown in Table 3.

Table 3. SBFL formulas.

Name	Formula
Ochiai	$Ochiai(e) = \dfrac{N_{CF}}{\sqrt{N_F \cdot (N_{CF}+N_{CS})}}$
Tarantula	$Tarantula(e) = \dfrac{N_{CF}/N_F}{N_{CF}/N_F+N_{CS}/N_S}$
DStar2	$DStar2(e) = \dfrac{N_{CF}^2}{N_{CS}+(N_F-N_{CF})}$
Jaccard	$Jaccard(e) = \dfrac{N_{CF}}{N_{CF}+N_{UF}+N_{CS}}$

SBFL only counts whether a single program element is covered by failed or passed tests. The propagation of faults is not considered in SBFL [10]. But the program elements are not independent, the elements influence each other. The dependency among program elements is also very important for fault localization.

2.2 Context-Based Fault Localization

Taking advantage of various types of contextual information can greatly enrich the information expression of entities. Therefore, researchers apply context information to fault localization in software testing [23]. Program elements are not all independent individuals. For structured programs such as sequence, selection, and loop, input statements, output statements, assignment statements, and conditional statements can all reflect the guiding role of context information. Regarding variables, the definition and utilization of variables also reflect the context information of the dependencies. Path coverage information through successful and failed test cases collected by SBFL also reflects context information of running status.

The context information of the program can be obtained through the control dependency graph and the data dependency graph. Our work mainly makes use of the context information contained from the data dependence of the variables in the program for fault localization. Data dependence is concerned with the interaction between the definition and utilization of variables.

According to the definition of data flow analysis by Herman [24], in the control dependency graph, if there is a control path between the *definition* node of the variable *x* and the *utilization* node, and there is no redefinition node of *x* along the path, these two nodes make up a Definition Use Pair (DUP), represented as a triple *(def, use, var)*. Where *def* represents the *definition* node of the variable, *use* represents the *utilization* node of the same variable, and *var* represents the variable. CSFL collects contextual information mainly along with the *def* and *use* of a *var*.

3   Approach

In this section, we introduce the basic framework of the CSFL firstly. Then, we describe how to obtain contextual information. Finally, in order to facilitate understanding, we show a case study.

3.1   Basic Framework

The basic framework of CSFL is shown in Fig. 1. We get the coverage information through the tests executing source code firstly. When the execution of test cases is finished, the elements will be divided into four categories: covered by failed tests, not covered by failed tests, covered by passed tests, not covered by passed tests. SBFL

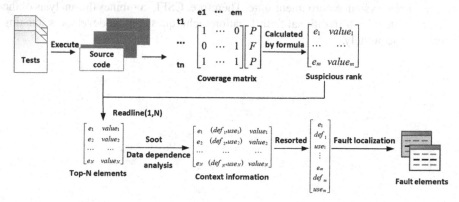

Fig. 1. Basic framework of CSFL

mainly performs statistical analysis on the statements covered by the failed test cases. Secondly, we calculate the suspicious value of the statements based on the coverage matrix by predefined formula. Sorting the statements in descending order of suspicious value. We use the *Readline()* method in Java to get the top N statements in the ranked list. Then, we analyze the data dependence of the top N statements by the tool Soot. Finally, we resort to the context information and the suspicious statements in the ranked list for fault localization.

A comprehensive context analysis will take a lot of time. In order to reduce the time cost, CSFL analyzes some of the statements in the list. After gaining the context information, we reorder the ranked list for fault localization. We add up the suspicious values of the data-dependent statements, and assign the sum to the suspicious statements as the new suspicious value. For example, the data dependence statements of e_1 contain e_i and e_j. The suspicious values of e_1, e_i and e_j are s_1, s_i and s_j respectively. We add the suspicious values s_1, s_i and s_j to *sum*, $sum = s_1 + s_i + s_j$, and assign *sum* to s_1. Then, we resort to the suspicious statements according to the new suspicious value. The new suspicious value rank list is the final results of CSFL, which is the basis for fault localization. Even if the fault element is not found in the ranked list, the context information of the suspicious statements can also provide a direction for the developer to locate the fault.

Generally, program elements can refer to classes, methods, or statements. Our work is carried out at statement granularity. There are three main reasons why we choose statement granularity. Firstly, context analysis is mainly for analyzing control dependence and data dependence, the class or method granularity is too coarse. Secondly, the large amount of code of our experiment object prompts us to research on statements, otherwise the developers still need to spend a lot of efforts to locate faults. Finally, the faults in the bug version are accurate to the statement, so our research is based on statement granularity.

3.2   The Algorithm of Context Analysis

The execution result of the software largely depends on the execution context of the program, including not only the execution traces, but also the data status of each variable, and the current system environment state. Therefore, CSFL combines the analysis of the program context with traditional fault location techniques to help developers locating faults more accurately.

Algorithm 1: Context Analysis Algorithm.

Inputs: S //source code of program
    $F = \{f_{Ochiai}, f_{Tarantula}, f_{Dstar2}, f_{Jaccard}\}$ //formulas of SBFL
    Ranklist //ranked list of suspicious value
Outputs: D // dataset of dependence elements
Procedure Begin :
1: **while** $F \neq \phi$ **do** :
2:   Calculate suspicious value of elements in S ;
3:   Rank the elements in descending order $\rightarrow$ *Ranklist* ;
4: **end while**
5: **for** N = 1, 3, 5, 10 **do** :
6:   Readline (1, N) ; $\leftarrow$ *Ranklist*   // read the top N statements
7:   loading the class file through the class name by tool Soot;
8:   converting the class file into a Jimple file ;
9:   variables in Jimple file $\rightarrow$ *valueBox* ;
10:    **for** *variable* in *valueBox* **do** :
11:     **if** (variable != constant) **then**   // judgment the Type of variable
12:     searching the data dependence variables in SootMethod or SootClass ;
13:     data dependence variables $\rightarrow$ D ;
14:     **return** D ;
15:    **end if**
16:    **end for**
17: **end for**

CSFL mainly uses the data dependence of variables in the statements as the context information, analyzing the dependence of variables through DUP [24]. Algorithm 1 describes the process of context analysis in detail and shows the key steps to obtain context information. Firstly, we calculate a sorted list of suspicious values through a certain formula of SBFL (lines 1–4). Secondly, we use the *Readline()* method in Java library to read the top N statements in the sorted list (lines 5–6), $N = \{1, 3, 5, 10\}$.

According to the class name contained in the statement, loading the class file and convert the class file into a Jimple file by Soot (line 7). We convert the Jimple file into soot related objects (such as *SootClass*, *SootMethod*, *ValueBox*) and store variables in Jimple file to *ValueBox* correspondingly (lines 8–9). Then, we traverse the variables in the *valueBox* and eliminate constants (lines 10–11). We search for the variable to be analyze among the soot objects (line 12). If a statement that contains the variable is found, the statement is added to the data dependence set (line 13). Finally, returning the data dependence set (line 14). After that, we use context information and suspicious statements for fault localization.

3.3 The Case Study of CSFL

We take the Chart project bug 5 in the Defects4J benchmark as an example for specific analysis, as shown in Table 4. The table shows the top 5 statements with the suspicious value calculated by *Ochiai* [19] (column 1), the data dependence statements (column 2) and the fault statements (column 3). The top 5 statements and the data dependence statements will be the final results for fault statements. We can observe that the top 5 suspicious statements do not include any fault statements. The context dependence statements of the second suspicious statement include the fault statement *org.jfree.data.xy.XYSeries.java#548*. It can be found from the examples that it is feasible to apply context analysis for fault localization.

Table 4. The case study of context analysis.

Top-5 statements	Data dependence statements	Buggylines of Chart_5
org.jfree.data.xy.XYSeries#527	null	org/jfree/data/xy/XYSeries.java#**548**#
org.jfree.data.xy.XYSeries#564	541/547/**548**/549/556	org/jfree/data/xy/XYSeries.java#544#
org.jfree.data.xy.XYSeries#563	563/352/692	
org.jfree.data.xy.XYSeries#570	570/388/689	
org.jfree.data.xy.XYSeries#541	null	

3.4 Time Cost Reduction

Context analysis requires static analysis of the code. The context within and between classes is complicated, and the time cost is a challenge for CSFL. In order to reduce the time cost, we have tried to apply program slicing technology to narrow the scope of context analysis, but the experimental results show that this method is not suitable for contextual fault localization. The reason may be that the program slicing destroyed the code structure.

At last, we have limited the depth of data dependence analysis to reduce the time cost. Because the propagation of faults is limited, the dependence will be reduced after multiple layers function calls among statements, and the probability of causing software faults will also be reduced. Therefore, we consider the data dependence within three layers function calls.

4   Evaluation

In this section, the research questions are proposed firstly, and then we introduce the subjects and implementation of the experiment. Finally, we describe the evaluation measurements.

4.1 Research Questions

This work explores the following questions:

RQ1: How does CSFL perform for real faults localization?

RQ2: How much effectiveness has CSFL improved compared with the traditional SBFL techniques?

RQ3: How About the Time Cost of CSFL?

4.2 Experimental Subjects

To investigate the RQs, we use the Defects4J benchmark [25] of version 2.0.0 that has been widely used in software testing. We use 6 subjects that contained 414 real faults. The detailed information of these subjects is shown in Table 5. Where *jfreechart* is a framework for creating charts, *closure-compiler* is a JavaScript compiler for optimization, *Apache commons-lang* and *commons-math* are supplements to the existing libraries in the JDK, and *joda-time* is a standard time library (column 2). We mainly use the project identifier to describe in the following (column 1).

Table 5. Details of Defects4J benchmark.

Identifier	Project	#Bugs	#Test	#KLoc
Chart	Jfreechart	26	2,205	96
Closure	Closure-compiler	154	9527	128
Lang	Commons-lang	64	2245	22
Math	Commons-math	106	3602	85
Mockito	Mockito	38	1366	23
Time	Joda-time	26	4130	28
Total		414	23075	382

In Table 5, the *#Bugs* represents the total number of faults in the benchmark (column 3), the *#Tests* represents the total number of test cases for each project (column 4), the *#KLoC* represents the number of lines of code in the program (column 5).

4.3 Implementation Details

We mainly introduce the implementation details of four different SBFL technologies and context analysis in this section. In Sect. 2, we have provided the formulas of SBFL, which are based on the code coverage information. We use the open-source tool Gzoltar [26] to count the coverage information and calculate the suspicious value of the corresponding element by Java program.

For the implementation of context analysis, we mainly analyze the context information of the data dependence of variables. Soot is a Java compilation optimization framework, which can be used to realize data flow analysis and control flow analysis of Java bytecode programs. Soot further generates the data flow graph by converting the Java program into the intermediate code Jimple program. We mainly parse the intermediate code Jimple file and output the dependent nodes of the variables.

4.4 Measurements

In order to evaluate the effectiveness of CSFL, we use three measurements: *Exam*, *Recall at Top-N* and *Percentage of Total_lines*, which are widely used in the researches [3, 11, 12].

Exam Score

Exam is used to measure the percentage of program elements that need to be checked by the developer among all candidate program elements before reaching the first expected fault element, reflecting the relative ranking of fault elements and the overall effectiveness of the fault localization. *Exam* shows the search cost for fault localization. Therefore, many previous studies [18, 27, 28] also used *Exam*, the calculation formula as follows.

$$Exam = \frac{Number\ of\ statements\ examined}{Total\ number\ of\ candidate\ statements\ in\ the\ list} \times 100\% \qquad (1)$$

Recall at Top-N

Top-N is used to measure how many faults can be located among the top N elements of all candidates. In a survey conducted by Kochhar et al. [20], 73% of developers thought it was acceptable to check 5 procedural elements, and almost all developers believed that checking 10 elements was the upper limit of its acceptable level. Therefore, we consider the number of faults contained in the top N elements, where $N \in \{1,3,5,10\}$. Note that even when multiple faulty elements of a fault are localized within top N, it is only counted once.

Percentage of Total_lines

In specific calculations, even if one element is matched, it will be counted as catching the fault, it is a coarse evaluation for faults with multiple elements. So we define *Percentage of Total_lines* that represents the ratio of fault elements be located to total fault elements, as shown in formula 2. If we find more fault elements in top N elements, the *Number of statements Located* will be larger. *Percentage of Total_lines* reflects the accuracy of techniques for fault localization to a certain extent.

$$Percentage\ of\ Total\_lines = \frac{Number\ of\ statements\ Located}{Total\ number\ of\ Buggylines} \times 100\% \qquad (2)$$

5 Results Analysis

5.1 RQ1: How Does CSFL Perform in Locating Real Faults?

To answer this question, we compare the effectiveness of CSFL with the SBFL technologies (*Ochiai, Tarantula, Dstar2 and Jaccard*). We combine the context analysis technology with the four technologies respectively, and conduct experiments to evaluate the effectiveness of fault localization. The detailed experimental results are from the perspective of the three measurements of *Top-N*, *Exam* and *Percentage of Total_lines*.

We first analyze the *Top-N* measurement. Table 6 shows the compared techniques (column 1), and the number of faults located in every range (columns 2–5). From Table 6, we can find that CSFL can locate more faults than other technologies, and *CSFL-Ochiai* can locate 61 more faults in Top-1 than *Ochiai*. *CSFL-Ochiai* has located 213 faults in the Top-10. It can be found that CSFL get better effect than pure spectrum-based techniques. CSFL supplements effective context information on the basis of SBFL for accurate fault localization. The experimental results prove that combining context analysis and SBFL to locate faults is feasible.

In addition, we can observe that the performance of *CSFL-Ochiai* in Top-3, Top-5 and Top-10 is better than *CSFL-Tarantula*, *CSFL-Dstar2* and *CSFL-Jaccard*, indicating that *Ochiai* is more fully utilized contextual information than the others. We mainly use *CSFL-Ochiai* as an example for comparison analysis.

Table 6. Effectiveness of different techniques.

Techniques	Top-1	Top-3	Top-5	Top-10
CSFL-Ochiai	96	149	182	213
CSFL-Tarantula	93	142	176	204
CSFL-Dstar2	84	132	163	188
CSFL-Jaccard	97	145	179	211
Ochiai	35	84	113	157
Tarantula	34	77	106	147
Dstar2	32	75	102	135
Jaccard	36	81	108	155

Table 6 is an overall reflection of the total number of faults located by all techniques in the Top-N range. Next, we will analyze the effectiveness of various technologies for each project in Table 7.

The Table 7 lists the Defects4J projects studied in this work (column 1), CSFL and the compared techniques (column 2). On the whole, the number of faults that CSFL located in the six projects is greater than that of the other four technologies (columns 3–6). Through observation, we can find that CSFL has improved the most on *Math* and *Lang* projects. The table contains the *Exam* score of technique for every project (column 7). We can find that the *Exam* score of CSFL is within an acceptable range, which is similar to other techniques.

In order to evaluate the effectiveness of CSFL more intuitively, we analyze the proportion of fault localization. It can be found from Fig. 2 that CSFL has the highest ratio compared to the other technologies in fault located, it has located 19.4% more faults than *Dstar2* in Top-5 most obviously. With the increase of range *Top-N*, the proportion of faults located also gradually increases. We can observe that the fault located ratios of *Tarantula*, *Dstar2* and *Jaccard* are small, especially the effects of *Tarantula* and *Dstar2* are very close. The reason may be that the principle of statistical analysis of code coverage is similar.

Table 7. Effectiveness of different techniques for every project.

Subjects	Techniques	Top-1	Top-3	Top-5	Top-10	Exam
Chart	Ochiai	3	7	10	14	0.15
	Tarantula	3	7	10	13	0.144
	Dstar2	4	6	10	11	0.17
	Jaccard	3	7	10	14	0.152
	CSFL	**10**	**15**	**19**	**20**	**0.149**
Closure	Ochiai	6	16	22	38	0.252
	Tarantula	6	13	20	31	0.253
	Dstar2	7	19	22	35	0.28
	Jaccard	6	15	22	35	0.253
	CSFL	**14**	**28**	**35**	**47**	**0.249**
Lang	Ochiai	4	13	19	33	0.204
	Tarantula	4	13	19	32	0.213
	Dstar2	3	12	19	28	0.267
	Jaccard	4	13	19	33	0.205
	CSFL	**18**	**28**	**37**	**45**	**0.216**
Math	Ochiai	15	26	34	42	0.154
	Tarantula	16	27	35	43	0.157
	Dstar2	9	18	25	32	0.22
	Jaccard	16	27	34	43	0.154
	CSFL	**36**	**48**	**55**	**61**	**0.176**
Mockito	Ochiai	5	14	18	19	0.066
	Tarantula	3	9	13	18	0.07
	Dstar2	5	13	17	18	0.084
	Jaccard	5	12	16	19	0.071
	CSFL	**11**	**18**	**22**	**24**	**0.07**
Time	Ochiai	2	8	10	11	0.156
	Tarantula	2	8	9	10	0.157
	Dstar2	4	7	9	11	0.155
	Jaccard	2	7	9	11	0.157
	CSFL	**7**	**12**	**14**	**16**	**0.157**

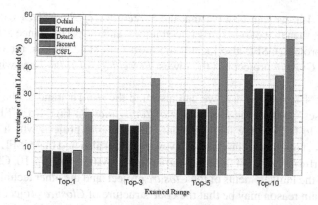

Fig. 2. Percentage of faults located by different techniques

With the range of search faults increases, more and more context information is added in CSFL. Will it bring higher search costs to developers? Fig. 3 shows the comparison between CSFL and the other techniques in *Exam*. From Fig. 3 we can observe that there is no significant difference between CSFL and other techniques in *Exam*. Compared with other techniques, the *Exam* of CSFL is higher than that of *Ochiai*, *Tarantula* and *Jaccard* in the *Lang* and *Math* projects, and it is very close to the *Exam* of these three technologies in the other four projects. CSFL can locate almost twice as many faults as the other four technologies, but the search cost has not increased. The main reason is that we performed a series of sorting when adding context information to the sorting list, which can advance the ranking of faults.

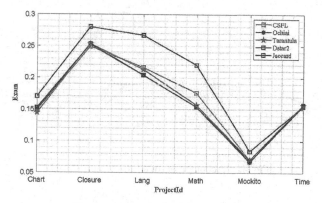

Fig. 3. Exam of different techniques

We also evaluate how many fault elements can be located by different techniques. We use the evaluation measurement *Percentage of Total_lines* to calculate the ratio of the number of located fault elements to total fault elements. The following analysis provides the *Percentage of Total_lines* for each project within *Top-N* ($N = \{1,3,5,10\}$) respectively.

From Fig. 4-a, we can observe that the *Percentage of Total_lines* within Top-1 of CSFL is higher than that of other SBFL techniques, and the performance is most obvious in the *Chart* project. CSFL also locates the most fault statements in the other projects within Top-1. *Closure* project has the lowest *Percentage of Total_lines* within Top-1 of all techniques.

In the Fig. 4-b, 4-c and 4-d, we can also find the similar trend as the search range *Top-N* increases, so does the *Percentage of Total_lines*. In Fig. 4-d, CSFL in Top-10 can locate up to 60% of the fault elements for the *Lang* project, which is more than double the effect of other techniques. However, we can also find that CSFL and the other techniques perform the worst in the *Closure* project. Within the Top-10, CSFL can only locate 12% of the fault elements of the *Closure* project, and the other techniques perform worse. The main reason may be that the code structure of *Closure* project is special, we will continue to study so as to achieve better effectiveness. Based on the above, CSFL performs better than the other techniques in any range for fault localization.

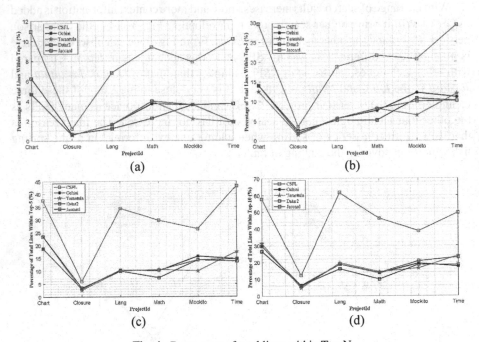

Fig. 4. Percentage of total lines within Top-N

5.2   RQ2: How Much Efficiency Has CSFL Improved?

To answer RQ2, we specifically introduce how much performance CSFL improves over traditional SBFL techniques. Figure 5 shows the percentage of faults located by CSFL compared to the other techniques in different search ranges. Figure 6 shows the average improved percentage of faults located.

Figure 5 shows the combination of context with four techniques and their own effectiveness for fault localization. Overall, we can find that *CSFL-Ochiai, CSFL-Tarantula, CSFL-Dstar2* and *CSFL-Jaccard* perform better than *Ochiai, Tarantula, Dstar2* and *Jaccard* respectively. *CSFL-Ochiai* has more than 14% improvement compared with *Ochiai* within Top-1. The highest growth occurred between *CSFL- Jaccard* and *Jaccard* in the Top-5 range, which is about 17%, which fully illustrates the advantages of CSFL.

We can observe that the combination of context and *Ochiai* performs best in every range. For example, *CSFL-Ochiai* is 2%, 3%, 1% higher than *CSFL-Tarantula, CSFL-Dstar2, CSFL-Jaccard* respectively within Top-5. The percentage of faults located by CSFL in Top-5 has increased more than that in Top-10 shows that the number of faults located is not entirely proportional to the search range.

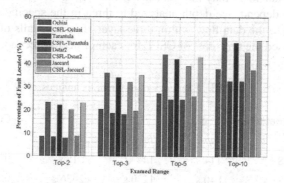

Fig. 5. Improvement of CSFL compared with other four techniques

From Fig. 6, it can be observed that the average improvement rate of CSFL in different search ranges is not less than 15%. The biggest improvement is in Top-5 range, and the lowest improvement is in Top-1 range. The main reason for that is the context information of statements contained in Top-1 is limited. With the expansion of the search scope to Top-5, the improvement rate of CSFL is also increasing.

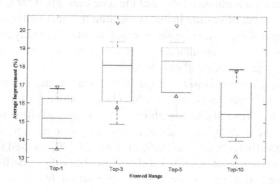

Fig. 6. Average improvement of CSFL

However, when the search range is expanded to Top-10, the improvement rate of CSFL is lower than that of Top-5. The main reason for the trend changed is that there is too much contextual information analyzed in Top-10, and a lot of useless redundant information will affect fault localization. Based on the above experimental evaluation, we can get that CSFL is better than the traditional SBFL techniques in the performance of fault localization.

5.3 RQ3: How About the Time Cost of CSFL?

CSFL combines context analysis with traditional SBFL techniques for fault localization, and the time complexity has always been a challenge for context analysis. The context of each program statement may have dozens of lines. In order to reduce the time cost, we limit the data dependence depth analyzed to three in the specific implementation. That is, we analyze the data flow within three-layers function calls of the variable. In Table 8, we assessed the time cost of CSFL for each project in second.

Table 8. Efficiency of different techniques.

Subjects	Context collection				Computation
	Top-1	*Top-3*	*Top-5*	*Top-10*	
Chart	48 s	114 s	144 s	318 s	0.12 s
Closure	528 s	840 s	1230 s	2436 s	0.24 s
Lang	96 s	174 s	306 s	834 s	0.12 s
Math	222 s	348 s	552 s	966 s	0.3 s
Mockito	258 s	378 s	576 s	1062 s	0.18 s
Time	54 s	78 s	204 s	330 s	0.12 s

Table 8 shows the experimental projects (column 1), the time consumed for collecting context information (columns 2–5), and the time consumed for CSFL computation (column 6). The computation time includes the time to generate the spectrum and sort the statements. From Table 8, we can observe that the time is mainly spent on collecting context information. The computation time is very small for the whole, and the most used is only 0.3 s, which is basically negligible.

For the largest project *Closure* and the widest search range Top-10, the time for collecting context information is 2436 s, which is acceptable for most researchers. For small projects such as *Time*, the time within Top-1 is less than 1 min, which is relatively low for the technique of fault localization. As the search range Top − N decreases, the time cost is also greatly reduced. The study of Xie et al. [20] showed that for more than 70% of researchers, the greatest afford ability is to check the code in Top-5. It can be found that the time cost of most projects in Top-5 is within 600 s.

5.4 Threats to Validity

Our experimental evaluation shows CSFL is more effective than using SBFL techniques for fault localization. However, there are threat to internal validity and external validity in CSFL.

The threat to internal validity is the potential mistake in our implementation of the CSFL. To reduce this threat, our implementation utilizes mature tools such as Gzoltar [26] and Soot [29]. Furthermore, we have checked most of the experimental results to verify their correctness manually.

The external validity threat mainly comes from the experimental subjects. The experimental evaluation in our work is based on the six projects of the Defects4J benchmark [15]. When CSFL is applied to other test benchmarks or other projects within the Defects4J benchmark, we cannot clearly state CSFL will achieve the same results. Only by conducting such analysis and experimental evaluation on other projects can eliminate this threat.

6 Related Work

In this section, we discuss related work with respect to two aspects. On one hand, we explain spectrum-based fault localization investigated in our work. On the other hand, we discuss the approaches that combine context with spectrum based for fault localization.

6.1 Spectrum-Based Fault Localization

Spectrum-based fault localization is one of the commonly used fault location techniques [1], which is broadly utilized in program debugging. In the previous decade, many SBFL techniques had been proposed. *Tarantula* [5] was a representative method proposed by Jones and Harrold early. Abreu et al. [6] did a more thorough study and proposed a better formula named *Ochiai*, which was widely in the fault localization domain. Wong et al. [21] proposed an approach named *DStar(D*)*, which can automatically suggest suspicious locations for fault localization without any prior information about program structure or semantics. It should be noted that * in the D* formula is usually assigned the value 2 [14]. Chen et al. [30] proposed *Jaccard* technique, which is a statistically based fault localization algorithm. Recently, some other formulas were proposed [9, 31, 32]. Although SBFL has many different formulas, they follow the same paradigm.

There were many studies compared the different spectrum-based fault localization formulas [7, 19]. However, there is no formula claiming that it can outperform all others under every scenario [18]. In addition to the influence of different formulas on the effectiveness for fault localization. Since SBFL mainly relies on coverage information of pass or fail tests, the attributes of the test suite directly affect fault localization [33, 34].

Furthermore, many studies tried to improve SBFL technique with other optimized information such as suspicious variables [35] and quality assessment [36] or incorporated techniques like data-augmented diagnosis [37] with SBFL. In contrast, we further explore the effectiveness of SBFL by combining context information.

6.2 Combination of Context and Spectrum-Based for Fault Localization

Researchers tried to improve SBFL through program context. Ma et al. [10] proposed a fault localization method based on the combination dependency network. By calculating the combination dependency probability of each sentence, and then the propagation context of the sentence was analyzed for fault localization. The difference between CSFL and Ma's work is that CSFL applies data dependence as context information, and reorders the sorted list of suspicious statements for fault localization.

Wang et al. [11] mentioned the addition of context information to improve the effectiveness of SBFL, but the definition of the context in the work is all suspicious program elements that have been executed by failed tests except the element itself. The definition of context information in CSFL is different from Wang's work. Our definition of context information is more specific and deeper. Ferenc et al. [12] proposed adding contextual information to the suspicion ranking table to provide feedback to developers. However, their work also needed the feedback from developers, and it was the key step of Ferenc's work. In the real process for fault localization, the developer is unable to provide accurate feedback. CSFL has a complete framework for fault localization that do not need much feedback from developers.

Not only that, but previous works mainly focused on artificial fault, and did not highlight the advantages of context analysis. In contrast, CSFL is carried out on the real software faults. The substantial increase in the amount of code in CSFL can further fully integrate the context analysis, the effectiveness of fault localization has also been improved significantly.

7 Conclusion

In this work, we propose an approach that combines context analysis with SBFL for fault localization. The experimental evaluation is carried out on 414 real software faults in the widely used Defects4J benchmark, which shows that CSFL can outperform the traditional SBFL techniques. For example, it can locate 61 more faults than the *Ochiai* within Top-1. The experimental results also show that the *Exam* score of CSFL is not obviously different from other techniques. In addition, we have investigated the time cost of CSFL, which is acceptable to most researchers.

Acknowledgment. The authors wish to thank the reviewers and editors for suggesting improvements and for their helpful comments. This work was supported in part by National Natural Science Foundation of China under grant No. 61673384.

References

1. Harrold, M.J., Rothermel, G., Sayre, K., Wu, R., Yi, L.: An empirical investigation of the relationship between spectra differences and regression faults. J. Softw. Test., Verication, Reliab. **10**(3), 171–194 (2000)
2. Mike, P., Yves, L.T.: Metallaxis-FL: mutation-based fault localization. J. Softw. Test., Verication, Reliab. **25**(5–7), 605–628 (2015)

3. Li, X., Li, W., Zhang, Y., Zhang, L.: DeepFL: integrating multiple fault diagnosis dimensions for deep fault localization. In: Proceedings of the 28th ACM SIGSOFT International Symposium on Software Testing and Analysis (ISSTA 2019), Association for Computing Machinery, pp. 169–180 (2019)
4. Reps, T., Ball, T., Das, M., Larus, J.: The use of program profiling for software maintenance with applications to the year 2000 problem. In: Jazayeri, M., Schauer, H. (eds.) ESEC/SIGSOFT FSE -1997. LNCS, vol. 1301, pp. 432–449. Springer, Heidelberg (1997). https://doi.org/10.1007/3-540-63531-9_29
5. Jones, J.A., Harrold, M.J.: Empirical evaluation of the tarantula automatic fault-localization technique. In: Proceedings of the 20th IEEE/ACM international Conference on Automated software engineering, pp. 273–282 (2005)
6. Abreu, R., Zoeteweij, P., Van Gemund, A.J.: An evaluation of similarity coefficients for software fault localization. In: Dependable Computing, 2006. PRDC06. 12th Pacifjc Rim International Symposium on, pp. 39–46 (2006)
7. Wong, W.E., Debroy, V., Li, Y., Gao, R.: Software fault localization using dstar (d*). In: Software Security and Reliability (SERE), In: 2012 IEEE Sixth International Conference on, pp. 21–30 (2012)
8. Abreu, R., Zoeteweij, P., Van Gemund, A.J.: On the accuracy of spectrum-based fault localization. In: Testing: Academic and Industrial Conference Practice and Research Techniques-MUTATION, TAICPART-MUTATION 2007, pp. 89–98 (2007)
9. Naish, L., Lee, H.J., Ramamohanarao, K.: A model for spectra based software diagnosis. ACM Trans. Softw. Eng. Methodol. (TOSEM) **20**(3), 11 (2011)
10. Ma, P., Wang, Y., Su, X., Wang, T.: A novel fault localization method with fault propagation context analysis. In: 2013 Third International Conferenceon Instrumentation, Measurement, Computer, Communication and Control, Shenyang, pp. 1194–1199 (2013)
11. Wang, Y., Huang, Z., Li, Y., Fang, B.: Lightweight fault localization combined with fault context to improve fault absolute rank. Sci. China Inf. Sci. **60**(9), 092113:1-092113:16 (2017)
12. Horvth, F., Lacerda, V.S., Beszdes, Á., Vidcs, L., Gyimthy, T.: A new interactive fault localization method with context aware user feedback. In: 2019 IEEE 1st International Workshop on Intelligent Bug Fixing (IBF), pp. 23–28 (2019)
13. Zhang, Z., Tan, Q., Mao, X., et al.: Effective fault localization approach based on enhanced contexts. J. Softw. **30**(2), 266–281 (2019)
14. Pearson, S., et al.: Evaluating and improving fault localization. In: International Conference on Software Engineering, pp. 609–620 (2017)
15. Just, R., Jalali, D., Ernst, M.D.: Defects4J: a database of existing faults to enable controlled testing studies for Java programs. In: Proceedings of the International Symposium on Software Testing and Analysis (ISSTA), pp. 437–440 (2014)
16. Collofello, J.S., Cousins, L.: Towards automatic software fault localization through decision-to-decision path analysis. In: Proceedings of National Computer Conference, pp. 539–544 (1987)
17. Agrawal, H., DeMillo, R.A., Spafford, E.H.: An execution backtracking approach to program debugging. IEEE Softw. **8**(5), 21–26 (1991)
18. Wong, W.E., Gao, R., Li, Y., Abreu, R., Wotawa, F.: A survey on software fault localization. IEEE Trans. Softw. Eng. **42**(8), 707–740 (2016)
19. Xie, X., Wong, W., Chen, T., Xu, B.: Spectrum-based fault localization: testing oracles are no longer mandatory. In: Proceedings of the 11th International Conference on Quality Software, pp. 1–10 (2011)
20. Xie, X., Chen, T.Y., Kuo, F.-C., Baowen, X.: A theoretical analysis of the risk evaluation formulas for spectrum-based fault localization. ACM Trans. Softw. Eng. Methodol. **22**(4), 1–40 (2013). https://doi.org/10.1145/2522920.2522924

21. Wong, W.E., Debroy, V., Gao, R., Li, Y.: The dstar method for effective software fault localization. IEEE Trans. Reliab. **63**(1), 290–308 (2014)
22. Artzi, S., Kiezun, A., et al.: Finding bugs in web applications using dynamic test generation and explicit-state model checking. IEEE Trans. Softw. Eng. **36**(4), 474–494 (2010)
23. https://bitbucket.org/rjust/fault-localization-data
24. Herman, P.M.: A data flow analysis approach to program testing. Aust. Comput. J. **8**(3), 92–96 (1976)
25. Martinez, M., Durieux, T., Xuan, J., Sommerard, R., Monperrus, M.: Automatic repair of real bugs: an experience report on the defects4j dataset (2015). arXiv preprintarXiv:1505.07002
26. https://gzoltar.com/
27. Jiang, J., Wang, R., Xiong, Y., Chen, X., Zhang, L.: combining spectrum-based fault localization and statistical debugging: an empirical study. In: 2019 34th IEEE/ACM International Conference on Automated Software Engineering (ASE), pp. 502–514 (2019)
28. Reis, S., Abreu, R., d'Amorim, M.: Demystifying the combination of dynamic slicing and spectrum-based fault localization. In: Twenty Eighth International Joint Conference on Artificial Intelligence IJCAI 19, pp. 4760–4766 (2019)
29. https://github.com/soot-oss/soot
30. Chen, M.Y., Kiciman, E., Fratkin, E., Fox, A., Brewer, E.: Pinpoint: problem determination in large, dynamic Internet services. In: Proceedings International Conference on Dependable Systems and Networks, pp. 595–604 (2002)
31. Wong, W.E., Debroy, V., Choi, B.: A family of code coverage-based heuristics for effective fault localization. J. Syst. Softw. **83**(2), 188–208 (2010)
32. Zeller, A.: Isolating cause-effect chains from computer programs. In: Proceedings of the 10th ACM SIGSOFT Symposium on Foundations of Software Engineering, pp. 1–10 (2002)
33. Baudry, B., Fleurey, F., Traon, Y.L.: Improving test suites for efficient fault localization. In: 28th international conference on Software engineering, pp. 82–91 (2006)
34. Yu, Y., Jones, J.A., Harrold, M.J.: An empirical study of the effects of test-suite reduction on fault localization. In: International Conference on Software Engineering (ICSE), pp. 201–210 (2008)
35. Kim, J., Kim, J., Lee, E.: Vfl: Variable-based fault localization. Inf. Softw. Technol. **107**, 179–191 (2019)
36. Liu, C., Ma, C., Zhang, T.: Improving spectrum-based fault localization using quality assessment and optimization of a test suite. In: 2020 IEEE 20th International Conference on Software Quality, Reliability and Security Companion (QRS-C), pp. 72–78 (2020)
37. Elmishali, A., Stern, R., Kalech, M.: Data-augmented software diagnosis. In: Proceedings of the Thirtieth AAAI Conference on Artificial Intelligence, pp. 4003–4009 (2016)

A Distributed Simplex Architecture for Multi-agent Systems

Usama Mehmood[1]([⊠]), Scott D. Stoller[1], Radu Grosu[2], Shouvik Roy[1], Amol Damare[1], and Scott A. Smolka[1]

[1] Department of Computer Science, Stony Brook University, Stony Brook, USA
`umehmood@cs.stonybrook.edu`
[2] Department of Computer Engineering, Technische Universität Wien,
Vienna, Austria

Abstract. We present the *Distributed Simplex Architecture* (DSA), a new runtime assurance technique that provides safety guarantees for multi-agent systems (MASs). DSA is inspired by the Simplex control architecture of Sha et al., but with some significant differences. The traditional Simplex approach is limited to single-agent systems or a MAS with a centralized control scheme. DSA addresses this limitation by extending the scope of Simplex to include MASs under distributed control. In DSA, each agent runs a local instance of traditional Simplex such that the preservation of safety in the local instances implies safety for the entire MAS. Control Barrier Functions play a critical role. They are used to define DSA's core components (the baseline controller and the decision module's switching logic between advanced and baseline controllers) and to verify the safety of a DSA instance in a distributed manner. We provide a general proof of safety for DSA, and present experimental results for several case studies, including flocking with collision avoidance, safe navigation of ground rovers through way-points, and the safe operation of a microgrid.

Keywords: Runtime assurance · Simplex architecture · Control barrier functions · Distributed flocking · Reverse switching

1 Introduction

A multi-agent system (MAS) is a group of autonomous, intelligent agents that work together to solve tasks and carry out missions. MAS applications include the design of power systems and smart-grids [1, 2], autonomous control of robotic swarms for monitoring, disaster management, military battle systems, etc. [3], and sensor networks [4]. Many MAS applications are safety-critical. It is therefore paramount that MAS control strategies ensure safety.

This work is supported in part by NSF awards OIA-2040599, CCF-1918225, CCF-1954837, CPS-1446832 and ONR award N000142012751.

S. Qin et al. (Eds.): SETTA 2021, LNCS 13071, pp. 239–257, 2021.
https://doi.org/10.1007/978-3-030-91265-9_13

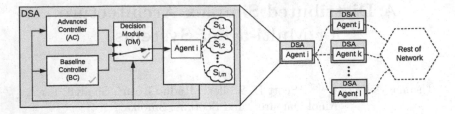

Fig. 1. Architectural overview of DSA. Agents are homogeneous and operate under DSA control; the figure zooms in on DSA components for agent i. Sensed state of agent i's j^{th} neighbor denoted as $S_{i,j}$. AC, BC, and DM take as input the state of the agent and its neighbors.

In this paper, we present the *Distributed Simplex Architecture* (DSA), a new runtime assurance technique that provides safety guarantees for MASs under distributed control. DSA is inspired by Sha et al.'s Simplex Architecture [5,6], but differs from it in significant ways. The Simplex Architecture provides runtime assurance of safety by switching control from an unverified (hence potentially unsafe) *advanced controller* (AC) to a verified-safe *baseline controller* (BC), if the action produced by the AC could result in a safety violation in the near future. The switching logic is implemented in a verified *decision module* (DM). The applicability of the traditional Simplex Architecture is limited to systems with a centralized control architecture.

DSA, illustrated in Fig. 1, addresses this limitation by re-engineering the traditional Simplex architecture to widen its scope to include MASs. Also, as in [7], it implements *reverse switching* by reverting control back to the AC when it is safe to do so.

In DSA, for each agent, there is a verified-safe BC and a verified switching logic such that if all agents operate under DSA, then safety of the MAS is guaranteed. The BC and DM along with the AC are distributed and depend only on local information. DSA itself is *distributed* in that it involves one local instance of traditional Simplex per agent such that the conjunction of their respective safety properties yields the desired safety property for the entire MAS. For example, consider our flocking case study, where a group of robotic agents is moving cohesively, and we want to establish collision-freedom for the entire MAS. This can be accomplished in a distributed manner by showing that each local instance of Simplex, say for agent i, ensures collision-freedom for agent i and its neighboring agents.

DSA allows agents to switch their mode of operation independently. At any given time, some agents may be operating in AC mode while others are operating in BC mode. Our approach to the design of the BC and DM leverages *Control Barrier Functions* (CBFs), which have been used to synthesize safe controllers [8–10], and are closely related to Barrier Certificates used for safety verification of closed dynamical systems [11,12]. A CBF is a mapping from the system's (i.e., plant's) state space to a real number, with its zero level-set partitioning the state space into safe and unsafe regions. If certain inequalities on the derivative of the

CBF in the direction of the state trajectories (also known as Lie derivative) are satisfied, then the corresponding control actions are considered safe (admissible).

In DSA, the BC is designed as an optimal controller with the goal of increasing a utility function based on the Lie derivatives of the CBFs. As CBFs are a measure of the safety of a state, optimizing for control actions with a higher Lie derivative values provides a direct way to make the state safer. The safety of the BC is further guaranteed by constraining the control action to remain in a set of admissible actions that satisfy certain inequalities on the Lie derivatives of the CBFs. CBFs are also used in the design of the switching logic, as they provide an efficient method for checking whether an action could lead to a safety violation during the next time step.

We demonstrate the effectiveness of DSA on several example MASs, including a flock of robots moving coherently while avoiding inter-agent collisions, ground rovers safely navigating through a series of way-points, and safe operation of a microgrid.

2 Background

2.1 Simplex Architecture

The Simplex Control Architecture relies on a verified-safe baseline controller (BC) in conjunction with the verified switching logic of the Decision Module (DM) to guarantee the safety of the plant, while permitting the use of an unverifiable, high-performance advanced controller (AC); see agent i in Fig. 1.

Let the *admissible* states of a system be those which satisfy all safety constraints and operational limits. All other states are *inadmissible*. The goal of the Simplex Architecture is to ensure that the system never enters an inadmissible state. The set $\mathcal{R}$ of *recoverable* states is a subset of the admissible states such that the BC, starting from any state in $\mathcal{R}$, guarantees that all future states are also in $\mathcal{R}$. The recoverable set takes into account the inertia of the physical system, giving the BC enough time to preserve safety.

The DM's *forward switching condition* (FSC) evaluates the control action proposed by the AC and decides whether to switch to the BC. A common technique used to develop an FSC is to shrink the recoverable region by a margin based on the maximum time derivative of the state and the length of a time step, and switch to BC if the current state lies outside this smaller set.

2.2 Control Barrier Functions

Control Barrier Functions (CBFs) [13,14] are an extension of the Barrier Certificates used for safety verification of hybrid systems [11,12]. CBFs are a class of Lyapunov-like functions used to guarantee safety for nonlinear control systems by assisting in the design of a class of safe controllers that establish the forward-invariance of safe sets [10,15]. Our presentation of CBFs is based on [14].

Consider a nonlinear affine control system

$$\dot{x} = f(x) + g(x)u \tag{1}$$

with state $x \in D \subset \mathbb{R}^n$, control input $u \in U$, and functions f and g that are locally Lipschitz. The set $\mathcal{R}$ of recoverable states is defined as the super-level set of a continuously differentiable function $h : D \subset \mathbb{R}^n \to \mathbb{R}$. The recoverable set $\mathcal{R}$ and its boundary $\partial \mathcal{R}$ are given by:

$$\mathcal{R} = \{x \in D \subset \mathbb{R}^n | h(x) \geq 0\} \tag{2}$$

$$\partial \mathcal{R} = \{x \in D \subset \mathbb{R}^n | h(x) = 0\} \tag{3}$$

The time derivative of $h(x)$ along the direction of the state evolution is

$$\frac{dh(x)}{dt} = \frac{\partial h(x)}{\partial x}\dot{x} = \frac{\partial h(x)}{\partial x}(f(x) + g(x)u) \tag{4}$$

which can be restated in the Lie derivative formulation as

$$\frac{dh(x)}{dt} = L_f h(x) + L_g h(x)u. \tag{5}$$

For all $x \in \mathcal{D}$, if there exists an extended class $\mathcal{K}$ function $\alpha : \mathbb{R} \to \mathbb{R}$ (strictly increasing and $\alpha(0) = 0$) such that the following condition on the Lie derivative of h is satisfied:

$$\sup_{u \in U} [L_f h(x) + L_g h(x)u + \alpha(h(x))] \geq 0 \tag{6}$$

then h is a valid CBF. Condition (6) implies the existence of a control action for all $x \in D$, such that the Lie derivative of h is bounded from below by $-\alpha(h(x))$. Furthermore, for $x \in \partial \mathcal{R}$, condition (6) reduces to a result for set invariance known as Nagumo's theorem [16,17]. Condition (6) is used to define the set $K(x)$ of control actions that establish the forward invariance of set $\mathcal{R}$; i.e., starting from $x \in \mathcal{R}$, the state will always remain inside the set $\mathcal{R}$:

$$K(x) = \{u \in U : L_f h(x) + L_g h(x)u + \alpha(h(x)) \geq 0\} \tag{7}$$

The following theorem is from [14].

Theorem II.1. *For the control system given in Eq. (1) and recoverable set $\mathcal{R}$ defined in (2) as the super-level set of some continuously differentiable function $h : \mathbb{R}^n \to \mathbb{R}$, if h is a CBF for all $x \in D$ and $\frac{\partial h}{\partial x} \neq 0$ for all $x \in \partial \mathcal{R}$, then any controller u such that $\forall x \in D : u(x) \in K(x)$ ensures forward-invariance of the set $\mathcal{R}$.*

Proof. See [14]. Condition (6) on the Lie derivative of h reduces, on the boundary of $\mathcal{R}$, to the set invariance condition of Nagumo's theorem: for $x \in \partial \mathcal{R}$, $\dot{h} \geq -\alpha(h(x)) = 0$. Hence, according to Nagumo's theorem [16,17], the set $\mathcal{R}$ is forward-invariant.

A widely used technique for the synthesis of CBFs is SOS-optimization [18] based search, which can be applied to a polynomial approximation of the systems dynamics. Other methods of synthesizing CBFs are surveyed in [14].

3   Distributed Simplex Architecture

This section describes the Distributed Simplex Architecture (DSA). We formally introduce the MAS safety problem and then discuss the main components of DSA, namely, the distributed baseline controller (BC) and the distributed decision module (DM).

Let an instance of DSA be *symmetric* if every agent uses the same switching condition and baseline controller. Moreover, DSA, or more precisely the MAS it is controlling, is *homogeneous* if every constituent agent is an instance of the same plant model.

Consider a MAS consisting of k homogeneous agents, denoted as $\mathcal{M} = \{1, ..., k\}$, where the nonlinear control affine dynamics for the ith agent are:

$$\dot{x}_i = f(x_i) + g(x_i)u_i \tag{8}$$

where $x_i \in D \in \mathbb{R}^n$ is the state of agent i and $u_i \in U \subset \mathbb{R}^m$ is its control input. For an agent i, we define the set of its *neighbors* $\mathcal{N}_i \subseteq \mathcal{M}$ as the agents whose state is accessible to i either through sensing or communication. Depending on the application, the set of neighbors could be fixed or vary dynamically. For example, in our flocking case study (Sect. 4), agent i's neighbors (in a given state) are the agents within a fixed distance r of agent i; we assume agent i can accurately sense the positions and velocities of these agents.

We denote a combined state of all of the agents in the MAS as the vector $x = \{x_1^T, x_2^T, \dots x_k^T\}^T$ and denote a state of the neighbors of agent i (including i itself) as $x_{\mathcal{N}_i}$. DSA uses discrete-time control: the DMs and controllers execute every η seconds. We assume that all agents execute their DM and controllers simultaneously; this assumption simplifies the analysis.

Admissible States. The set of admissible states $\mathcal{A} \subset \mathbb{R}^{kn}$ consists of all states that satisfy the safety constraints. A constraint $C : D^k \to \mathbb{R}$ is a function from k-agent MAS states to the reals. In this paper, we are primarily concerned with *binary constraints* (between neighboring agents) of the form $C_{ij} : D \times D \to \mathbb{R}$, and *unary constraints* of the form $C_i : D \to \mathbb{R}$. Hence, the set of admissible states, $\mathcal{A} \subset \mathbb{R}^{kn}$ are the MAS states of $\mathbf{x} \in \mathbb{R}^{kn}$ such that all of the unary and binary constraints are satisfied.

Formally, a symmetric instance of DSA is tasked with solving the following problem. Given a MAS defined as in Eq. (8) and $\mathbf{x}(0) \in \mathcal{A}$, design a BC and DM to be used by all agents such that the MAS remains safe; i.e. $\mathbf{x}(t) \in \mathcal{A}, \forall t > 0$.

Recoverable States. For each agent i, the local admissible set $\mathcal{A}_i \subset \mathbb{R}^n$ is the set of states $x_i \in \mathbb{R}^n$ that satisfy all unary constraints. The set $\mathcal{S}_i \subset \mathcal{A}_i$ is defined as the super-level set of the CBF $h_i : \mathbb{R}^n \to \mathbb{R}$, which is designed to ensure forward-invariance of $\mathcal{A}_i$. Similarly, for a pair of neighboring agents i, j where $i \in \mathcal{M}, j \in \mathcal{N}_i$, the pairwise-admissible set $\mathcal{A}_{ij} \subset \mathbb{R}^{2n}$ is the set of pairs of states that satisfy all binary constraints. The set $\mathcal{S}_{ij} \subset \mathcal{A}_{ij}$ is defined as the super-level set of the CBF $h_{ij} : \mathbb{R}^{2n} \to \mathbb{R}$ designed to ensure forward-invariance of $\mathcal{A}_{ij}$. The recoverable set $\mathcal{R}_{ij} \subset \mathbb{R}^{2n}$, for a pair of neighboring agents i, j where $i \in \mathcal{M}, j \in \mathcal{N}_i$, is defined in terms of $\mathcal{S}_i, \mathcal{S}_j$ and $\mathcal{S}_{ij}$.

$$\mathcal{S}_i = \{x_i \in \mathbb{R}^n | h_i(x_i) \geq 0\} \tag{9}$$

$$\mathcal{S}_{ij} = \{(x_i, x_j) \in \mathbb{R}^{2n} | h_{ij}(x_i, x_j) \geq 0\} \tag{10}$$

$$\mathcal{R}_{ij} = (\mathcal{S}_i \times \mathcal{S}_j) \cap \mathcal{S}_{ij} \tag{11}$$

The recoverable set $\mathcal{R} \subset \mathcal{A}$ for the entire MAS is defined as the set of system states for which $(x_i, x_j) \in \mathcal{R}_{ij}$ for every pair of neighboring agents i, j. Note that if agent i and j's controllers satisfy the following constraints based on the Lie derivatives of h_i, h_j and h_{ij}, similar to the constraints in (7), the pairwise state of agents i and j will remain in $\mathcal{R}_{ij}$ according to Theorem II.1.

$$L_f h_i(x_i) + L_g h_i(x_i) u_i + \alpha(h_i(x_i)) \geq 0 \tag{12a}$$

$$L_f h_j(x_j) + L_g h_j(x_j) u_j + \alpha(h_j(x_j)) \geq 0 \tag{12b}$$

$$L_f h_{ij}(x_i, x_j) + L_g h_{ij}(x_i, x_j) \begin{bmatrix} u_i \\ u_j \end{bmatrix} + \alpha(h_{ij}(x_i, x_j)) \geq 0 \tag{12c}$$

Constraint Partitioning. Note that the constraints in (12) are linear in the control variable. For ease of notation, we write the unary constraints as $A_i u_i \leq b_i$ and the binary constraints as $[P_{ij} \ Q_{ij}] [\begin{smallmatrix} u_i \\ u_j \end{smallmatrix}] \leq b_{ij}$.

The binary constraint in (12c) is a condition on the control actions of a pair of agents. For a centralized MAS, the global controller can pick coordinated actions for agents i and j to ensure the binary constraint (12c) is satisfied. For a decentralized MAS, however, the distributed control of the two agents cannot independently satisfy the binary constraint without running an agreement protocol.

As DSA is a distributed control framework, we solve the problem of the satisfaction of binary constraints by partitioning a binary constraint into two unary constraints such that the satisfaction of the unary constraints by agents i and j implies the satisfaction of the binary constraint (but not necessarily vice versa) [10].

$$\left. \begin{array}{c} P_{ij} u_i \leq b_{ij}/2 \\ Q_{ij} u_j \leq b_{ij}/2 \end{array} \right\} \Rightarrow [P_{ij} \ Q_{ij}] \begin{bmatrix} u_i \\ u_j \end{bmatrix} \leq b_{ij} \tag{13}$$

Moreover, the equal partitioning of the binary constraint ensures that the agents share an equal responsibility in maintaining it. The admissible control space for agent i, denoted by $\mathcal{L}_i$, is the intersection of half-spaces of the hyper-planes defined by the linear constraints.

$$\mathcal{L}_i = \{u_i \in U \mid \forall j \in \mathcal{N}_i : A_i u_i \leq b_i \wedge P_{ij} u_i \leq b_{ij}/2\} \tag{14}$$

Theorem III.1. *Given a MAS indexed by $\mathcal{M}$ and with dynamics as in (8), if the controller for each agent $i \in \mathcal{M}$ chooses an action $u_i \in \mathcal{L}_i$, thereby satisfying the Lie derivative constraints on the respective CBFs, and $\mathbf{x}(0) \in \mathcal{R}$, then the MAS is guaranteed to remain safe.*

Proof. If all agents choose an action from their respective admissible control spaces $\mathcal{L}_i$, then the forward-invariance of the set $\mathcal{S}_i$ for all $i \in \mathcal{M}$ and $\mathcal{S}_{ij}$ for all $i \in \mathcal{M}, j \in \mathcal{N}_i$ is established by Theorem II.1. Therefore, $\mathcal{R}_{ij}$ is forward-invariant for all $i \in \mathcal{M}, j \in \mathcal{N}_i$ and consequently $\mathcal{R}$ is forward-invariant.

3.1 Baseline Controller

The BC is a distributed controller tasked with keeping the state of an agent in the safe region. For an agent i, the BC's control law depends on i's state x_i and the states of its neighbors $x_j, \forall j \in \mathcal{N}_i$. In our design, the BC is strictly focused on safety, leaving mission-critical objectives to the AC. Specifically, the BC is designed to move the system away from unsafe states and toward safer states as quickly as possible.

We design the BC as the solution to the following constrained multi-objective optimization (MOO) problem where the utility function is the weighted sum of objective functions based on the Lie derivatives of the CBFs h_i and h_{ij} introduced above:

$$u_i^* = \underset{u_i}{argmax} \quad \frac{1}{h_i}(L_f h_i + L_g h_i u_i) + \sum_{j \in \mathcal{N}_i} \frac{1}{h_{ij}}(L_f h_{ij} + L_g h_{ij} \begin{bmatrix} u_i \\ 0 \end{bmatrix}) \tag{15}$$
$$\text{s.t.} \quad u_i \in \mathcal{L}_i$$

The bottom component of the column vector in the last term is agent i's prediction for agent j's next control action u_j. Since we consider MASs in which agents are unable to communicate their planned control actions, agent i simply predicts that $u_j = 0$. This approach has been shown to work well in prior work on distributed model-predictive control for flocking [19] , where the control actions are accelerations. Despite its complex form, at any given time, the utility function in Eq. (15) is linear in u_i, as the values of all other quantities are fixed. Since the constraints are also linear, the optimization problem in Eq. (15) is a linear program and hence can be efficiently solved in real-time.

Recall that, by definition, the CBFs quantify the degree of safety of a state with respect to the given safety constraints, with larger (positive) values indicating safer states. A positive value of the Lie derivative indicates that the proposed action will lead to a state that has a higher CBF value and therefore is safer.

The solution to the optimization problem (15) is a control action that maximizes the weighted sum of the Lie derivatives of the CBFs. We note that in a weighted-sum formulation of a MOO problem, it is possible that some objective functions are negative in the optimal solution. We ensure the selected action u_i is safe by constraining u_i to be in the admissible control space $\mathcal{L}_i$, defined in Eq. (14).

The weights in the utility function in Eq. (15) prioritize certain safety constraints over others. We use state-dependent weights in the form of inverses of the CBFs, thereby giving more weight to maximizing the Lie derivatives of CBFs corresponding to safety constraints that are closer to being violated.

3.2   Decision Module

Each agent's DM implements the switching logic for both forward and reverse switching. Control is switched from the AC to the BC if the *forward switching condition* (FSC) is true. Similarly, control is reverted back to the AC (from the BC) if the *reverse switching condition* (RSC) is true. For an agent i, the state of the DM is denoted as $DM_i \in \{AC, BC\}$, with $DM_i = AC$ ($DM_i = BC$) indicating that the advanced (baseline) controller is in control. DSA starts with all agents in the AC mode; i.e., $DM_i(t) = AC$ for all $t \leq 0$ and $i \in \mathcal{M}$; this is justified by the assumption that $\mathbf{x}(0) \in \mathcal{R}$.

We derive the switching conditions from the CBFs as follows. To ensure safety, the FSC must be true in a state $x_{\mathcal{N}_i}(t)$ if an unrecoverable state is reachable from $x_{\mathcal{N}_i}(t)$ in one time step η. The check for one-step reachability of an unrecoverable state is based on computing the Taylor series approximation of the CBF at the current time t, and evaluating it one time step in the future, i.e., at time $t + \eta$. The Taylor series approximation of the CBF is a function of its time-derivatives and can be regarded as a function of time based on the dynamics of the system for a given value of the control input; we take the control input of agent i to be the command proposed by the AC at time t and use the worst-case commands as the control inputs for the neighboring agents $j \in \mathcal{N}_i$. The worst-case commands are defined as the control inputs that minimize the value of the Taylor approximation of the CBF. If the Taylor series approximation of any of the CBFs is negative during the next time step η, we switch control to the BC. We denote the Taylor series approximation of the CBF h as $\hat{h}$. This results in an FSC of the following form:

$$FSC(x_{\mathcal{N}_i}, t) = \exists t_c \in (t,\, t + \eta] \mid (\hat{h}_i(t_c) < 0) \vee (\exists j \in \mathcal{N}_i \mid \hat{h}_{ij}(t_c) < 0) \quad (16)$$

We derive the RSC using a similar approach, except the inequalities are reversed, the worst-case commands are used as the control inputs for all the agents, and an m-time-step reachability check with $m > 1$ is used; the latter is to prevent frequent back-and-forth switching between the AC and BC. The RSC holds if the Taylor series approximations of all the CBFs remain positive during the next $m \cdot \eta$ seconds.

$$RSC(x_{\mathcal{N}_i}, t) = \forall t_c \in (t,\, t + m \cdot \eta] \mid (\hat{h}_i(t_c) > 0) \wedge (\forall j \in \mathcal{N}_i \mid \hat{h}_{ij}(t_c) > 0) \quad (17)$$

We experimented with various orders of Taylor series approximations in our case studies. Since the time step η is typically small, even low-order Taylor series approximation gives very good results, i.e., $\hat{h}(t + \eta)$ is very close to the exact value $h(t + \eta)$. The switching condition can be made more rigorous by taking into account the remainder error in the Taylor series approximation; Taylor's theorem provides a bound on the remainder error. We will explore this idea in future work.

3.3 Safety Theorem

Our main result is the following safety theorem for DSA.

Theorem III.2. *Given a MAS indexed by $\mathcal{M}$ with dynamics specified as in Eq. (8), if each agent operates under DSA with the BC as in Eq. (15), the switching logic as in Eqs. (16) and (17), and $\mathbf{x}(0) \in \mathcal{R} \subset \mathbb{R}^{kn}$, then the MAS will remain safe.*

Proof. The proof proceeds by considering both possible DM states for an arbitrary agent i, and establishing that i's next state is safe. First, consider agent i at time t with $DM_i(t) = AC$. As the FSC is false, the one-step reachability check associated with the FSC ensures that the CBFs for unary and binary safety constraints are strictly positive in the next state $x_i(t+\eta)$; i.e. $h_i(x_i(t+\eta)) > 0$ and $\forall j \in \mathcal{N}_i : h_{ij}(x_i(t+\eta), x_j(t+\eta)) > 0$. Hence the next state is recoverable.

Subsequently, consider agent i at time t with $DM_i(t) = BC$. The unary safety constraint is satisfied for agent i as the BC's action is constrained within the admissible control space. Next, we show that the binary safety constraints with all neighboring agents are also satisfied. We divide the neighbors of i into two sets based on their DM states: the set of neighbors in AC mode and the set of neighbors in BC mode are denoted as $\mathcal{N}_i^{AC}$ and $\mathcal{N}_i^{BC}$, respectively. The neighbors in BC mode choose their control actions from their corresponding admissible control spaces as in Eq. (14). As agent i also chooses its control action from its admissible control space, according to *Theorem* III.1, the neighbors in BC mode will satisfy the binary safety constraints with agent i. As for neighbors in AC mode, due to the one-step reachability check in their FSC, in state $x_i(t+\eta)$, the pairwise CBFs satisfy $h_{ij}(x_i(t+\eta), x_j(t+\eta)) \geq 0$ for all $j \in \mathcal{N}_i^{AC}$. Hence, $x_i(t+\eta)$ is recoverable for $DM_i(t) = BC$. We have proven that for any agent i and time step t, if $x_i(t)$ is recoverable, then $x_i(t+\eta)$ is recoverable. By assumption, $\mathbf{x}(0) \in \mathcal{R}$. Therefore, by induction, $\mathbf{x}(t) \in \mathcal{R}$ for $t > 0$.

4 Flocking Case Study

We evaluate DSA on the distributed flocking problem with the goal of preventing inter-agent collisions. Consider a MAS consisting of k robotic agents with double integrator dynamics, indexed by $\mathcal{M} = \{1, \dots, k\}$:

$$\begin{bmatrix} \dot{p}_i \\ \dot{v}_i \end{bmatrix} = \begin{bmatrix} 0 & I_{2\times2} \\ 0 & 0 \end{bmatrix} \begin{bmatrix} p_i \\ v_i \end{bmatrix} + \begin{bmatrix} 0 \\ I_{2\times2} \end{bmatrix} a_i \tag{18}$$

where $p_i, v_i, a_i \in \mathbb{R}^2$ are the position, velocity and acceleration of agent $i \in \mathcal{M}$, respectively. The magnitudes of velocities and accelerations are bounded by $\bar{v}$ and $\bar{a}$, respectively. Acceleration a_i is the control input for agent i. As DSA is a discrete-time protocol, the state of the DM and the a_i's are updated every η seconds. The *state* of an agent i is denoted by the vector $s_i = [p_i^T v_i^T]^T$. The *state* of the entire flock at time t is denoted by the vector $\mathbf{s}(t) = [\mathbf{p}(t)^T \ \mathbf{v}(t)^T]^T \in \mathbb{R}^{4n}$, where $\mathbf{p}(t) = [p_1^T(t) \cdots p_n^T(t)]^T$ and $\mathbf{v}(t) = [v_1^T(t) \cdots v_n^T(t)]^T$ are the vectors respectively denoting the positions and velocities of the flock at time t.

We assume that an agent can accurately sense the positions and velocities of nearby agents within a fixed distance r. The set of the *spatial neighbors* of agent i is defined as $\mathcal{N}_i(\mathbf{p}) = \{j \in \mathcal{M} \mid j \neq i \wedge \|p_i - p_j\| < r\}$, where $\|\cdot\|$ denotes the Euclidean norm. For ease of notation, we sometimes use $\mathbf{s}$ and $\mathbf{s}_i$ to refer to the state variables $\mathbf{s}(t)$ and $\mathbf{s}_i(t)$, respectively, without the time index.

The MAS is characterized by a set of operational constraints which include physical limits and safety properties. States that satisfy the operational constraints are called *admissible*, and are denoted by the set $\mathcal{A} \in \mathbb{R}^{4k}$. The desired safety property is that no pair of agents is in a "state of collision". A pair of agents is considered to be in a *state of collision* if the Euclidean distance between them is less than a threshold distance $d_{min} \in \mathbb{R}^+$, resulting in a binary safety constraint of the form: $\|p_i - p_j\| - d_{min} \geq 0 \ \forall \ i \in \mathcal{M}, j \in \mathcal{N}_i$. Similarly, a state $\mathbf{s}$ is *recoverable* if all pairs of agents can brake (de-accelerate) relative to each other without colliding. Otherwise, the state $\mathbf{s}$ is considered *unrecoverable*.

4.1 Synthesis of Control Barrier Function

Let $\mathcal{R}_{ij} \subset \mathbb{R}^8$ be the set of recoverable states for a pair of agents $i, j \in \mathcal{M}$. The flock-wide set of recoverable states, denoted by $\mathcal{R} \subset \mathbb{R}^{4k}$, is defined in terms of $\mathcal{R}_{ij}$. As in [15], the set $\mathcal{R}_{ij}$ is defined as the super-level set of a pairwise CBF $h_{ij} : \mathbb{R}^8 \to \mathbb{R}$: $\mathcal{R}_{ij} = \{s_i, s_j \mid h_{ij}(s_i, s_j) \geq 0\}$. The flock-wide set of recoverable states $\mathcal{R} \subset \mathcal{A}$ is defined as the set of system states in which $(s_i, s_j) \in \mathcal{R}_{ij}$, for every pair of neighboring agents i, j.

In accordance with [15], the function $h_{ij}(s_i, s_j)$ is based on a safety constraint over a pair of agents $i, j \in \mathcal{M}$. The safety constraint ensures that for any pair of agents, the maximum braking force can always keep the agents at a distance greater than d_{min} from each other. As introduced earlier, d_{min} is the threshold distance that defines a collision. Considering that the tangential component of the relative velocity, denoted by Δv, causes a collision, the constraint regulates Δv by application of maximum acceleration to reduce Δv to zero. Hence, the safety constraint can be represented as the following condition on the inter-agent distance $\|\Delta \mathbf{p}_{ij}\| = \|p_i - p_j\|$, the braking distance $(\Delta v)^2/4\bar{a}$, and the safety threshold distance d_{min}:

$$\|\Delta \mathbf{p}_{ij}\| - \frac{(\Delta v)^2}{4\bar{a}} \geq d_{min} \tag{19}$$

$$h_{ij}(s_i, s_j) = \sqrt{4\bar{a}(\|\Delta \mathbf{p}_{ij}\| - d_{min})} - \Delta v \geq 0 \tag{20}$$

The braking distance is the distance covered while the relative speed reduces from Δv to zero under a deceleration of $2\bar{a}$. The constraint in Eq. (19) is rearranged to get the CBF h_{ij} given in Eq. (20).

Combining Eqs. (20) and (12c), we arrive at the linear constraint on the accelerations for agents i and j, which constrains the Lie derivative of the CBF in (20) to be greater than $-\alpha(h_{ij})$. We set $\alpha(h_{ij}) = \gamma h_{ij}^3$, as in [15], where $\gamma \in \mathbb{R}^+$, resulting in the following constraint on the accelerations of agents i, j:

$$\frac{\Delta \mathbf{p}_{ij}^T (\Delta \mathbf{a}_{ij})}{\|\Delta \mathbf{p}_{ij}\|} - \frac{(\Delta \mathbf{v}_{ij}^T \Delta \mathbf{p}_{ij})^2}{\|\Delta \mathbf{p}_{ij}\|^3} + \frac{\|\Delta \mathbf{v}_{ij}\|^2}{\|\Delta \mathbf{p}_{ij}\|}$$

$$+ \frac{2\bar{a} \Delta \mathbf{v}_{ij}^T \Delta \mathbf{p}_{ij}}{\|\Delta \mathbf{p}_{ij}\| \sqrt{4\bar{a}(\|\Delta \mathbf{p}_{ij}\| - d_{min})}} \geq -\gamma h_{ij}^3 \qquad (21)$$

where the left-hand side is the Lie derivative of the CBF h_{ij} and $\Delta \mathbf{p}_{ij} = p_i - p_j$, $\Delta \mathbf{v}_{ij} = v_i - v_j$, and $\Delta \mathbf{a}_{ij} = a_i - a_j$ are the vectors representing the relative position, the relative velocity, and the relative acceleration of agents i and j, respectively. We further note that the binary constraint (21) can be reformulated as $[P_{ij}\ Q_{ij}][\begin{smallmatrix} a_i \\ a_j \end{smallmatrix}] \leq b_{ij}$, and hence can be split into two unary constraints $P_{ij}u_i \leq b_{ij}/2$ and $Q_{ij}u_j \leq b_{ij}/2$, following the convention in Eq. (13). The set of safe accelerations for an agent i, denoted by $\mathcal{K}_i(\mathbf{s}_i) \subset \mathbb{R}^2$, is defined as the intersection of the half-planes defined by the Lie-derivative-based constraints, where each neighboring agent contributes a single constraint:

$$\mathcal{K}_i(\mathbf{s}_i) = \left\{ a_i \in \mathbb{R}^2 \mid P_{ij}u_i \leq b_{ij}/2, \ \forall j \in \mathcal{N}_i \right\} \qquad (22)$$

With the CBFs for collision-free flocking defined in (20) and the admissible control space defined in (22), the BC, FSC, and RSC follow from (15), (16), and (17), respectively. We use Taylor approximation of order one to compute FSC and RSC.

4.2 Advanced Controller

We use the Reynolds flocking model [20] as the AC. In the Reynolds model, the accelerations a_i for each agent is a weighted sum of three acceleration terms based on simple rules of interaction with neighboring agents: *separation* (move away from your close-by neighbors), *cohesion* (move towards the centroid of your neighbors), and *alignment* (match your velocity with the average velocity of your neighbors). The acceleration for agent i is $a_i = w_s a_i^s + w_c a_i^c + w_{al} a_i^{al}$, where $w_s, w_c, w_{al} \in \mathbb{R}^+$ are scalar weights and $a_i^s, a_i^c, a_i^{al} \in \mathbb{R}^2$ are the acceleration terms corresponding to separation, cohesion, and alignment, respectively. We note that the Reynolds model does not guarantee collision avoidance. Nevertheless, when the flock stabilizes, the average distance to the closest neighbors is determined by the weights of the interaction terms.

4.3 Experimental Results

The number of agents in the MAS is $k = 15$. The other parameters used in the experiments are $r = 4$, $\bar{a} = 5$, $\bar{v} = 2.5$, $d_{min} = 2$, and $\eta = 0.1$s. The length of the simulations is 50 s. The initial positions and the initial velocities are uniformly sampled from $[-10, 10]^2$ and $[-1, 1]^2$, respectively, and we ensure that the initial state is recoverable. The weights of the Reynolds model terms are chosen experimentally to ensure that no pair of agents are in a state of collision in the steady state. They are set to $w_s = 3$, $w_c = 1.5$, and $w_{al} = 0.5$.

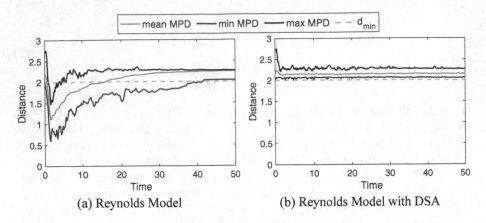

Fig. 2. The minimum pairwise distance (MPD) for a flock of size 15, calculated over 100 simulation runs, with and without DSA.

To demonstrate the effectiveness of DSA in preventing inter-agent collisions, we generated 100 simulation runs using two different control strategies, starting from the same set of random initial configurations. In the first set of 100 simulations, Reynolds model is used to control all agents for the duration of the simulations. In the second set of 100 simulations, Reynolds model is wrapped with a verified safe BC and DM designed using DSA.

We define the *minimum pairwise distance* (MPD), as the minimum Euclidean distance between any pairs of agents in the flock, i.e., $\min_{i,j \in \mathcal{M}} \|p_i - p_j\|$. Figure 2 shows the spread of MPD at each time step, by plotting its mean, minimum, and maximum values, calculated over 100 simulation runs.

As evident from Fig. 2(b), the minimum MPD is greater than d_{min} for the entire duration of the simulation runs, indicating that DSA is able to prevent inter-agents collisions for the 100 simulations. In contrast, as shown in Fig. 2(a), Reynolds model results in safety violations during the first 42 s (Only the last 8 s are collision-free in all 100 simulations) and the mean MPD crosses the safety threshold at around 16 s. Moreover, operating under DSA, the distribution of MPD is relatively uniform over the duration of the simulations. We further note that the average time the agents spend in BC mode is only 3.44% of the total duration of the simulation, indicating that DSA is largely non-invasive. Videos of flocking under both control strategies are available online.[1]

The simulation results clearly demonstrate the effectiveness of DSA in guaranteeing inter-agent collision avoidance. We also ran simulations where all agents are solely under the control of the BC. As the BC is strictly focused on safety, we observed that the flock fragments as agents safely move out of the sensing ranges of other agents.

The flocking case study clearly illustrate the guiding principles and benefits of DSA. In particular, it shows that: (a) the AC is not always safe, but (b) the combination of the AC and BC in DSA is safe, and (c) DSA outperforms the BC.

---

[1] https://youtu.be/E_ufaJRnfvo, https://youtu.be/PZz6nUA5fD8.

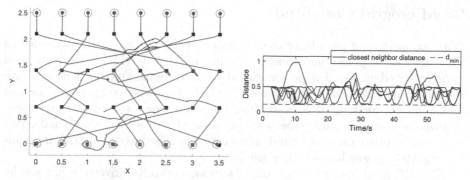

(a) Trajectories of agents passing through WPs. Red/blue segments indicate AC/BC mode.

(b) Distance to closest neighbor for all agents.

Fig. 3. Experimental results for way-point case study. (Color figure online)

5   Way-Point Case Study

This section describes the problem setup and experimental results for the way-point (WP) control case study. The agent model is the same as the one used for the flocking case study, given in Eq. (18). The experimental setup is shown in Fig. 3, where the agents, initially positioned along the top of the figure, are to navigate through a series of WPs while maintaining a safe distance from one another. The WPs are represented by the black squares. The CBFs, BC and DM are same as those defined for the flocking problem; see Sect. 4

The AC is a rule-based controller where each agent accelerates towards its next WP (ignoring the other agents) until the final WP is reached. Agents are assigned one WP from each row such that they are on a collision course if they follow the AC's commands.

5.1   Experimental Results

The number of agents used in the experiment is eight and the number of WPs an agent is required to visit is four (one in each row). Initially, the agents are at rest with their positions represented by the red dots in Fig. 3(a). The final positions are shown as green dots. The duration of the simulation is 60 s. The other parameters used in the experiments are $r = 1.0$, $\bar{a} = 0.8$, $\bar{v} = 0.2$, $d_{min} = 0.15$, and $\eta = 0.05$ s. The trajectories of the agents are given in Fig. 3(a), where the segments in blue indicate when the BC is in control. Figure 3(b) plots the smallest inter-agent distances, indicating that the agents maintain a safe distance from one another. A video of the simulation is available online.[2]

---

[2] https://youtu.be/AcC8iUI0TjU.

6   Microgrid Case Study

With an increasing prevalence of distributed energy resources (DERs) such as wind and solar power, electrification using microgrids (MGs) has witnessed unprecedented growth. Unlike traditional power systems, MG DERs do not have rotating components such as turbines. The lack of rotating components can lead to low inertia, making MGs susceptible to oscillations resulting from transient disturbances [21]. Ensuring the safe operation of an MG is thus a challenging problem. In this case study, we demonstrate the effectiveness of DSA in maintaining MG voltage levels within safe limits.

The MG we consider is a network of k droop-controlled inverters, indexed by $\mathcal{M} = \{1, \ldots, k\}$. The dynamics of each inverter is modeled as [21–24]:

$$\dot{\theta}_i = \omega_i \tag{23a}$$

$$\tau_i \dot{\omega}_i = \omega_i^0 - \omega_i + \lambda_i^p (P_i^{set} - P_i) \tag{23b}$$

$$\tau_i \dot{v}_i = v_i^0 - v_i + \lambda_i^q (Q_i^{set} - Q_i) \tag{23c}$$

where θ_i, ω_i, and v_i are respectively the phase angle, frequency, and voltage of inverter i, $i \in \mathcal{M}$. The state vector for the MG is denoted by $\mathbf{s} = [\theta^T \ \omega^T \ v^T]^T \in \mathbb{R}^{3k}$, where θ, ω, and v are respectively vectors representing the voltage phase angle, frequency, and voltage at each node of the MG. A pair of inverters are considered neighbors if they are connected by a transmission line. Also, λ_i^p and λ_i^q are droop coefficients of "active power vs frequency" and "reactive power vs voltage" droop controllers, respectively. $\tau_i \in \mathbb{R}^+$ is the time constant used for the low-pass filters that are processing the active and reactive power measurements. Finally, ω_i^0 and v_i^0 are the nominal frequency and voltage values.

P_i and Q_i are the active and reactive powers injected by inverter i into the system:

$$
\begin{aligned}
P_i &= v_i \sum_{j \in \mathcal{N}_i} v_j (G_{i,j} \cos \theta_{i,j} + B_{i,j} \sin \theta_{i,j}) \\
Q_i &= v_i \sum_{j \in \mathcal{N}_i} v_j (G_{i,j} \sin \theta_{i,j} - B_{i,j} \cos \theta_{i,j})
\end{aligned}
\tag{24}
$$

where $\theta_{i,j} = \theta_i - \theta_j$, and $\mathcal{N}_i \subseteq \mathcal{M}$ is the set of neighbors. $G_{i,j}, B_{i,j}$ are respectively conductance and susceptance values of the transmission line connecting inverters i and j.

P_i^{set} and Q_i^{set} are the active power and reactive power setpoints. The inverters have the ability to change their respective power setpoints according to the MG's operating conditions. This is modeled as:

$$P_i^{set} = P_i^0 + u_i^p, \ Q_i^{set} = Q_i^0 + u_i^q \tag{25}$$

where P_i^0 and Q_i^0 are the setpoints for the nominal operating condition, and u_i^p and u_i^q are control inputs.

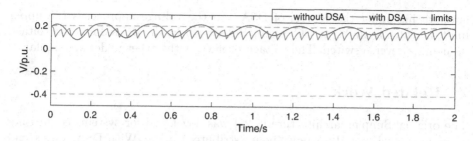

Fig. 4. Voltage graph at node 4 of the MG network.

6.1   Synthesis of Control Barrier Function

The safety property for the MG network is a set of unary constraints restricting the voltages at each node to remain within safe limits. The recoverable set $\mathcal{R}_i \subset \mathbb{R}^3$ for inverter i is defined as the super-level set of a CBF $h_i : \mathbb{R}^3 \to \mathbb{R}$. We follow the SOS-optimization technique given in [24] to synthesize the CBFs. Since the power flow Eq. (23) are nonlinear, we apply a third-order Taylor series expansion to approximate the dynamics in polynomial form. We then follow the three-step process given in [24] to obtain the CBF for each MG node. We then calculate the admissible control space according to Eq. (14), and the BC, FSC, and RSC follow from Eqs. (15), (16), and (17), respectively. We have experimented with various orders of Taylor approximations for the computation of FSC and RSC.

6.2   Advanced Controller

The AC sets the active/reactive power setpoints to their nominal values. Thus, the AC does not limit voltage and frequency magnitudes but is only concerned with stabilizing frequency and voltage magnitudes to their nominal values.

6.3   Experimental Results

We consider a 6-bus MG [24]. Disconnecting the MG from the main utility, we replace bus 0 with a droop-controlled inverter (Eq. (23)), with inverters also placed on buses 1, 4 and 5. Bus 0 is the reference bus for the phase angle. Nominal values of voltage and frequency, as well as the active/reactive power set-points, were obtained by solving the steady-state power-flow equations given in Eq. (24); these were then used to shift the equilibrium point to the origin. Droop coefficients λ_i^p and λ_i^q were set to 2.43 rad/s/p.u. and 0.20 p.u./p.u., τ_i was set to 0.5 s, and the control period η was set to 0.01 s. Loads are modeled as constant power loads, and a Kron-reduced network [25] with only the inverter nodes was used for analysis. The safe set is defined in terms of the shifted (around the 0 p.u.) nodal voltage magnitudes as follows: $v_i \geq -0.4$ p.u. $\wedge$ $v_i \leq 0.2$ p.u.

The duration of the simulation is two seconds. Our results show that with DSA, the voltage at each node remains within safe limits; without DSA, safety limits are exceeded. Figure 4 gives the voltage plot at node 4. When the MG is operating under the control of DSA and the voltage approaches the upper limit, a switch from AC to BC occurs. Subsequently, the BC reduces the voltage inducing a reverse switch. The voltage profiles at the other nodes are similar.

7 Related Work

The original Simplex architecture [5,26] was developed for systems comprising a single controller and a single (non-distributed) plant. With DSA, we extend the scope of Simplex to MASs under distributed control. RTA [27,28] is a runtime assurance technique that can be applied to component-based systems. In this case, however, each RTA wrapper (i.e., each Simplex-like instance) independently ensures a local safety property of a component. For example, in [27], RTA instances for an inner-loop controller and a guidance system are uncoordinated and operate independently. In contrast, in DSA, each agent takes the states of neighboring agents into account when making control decisions, in order to ensure that pairwise safety constraints are satisfied.

A runtime verification framework for dynamically adaptive multi-agent systems (DAMS-RV) is proposed in [29]. DAMS-RV is activated every time the system adapts to a change in the system itself or its environment. This method relies on a *monitoring* phase to observe and identify changes that occur in agent collaboration so that verification can be carried out on the system operating in new contexts. In contrast, DSA does not require such intermediary supervision. In [30], a dynamic policy model that can be used to express constraints on agent behavior is presented. These constraints limit agent autonomy to lie within well-defined boundaries. Constraint specifications are kept simple by allowing the policy designer to decompose a specification into components and define the overall policy as a composition of these smaller units. In contrast, DSA uses CBFs to compute the requisite safety regions.

In [10,14,15,31], CBF-based methodologies have been used for runtime safety assurance of MASs. For example, in [10,15], a formal framework for collision avoidance in multi-robot systems is presented. A CBF-based wrapper around an advanced controller guarantees forward invariance of a safe set. The wrapper solves an optimization problem involving the Lie derivative of the CBF to compute minimal changes to the AC's output needed to ensure safety. In contrast, in DSA, no attempt is made to minimally perturb the AC's output. Instead we rely on CBF-based switching logic in the DM to forward switch to the BC if the AC's output is not recoverable.

In [32], a shield-based technique for runtime verification of multi-agent systems is presented. In this approach, which does not require global information, every agent has a shield consisting of two components: a pathfinder that corrects the behavior of the agent, and an ordering mechanism that dynamically modifies the priority of the agent. An upper bound is derived on the maximum deviation for any agent from its original behavior. In contrast, DSA relies on forward and reverse switching between an agent's advanced and baseline controllers to safely allow completion of mission goals.

8   Conclusion

We have presented the Distributed Simplex Architecture, a runtime assurance technique for the safety of multi-agent systems. DSA is distributed in the sense that it involves one local instance of traditional Simplex per agent such that the conjunction of their respective safety properties yields the desired safety property for the entire MAS. Moreover, an agent's switching logic depends only on its own state and that of neighboring agents. We demonstrated the effectiveness of DSA by successfully applying it to flocking, way-point visiting, and microgrid control. As future work, we plan to apply DSA to non-homogenous MASs and implement it on a physical platform.

In some situations, the BC's optimization problem might become infeasible. For example, for the flocking case study, infeasibility of the BC's optimization problem is possible if the agents are crowded in a small region. One possible solution for infeasibility is to design aggressive control barrier functions that guarantee feasibility at the cost of performance. For the flocking case study, one such solution is a CBF that enforces the braking manoeuvre [10].

References

1. Nasir, M., Jin, Z., Khan, H.A., Zaffar, N.A., Vasquez, J.C., Guerrero, J.M.: A decentralized control architecture applied to DC nanogrid clusters for rural electrification in developing regions. IEEE Trans. Power Electron. **34**(2), 1773–1785 (2019)
2. Boussaada, Z., Curea, O., Camblong, H., Bellaaj Mrabet, N., Hacala, A.: Multi-agent systems for the dependability and safety of microgrids. Int. J. Interact. Design Manuf. (IJIDeM) **10**(1), 1–13 (2014). https://doi.org/10.1007/s12008-014-0257-9
3. Tahir, A., Böling, J., Haghbayan, M.-H., Toivonen, H.T., Plosila, J.: Swarms of unmanned aerial vehicles - a survey. J. Ind. Inf. Integr. **16**, 100106 (2019)
4. Tynan, R., O'Hare, G.M.P., Marsh, D., O'Kane, D.: Multi-agent system architectures for wireless sensor networks. In: Sunderam, V.S., van Albada, G.D., Sloot, P.M.A., Dongarra, J. (eds.) ICCS 2005. LNCS, vol. 3516, pp. 687–694. Springer, Heidelberg (2005). https://doi.org/10.1007/11428862_94
5. Seto, D., Sha, L.: A case study on analytical analysis of the inverted pendulum real-time control system. Software Engineering Institute, Carnegie Mellon University, Pittsburgh, PA, Technical report CMU/SEI-99-TR-023 (1999)
6. Sha, L.: Using simplicity to control complexity. IEEE Softw. **18**(4), 20–28 (2001)
7. Phan, D.T., Grosu, R., Jansen, N., Paoletti, N., Smolka, S.A., Stoller, S.D.: Neural simplex architecture. In: Lee, R., Jha, S., Mavridou, A., Giannakopoulou, D. (eds.) NFM 2020. LNCS, vol. 12229, pp. 97–114. Springer, Cham (2020). https://doi.org/10.1007/978-3-030-55754-6_6
8. Gurriet, T., Singletary, A., Reher, J., Ciarletta, L., Feron, E., Ames, A.: Towards a framework for realizable safety critical control through active set invariance. In: 2018 ACM/IEEE 9th International Conference on Cyber-Physical Systems (ICCPS), pp. 98–106 (2018)

9. Egerstedt, M., Pauli, J.N., Notomista, G., Hutchinson, S.: Robot ecology: constraint-based control design for long duration autonomy. Annu. Rev. Control. **46**, 1–7 (2018)
10. Wang, L., Ames, A.D., Egerstedt, M.: Safety barrier certificates for heterogeneous multi-robot systems. In: 2016 American Control Conference (ACC), pp. 5213–5218. IEEE (2016)
11. Prajna, S., Jadbabaie, A.: Safety verification of hybrid systems using barrier certificates. In: Alur, R., Pappas, G.J. (eds.) HSCC 2004. LNCS, vol. 2993, pp. 477–492. Springer, Heidelberg (2004). https://doi.org/10.1007/978-3-540-24743-2_32
12. Prajna, S.: Barrier certificates for nonlinear model validation. Autom. **42**(1), 117–126 (2006)
13. Wieland, P., Allgöwer, F.: Constructive safety using control barrier functions. IFAC Proc. Vol. **40**(12), 462–467 (2007). 7th IFAC Symposium on Nonlinear Control Systems
14. Ames, A.D., Coogan, S., Egerstedt, M., Notomista, G., Sreenath, K., Tabuada, P.: Control barrier functions: Theory and applications. In: 18th European Control Conference, ECC 2019, pp. 3420–3431. IEEE, Naples (2019)
15. Borrmann, U., Wang, L., Ames, A.D., Egerstedt, M.: Control barrier certificates for safe swarm behavior. In: Egerstedt, M., Wardi, Y. (eds.) ADHS. Series IFAC-PapersOnLine, vol. 48, no. 27, pp. 68–73. Elsevier (2015)
16. Blanchini, F., Miani, S.: Set-Theoretic Methods in Control. 1st edn. Birkhäuser Basel (2007)
17. Blanchini, F.: Set invariance in control. Automatica **35**(11), 1747–1767 (1999)
18. Wang, L., Han, D., Egerstedt, M.: Permissive barrier certificates for safe stabilization using sum-of-squares. In: 2018 Annual American Control Conference, ACC 2018, pp. 585–590. IEEE (2018)
19. Mehmood, U., et al.: Declarative vs rule-based control for flocking dynamics. In: Proceedings of 33rd Annual ACM Symposium on Applied Computing (2018)
20. Reynolds, C.W.: Flocks, herds and schools: a distributed behavioral model. SIGGRAPH Comput. Graph. **21**(4), 25–34 (1987)
21. Pogaku, N., Prodanovic, M., Green, T.C.: Modeling, analysis and testing of autonomous operation of an inverter-based microgrid. IEEE Trans. Power Electron. **22**(2), 613–625 (2007)
22. Schiffer, J., Ortega, R., Astolfi, A., Raisch, J., Sezi, T.: Conditions for stability of droop-controlled inverter-based microgrids. Automatica **50**(10), 2457–2469 (2014)
23. Coelho, E.A.A., Cortizo, P.C., Garcia, P.F.D.: Small-signal stability for parallel-connected inverters in stand-alone AC supply systems. IEEE Trans. Ind. Appl. **38**(2), 533–542 (2002)
24. Kundu, S., Geng, S., Nandanoori, S.P., Hiskens, I.A., Kalsi, K.: Distributed barrier certificates for safe operation of inverter-based microgrids. In: 2019 American Control Conference (ACC), pp. 1042–1047 (2019)
25. Kundur, P., Balu, N., Lauby, M.: Power System Stability and Control. EPRI Power System Engineering Series. McGraw-Hill Education (1994)
26. Seto, D., Krogh, B., Sha, L., Chutinan, A.: The simplex architecture for safe online control system upgrades. In: Proceedings of the 1998 American Control Conference, vol. 6, pp. 3504–3508 (1998)
27. Aiello, M., Berryman, J., Grohs, J., Schierman, J.: Run-time assurance for advanced flight-critical control systems (2010)
28. Schierman, J., et al.: Run-time verification and validation for safety-critical flight control systems (2012)

29. Lim, Y.J., Hong, G., Shin, D., Jee, E., Bae, D.-H.: A runtime verification framework for dynamically adaptive multi-agent systems. In: 2016 International Conference on Big Data and Smart Computing (BigComp), pp. 509–512 (2016)
30. Alotaibi, H., Zedan, H.: Runtime verification of safety properties in multi-agents systems. In: 2010 10th International Conference on Intelligent Systems Design and Applications, pp. 356–362 (2010)
31. Ames, A.D., Xu, X., Grizzle, J.W., Tabuada, P.: Control barrier function based quadratic programs for safety critical systems. IEEE Trans. Autom. Control **62**(8), 3861–3876 (2017)
32. Raju, D., Bharadwaj, S., Topcu, U.: Online synthesis for runtime enforcement of safety in multi-agent systems. Preprint ArXiv:1910.10380 (2019)

Satisfiability, Reachability and Model Checking

OURS: Over- and Under-Approximating Reachable Sets for Analytic Time-Invariant Differential Equations

Ruiqi Hu, Meilun Li, and Zhikun She[(✉)]

SKLSDE, LMIB and School of Mathematical Sciences, Beihang University,
Beijing 100191, China
{by1809102,zhikun.she}@buaa.edu.cn, hyniac.li@cloudwise.com

Abstract. We present **OURS**, a precision-oriented **MATLAB** tool for computing *Over- and Under- approximations of Reachable Sets* for analytic time-invariant differential equations. The main theoretical framework behind **OURS** is introduced, including the concept of evolution function, whose zero sub-level sets are used to describe reachable sets, and a series representation of evolution function. Using the partial sums of this series, **OURS** finds over- and under-approximations of evolution function at time-instants: it consecutively estimates each remainder of the corresponding partial sum of the series with interval arithmetics until one remainder satisfies the designated precision, and then builds over- and under-approximations with this remainder. The structure of **OURS** is also presented, such as the forms of inputs and outputs, and technical implementations of the crucial steps inside. We also compare **OURS** with two other existing methods.

1 Overview of OURS

Safety verification and system falsification [1] are two crucial issues in various realistic problems. However, it is impossible to obtain the exact reachable set in general, especially for non-linear systems. In most cases, it is practical and convenient to find over- or under-approximations of the reachable set instead. Over-approximations of the reachable set can be used to prove that the system avoids the unsafe set, on the other hand, under-approximations of the reachable set can be used to prove that the system reaches the target set [2].

In this paper we present **OURS**, a **MATLAB** tool for computing both **O**ver- and **U**nder-approximations of **R**eachable **S**ets for *analytic time-invariant differential equations* (ATDEs). Following the theoretical analysis in [3,4], we start with the concept of *evolution function* (EF) of an ATDE and find a series representation of EF w.r.t. time t, named *t-expansion*. Therefore we can get the EF without analytic solutions to the ATDE. **OURS** consecutively conducts *remainder estimations* (RE) for the partial sums of t-expansion with interval

This work was supported by the Beijing Natural Science Foundation (Z180005).

S. Qin et al. (Eds.): SETTA 2021, LNCS 13071, pp. 261–278, 2021.
https://doi.org/10.1007/978-3-030-91265-9_14

arithmetics until one remainder satisfies the designated precision, and then builds over-/under-approximations of EF, leading to the over-/under-approximations of the reachable set. The main features of **OURS** are the following:

1. Equipped with sub-level sets, **OURS** can directly handle non-convex and even non-connected sets (see Fig. 2c). Moreover, it can obtain over- and under-approximations of reachable set at any desired instant in the time interval from obtained explicit expressions without repeated computations.
2. Due to the use of interval arithmetics, the current version of **OURS** allows rational functions, and even trigonometric (see Examples 4 and 7) and exponential functions with arbitrary nestings in the input.
3. Different from [3], **OURS** uses the information not only from forward reachable sets but also form backward reachable sets (see Theorem 1 and Algorithm 1), guaranteeing the output over- and under-approximations to be bounded by designated precision (see Theorem 3). Moreover, we particularly illustrate many of the details on implementation in this paper.

Related Work. In recent years, various methods have been discussed in the literature for computing over- and under- approximations of reachable sets, such as the abstraction method [5,6], the Lagrangian method [7,8], the Taylor expansion method [9,10], the support function method [11,12], the constraint solving method [13], the level set method [14,15], etc. Their corresponding tools have also been developed. **CORA** [16], a typical abstraction based tool proposed by M. Althoff, is designed for various kinds of systems with purely continuous dynamics (linear systems, nonlinear systems, differential-algebraic systems, parameter-varying systems, etc.) and supports over-approximative computation of reachable sets. Moreover, **CORA** [17] is also able to extract under-approximations of reachable sets. Lagrangian method [18] studies the continual reachability set and its connection to other backward reachability constructs, further it can be generalized to characterize robust reachable sets or viability kernels [19]. **Flow*** [20], a Taylor expansion based tool used to generate flowpipes for non-linear hybrid systems, can handle discrete transitions on Taylor model flowpipe construction based on domain contraction and range over-approximation, allowing **Flow*** to represent non-convex sets [21]. **SpaceEx** [12], a support function based tool focuses on the verification of safety properties of hybrid systems with piecewise constant bounds on the derivatives, and solves the scalability issues by making use of a wrapping-free algorithm for linear continuous systems. The recent method in [22], a tool based on constraint solving, reduces the computation of approximations to a semi-definite programming problem and then solves this convex optimization by sum-of-squares decomposition tools. A toolbox of level set was given in [14]. It describes reachable sets as the sub-level sets of the viscosity solutions of the time-dependent Hamilton-Jacobi partial differential equations, and then uses an efficient toolbox of level set method [15] to numerically solve them by gridding the state space so that one can tune the accuracy of the results by varying the number of grid points.

2   Main Theoretical Features

OURS deals with analytic time-invariant differential equations (ATDEs) of form

$$\dot{\mathbf{x}} = \mathbf{f}(\mathbf{x}), \ \mathbf{x} \in \mathbb{D}, \tag{1}$$

where $\mathbf{x}$ is an n-dimensional vector, $\mathbb{D} \subseteq \mathbb{R}^n$ is a domain and $\mathbf{f}(\mathbf{x}) : \mathbb{D} \to \mathbb{R}^n$ is an analytic real function. We define $\phi(\mathbf{x}_0, t)$ as the solution to (1), where $\mathbf{x}_0$ is the initial state. Moreover, we use $(T_{\mathbf{x}_0}^-, T_{\mathbf{x}_0}^+)$ to represent the maximal time interval of $\phi(\mathbf{x}_0, t)$, and define $\mathcal{R}^- \equiv \{(\mathbf{x}, t) \mid \mathbf{x} \in \mathbb{D} \wedge t \in (T_{\mathbf{x}}^-, T_{\mathbf{x}}^+)\}$.

2.1   EF Based Description of Reachable Set

We define *reachable set* starting from the initial set of states as follows.

Definition 1. *For given initial set of states* $\mathbf{X}_0$ *and time instant* t, *the* reachable set $Reach_{\mathbf{f}, \mathbf{X}_0}^t$ *of the ATDE* (1) *from* $\mathbf{X}_0$ *at instant* t *is defined as* $Reach_{\mathbf{f}, \mathbf{X}_0}^t = \{\phi(\mathbf{x}_0, t) \in \mathbb{R}^n \mid \mathbf{x}_0 \in \mathbf{X}_0\}$. *And the reachable set within the time interval* $[T_1, T_2]$ *is defined as* $\boldsymbol{Reach}_{\mathbf{f}, \mathbf{X}_0}^{[T_1, T_2]} = \bigcup_{t \in [T_1, T_2]} Reach_{\mathbf{f}, \mathbf{X}_0}^t$. *For simplicity, we additionally denote* $\boldsymbol{Reach}_{\mathbf{f}, \mathbf{X}_0}^{[0, T]}$ *as* $\boldsymbol{Reach}_{\mathbf{f}, \mathbf{X}_0}^T$.

Throughout this paper, if the initial set $\mathbf{X}_0$ can be described by the zero sublevel set $\mu(g)$ of a function $g(\mathbf{x})$, i.e., $X_0 = \mu(g) := \{\mathbf{x} \in \mathbb{R}^n \mid g(\mathbf{x}) \leq 0\}$, we use $Reach_{\mathbf{f}, g}^t$ ($\boldsymbol{Reach}_{\mathbf{f}, g}^T$) as an alias of $Reach_{\mathbf{f}, \mathbf{X}_0}^t$ ($\boldsymbol{Reach}_{\mathbf{f}, \mathbf{X}_0}^T$). Then, we will define evolution function as follows, which will be used for representing the reachable set $Reach_{\mathbf{f}, \mathbf{X}_0}^t$ in Proposition 1.

Definition 2. *For an analytic function* $g(\mathbf{x}) : \mathbb{R}^n \to \mathbb{R}$, *the evolution function of the ATDE* (1) *with* $g(\mathbf{x})$ *is defined as* $Evo_{\mathbf{f}, gv}(\mathbf{x}, t) = g(\phi(\mathbf{x}, -t)), \forall (\mathbf{x}, t) \in \mathcal{R}^-$.

The relationship between $Reach_{\mathbf{f}, g}^t$ and $Evo_{\mathbf{f}, gv}(\mathbf{x}, t)$ can be illustrated as follows.

Proposition 1. *For ATDE* (1) *and analytic* $g(\mathbf{x}) : \mathbb{R}^n \to \mathbb{R}$, $Reach_{\mathbf{f}, g}^t = \{\mathbf{x} \in \mathbb{R}^n \mid Evo_{\mathbf{f}, gv}(\cdot, t) \leq 0\}$.

Proposition 1 shows that, we can compute evolution function to represent the reachable set. However, evolution function depends on the solution of (1) which is generally unaccessible. Alternatively, we consider the Taylor expansion of EF w.r.t. time t, named *t-expansion*:

$$Evo_{\mathbf{f}, gv}(\mathbf{x}, t) = \sum_{i=0}^{+\infty} \frac{\mathcal{M}_{\mathbf{f}, g}^i(\mathbf{x})}{i!} (-t)^i, \tag{2}$$

where $\mathcal{M}_{\mathbf{f}, g}^i(\mathbf{x})$ is defined inductively as $\mathcal{M}_{\mathbf{f}, g}^0(\mathbf{x}) = g(\mathbf{x})$ and $\mathcal{M}_{\mathbf{f}, g}^{i+1}(\mathbf{x}) = \frac{\partial \mathcal{M}_{\mathbf{f}, g}^i(\mathbf{x})}{\partial \mathbf{x}} \cdot \mathbf{f}(\mathbf{x})$ for all $\mathbf{x} \in \mathbb{D}$. Moreover, we denote $Evo_{\mathbf{f}, g}^N(\mathbf{x}, t)$ as the Nth partial sum of t-expansion, i.e. $Evo_{\mathbf{f}, g}^N(\mathbf{x}, t) \equiv \sum_{i=0}^N \frac{(-t)^i \mathcal{M}_{\mathbf{f}, g}^i(\mathbf{x})}{i!}$.

2.2   RE Based Approximation of Reachable Sets

We denote the remainder of the Nth partial sum of $Evo_{\mathbf{f},gv}(\mathbf{x},t)$ as $Rem_{\mathbf{f},g}^{N}(\mathbf{x},t) = Evo_{\mathbf{f},gv}(\mathbf{x},t) - Evo_{\mathbf{f},g}^{N}(\mathbf{x},t)$. It is proved in [3] that $Rem_{\mathbf{f},g}^{N}(\mathbf{x},t)$ can be represented as $Rem_{\mathbf{f},g}^{N}(\mathbf{x},t) = -\int_{0}^{t} \frac{(r-t)^{N}}{N!} \mathcal{M}_{\mathbf{f},g}^{N+1}(\phi(\mathbf{x},-r))dr$. Thus, if we can find upper and lower bounds of $\mathcal{M}_{\mathbf{f},g}^{N+1}(\phi(\mathbf{x},-r))$, we can estimate $Rem_{\mathbf{f},g}^{N}(\mathbf{x},t)$, arriving at over- and under-approximations of evolution function[1] as shown in Theorem 1.

Theorem 1. *For given ATDE, $g : \mathbb{R}^n \to \mathbb{R}$, degree N and time bound T, assume that S and S' are compact sets of states such that $\mathbb{D} \supseteq S \supseteq \mathbf{Reach}_{\mathbf{f},g}^{T}$ and $S' \supseteq \mathbf{Reach}_{-\mathbf{f},S}^{T}$. If we can find constants L_{N+1} and U_{N+1}, satisfied that $L_{N+1} \leq \mathcal{M}_{\mathbf{f},g}^{N+1}(\mathbf{y}) \leq U_{N+1}$, $\forall \mathbf{y} \in S'$, then for all $t \in [0,T]$,*

1. *if N is odd, $Evo_{\mathbf{f},g}^{N}(\mathbf{x},t) + L_{N+1}\frac{t^{N+1}}{(N+1)!}$ and $Evo_{\mathbf{f},g}^{N}(\mathbf{x},t) + U_{N+1}\frac{t^{N+1}}{(N+1)!}$ are the over- and under-approximations of $Evo_{\mathbf{f},gv}(\mathbf{x},t)$ respectively over S;*
2. *if N is even, $Evo_{\mathbf{f},g}^{N}(\mathbf{x},t) - U_{N+1}\frac{t^{N+1}}{(N+1)!}$ and $Evo_{\mathbf{f},g}^{N}(\mathbf{x},t) - L_{N+1}\frac{t^{N+1}}{(N+1)!}$ are the over- and under-approximations of $Evo_{\mathbf{f},gv}(\mathbf{x},t)$ respectively over S;*
3. *all precisions for above approximations are bounded by $(U_{N+1} - L_{N+1})\frac{t^{N+1}}{(N+1)!}$.*

To find over- and under-approximations of EF, we need to estimate upper and lower bounds of $\mathcal{M}_{\mathbf{f},g}^{N+1}(\phi(\mathbf{x},-r))$. Since $x \in S$ and $-r \in (-t,0)$, we have $\mathbf{y} = \phi(\mathbf{x},-r) \in \mathbf{Reach}_{-\mathbf{f},S}^{T}$. Considering that it is inconvenient to use $\mathbf{Reach}_{-\mathbf{f},S}^{T}$ directly as the bound of $\mathbf{y}$ to estimate $\mathcal{M}_{\mathbf{f},g}^{N+1}(\mathbf{y})$, so we use a box S' containing the reachable set as the bound. Then we can iteratively compute upper bound U_{N+1} and lower bound L_{N+1} of each $\mathcal{M}_{\mathbf{f},g}^{N+1}(\mathbf{y})$ for increasing N until $U_{N+1} - L_{N+1} \leq \frac{\epsilon \cdot (N+1)!}{T^{N+1}}$, such that the precision for over- and under-approximations of EF are bounded by ϵ, and then generate over- and under-approximations of EF as described in Theorem 1.

Remark 1. There is another method based on quantifier elimination in [3] to estimate over- and under-approximations of EF, that is, with the same precondition as Theorem 1, for given $\varepsilon > 0$, if a function $P(\mathbf{x},t)$ satisfies $P(\mathbf{x},0) = g(\mathbf{x})$ and $-\varepsilon \leq (0 \leq)\frac{\partial P(\mathbf{x},t)}{\partial \mathbf{x}} \cdot \mathbf{f}(\mathbf{x}) + \frac{\partial P(\mathbf{x},t)}{\partial t} \leq 0(\leq \varepsilon)$ for all $(\mathbf{x},t) \in S' \times [0,T]$, then $P(\mathbf{x},t)$ is an over- (under-) approximation of EF over S, i.e., for all $t \in [0,T]$ and $\mathbf{x} \in S$, $0 \leq (-\varepsilon t \leq)Evo_{\mathbf{f},gv}(\mathbf{x},t) - P(\mathbf{x},t) \leq \varepsilon t(\leq 0)$. Since this method is based on quantifier elimination [23], it is not suitable for precision-oriented requirement and thus we here only use the method based on RE to design **OURS**.

3   Main Implementation Features

The structure of **OURS** is shown in Fig. 1. First, **OURS** reads the inputs including the description of ATDE, initial set, time bound, etc., and splits the

---

[1] For two n-dimensional scale functions $f_1(\mathbf{x})$ and $f_2(\mathbf{x})$, $f_1(\mathbf{x})$ is an *over- (or under-) approximation* of $f_2(\mathbf{x})$ over S if $f_1(\mathbf{x}) \leq (or \geq)f_2(\mathbf{x}), \forall \mathbf{x} \in S$.

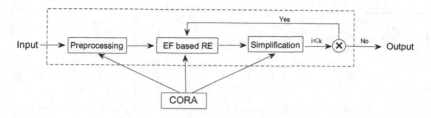

Fig. 1. Structure of **OURS**

time bound into segments with equal length. Then, before operating in each time segment, **OURS** computes a series of rough enclosures for reachable sets (*Preprocessing*). For each segment, **OURS** first iteratively computes upper and lower bounds of each remainder of the partial sums for increasing degree until one remainder satisfies the designated precision, and then constructs over- and under-approximations according to Theorem 1 (*EF based RE*); further, **OURS** simplifies the results for output (*Simplification*). **OURS** repeats this procedure for all time-segments and returns piecewise over- and under-approximations of EF, with a list of bounds for reachable sets for the corresponding segments.

3.1   Inputs and Outputs

We use the following example as the running example

$$\begin{cases} \dot{x}_1 = x_2 \\ \dot{x}_2 = -0.2x_1 + x_2 \end{cases},$$

with the initial set $\{(x_1, x_2) \in \mathbb{R}^2 \mid (x_1^2 - 1)^2 + (x_2^2 - 1)^2 \le 1\}$ (drawn in Fig. 2a) and the time bound $T = 1$, to illustrate the input and output of **OURS**.

The input of **OURS** contains: varList, f, g, S, epsilon, T, K, r.

- varList is the symbolic list of names for all dimensions in the dynamical system. Therefore the length of varList is the dimension of the input system variables. In the running example, varList := [x1,x2].
- f is the vector field and g determines the initial set $X_0 = \mu(g)$. In the running example, f := [x2, -x1/5+x2], g := (x1^2-1)^2+(x2^2-1)^2-1. Notice that if f or g is non-polynomial, so is the output of **OURS**. Current version of **OURS** allows rational functions, and even trigonometric and exponential functions with arbitrary nestings in f and g.
- S is a box containing X_0. In the running example, S := [-2,2,-2,2] is a proper choice of S, indicating that $-2 \le$ x1 ≤ 2 and $-2 \le$ x2 ≤ 2.
- epsilon is the precision requirement for the results. Since **OURS** is a precision-oriented method, we need to designate epsilon for over- and under-approximations of EF. In the running example we set epsilon:=1e-2.
- T is the time bound. In the running example we set T := 1, indicating that we estimate the EF $Evo_{f,gv}(\mathbf{x}, t)$ for $t \in [0, 1]$.

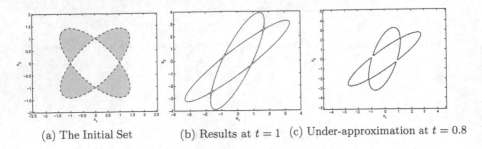

(a) The Initial Set   (b) Results at $t = 1$ (c) Under-approximation at $t = 0.8$

Fig. 2. Running Example for **OURS**.

- K is a natural number to split time bound. Since **OURS** uses time-splitting technique, K is required to separate the given time interval. In the running example, we set K := 10, so that each time-segment is $[0, 0.1]$.
- r is a number within $(0, 1]$. It represents the negotiation rate of precision allocation: **OURS** will allocate a part of precision, r∗epsilon, to *EF based RE* and the rest, $(1 - r)$∗epsilon, to *Simplification*. In the running example and examples in Sect. 4, we set r := 0.2.

The output of **OURS** contains: Over, Under, Bound.

- Over and Under are two lists of functions representing over- and under-approximations of EF over Bound respectively. They can be treated as piecewise functions $Over(\mathbf{x}, t)$ and $Under(\mathbf{x}, t)$ such that for the ith segment, $Over^i(\mathbf{x}, t)$ and $Under^i(\mathbf{x}, t)$ are stored in Over(i) and Under(i) (i.e. $Over^i(\mathbf{x}, t) = $ Over(i) and $Under^i(\mathbf{x}, t) = $ Under(i)) for $\mathbf{x} \in$ Bound(i). Thus, $Over(\mathbf{x}, t) = Over^j(\mathbf{x}, t - \frac{j-1}{K}T)$, $Under(\mathbf{x}, t) = Under^j(\mathbf{x}, t - \frac{j-1}{K}T)$ for all $\mathbf{x} \in$ Bound(i) and $t \in [\frac{j-1}{K}T, \frac{j}{K}T], 1 \le j \le K$.
- Bound is the list of enclosures for reachable sets in each time-segment.

Results of the running example at $t = 1$ are depicted in Fig. 2b using ezplot in **MATLAB**. The red/blue lines represent the boundaries of the over-/under-approximation of reachable set at $t = 1$ respectively. It is worthy to note that **OURS** can deal with non-convex even disconnected sets. For example, in the running example, the under-approximation of EF at $t = 0.8$ is 0.81682*x1^4- 1.8506*x1^3*x2+1.5878*x1^2*x2^2-1.8307*x1^2-0.56579*x1*x2^3 +1.872 5*x1* x2+0.11316*x2^4-0.91999*x2^2+1.0039. The corresponding zero sub-level set in Bound(8) is non-connected, as shown in Fig. 2c.

3.2   Technical Implementation

Based on the structure of **OURS** in the previous subsection, we here present the pseudo-code of **OURS** in Algorithm 1. **OURS** first defines time length $\Delta T :=$ T/K and precision requirement $\Delta \epsilon :=$ epsilon/K for time-segment, and consecutively calls procedures *Preprocessing* and *EF based RE* for computing over- and under-approximations of EF. Therein, for each iteration, we denote

---

Algorithm 1. Tool **OURS**

Input: varList, f, g, S, epsilon, T, K, r;
Output: Over, Under, Bound.

1:   $\Delta T := \text{T/K}, \Delta\epsilon := \text{epsilon/K}$;
2:   Initialize $Init(\mathbf{x}) \Leftarrow g$, $Tail_o \Leftarrow 0$, $Tail_u \Leftarrow 0$, $i \Leftarrow 1$;
3:   Call *Preprocessing* (i.e, Algorithm 2) for **Bound** and **Interval**;
4:   **while** $i \leq \text{K}$ **do**
5:      $S' \Leftarrow \text{Interval}(i-1)$, $S \Leftarrow \text{Interval}(i)$;
6:      Call *EF based RE* (i.e., Algorithm 3) for $Tr(\mathbf{x}, t)$, $Tail_o'(t)$, $Tail_u'(t)$;
7:      Call *Simplification* (i.e., Algorithm 4) for $Tr(\mathbf{x}, t)$;
8:      $\text{Over}^i \Leftarrow Tr(\mathbf{x}, t) + Tail_o - \frac{(1-\text{r})\Delta\epsilon}{2} + Tail_o'(t)$;
9:      $\text{Under}^i \Leftarrow Tr(\mathbf{x}, t) + Tail_u + \frac{(1-\text{r})\Delta\epsilon}{2} + Tail_u'(t)$;
10:     $Tail_o \Leftarrow Tail_o - \frac{(1-\text{r})\Delta\epsilon}{2} + Tail_o'(\Delta T)$, $Tail_u \Leftarrow Tail_u + \frac{(1-\text{r})\Delta\epsilon}{2} + Tail_u'(\Delta T)$;
11:     $Init(\mathbf{x}) \Leftarrow Tr(\mathbf{x}, \Delta T)$ and $i \Leftarrow i+1$;
12: $\text{Over} := \text{Over}^j(\mathbf{x}, t - \frac{j-1}{\text{K}}\text{T}), \forall t \in [\frac{j-1}{\text{K}}\text{T}, \frac{j}{\text{K}}\text{T}], 1 \leq j \leq \text{K}$;
13: $\text{Under} := \text{Under}^j(\mathbf{x}, t - \frac{j-1}{\text{K}}\text{T}), \forall t \in [\frac{j-1}{\text{K}}\text{T}, \frac{j}{\text{K}}\text{T}], 1 \leq j \leq \text{K}$;

---

the initial function as $Init(\mathbf{x})$ and $Evo_{f,g}^N(\mathbf{x}, t)$ as $Tr(\mathbf{x}, t)$. Further, **OURS** calls procedures *Simplification* to simplify $Tr(\mathbf{x}, t)$ and then obtain both over- and under-approximations of evolution function with less terms, as shown in Line 8–9 in Algorithm 1. Therefore, their performances are crucial to the efficacy of **OURS**. In this subsection we explain how *Preprocessing*, *EF based RE* and *Simplification* work when calling **OURS**.

Preprocessing. In *Preprocessing*, **OURS** computes a rough enclosure of the reachable set for each segment as follows, which is necessary for using Theorem 1. First, starting from the input S, **OURS** successively calls **CORA**[2] to get an enclosure **Bound** for the reachable set in each time segment based on the previous enclosure. **CORA** can compute the over-approximation of reachable set within given time-interval and return the resulting boxes, which is really suitable for our purpose. Then, **OURS** uses **CORA** for each time segment to calculate the over-approximation of the backward reachable set of previous over-approximation, denoted as **Interval**. Here **Bound** and **Interval** satisfy that: $\text{Reach}_{f,g}^{[(i-1)\Delta T, i\Delta T]} \subseteq \text{Bound}(i)$ for all $1 \leq i \leq \text{K}$, $\text{Bound}(\text{K}) = \text{Interval}(\text{K})$, and $\text{Reach}_{-f,\text{Interval}(\text{K})}^{[(\text{K}-i)\Delta T, \text{K}-i+1\Delta T]} \subseteq \text{Interval}(i-1)$ for all $1 \leq i \leq \text{K}$. Note that for the ith segment, the initial set is $\mathbf{X}_{i-1} = \text{Reach}_{f,g}^{(i-1)\Delta T}$, $\text{Reach}_{f,\mathbf{X}_{i-1}}^{\Delta T} \subseteq \text{Bound}(i)$ and $\text{Reach}_{-f,\text{Bound}(i)}^{\Delta T} \subseteq \text{Interval}(i-1)$; moreover, $\text{Bound}(i)/\text{Interval}(i-1)$ will be the enclosure S/S' used for Theorem 1 respectively.

---

[2] The version we use is **CORA** $-$ 2020. We can also replace **CORA** with some other tools that can calculate a rough enclosure of the reachable set, such as **VNODE-LP** [25] and **RealPaver** [26] etc.

Algorithm 2. *Preprocessing* in **OURS**

Input: f, S, ΔT, K;
Output: Bound, Interval.
1: $i \Leftarrow 1$, $S \Leftarrow$ S;
2: **while** $i \leq$ K **do**
3:     Call **CORA**(f, S, ΔT) to update S, and Bound(i) $\Leftarrow S$;
4:     $i \Leftarrow i + 1$;
5: $i \Leftarrow$ K, Interval(K) $\Leftarrow$ Bound(K);
6: **while** $i \geq 1$ **do**
7:     $i \Leftarrow i - 1$;
8:     Call **CORA**(-f, S, ΔT) to update S, and Interval(i) $\Leftarrow S$;

Algorithm 3. *EF based RE* in **OURS**

Input: f, $Init(\mathbf{x})$, S', ΔT, $\mathbf{r}\Delta\epsilon$;
Output: $Tr(\mathbf{x}, t)$, $Tail'_o(t)$, $Tail'_u(t)$.
1: Initialize $Tr(\mathbf{x}, t) \Leftarrow Init(\mathbf{x})$, $\mathbf{f}(\mathbf{x}) \Leftarrow \mathbf{f}$, $M(\mathbf{x}) \Leftarrow \frac{\partial g(\mathbf{x})}{\partial \mathbf{x}} \cdot \mathbf{f}(\mathbf{x})$, and $N \Leftarrow 0$;
2: Call **CORA** for L and U of $M(\mathbf{x})$ in S';
3: **while not** $U - L \leq \frac{\mathbf{r}\Delta\epsilon \cdot (N+1)!}{T^{N+1}}$ **do**
4:     $Tr(\mathbf{x}, t) \Leftarrow Tr(\mathbf{x}, t) + \frac{(-t)^{N+1}}{(N+1)!} M(\mathbf{x})$;
5:     $M(\mathbf{x}) \Leftarrow \frac{\partial M(\mathbf{x})}{\partial \mathbf{x}} \cdot \mathbf{f}(\mathbf{x})$, $N \Leftarrow N + 1$;
6:     Call **CORA** for L and U of $M(\mathbf{x})$ in S';
7: Compute the remainder $Tail'_o(t)$ and $Tail'_u(t)$ according to Theorem 1;

EF Based RE. In *EF based RE*, **OURS** computes the over- and under-approximations of evolution function satisfying the designated precision in S, according to Theorem 1. Specifically, for given f, $Init(\mathbf{x})$, S', ΔT and designated precision $\mathbf{r}\Delta\epsilon$, **OURS** iteratively increases the degree N and estimate the lower bound L and upper bound U of $\mathcal{M}_{\mathbf{f},g}^{N+1}(\mathbf{x})$ over S' with interval arithmetics in **CORA** until $U - L \leq \frac{\mathbf{r}\Delta\epsilon \cdot (N+1)!}{T^{N+1}}$. Then **OURS** returns the current partial sum of t-expansion $Tr(\mathbf{x}, t) = Evo_{\mathbf{f}, Init}^N(\mathbf{x}, t)$, and the remainders of over- and under-approximations ($Tail'_o(t)$, $Tail'_u(t)$) of EF in S, obtained based on Theorem 1:

- $Tail'_o(t) = L\frac{t^{N+1}}{(N+1)!}$, $Tail'_u(t) = U\frac{t^{N+1}}{(N+1)!}$, if N is odd.
- $Tail'_o(t) = -U\frac{t^{N+1}}{(N+1)!}$, $Tail'_u(t) = -L\frac{t^{N+1}}{(N+1)!}$, if N is even.

Theorem 1 further shows us that $|Tail'_o(t) - Tail'_u(t)|$, the error of the current step, is not greater than $\mathbf{r}\Delta\epsilon$.

Moreover, for each time-segment, the corresponding initial functions $g(\mathbf{x})$ for the over-approximation and the under-approximation are $Init(\mathbf{x}) + Tail_o$ and $Init(\mathbf{x}) + Tail_u$, respectively. Observing that $Tail_o$ and $Tail_u$ are constants, it is easy to see that even though these two initial functions $Init(\mathbf{x}) + Tail_o$ and $Init(\mathbf{x}) + Tail_u$ are different, for all $i \geq 0$, $\mathcal{M}_{\mathbf{f},g}^{i+1}(\mathbf{x}) = \frac{\partial \mathcal{M}_{\mathbf{f},g}^i(\mathbf{x})}{\partial \mathbf{x}} \cdot \mathbf{f}(\mathbf{x}) = \frac{\partial \mathcal{M}_{\mathbf{f}, Init}^i(\mathbf{x})}{\partial \mathbf{x}} \cdot \mathbf{f}(\mathbf{x}) = \mathcal{M}_{\mathbf{f}, Init}^{i+1}(\mathbf{x})$ holds for these two different initial functions,

---

Algorithm 4. *Simplification* in **OURS**

Input: $Tr(\mathbf{x}, t), S, \Delta T, \frac{(1-r)\Delta\epsilon}{2}$
Output: Updated $Tr(\mathbf{x}, t)$.
1: List all terms in $Tr(\mathbf{x}, t)$, denoted as P;
2: Compute an upper bound L of absolute value of each element in P in S by **CORA**;

3: $\bar{P} := sortrow([P, L], 2), M \Leftarrow 1$;
4: **while not** sum $(\bar{P}(1 : M, 2)) \geq \frac{(1-r)\Delta\epsilon}{2}$ **do**
5:     $M \Leftarrow M + 1$;
6: $Tr(\mathbf{x}, t) \Leftarrow sum(\bar{P}(M : end, 1))$;

---

indicating that $Tail_o$ and $Tail_u$ do not influence the satisfaction of $U - L \leq \frac{r\Delta\epsilon \cdot (N+1)!}{T^{N+1}}$ in *EF based RE* and only the $Init(\mathbf{x})$ that appears in both $Init(\mathbf{x}) + Tail_o$ and $Init(\mathbf{x}) + Tail_u$ matters. Consequently, in each iteration, we can always generate both over- and under-approximations of EF in a single sweep.

Simplification. We noticed that during time-splitting, if we directly use $Tr(\mathbf{x}, t)$ obtained from *EF based RE* to initialize the successive iteration, as shown in Line 11 in Algorithm 1, the scale of $Init(\mathbf{x})$ will grow rapidly when i increases. So as a remedy, we introduce procedure *Simplification* into **OURS**. In *Simplification*, **OURS** lists all terms in the result $Tr(\mathbf{x}, t)$ of *EF based RE* as a list P, and then calls **CORA** to compute an upper bound of absolute value of each element in P in S. After sorting P by the upper bound in ascending order, denoted as $\bar{P}$, **OURS** gathers the terms in P until the sum of the corresponding upper bound of the collected terms exceeds $\frac{(1-r)\Delta\epsilon}{2}$ and removes the previously collected terms. Then **OURS** update $Tr(\mathbf{x}, t)$ with the remaining terms, and adds $-\frac{(1-r)\Delta\epsilon}{2} / \frac{(1-r)\Delta\epsilon}{2}$ to the over/under approximation respectively in the output.

3.3   Correctness Analysis of OURS

Now we prove that $\text{Over}(\mathbf{x}, t)$ and $\text{Under}(\mathbf{x}, t)$ satisfy the set inclusion relation and designated precision requirement. Specifically, we prove that, the errors of over- and under-approximations of EF are bounded in each segment (see Theorem 2), and correctness is maintained after iteration (see Theorem 3).

Theorem 2. *In the ith segment, Over^i and Under^i satisfy that: for all $(\mathbf{x}, t) \in \text{Interval}(i) \times [0, \Delta T]$, $0 \leq \text{Under}^i(\mathbf{x}, t) - \text{Over}^i(\mathbf{x}, t) \leq i\Delta\epsilon$.*

Proof. Based on Algorithm 3, with the terminating condition of the **while** loop and Theorem 1, the output of *EF based RE* satisfies $|Tail_o'(t) - Tail_u'(t)| < r\Delta\epsilon$, $\forall(\mathbf{x}, t) \in \text{Interval}(i) \times [0, \Delta T]$. Moreover, according to the configuration of $Tail_o$ and $Tail_u$, shown in Line 10 in Algorithm 1, $|Tail_o - Tail_u|$ increases no greater than $\Delta\epsilon$ for each segment. Thus, according to the configuration of Over^i and Under^i, shown in Lines 8–9 in Algorithm 1, we complete the proof.   □

Remark 2. According to Theorem 1 and Lines 8–9 in Algorithm 1, we can derive that $-\Delta\epsilon \leq \mathtt{Over}^i(\mathbf{x},t) - Evo_{\mathtt{f},\mathtt{Over}^{i-1}(\mathbf{x},\Delta T)v}(\mathbf{x},t) \leq 0$ and $0 \leq \mathtt{Under}^i(\mathbf{x},t) - Evo_{\mathtt{f},\mathtt{Under}^{i-1}(\mathbf{x},\Delta T)v}(\mathbf{x},t) \leq \Delta\epsilon$ for all $(\mathbf{x},t) \in \mathtt{Interval}(i) \times [0,\Delta T]$, where $\mathtt{Over}^{i-1}/\mathtt{Under}^{i-1}(\mathbf{x},\Delta T) = Init(\mathbf{x}) + Tail_o/Tail_u$.

Theorem 3. *The piecewise functions* $\mathtt{Over}(\mathbf{x},t)$ *and* $\mathtt{Under}(\mathbf{x},t)$ *returned by* **OURS** *satisfy that: for all* $(\mathbf{x},t) \in Bound(K) \times [0,T]$, $-\epsilon \leq \mathtt{Over}(\mathbf{x},t) - Evo_{\mathtt{f},gv}(\mathbf{x},t) \leq 0$ *and* $0 \leq \mathtt{Under}(\mathbf{x},t) - Evo_{\mathtt{f},gv}(\mathbf{x},t) \leq \epsilon$.

Proof. We inductively prove this theorem for $\mathtt{Interval}(i)$ since $Bound(K) \subseteq \mathtt{Interval}(i)$. For simplicity, denote $\mathtt{Interval}(i) \times [(i-1)\Delta T, i\Delta T]$ as $Range(i)$.

In the first segment, due to Remark 2, $-\Delta\epsilon \leq \mathtt{Over}^1(\mathbf{x},t) - Evo_{\mathtt{f},gv}(\mathbf{x},t) \leq 0$ and $0 \leq \mathtt{Under}^1(\mathbf{x},t) - Evo_{\mathtt{f},gv}(\mathbf{x},t) \leq \Delta\epsilon$, $\forall(\mathbf{x},t) \in Range(1)$.

Assume that in the ith segment, we have $-i\Delta\epsilon \leq \mathtt{Over}^i(\mathbf{x},t-(i-1)\Delta T) - Evo_{\mathtt{f},gv}(\mathbf{x},t) \leq 0$ and $0 \leq \mathtt{Under}^i(\mathbf{x},t-(i-1)\Delta T) - Evo_{\mathtt{f},gv}(\mathbf{x},t) \leq i\Delta\epsilon$, $\forall(\mathbf{x},t) \in Range(i)$. From Algorithm 2, $\mathtt{Interval}(i)$ is an enclosure of the backward reachable set and thus $\mathtt{Interval}(i+1) \subseteq \mathtt{Interval}(i) \subseteq \mathbf{Reach}^{\Delta T}_{\mathtt{f},\mathtt{Interval}(i)}$. Hence, due to the assumption, $Evo_{\mathtt{f},\mathtt{Over}^i(\mathbf{x},\Delta T)v}(\mathbf{x},t-i\Delta T) - Evo_{\mathtt{f},gv}(\mathbf{x},t) \leq 0$ and $0 \leq Evo_{\mathtt{f},\mathtt{Under}^i(\mathbf{x},\Delta T)v}(\mathbf{x},t-i\Delta T) - Evo_{\mathtt{f},gv}(\mathbf{x},t), \forall(\mathbf{x},t) \in Range(i+1)$.

Let us consider the $(i+1)$th segment. Due to Remark 2, for all $(\mathbf{x},t) \in Range(i+1)$, $\mathtt{Over}^{i+1}(\mathbf{x},t-i\Delta T) - Evo_{\mathtt{f},\mathtt{Over}^i(\mathbf{x},\Delta T)v}(\mathbf{x},t-i\Delta T) \leq 0$ and $0 \leq \mathtt{Under}^{i+1}(\mathbf{x},t-i\Delta T) - Evo_{\mathtt{f},\mathtt{Under}^i(\mathbf{x},\Delta T)v}(\mathbf{x},t-i\Delta T)$. Thus, combining with the result obtained in the above paragraph, we have that $\mathtt{Over}^{i+1}(\mathbf{x},t-i\Delta T) \leq Evo_{\mathtt{f},gv}(\mathbf{x},t) \leq \mathtt{Under}^{i+1}(\mathbf{x},t-i\Delta T)$, $\forall(\mathbf{x},t) \in Range(i+1)$. Further, from Theorem 2, we have that $-(i+1)\Delta\epsilon \leq \mathtt{Over}^{i+1}(\mathbf{x},t) - \mathtt{Under}^{i+1}(\mathbf{x},t) \leq 0$, $\forall(\mathbf{x},t) \in Range(i+1)$. Thus, we can infer that for all $(\mathbf{x},t) \in Range(i+1)$, $-(i+1)\Delta\epsilon \leq \mathtt{Over}^{i+1}(\mathbf{x},t-i\Delta T) - Evo_{\mathtt{f},gv}(\mathbf{x},t) \leq 0$ and $0 \leq \mathtt{Under}^{i+1}(\mathbf{x},t-i\Delta T) - Evo_{\mathtt{f},gv}(\mathbf{x},t) \leq (i+1)\Delta\epsilon$, which completes the proof.   □

4   Comparisons with Examples

We show the performance of **OURS** by comparing it with the method in [22] and the **ToolboxLS** from [27] with seven examples. Especially, Example 1 deals with a disconnected set, Example 4 deals with a 2-dimensional non-polynomial system, and Example 7 deals with a 8-dimensional non-polynomial systems. Some data of the results of these seven examples are listed in Table 1, where we use '-' to represent all unavailable data, for example, we cannot determine the highest degree of variables in Examples 4 and 7 since the outputs contain trigonometric functions. Moreover, we also changed the time interval and designated precision for **OURS** and more data are listed in Table 2 with discussions. Note that we have been authorized by the authors of [22] to run their source code in the same machine used in the paper. The data are all given on a Laptop 1.8GHz Intel Core i7 (4 cores) and 8 Gb of RAM.

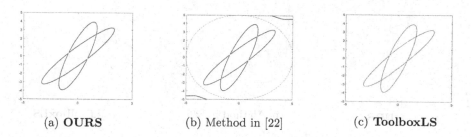

(a) **OURS**   (b) Method in [22]   (c) **ToolboxLS**

Fig. 3. Results of Example 1 at $t = 1$.

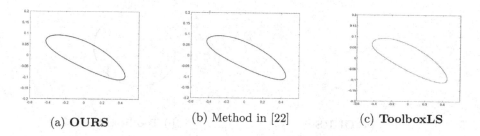

(a) **OURS**   (b) Method in [22]   (c) **ToolboxLS**

Fig. 4. Results of Example 2 at $t = 1$.

Example 1. We consider the running example with $\epsilon = 10^{-8}$. Additionally, we set degree-14 for the method in [22] which makes the precision be 1.05×10^{-8}, and g.dx $= 2/100$ and accuracy $-$ 'medium' for **ToolboxLS**. The results at $t = 1$ are shown in Fig. 3. Note that the dashed curve in Fig. 3b is the boundary of an appropriate compact set $\mathcal{Y} \subset \mathbb{R}^n$ (see Definition 3 in [22] for details).

Example 2. We consider the non-linear system from [3,22]

$$\begin{cases} \dot{x}_1 = x_1 - 2x_2 \\ \dot{x}_2 = x_1 x_2 + 0.5 x_2^2 \end{cases},$$

with the initial set $\{\mathbf{x} \mid x_1^2 + x_2^2 \leq 0.01\}$. We want to compute the approximations of $Reach^t_{f,g}$ with $t \in [0, 1]$. We set $\epsilon = 10^{-4}$ for **OURS**, degree=20 for the method in [22] which makes the precision be 1.31×10^{-4}, and g.dx $= 1/100$ and accuracy $=$ 'medium' for **ToolboxLS**. The results at $t = 1$ are shown in Fig. 4.

Example 3. Consider the classical Van der Pol circuit system:

$$\begin{cases} \dot{x}_1 = \dfrac{1}{C} x_2 \\ \dot{x}_2 = \dfrac{1}{L} \cdot (-x_1 + \mu x_2 - x_2^3) \end{cases}.$$

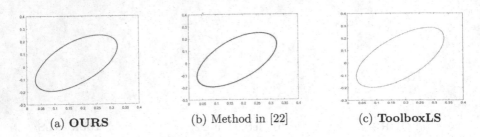

(a) **OURS**   (b) Method in [22]   (c) **ToolboxLS**

Fig. 5. Results of Example 3 at $t = 1$.

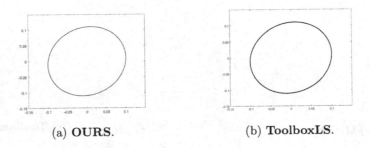

(a) **OURS**.   (b) **ToolboxLS**.

Fig. 6. Results of Example 4 at $t = 1$.

We assume that $C = \mu = L = 1$, the initial set is $\{\mathbf{x} \mid (x_1 - 0.1)^2 + (x_2 - 0.1)^2 \leq 0.01\}$. We want to compute the approximations of $Reach_{\mathbf{f},g}^t$ with $t \in [0, 1]$. We set $\epsilon = 10^{-4}$ for **OURS**, degree=10 for the method in [22] which makes the precision be 2.03×10^{-4}, and g.dx=1/100 and accuracy='medium' for **ToolboxLS**. The results at $t = 1$ are shown in Fig. 5.

Example 4. Consider the non-polynomial system from [3]:

$$\begin{cases} \dot{x}_1 = 0.1 \sin(x_2) \\ \dot{x}_2 = 0.1 x_2 - 0.02 \sin(x_1)^2 \end{cases},$$

with the initial set $\{\mathbf{x} \mid x_1^2 + x_2^2 \leq 0.01\}$. We want to compute the approximations of $Reach_{\mathbf{f},g}^t$ with $t \in [0, 1]$. We set $\epsilon = 10^{-4}$ for **OURS**, and g.dx=1/100 and accuracy='medium' for **ToolboxLS**. The results at $t = 1$ are shown in Fig. 6. Note that the method in [22] cannot handle this example directly since it is a non-polynomial system.

Example 5. We consider the 3-dimensional Lotka-Volterra system from [22]:

$$\begin{cases} \dot{x}_1 = -x_1 x_2 + x_1 x_3 \\ \dot{x}_2 = -x_2 x_3 + x_2 x_1 \\ \dot{x}_3 = -x_3 x_1 + x_3 x_2 \end{cases},$$

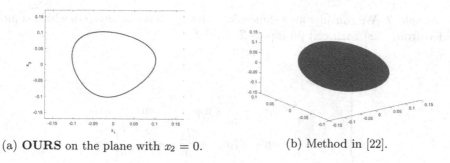

(a) **OURS** on the plane with $x_2 = 0$.   (b) Method in [22].

Fig. 7. Results of Examples 5 at $t = 1$.

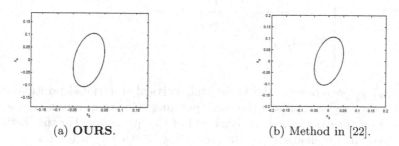

(a) **OURS**.   (b) Method in [22].

Fig. 8. Results of Example 6 at $t - 1$ on the plane with $x_1 = x_2 = 0$.

with the initial set $\{\mathbf{x} \mid x_1^2 + x_2^2 + x_3^2 \leq 0.01\}$. We want to compute the approximations of $Reach_{\mathbf{f},g}^t$ with $t \in [0,1]$. We set $\epsilon = 10^{-4}$ for **OURS** and g.dx = $1/100$ and accuracy = 'medium' for **ToolboxLS**. The result of **OURS** at $t = 1$ on the plane with $x_2 = 0$ is shown in Fig. 7a and the result of **ToolboxLS** at $t = 1$ is shown in Fig. 7b. But the method in [22] cannot achieve the precision $\epsilon = 10^{-4}$.

Example 6. We consider a 4-dimensional system from [3,24] which is the dynamics of an enzymatic reaction:

$$\begin{cases} \dot{x}_1 = -k_f x_1 x_2 + (k_b + k_m) x_3 \\ \dot{x}_2 = -k_f x_1 x_2 + k_b x_3 \\ \dot{x}_3 = k_f x_1 x_2 - (k_b + k_m) x_3 \\ \dot{x}_4 = k_m x_3 \end{cases}$$

We assume that $k_m = k_f = 0.5$, $k_b = 0.1$, the initial set is $\{\mathbf{x} \mid x_1^2 + x_2^2 + x_3^2 + x_4^2 \leq 0.01\}$. We want to compute the approximations of $Reach_{\mathbf{f},g}^t$ with $t \in [0,1]$. We set $\epsilon = 10^{-2}$ for **OURS**, degree=6 for the method in [22] which makes the precision be 2.2×10^{-2}, and g.dx=$1/100$ and accuracy='medium' for **ToolboxLS**. The results of **OURS** and the method in [22] at $t = 1$ on the plane with $x_1 = x_2 = 0$ are shown in Fig. 8. Note that it is difficult to obtain the result of **ToolboxLS** at $t = 1$ on the same plane since the corresponding result has only discrete data.

Example 7. We consider an 8-dimensional non-polynomial system which is modified from   [28] with certain inputs T_1 and T_2:

$$\begin{cases} \dot{p}_x = v_x \\ \dot{p}_y = v_y \\ \dot{v}_x = -\dfrac{1}{m}C_D^v v_x - \dfrac{T_1}{m}\sin\phi - \dfrac{T_2}{m}\sin\phi \\ \dot{v}_y = -\dfrac{1}{m}(mg + C_D^v v_y) + \dfrac{T_1}{m}\cos\phi + \dfrac{T_2}{m}\cos\phi \\ \dot{\phi} = \omega \\ \dot{\omega} = -\dfrac{1}{I_{yy}}C_D^\phi \omega + \dfrac{l}{I_{yy}}T_1 + \dfrac{l}{I_{yy}}T_2 \\ \dot{T}_1 = \alpha T_2 \\ \dot{T}_2 = -\alpha T_1 \end{cases},$$

where p_x, p_y, ϕ represent the horizontal, vertical, rotational positions of the quadrotor, v_x, v_y, ω represent the corresponding velocities, respectively, and T_1, T_2 are input thrusts exerted on either end of the quadrotor. For the coefficients in the system, we choose $C_D^v = 0.1, m = 5, g = 9.8, C_D^\phi = 0.1, l = 0.5, I_{yy} = 10$ and $\alpha = 1$. The initial set $\mu(g)$ is represented by an 8-dimensional ball with radius 0.2, centering at $(0, 0, 2, 1, \frac{\pi}{6}, 0.1, 10, -10)$. We compute the over- and under-approximations of $Reach_{f,g}^t$ with $t \in [0, 1]$. Note that the method in [22] cannot operate directly; and because of the high dimension and large computation interval, **ToolboxLS** is not easy to deal with this example either.

Figure 9a shows the projected results at time instants $t = 0.1, 0.2, ..., 1$ onto the corresponding $p_x - p_y$ planes defined by letting $(v_x, v_y, \phi, \omega, T_1, T_2) = (\Phi_2(t), \Phi_4(t), \Phi_5(t), \Phi_6(t), \Phi_7(t), \Phi_8(t))$, where $\Phi(t)$ is the simulated trajectory starting from the center $\mathbf{x}_0 = (0, 0, 2, 1, \frac{\pi}{6}, 0.1, 10, -10)^T$. Similarly, Fig. 9b, Fig. 9c and Fig. 9d show the projected results at time instants $t = 0.1, 0.2, ..., 1$ onto the corresponding $v_x - v_y$, $\phi - \omega$ and $T_1 - T_2$ planes, respectively.

In Table 1, we list certain data of the obtained results for **OURS**/the method in [22]/**ToolboxLS**, i.e. the running times(RT), the maximal number of terms(NT) in outputs, the highest degree of all variables $deg_{x,t}$ and the degree of time variable deg_t. Moreover, after assigning $t = T$ for the outputs, we also list the highest degree of variables deg_x and the number of terms in the corresponding results. Considering that the results obtained by **ToolboxLS** are numerical data, it is meaningless to list them except the running times of **ToolboxLS**. Additionally, Examples 4 and 7 are non-polynomial and thus the method in [22] cannot directly handle them; and for Example 5, the method in [22] cannot achieve the given precision $\epsilon = 10^{-4}$.

Different from **ToolboxLS**, the outputs obtained by **OURS** and the method in [22] are forms of algebraic inequalities, which can be directly used to obtain the results at any time instant within the time interval and are more convenient for the next call. Moreover, for higher-dimensional systems (see Example 6), the

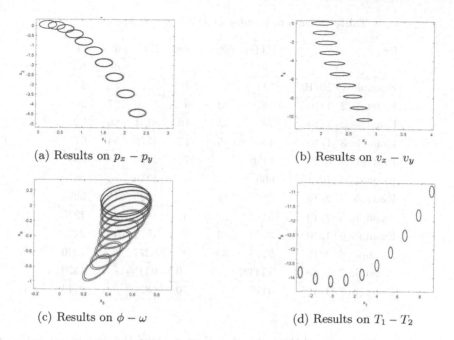

(a) Results on $p_x - p_y$

(b) Results on $v_x - v_y$

(c) Results on $\phi - \omega$

(d) Results on $T_1 - T_2$

Fig. 9. Results of Example 7 at time instants $t = 0.1, 0.2, ..., 1$.

Table 1. Data of results for examples.

Ex.	RT(s)	$deg_{x,t}$	deg_t	NT	at t = 1	
					deg_x	NT
Example 1	18/29/58	11/14/–	8/14/–	56/680/–	4/14/–	9/120/–
Example 2	53/456/3	15/20/–	6/20/–	410/1771/–	10/20/–	95/231/–
Example 3	74/7/5	20/10/–	5/10/–	370/286/–	18/10/–	121/33/–
Example 4	6/–/2	–/–/–	2/–/–	5/–/–	–/–/–	4/–/–
Example 5	41/–/2	9/–/–	4/–/–	174/–/–	7/–/–	70/–/–
Example 6	26/267/43	7/6/–	4/6/–	111/462/–	6/6/	42/210/–
Example 7	821/–/–	–/–/–	8/–/–	4198/–/–	–/–/–	915/–/–

results of **OURS** and the method in [22] can be more easily used to obtain the results at any cross section by directly operating on the obtained algebraic inequalities with variable assignments (see Fig. 8), while **ToolboxLS** has only discrete data. Additionally, according to Table 1, **ToolboxLS** requires more time for higher-dimensional systems (see Examples 6 and 7); and **OURS** has better time performance than the method in [22] except Example 3 since Example 3 is very sensitive to the size of the initial set and the length of the time horizon; moreover, compared with the method in [22], **OURS** can directly handle non-polynomial systems (see Examples 4 and 7).

Table 2. Data of Results for Different Parameters.

| Ex. | T/ϵ | RT(s) | $deg_{x,t}$ | deg_t | NT | at t = T | |
						deg_x	NT
Example 1	$10/10^{-32}$	72	51	49	352	4	9
Example 2	$1/10^{-8}$	286	30	9	1710	27	248
Example 2	$1/10^{-16}$	998	53	16	8731	46	725
Example 3	$1/10^{-8}$	490	65	12	4276	54	671
Example 4	$5/10^{-8}$	1156	–	7	1690	–	355
Example 4	$10/10^{-4}$	660	–	5	1310	–	387
Example 5	$2/10^{-4}$	846	17	5	1625	15	505
Example 5	$2/10^{-8}$	5692	27	8	10211	23	1975
Example 6	$1/10^{-8}$	313	14	7	1171	11	242
Example 6	$3/10^{-4}$	2215	30	9	8277	25	1240
Example 7	$2/10^{-2}$	124327	–	10	93485	–	13792
Example 7	$1/10^{-4}$	4179	–	10	18127	–	2714

We have also increased the time interval or changed the designated precision for these examples, and listed the corresponding data of results in Table 2. Since **OURS** need to increase time segmentation to deal with longer time intervals and increase the degree of t-expansion to achieve the higher precision requirement, these will definitely lead to an increase of running time and number of terms in the output of **OURS**. Note that the current version of **CORA** has an error of 'reachable set explosion' when handling high-order systems with long time interval, which affects the scalability of **OURS**. We have reported this problem to the authors and it may be addressed in the future version.

In general, for the low degree and trigonometric system, **OURS** shows good performance. The output of **OURS** has low degree and few terms, such that **OURS** can carry out more expansion to deal with higher dimensional systems, achieve higher precision requirements and extend to a longer time. Moreover, in future version, we will consider to realize automatic segmentation of input time bound, and to design a better simplification program to further deal with the problem of excessive exponential growth caused by Taylor expansion.

5   Conclusion

In this paper, we have presented the **MATLAB** tool **OURS** to construct over- and under-approximations of evolution functions, leading to over- and under-approximations of reachable sets, via estimating the corresponding remainder of the partial sum of t-expansion with interval arithmetics. We have confirmed the efficacy and promise of **OURS** by comparing to other methods with examples. In the future, we will investigate systems with disturbances described by uncertain parameters and even time-varying inputs.

References

1. Plaku, E., Kavraki, L., Vardi, M.: Hybrid systems: from verification to falsification by combining motion planning and discrete search. Formal Methods Syst. Design **34**, 157–182 (2009)
2. Goubault, E., Putot, S.: Inner and outer reachability for the verification of control systems. In: HSCC 2019, pp. 11–22 (2019)
3. Li, M., She, Z.: Over- and under-approximations of reachable sets with series representations of evolution functions. IEEE Trans. Automat. Contr. **66**(3), 1414–1421 (2021)
4. Li, M., Mosaad, P.N., Fränzle, M., She, Z., Xue, B.: Safe over- and under-approximation of reachable sets for autonomous dynamical systems. In: Jansen, D.N., Prabhakar, P. (eds.) FORMATS 2018. LNCS, vol. 11022, pp. 252–270. Springer, Cham (2018). https://doi.org/10.1007/978-3-030-00151-3_15
5. Ratschan, S., She, Z.: Safety verification of hybrid systems by constraint propagation-based abstraction refinement. ACM Trans. Embed. Comput. Syst. **6**(1), 1–23 (2007). Article No. 8
6. Kurzhanskiy, A.A., Varaiya, P.: Ellipsoidal toolbox (ET). In: Proceedings of the 45th IEEE Conference on Decision and Control, pp. 1498–1503 (2006)
7. Girard, A., Le Guernic, C., Maler, O.: Efficient computation of reachable sets of linear time-invariant systems with inputs. In: HSCC 2006, pp. 257–271. ACM (2006)
8. Dang, T., Maler, O., Testylier, R.: Accurate hybridization of nonlinear systems. In: HSCC 2010, pp. 11–20. ACM (2010)
9. Althoff, M.: Reachability analysis of nonlinear systems using conservative polynomialization and non-convex sets. In: HSCC 2013, pp. 173–182. ACM (2013)
10. Goubault, E., Putot, S.: Robust under-approximations and application to reachability of non-linear control systems with disturbances. IEEE Control Syst. Lett. **4**(4), 928–933 (2020)
11. Frehse, G.: PHAVer: algorithmic verification of hybrid systems past HyTech. Int. J. Softw. Tools Technol. Transf. **10**, 263–279 (2008)
12. Frehse, G., et al.: SpaceEx: scalable verification of hybrid systems. In: Gopalakrishnan, G., Qadeer, S. (eds.) CAV 2011. LNCS, vol. 6806, pp. 379–395. Springer, Heidelberg (2011). https://doi.org/10.1007/978-3-642-22110-1_30
13. Wang, T.C., Lall, S., West, M.: Polynomial level-set method for polynomial system reachable set estimation. IEEE Trans. Automat. Contr. **58**(10), 2508–2521 (2013)
14. Mitchell, I.M., Bayen, A.M., Tomlin, C.J.: A time-dependent Hamilton-Jacobi formulation of reachable sets for continuous dynamic games. IEEE Trans. Automat. Contr. **50**(7), 947–957 (2005)
15. Mitchell, I.M.: The flexible, extensible and efficient toolbox of level set methods. J. Sci. Comput. **35**(2), 300–329 (2008)
16. Althoff, M.: An introduction to CORA 2015. In: Proceedings of the Workshop on Applied Verification for Continuous and Hybrid Systems, pp. 120–151 (2015)
17. Kochdumper, N., Althoff, M.: Computing non-convex inner-approximations of reachable sets for nonlinear continuous systems. In 59th IEEE Conference on Decision and Control (CDC), pp. 2130–2137 (2020)
18. Kaynama, S., Oishi, M., Mitchell, I.M., Dumont, G.A.: The continual reachability set and its computation using maximal reachability techniques. In: 50th IEEE Conference on Decision and Control (CDC), pp. 6110–6115 (2011)

19. Kaynama, S., Maidens, J., Oishi, M., Mitchell, I.M., Dumont, G.A.: Computing the viability kernel using maximal reachable sets. In: HSCC 2012, pp. 55–64. ACM (2012)
20. Chen, X., Ábrahám, E., Sankaranarayanan, S.: Flow*: an analyzer for non-linear hybrid systems. In: Sharygina, N., Veith, H. (eds.) CAV 2013. LNCS, vol. 8044, pp. 258–263. Springer, Heidelberg (2013). https://doi.org/10.1007/978-3-642-39799-8_18
21. Chen, X., Ábrahám, E., Sankaranarayanan, S.: Taylor model flowpipe construction for non-linear hybrid systems. In: RTSS 2012, pp. 183–192. IEEE Computer Society (2012)
22. Xue, B., Fränzle, M., Zhan, N.: Under-approximating reach sets for polynomial continuous systems. In: HSCC 2018, pp. 51–60 (2018)
23. Ratschan, S., She, Z.: Providing a basin of attraction to a target region of polynomial systems by computation of Lyapunov-like functions. SIAM J. Control Optim. 48(7), 4377–4394 (2010)
24. Julius, A.A., Pappas, G.J.: Trajectory based verification using local finite-time invariance. In: Majumdar, R., Tabuada, P. (eds.) HSCC 2009. LNCS, vol. 5469, pp. 223–236. Springer, Heidelberg (2009). https://doi.org/10.1007/978-3-642-00602-9_16
25. Nedialkov, N.S.: Implementing a rigorous ode solver through literate programming. In: Rauh, A., Auer, E. (eds.) Modeling, Design, and Simulation of Systems with Uncertainties. Mathematical Engineering, vol. 3, pp. 3–19. Springer, Berlin (2011). https://doi.org/10.1007/978-3-642-15956-5_1
26. Granvilliers, L., Benhamou, F.: RealPaver: an interval solver using constraint satisfaction techniques. ACM Trans. Math. Softw. 32(1), 138–156 (2006)
27. http://www.cs.ubc.ca/~mitchell/ToolboxLS
28. Chen, M., Herbert, S.L., Vashishtha, M.S., Bansal, S., Tomlin, C.J.: Decomposition of reachable sets and tubes for a class of nonlinear systems. IEEE Trans. Automat. Contr. 63(11), 3675–3688 (2018)

ESAMPLER: Efficient Sampling of Satisfying Assignments for Boolean Formulas

Yongjie Xu[1], Fu Song[1(✉)], and Taolue Chen[2]

[1] ShanghaiTech University, Shanghai, China
songfu@shanghaitech.edu.cn
[2] Birkbeck, University of London, London, UK

Abstract. Boolean satisfiability (SAT) has played a key role in diverse areas spanning planning, inferencing, data mining, testing and optimization. Apart from the classical problem of checking Boolean satisfiability, generating random satisfying assignments has attracted significant theoretical and practical interests over the years. For practical applications, a large number of satisfying assignments for a given Boolean formula are needed, the generation of which turns out to be a hard problem in both theory and practice. In this work, we propose a novel approach to derive a large set of satisfying assignments from a given one in an efficient way. Our approach is orthogonal to the previous techniques for generating satisfying assignments and could be integrated into the existing SAT samplers. We implement our approach as an open-source tool ESAMPLER and conduct extensive experiments on real-world benchmarks. Experimental results show that ESAMPLER performs better than three state-of-the-art samplers on a large portion of the benchmarks, and is at least comparable on the others, showcasing the efficacy of our approach.

Keywords: Boolean satisfiability · Constraint-based sampling · SAT solving

1 Introduction

Boolean satisfiability, also known as SAT, concerns determining whether a given Boolean formula is satisfiable. There have been strong theoretical and practical interests in the SAT problem, which has played a key role in diverse areas spanning planning, inferencing, data mining, testing and optimization [1,6]. Apart from the classical problem of checking Boolean satisfiability, generating random satisfying assignments has attracted significant theoretical and practical interests

This work is supported by the National Natural Science Foundation of China (NSFC) under Grants No. 62072309 and No. 61872340, an oversea grant from the State Key Laboratory of Novel Software Technology, Nanjing University (KFKT2018A16), and Birkbeck BEI School Project (ARTEFACT).

© Springer Nature Switzerland AG 2021
S. Qin et al. (Eds.): SETTA 2021, LNCS 13071, pp. 279–298, 2021.
https://doi.org/10.1007/978-3-030-91265-9_15

over the years [3, 4, 18, 29–32, 39, 40, 43, 45–47]. In several practical applications, a large number of satisfying assignments for a given Boolean formula are needed. For instance, simulation-based verification is a commonly adopted technique to test hardware design. In this scenario, the simulated behavior is compared with the expected behavior where any mismatch is flagged as an indication of a bug [29, 47]. It is a common practice to generate a large number of stimuli satisfying a given set of constraints in the form of Boolean formulas. These constraints typically arise from various sources such as application-specific knowledge and environmental requirements. Another application scenario is the generation of adversarial examples for adversarial training [11, 48]. Adversarial training is a widely adopted technique to improve the robustness of neural networks against adversarial attacks where a large number of adversarial inputs (e.g., images) would be generated explicitly or implicitly. For instance, to adversarially train a binarized neural network [19, 44], adversarial images were generated by encoding a binarized neural network as a Boolean formula based on which satisfying assignments were sampled [24, 28].

Sampling satisfying assignments for a given Boolean formula is, however, challenging. It is well-known that the SAT problem is **NP**-complete [12]. In recent years, we have seen a tremendous progress in SAT solving, supported by techniques such as conflict-driven clause learning (CDCL [21, 33, 34]), yielding powerful solvers such as CryptoMiniSAT [37].

However, generating a large number of satisfying assignments is still computationally prohibitive and often infeasible in practical settings [14, 23]. In this work, we develop ESAMPLER, aiming for generating a large number of satisfying assignments efficiently for a given Boolean formula. The general strategy is to use an existing sampler to produce a seed sample as a satisfying assignment, from which we derive more satisfying assignments by flipping some variables of the given Boolean formula. Clearly, naively flipping variables may yield unsatisfying assignments. To tackle this problem, we propose a novel derivation procedure which explores the semantics of the Boolean formula under the seed sample, so that the resulting assignments can be guaranteed to satisfy the Boolean formula. The advantage of our approach lies in that it can be integrated with the existing SAT samplers, so would enjoy considerably wider applicability.

To demonstrate our approach, we implement a sampler ESAMPLER based on the recent sampler QUICKSAMPLER [14]. We carry out extensive experiments on the publicly available benchmarks from UNIGEN [10] which include Boolean formulas from real-world testing and verification applications. Our experimental results show that ESAMPLER performs considerably better than the three state-of-the-art samplers QUICKSAMPLER, SEARCHTREESAMPLER (STS in short) [16] and UNIGEN3 [36], indicating the effectiveness of our approach.

Our main contributions can be summarized as follows.

- We introduce a novel approach for deriving a large set of satisfying assignments from a given seed. It is generic and could be integrated with the existing samplers. To the best of our knowledge, it is the first work to generate satisfying assignments from a given seed.

- We implement an integrated sampler ESAMPLER. Our tool is available at https://github.com/ESampler/Esampler.
- We conduct extensive experiments on hundreds of Boolean formulas from real-world applications and ESAMPLER performs considerably better than the three state-of-the-art samplers QUICKSAMPLER, STS and UNIGEN3.

Related Work. Various techniques have been proposed to tackle the problem of the satisfying assignment generation for Boolean formulas [26]. Binary decision diagrams (BDD) and Markov Chain Monte Carlo (MCMC) algorithms such as simulated annealing and Metropolis-Hastings are widely used for generating satisfying assignments [22,42,43]. These techniques usually provide theoretical guarantees of uniformity but are limited in scalability and efficiency. Therefore, heuristics are proposed to speed up at the cost of theoretical guarantees of uniformity [22,25,41]. Another class of satisfying assignment generation techniques with theoretical guarantees of uniformity is based on hashing [5,8–10,15,17,35,36]. Hashing-based techniques add hash functions (e.g., XOR of a random subset of variables) to the Boolean formula in order to partition the search space uniformly and then randomly pick a satisfying assignment from a randomly chosen cell. These algorithms are also limited in scalability and efficiency. In comparison, our approach primarily aims for efficiency, using fewer solver calls to generate a large number of solutions. We also provide a parameter to balance the uniformity of the generated samples and the efficiency of the procedure. Although we do not provide a theoretical guarantee of uniformity, the experimental results demonstrate that our approach is able to produce solutions nearly uniformly when the maximal number of solutions per seed is set in a reasonable range.

Recently, SAT samplers aiming to quickly generate a large number of assignments have been proposed. Both QUICKSAMPLER [14] and STS [16] share the same goal as our work, namely, fast generation of a larger number of assignments. QUICKSAMPLER uses the MaxSAT solver [7] to generate random satisfying assignments, and then find more assignments that are close to satisfying assignments using the diffs of discovered satisfying assignments. However, the assignments generated by QUICKSAMPLER may not satisfy the Boolean formula, hence a follow-up checking is often needed. In contrast, our approach only mutates proper variables by which the formula is guaranteed to be satisfied. STS explores the tree of variable assignments in a breadth-first way with the MiniSat SAT solver [38] as an oracle. During this procedure, it generates *pseudosolutions*, which are partial assignments to the variables that can be completed to full satisfying assignments. However, it has to invoke the SAT solver multiple times during the breadth-first exploration. In contrast, ESAMPLER does not require SAT solving when generating satisfying assignments from a seed.

Technically, our derivation procedure aims to generate a large set of satisfying assignments from a given seed, and is orthogonal to the existing SAT samplers. It can be integrated into the existing samplers to improve their efficiency as we demonstrated using QUICKSAMPLER.

Sampling of satisfying assignments is also closely related to the model-counting problem which counts the number of satisfying assignments for a

Boolean formula. Model-counting techniques have been used for sampling satisfy-ing assignments (e.g., SPUR [2]) while satisfying assignment sampling techniques can also be used for model-counting (e.g., STS [16] and ApproxCount [42]).

Outline. The remainder of this paper is organized as follows. In Sect. 2, we briefly revisit related concepts of Boolean formulas. We present our derivation procedure in Sect. 3, and show how to integrate it into existing SAT samplers in Sect. 4. We report evaluation results in Sect. 5 and conclude this work in Sect. 6.

2 Preliminaries

We first recap some basic notions and notations which are used in this work.

Boolean Formulas. Let us fix a set of Boolean variables $\mathcal{V}$. A literal l is either a Boolean variable $x \in \mathcal{V}$ or its negation $\neg x$. We denote by $\text{var}(l)$ the variable x used in the literal l, namely, $\text{var}(x) = \text{var}(\neg x) = x$.

A *Boolean formula* Φ is a Boolean combination of literals using logical-AND ($\wedge$) and logical-OR ($\vee$) operators. As a convention, we assume that Boolean formulas are given in the conjunctive normal form (CNF) $\bigwedge_{j=1}^{m} \bigvee_{i=1}^{n_j} l_i^j$, where for each $1 \leq j \leq m$ and $1 \leq i \leq n_j$, l_i^j is a literal, and $\bigvee_{i=1}^{n_j} l_i^j$ is referred to a *clause* for each $1 \leq j \leq m$. Given a Boolean formula Φ and a literal l, let Φ_l denote the set of clauses that contain the literal l. For each clause $\phi = \bigvee_{i=1}^{n_j} l_i^j$, we assume that all literals in ϕ are distinct, and denote by $|\phi|$ the number n_j of literals in the clause ϕ.

Assignments. An *assignment* is a function $v \colon \mathcal{V} \to \{0,1\}$ which assigns a Boolean value to each Boolean variable $x \in \mathcal{V}$. Given a Boolean formula Φ and an assignment v, v is a *satisfying assignment* of Φ, denoted by $v \models \Phi$, if the Boolean formula Φ evaluates to 1 under the assignment v. For each assignment v, variable $x \in \mathcal{V}$ and value $i \in \{0,1\}$, we denote by $v[x \mapsto i]$ the assignment that agrees with v except for the variable x, i.e., for each variable $y \in \mathcal{V}$, $v[x \mapsto i](y) = v(y)$ if $y \neq x$, $v[x \mapsto i](y) = i$ otherwise.

Satisfiability and Maximum Satisfiability. Given a Boolean formula Φ, the *satisfiability problem* (SAT) is to determine whether a satisfying assignment of Φ exists or not. If Φ is satisfied, then a solution is produced as a witness. It is well-known that the SAT problem is **NP**-complete [12].

Given a pair of Boolean formulas (Φ, Ψ), the *maximum satisfiability problem* (MaxSAT) is to find a satisfying assignment that satisfies the Boolean formula Φ and meanwhile maximizes the number of satisfied clauses in Ψ. The clauses in Φ are usually called *hard* constraints, while the clauses in Ψ are called *soft* constraints. It is easy to see that the MaxSAT problem is at least **NP**-hard and can be solved by the state-of-the-art solvers such as Z3 [7].

In this work, by solvers we mean tools that are able to produce one satisfying assignment of the (Max)SAT problem whilst by samplers we mean those that are able to generate more than one satisfying assignments.

Independent Support. Given a Boolean formula Φ, an *independent support* Supp of Φ [10], is a set of variables such that for each pair of satisfying assignments (v, v') of Φ, if $v(x) = v'(x)$ holds for all variables $x \in$ Supp, then $v(y) = v'(y)$ holds for all variables $y \in \mathcal{V} \backslash$ Supp. Intuitively, the truth values of the independent support Supp_Φ uniquely determine the truth values of the other variables. In other words, flipping the truth value of any variable $y \in \mathcal{V} \backslash$ Supp in the satisfying assignment v only will make the resulting assignment $v[y \mapsto \neg v(y)]$ fail to satisfy Φ.

It is easy to see that any superset of an independent support of Φ is also an independent support. There are tools, such as MIS and SMIS [20], that are able to compute minimal and minimum independent supports for Boolean formulas, where *minimal* means removing any variable from the independent support X will lead to a non-independent support, and *minimum* means there does not exist any independent support whose size is smaller. Remark that the problem of deciding whether a set of variables is a minimal independent support of a Boolean formula Φ is **DP**-complete, where $\textbf{DP} := \{A - B \mid A, B \in \textbf{NP}\}$.

3   Derivation Procedure

In this section, we first present a motivating example which exemplifies the key insight behind our approach for efficiently generating a large number of satisfying assignments. We then provide a derivation procedure which is able to derive more satisfying assignments from a seed by flipping the truth values of properly chosen variables without invoking computationally expensive SAT solving. The derivation procedure is the basis for efficiently generating a large number of satisfying assignments, and can be integrated into other samplers.

3.1   Motivating Example

To exemplify the key insight behind our approach, let us consider the following Boolean formula

$$\Phi_e \equiv (\neg a \vee b \vee c) \wedge (a \vee \neg c \vee \neg d) \wedge (\neg b \vee c) \wedge (b \vee d).$$

Suppose we have already obtained one satisfying assignment v (called *seed*) of Φ_e with $v(a) = v(b) = v(c) = v(d) = 1$. We can observe that the clause $\neg a \vee b \vee c$ (resp. $b \vee d$) contains two literals b and c (resp. b and d) whose values are 1 under the assignment v. Moreover, the common literal b does not appear in other clauses, namely, $a \vee \neg c \vee \neg d$ and $\neg b \vee c$. By flipping the value $v(b)$ of the variable b in the assignment v, we can obtain a new assignment $v[b \mapsto \neg v(b)]$, which is also a satisfying assignment of Φ_e.

However, by flipping the value $v(c)$ of the variable c in the assignment v, the new assignment $v[c \mapsto \neg v(c)]$ is not a satisfying assignment of Φ_e. This is because the clause $\neg b \vee c$ contains only one literal c whose value is 1 under the assignment v. After flipping the value $v(c)$ of the variable c in the assignment v, the clause $(\neg b \vee c)$ is no more satisfied.

Algorithm 1. Deriving satisfying assignments from a seed

```
1: procedure DERIVATION(Φ, v, MaxNum, Supp)
2:     Derived = {v};
3:     Queue = [v];
4:     while Queue ≠ ∅ ∧ |Derived| ≤ MaxNum do
5:         v = Queue.DEQUEUE();
6:         L = {x ∈ Supp | v(x) = 1} ∪ {¬x | v(x) = 0 ∧ x ∈ Supp};
7:         for all l ∈ L do
8:             if for each ⋁ᵢ₌₁ᵐ lᵢ ∈ Φₗ, there exists 1 ≤ i ≤ m. (l ≠ lᵢ ∧ lᵢ ∈ L) then
9:                 x = var(l);
10:                v' = v[x ↦ ¬v(x)];
11:                if v' ∉ Derived then
12:                    Derived = Derived ∪ {v'};
13:                    Queue.ENQUEUE(v');
14:                end if
15:            end if
16:        end for
17:    end while
18:    return Derived;
19: end procedure
```

This simple observation suggests that, for a seed v, we may identify proper variables (such as b but not c in the above example) so that when the value of one such variable is flipped it is still a satisfying assignment. Furthermore, the new satisfying assignments can be used as seeds to derive more satisfying assignments. This often allows generation of a larger number of satisfying assignments without invoking computationally expensive SAT solving.

3.2 Derivation Algorithm

In this subsection, we present a derivation procedure for deriving new satisfying assignments from a given seed. Given a Boolean formula Φ, a seed v and an independent support Supp of Φ, and the maximal number MaxNum of expected satisfying assignments, the procedure DERIVATION in Algorithm 1 iteratively derives new satisfying assignments from the seed v until no new satisfying assignment can be found or the number of generated satisfying assignments hits the threshold MaxNum. It returns the set of generated satisfying assignments including the original seed v.

To start, Algorithm 1 initializes the set Derived for recording all the generated satisfying assignments (Line 2) and the queue Queue for storing the seeds (Line 3). It then repeats the following procedure until no new satisfying assignments can be found or the number of the generated satisfying assignments exceeds the threshold MaxNum (While-loop).

For each seed v in Queue (Line 5), it first identifies all the literals l whose value is 1 under the assignment v(Line 6). After that, for each literal $l \in L$ whose variable var(l) ∈ Supp (Line 7), it checks, for each clause $\bigvee_{i=j}^{m} l_j$ that contains the literal l (i.e., $\bigvee_{i=j}^{m} l_j \in \Phi_l$), whether $\bigvee_{i=j}^{m} l_j$ contains a distinct literal l_i whose value is also 1, i.e., $l_i \in L$ (Line 8). If this is the case, we can deduce that the assignment $v[x \mapsto \neg v(x)]$ obtained from the assignment v by flipping the variable $x = \mathtt{var}(l)$ is also a satisfying assignement of Φ. Therefore, we extract the variable x from the literal l (Line 9) and construct the assignment $v' = v[x \mapsto \neg v(x)]$ (Line 10). If the assignment v' has not been generated before, it is inserted to Derived and Queue (Lines 12 and 13).

One may notice that only variables in Supp are considered for flipping (Line 7). In general, we can take all the variables into account for flipping. However, as mentioned before (cf. Sect. 2), flipping variables outside of Supp will definitely lead to unsatisfying assignments. Therefore, it suffices to consider variables from Supp for flipping. Due to this, the values of each variable outside of Supp are the same in all the generated satisfying assignments from a given seed.

We remark that the derivation procedure DERIVATION could alternatively be presented as a recursive procedure which invokes itself when a new satisfying assignment is generated, or equivalently, use a stack rather than a queue to store the generated seeds. Intuitively, using the queue Queue to store the seeds, our algorithm works in a breadth-first fashion, while the other two ways would follow a depth-first fashion. We adopt the current way because it is more efficient than the other two.

Theorem 1. *Given a Boolean formula Φ, a seed v and an independent support* Supp *of Φ, the set* Derived *returned by Algorithm 1 contains only satisfying assignments of Φ. Moreover, these assignments agree on the variables outside of* Supp.

Proof. We show that the set Derived returned by Algorithm 1 contains only satisfying assignments of Φ by applying induction on the sequence $v_0 v_1 \cdots$ of the assignments added into Derived. The base case is trivial as the seed v_0 satisfies the Boolean formula Φ. We prove the inductive step below.

Suppose $v_0, v_1 \cdots v_{k-1}$ have been added into the set Derived and the inductive step adds the assignment v_k into the set Derived. Then, v_k must be added due to one v of the previously added satisfying assignments $v_0, v_1 \cdots v_{k-1}$. There necessarily exists a literal l such that $x = \mathtt{var}(l)$ and $v_k = v[x \mapsto \neg v(x)]$.

To show that v_k satisfies Φ, it is sufficient to prove that v_k satisfies all the clauses of Φ. Let us consider a clause $\bigvee_{i=j}^{m} l_j$ of Φ,

- If $\bigvee_{i=j}^{m} l_j$ does not contain the literal l, then by applying induction hypothesis, v satisfies the Boolean formula Φ and hence v satisfies the clause $\bigvee_{i=j}^{m} l_j$. Since $v_k = v[x \mapsto \neg v(x)]$ and $x = \mathtt{var}(l)$, the truth of the clause $\bigvee_{i=j}^{m} l_j$ does not change when the value of x in v is flipped. Therefore, we get that the assignment v_k satisfies the clause $\bigvee_{i=j}^{m} l_j$.
- If $\bigvee_{i=1}^{m} l_i$ contains the literal l, then there exists another literal $l_i \in \{l_1, \cdots, l_m\}$ such that $l_i \neq l$ and $l_i \in L = \{x \mid v(x) = 1\} \cup \{\neg x \mid v(x) = 0\}$. From $l_i \in L = \{x \mid v(x) = 1\} \cup \{\neg x \mid v(x) = 0\}$, we deduce that the literal l_i, hence the clause $\bigvee_{i=1}^{m} l_i$, holds under the assignment v_k.

$$\Phi_e : \quad (\neg a \lor b \lor c) \land (a \lor \neg c \lor \neg d) \land (\neg b \lor c) \land (b \lor d)$$

$v_1 : \quad (\ 0 \lor 1 \lor 1) \land (1 \lor \ 0 \ \lor \ \ 0) \land (\ 0 \lor 1) \land (1 \lor 1)$
flip b and d respectively $\Downarrow$
$v_2 : \quad (\ 0 \lor \mathbf{0} \lor 1) \land (1 \lor \ 0 \ \lor \ \ 0) \land (\ \mathbf{1} \lor 1) \land (\mathbf{0} \lor 1)$
$v_3 : \quad (\ 0 \lor 1 \lor 1) \land (1 \lor \ 0 \ \lor \ \ 1) \land (\ 0 \lor 1) \land (1 \lor \mathbf{0})$
flip a $\Downarrow$
$v_4 : \quad (\ \mathbf{1} \lor 1 \lor 1) \land (\mathbf{0} \lor 0 \ \lor \ \ 1) \land (\ 0 \lor 1) \land (1 \lor 0)$

Fig. 1. Derivation steps of the motivating example

Example 1. Recall the motivating example Φ_e. Suppose the input seed is v_1 with $v_1(a) = v_1(b) = v_1(c) = v_1(d) = 1$ and the independent support $\mathsf{Supp} = \{a, b, d\}$. The derivation steps are shown in Fig. 1. At the beginning of the first iteration of the while-loop, $v = v_1$ and $L = \{a, b, c, d\}$.

1. Suppose the variable a is chosen for flipping (Line 7), the clause $a \lor \neg c \lor \neg d$ does not have any literals other than a that occur in L, then Algorithm 1 will not flip the variable a.
2. Next, the variable b is chosen for flipping (Line 7), both clauses $\neg a \lor b \lor c$ and $b \lor d$ contain literals c and d that occur in L, then Algorithm 1 will flip the variable b (Line 9) and produce a new satisfying assignment $v_2 = v_1[b \mapsto 0]$ (Line 10).
3. Finally, the variable d is chosen for flipping (Line 7), the clause $b \lor d$ contains literal b that occurs in L, then Algorithm 1 will flip the variable d (Line 9) and produce a new satisfying assignment $v_3 = v_1[d \mapsto 0]$ (Line 10).

At the end of the first iteration of the while-loop, $\mathsf{Derived} = \{v_1, v_2, v_3\}$ and $\mathsf{Queue} = [v_2, v_3]$. After entering the second iteration of the while-loop, $v = v_2$, Queue (resp. L) becomes $[v_3]$ (resp. $\{a, \neg b, c, d\}$). By applying similar steps as above, the satisfying assignment v_2 is regenerated but will not be inserted to $\mathsf{Derived}$ or Queue.

At the end of the second iteration of the while-loop, $\mathsf{Derived} = \{v_1, v_2, v_3\}$ and $\mathsf{Queue} = [v_3]$. After entering the third iteration of the while-loop, $v = v_3$, Queue (resp. L) becomes $\emptyset$ (resp. $\{a, b, c, \neg d\}$). By applying similar steps as above, Algorithm 1 will flip the variable a and produce a new satisfying assignment $v_4 = v_3[a \mapsto 0]$. In the end, no more new satisfying assignments can be generated and Algorithm 1 returns the set $\{v_1, v_2, v_3, v_4\}$. □

4   ESAMPLER

In this section, we show that our derivation procedure is of generic nature in the sense that it can be integrated with other samplers. The basic idea is to generate seeds by invoking an existing sampler as an iterator, which returns a unique satisfying assignment each time. For each seed, we derive more satisfying

---

Algorithm 2. Integrated our derivation procedure into an existing sampler

---

```
 1: procedure INTEGRATEDSAMPLER(Sampler, Φ, T, MaxPerSeed, Supp, RT, DT)
 2:     Solutions = ∅;
 3:     Derivable = false;
 4:     Round = 0;
 5:     Iterator = Sampler(Φ, Supp);
 6:     repeat
 7:         v = Iterator.next();
 8:         if v == Null ∨ v ∈ Solutions then
 9:             break;
10:         end if
11:         if Derivable == true ∨ Round<RT then
12:             Derived = DERIVATION(Φ, MaxPerSeed, v, Supp);
13:             Solutions = Solutions ∪ Derived;
14:             if |Derived| ≥ DT then
15:                 Derivable = true;
16:             else
17:                 Round = Round + 1;
18:             end if
19:         else
20:             Solutions = Solutions ∪ {v};
21:         end if
22:     until T is satisfied
23:     return Solutions;
24: end procedure
```

---

assignments by invoking our derivation procedure. However, our derivation procedure may not be effective on some Boolean formulas. Therefore, we propose a heuristic to determine whether our derivation procedure is able to derive a large number of satisfying assignments or not. If it can derive a large number of satisfying assignments, we apply the derivation procedure for each satisfying assignment generated by the sampler, otherwise we disable it.

Our idea is formalized as the procedure INTEGRATEDSAMPLER in Algorithm 2, which takes, as input, an off-the-shelf sampler Sampler, a Boolean formula Φ, a threshold T as the termination condition, the maximum number MaxPerSeed of satisfying assignments per seed, an independent support Supp of the Boolean formula Φ, two thresholds RT and DT to determine whether our derivation procedure is able to derive a large number of satisfying assignments, and returns a set Solutions of satisfying assignments of the formula Φ.

The procedure INTEGRATEDSAMPLER first initializes the set Solutions, the Boolean flag Derivable, the counter Round and the iterator Iterator of the sampler using the independent support Supp and Boolean formula Φ (Lines 2–5), where the Boolean flag Derivable and counter Round are used to determine if our derivation procedure is able to derive a large number of satisfying assignments. Then, it repeats the following procedure until the threshold T is hit.

During each iteration, INTEGRATEDSAMPLER first invokes the iterator to get a satisfying assignment v, where v is Null if Φ is unsatisfiable or the iterator cannot find new satisfying assignments. If v is NULL or already exists in Solutions, it breaks the loop (Line 9). Otherwise it checks if the Boolean flag Derivable is true or the number Round of iterations is less than the threshold RT.

- If neither holds, the derivation procedure is considered to be not able to derive a large number of satisfying assignments and will be skipped;
- Otherwise, the derivation procedure is invoked to generate more satisfying assignments which are added to the set Solutions (Lines 12–13). If the number of satisfying assignments generated by the derivation procedure exceeds the threshold DT, we consider that the derivation procedure is able to derive a large number of satisfying assignments and set the Boolean flag Derivable to true (Line 15). Otherwise, we increase the counter Round by one. In general, we probe the effectiveness of the derivation procedure by checking the number of satisfying assignments generated by the derivation procedure in the first RT iterations. In our experiments, we found few rounds are sufficient to detect for each benchmark whether a large number of satisfying assignments can be derived from a seed. Therefore, we set RT = 3 and DT = 16.

By Theorem 1, we obtain that

Theorem 2. *The set* Solutions *returned by Algorithm 2 contains only satisfying assignments of* Φ.

5   Implementation and Evaluation

We implement Algorithms 1 and 2 as an open-source tool ESAMPLER in C++, with QUICKSAMPLER as the underlying seed generator. QUICKSAMPLER takes a Boolean formula and its independent support as inputs, and outputs a set of assignments. However, as mentioned above, assignments produced by QUICKSAMPLER may be duplicated or not satisfy the formula. As we focus on satisfying assignments of each Boolean formula in this work, we modify it so that duplicated and unsatisfying assignments are omitted.

ESAMPLER takes a Boolean formula in the DIMACS [13] format and other required options as inputs, and outputs a set of satisfying assignments for the given Boolean formula. To reduce the memory usage of storing the satisfying assignments, we only store and output the satisfying assignments for the variables in the given independent support. Indeed, the truth values of the independent support determine those of the other variables, thereby the satisfying assignments can be easily completed.

We compare ESAMPLER with three state-of-the-art tools QUICKSAMPLER, STS and UNIGEN3 [36]. As done by [14], for a fair comparison, we modify STS so that the additional independent support information can be used by STS.

Benchmarks. To evaluate the performance, we conducted extensive experiments. Industrial testing and verification instances are typically proprietary and

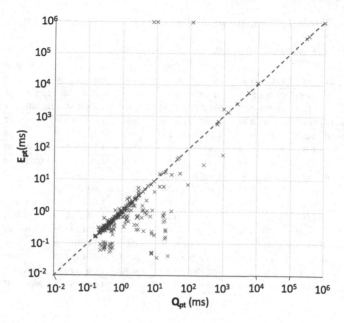

Fig. 2. ESAMPLER vs. QUICKSAMPLER

unavailable for published research. Therefore, we conducted experiments on the publicly available benchmarks from UNIGEN [10], which consist of 370 Boolean formulas in the DIMACS format and the independent supports thereof. Indeed, the independent supports of most Boolean formulas could be computed using MIS [20] in few seconds. These benchmarks come from four classes of problem instances:

1. ISCAS89: constraints arising from ISCAS89 circuits with parity conditions on randomly chosen subsets of outputs and next-state variables;
2. SMTLib: bit-blasted versions of SMTLib benchmarks;
3. ProgSyn: constraints arising from automated program synthesis; and
4. BMC: constraints arising in bounded model checking of circuits.

Note that the accompanied independent supports of these benchmarks may contain variables that are not involved in the corresponding Boolean formulas; such variables are removed from the independent supports in our experiments. We remark that our approach also works without the given independent supports, in which case the independent support of a Boolean formula contains all the involved variables. Since it does not make any sense to compute solutions for unsatisfiable Boolean formulas or the satisfiability cannot be solved, we checked the satisfiability of all these Boolean formulas with a timeout of one hour per Boolean formula using Z3 [27]. There are two unsatisfiable formulas (79.sk_4_40 and 36.sk_3_77), and four unsolvable formulas (logcount.sk_16_86, log2.sk_72_391, xpose.sk_6_134, and listReverse.sk_11_43). These formulas are not considered here, leaving 364 Boolean formulas.

Table 1. Comparison of QUICKSAMPLER and ESAMPLER

Benchmark	#Vars	#Cls	$Q_t(ks)$	Q_n	$Q_{pt}(ms)$	$E_t(ks)$	E_n	E_{dn}	$E_{pt}(ms)$	$\frac{Q_{pt}}{E_{pt}}$
s27_new_15_7	17	43	0.00	48	1.39	0.00	48	42	0.54	2.56
blasted_case.54	203	725	0.20	691,127	0.30	0.20	664,548	0	0.30	0.99
20.sk_1_51	15,475	60,994	3.94	491,074	8.02	1.67	1,520,152	~1,520k	1.10	7.31
s35932_7_4	17,849	44,425	4.22	245,506	17.17	0.63	1,270,247	~1,270k	0.50	34
blasted_case.126	302	1,129	0.34	1,007,411	0.34	0.34	1,022,991	0	0.33	1.03
blasted_case.40	245	650	0.41	1,149,017	0.35	0.41	1,149,017	0	0.36	0.99
s349_3_2	198	469	0.24	1,008,386	0.24	0.07	1,142,757	~1,088k	0.06	3.81
56.sk_6_38	4,842	17,828	1.97	1,004,037	1.96	1.18	1,093,080	~1,092k	1.08	1.81
blasted_case.107	618	1,661	0.82	1,149,017	0.72	0.84	1,149,017	0	0.73	0.98
s832a_15_7	693	2,017	0.53	1,001,732	0.53	0.52	1,000,093	4	0.52	1.01
s420_new_7_4	312	770	0.35	1,117,085	0.31	0.08	1,048,576	~1,043k	0.07	4.18
blasted_case.124	133	386	0.23	1,039,563	0.22	0.22	1,008,715	0	0.22	1.02
s35932_15_7	17,918	44,709	4.29	145,499	29.46	1.34	1,270,247	~1,270k	1.06	27
blasted_case.207	824	2,128	1.02	1,149,017	0.89	0.98	1,149,017	0	0.86	1.04
blasted_case.120	284	851	0.41	1,113,780	0.37	0.40	1,044,731	0	0.38	0.97
63.sk_3_64	7,242	24,379	4.04	917,681	4.41	0.30	1,200,120	~1,200k	0.25	17
s420_7_4	312	770	0.32	1,058,100	0.31	0.10	1,366,784	~1,363k	0.07	4.14

Experiment Setup. In our experiments, the maximal number MaxPerSeed of satisfying assignments per seed is 10,000 and the maximal number T of satisfying assignments to compute is 1,000,000, unless the recent 10 assignments/pseudosolutions already exist. As aforementioned, we set RT = 3 and DT = 16 for ESAMPLER. For STS and QUICKSAMPLER, we use their default parameter settings. All the experiments were conducted on Intel Xeon E5-2620 v4 2.10 GHz CPU with 256 RAM GB and the one-hour timeout.

5.1   Comparison with QUICKSAMPLER

Figure 2 shows the scatter plot comparing the average execution time per satisfying assignment between ESAMPLER and QUICKSAMPLER on all the 364 formulas. Timeout occurred along the top or right border; the red color indicates that Derivable is set true by Algorithm 2, namely, it determines that our derivation procedure is able to derive a large number of satisfying assignments. Points below (resp. above) the diagonal line indicate that ESAMPLER performs better (resp. worse) than QUICKSAMPLER.

Table 1 reports the performance of QUICKSAMPLER and ESAMPLER for a representative subset of the benchmarks. Columns benchmark, #Vars and #Cls respectively show the name, numbers of variables and clauses in each Boolean formula. Columns Q_t and E_t (resp. Q_{pt} and E_{pt}) give the total execution time in thousand seconds (ks) (resp. execution time per satisfying assignment in milliseconds (ms)) of QUICKSAMPLER and ESAMPLER, respectively. Columns Q_n and E_n show the total numbers of satisfying assignments generated by QUICKSAMPLER and ESAMPLER, respectively. Column E_{dn} gives the numbers of satisfying assignments generated by our derivation procedure. The last column provides

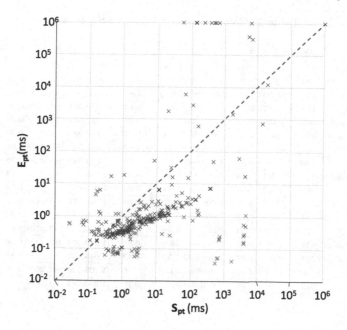

Fig. 3. ESAMPLER vs. STS

the ratio of execution time per satisfying assignment between QUICKSAMPLER and ESAMPLER, depicting the speedup of ESAMPLER. We can observe when our derivation procedure works, it can produce more satisfying assignments (e.g., 20.sk_1_51 and s35932_7_4) than QUICKSAMPLER in the same time budget, while when it does not work well, it often does not produce any satisfying assignments (e.g., blasted_case.54 and blasted_case.40). Note that, since QUICKSAMPLER is a randomized approach, QUICKSAMPLER and ESAMPLER may produce different satisfying assignments when our derivation procedure does not work, although ESAMPLER is built on QUICKSAMPLER.

Summary. ESAMPLER and QUICKSAMPLER respectively failed on 11 and 7 benchmarks due to the failure of MaxSAT solving. The difference between the numbers of the failed benchmarks indicates that the soft constraints generated randomly slightly affect MaxSAT solving. When ESAMPLER determined that the derivation procedure can generate a large number of satisfying assignments, ESAMPLER performed better than QUICKSAMPLER on almost all the benchmarks. While ESAMPLER determined that our derivation procedure was not able to generate a large number of satisfying assignments, ESAMPLER was comparable to QUICKSAMPLER. Specifically, ESAMPLER was faster than QUICKSAMPLER on 227 benchmarks. It was $1.66\times$ faster on average and more than $5\times$ faster on 41 benchmarks, while is 1.2 times slower on 16 benchmarks.

Table 2. Comparison of STS and ESAMPLER

Benchmark	#Vars	#Cls	$S_t(ks)$	S_n	$S_{pt}(ms)$	$E_t(ks)$	E_n	E_{dn}	$E_{pt}(ms)$	$\frac{S_{pt}}{E_{pt}}$
s27_new_15_7	17	43	0.00	48	0.85	0.00	48	42	0.54	1.57
blasted_case.54	203	725	1.45	961,782	1.51	0.20	664,548	0	0.30	5.06
20.sk_1_51	15,475	60,994	3.60	151,948	23.69	1.67	1,520,152	~1,520k	1.10	21
s35932_7_4	17,849	44,425	3.49	800	4,361	0.63	1,270,247	~1,270k	0.50	8,757
blasted_case.126	302	1,129	0.92	1,000,006	0.92	0.34	1,022,991	0	0.33	2.78
blasted_case.40	245	650	1.53	1,000,000	1.53	0.41	1,149,017	0	0.36	4.30
s349_3_2	198	469	0.31	1,000,028	0.31	0.07	1,142,757	~1,088k	0.06	4.94
56.sk_6_38	4,842	17,828	1.99	1,000,048	1.99	1.18	1,093,080	~1,092k	1.08	1.84
blasted_case.107	618	1,661	3.60	558,950	6.44	0.84	1,149,017	0	0.73	8.82
s832a_15_7	693	2,017	1.55	1,000,018	1.55	0.52	1,000,093	4	0.52	2.97
s420_new_7_4	312	770	0.72	1,000,001	0.72	0.08	1,048,576	~1,043k	0.07	9.68
blasted_case.124	133	386	0.32	1,000,013	0.32	0.22	1,008,715	0	0.22	1.47
s35932_15_7	17,918	44,709	3.50	800	4,380	1.34	1,270,247	~1,270k	1.06	4,140
blasted_case.207	824	2,128	3.60	276,250	13.03	0.98	1,149,017	0	0.86	15
blasted_case.120	284	851	1.59	1,000,000	1.59	0.40	1,044,731	0	0.38	4.13
63.sk_3_64	7,242	24,379	3.60	148,050	24.31	0.30	1,200,120	~1,200k	0.25	97
s420_7_4	312	770	0.74	1,000,038	0.74	0.10	1,366,784	~1,363k	0.07	9.93

5.2 Comparison with STS

Figure 3 shows the scatter plot comparing the average execution time per satisfying assignment between ESAMPLER and STS on all the 364 formulas. Recall that timeout occurred along the top or right border, the red color indicates that Derivable is set true by Algorithm 2, and points below the diagonal line indicate that ESAMPLER performs better than QUICKSAMPLER, and vice versa.

Table 2 reports the performance of STS and ESAMPLER for the same representative subset of the benchmarks. Column S_t (resp. S_{pt}) gives the total execution time in thousand seconds (ks) (resp. execution time per satisfying assignment in milliseconds (ms)) of STS. Column S_n shows the total number of satisfying assignments generated by STS for each Boolean formula. The last column provides the ratio of execution time per satisfying assignment between STS and ESAMPLER, depicting the speedup of ESAMPLER.

Summary. STS failed on 1 benchmark because the underlying SAT solver Minisat failed to solve the Boolean formula, while ESAMPLER failed on 11 benchmarks. In general, ESAMPLER performed better than STS on most benchmarks. It was faster on 316 benchmarks (5.47× faster on average and more than 10× faster on 93 benchmarks), while was 1.2 times slower on only 45 benchmarks.

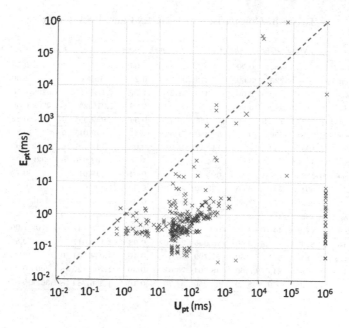

Fig. 4. ESAMPLER vs. UNIGEN3

5.3   Comparison with UNIGEN3

Figure 4 shows the scatter plot comparing the average execution time per satisfying assignment between ESAMPLER and UNIGEN3 on all the 364 formulas. Almost all the points are below the diagonal line, indicating ESAMPLER significantly outperforms UNIGEN3.

Table 3 reports the performance of UNIGEN3 and ESAMPLER on the same representative subset of benchmarks. Column U_t (resp. U_{pt}) gives the total execution time in thousand seconds (ks) (resp. execution time per satisfying assignment in milliseconds (ms)) of UNIGEN3. Column U_n shows the total number of satisfying assignments generated by UNIGEN3 for each Boolean formula. The last column provides the ratio of execution time per satisfying assignment between UNIGEN3 and ESAMPLER, depicting the speedup of ESAMPLER.

Summary. UNIGEN3 failed on 40 benchmarks. Recall that ESAMPLER failed on 11 benchmarks. No matter whether or not ESAMPLER determined that the derivation procedure was able to generate a large number of satisfying assignments, ESAMPLER performed significantly better than UNIGEN3 on almost all the benchmarks. Specifically, ESAMPLER was faster than STS on 348 benchmarks. It was 69.8× faster on average and more than 100× faster on 194 benchmarks, while was 1.2 times slower on only 7 benchmarks.

Table 3. Comparison of UNIGEN3 and ESAMPLER

Benchmark	#Vars	#Cls	$U_t(ks)$	U_n	$U_{pt}(ms)$	$E_t(ks)$	E_n	E_{dn}	$E_{pt}(ms)$	$\frac{U_{pt}}{E_{pt}}$
s27_new_15_7	17	43	0.00	48	20.83	0.00	48	42	0.54	19.83
blasted_case.54	203	725	3.60	158,168	22.76	0.20	664,548	0	0.30	3.33
20.sk_1_51	15,475	60,994	3.60	70,312	51.21	1.67	1,520,152	~1,520k	1.10	57.83
s35932_7_4	17,849	44,425	3.60	0	–	0.63	1,270,247	~1,270k	0.50	–
blasted_case.126	302	1,129	3.60	77,185	46.67	0.34	1,022,991	0	0.33	9.33
blasted_case.40	245	650	3.60	50,380	71.46	0.41	1,149,017	0	0.36	5.78
s349_3_2	198	469	3.60	144,279	24.95	0.07	1,142,757	~1,088k	0.06	1,643
56.sk_6_38	4,842	17,828	3.60	104,149	34.57	1.18	1,093,080	~1,092k	1.08	30.63
blasted_case.107	618	1,661	3.60	0	–	0.84	1,149,017	0	0.73	–
s832a_15_7	693	2,017	3.60	132,705	27.13	0.52	1,000,093	4	0.52	2.02
s420_new_7_4	312	770	3.60	98,934	36.39	0.08	1,048,576	~1,043k	0.07	3,966
blasted_case.124	133	386	3.60	89,376	40.28	0.22	1,008,715	0	0.22	14.92
s35932_15_7	17,918	44,709	3.60	0	–	1.34	1,270,247	~1,270k	1.06	–
blasted_case.207	824	2,128	3.60	15,026	239.92	0.98	1,149,017	0	0.86	16.89
blasted_case.120	284	851	3.60	51,799	69.5	0.40	1,044,731	0	0.38	3.12
63.sk_3_64	7,242	24,379	3.60	48,004	75.01	0.30	1,200,120	~1,200k	0.25	1,133
s420_7_4	312	770	3.60	95,260	37.79	0.10	1,366,784	~1,363k	0.07	3,990

5.4 Execution Time vs Number of Satisfying Assignments

To see the relation between the execution time and the number of satisfying assignments, we evaluate ESAMPLER on four randomly chosen benchmarks by varying the execution time and counting the number of satisfying assignments. Figure 5 shows the plot for the four randomly chosen benchmarks, where the x-axis is the execution time (in seconds) and the y-axis is number of satisfying assignments (#assignments). We can observe that the number of satisfying assignments for each benchmark is almost linear in the execution time. These results demonstrate the effectiveness of our derivation procedure.

5.5 Testing Uniformity

Since QUICKSAMPLER does not provide a guarantee of uniformity, neither does ESAMPLER. We empirically show that the uniformity of the solutions can be controlled by adjusting the maximal number of solutions per seed, i.e., the parameter MaxNumPerSeed. We run ESAMPLER on a randomly selected benchmark (i.e., 27.sk_3_32) on which our derivation procedure works, where duplicated solutions are recorded to measure uniformity and the mutation phase of QUICKSAMPLER is disabled to be more precise.

Figure 6 depicts the distributions of solutions when MaxNumPerSeed is 0, 10 and 100, where (x, y) denotes that there are y unique solutions each of which occurs x times. We can observe that the smaller the parameter MaxNumPerSeed is, the closer the distribution is to the normal distribution, meaning that the solutions generated by our tool are actually close to uniform.

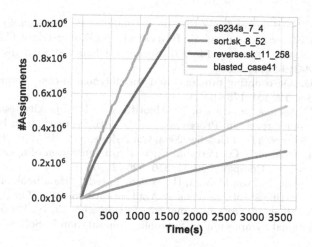

Fig. 5. Time vs. #assignments

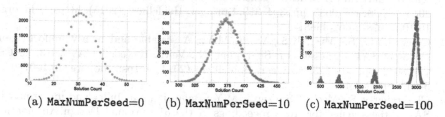

(a) `MaxNumPerSeed=0`   (b) `MaxNumPerSeed=10`   (c) `MaxNumPerSeed=100`

Fig. 6. Distribution of solutions

6   Conclusion

We have proposed a novel approach to generate a large set of satisfying assignments from a seed assignment without invoking computationally expensive SAT solving. Our approach is orthogonal to the previous techniques and could be integrated into the existing SAT samplers. We have also developed a new tool ESAMPLER, based on the recent sampler QUICKSAMPLER as the seed generator. We have carried out extensive experiments on real-world benchmarks. The experimental results confirmed the effectiveness and efficiency of our approach.

In future, we plan to further improve the performance of our tool ESAMPLER, which will be applied in emerging practical scenarios such as adversarial training of binaried neural networks and constrained hardware design fuzz testing.

References

1. Abed, S., Abdelaal, A.A., Alshayeji, M.H., Ahmad, I.: Sat-based and CP-based declarative approaches for top-rank-k closed frequent itemset mining. Int. J. Intell. Syst. **36**(1), 112–151 (2021)

2. Achlioptas, D., Hammoudeh, Z.S., Theodoropoulos, P.: Fast sampling of perfectly uniform satisfying assignments. In: Beyersdorff, O., Wintersteiger, C.M. (eds.) SAT 2018. LNCS, vol. 10929, pp. 135–147. Springer, Cham (2018). https://doi.org/10.1007/978-3-319-94144-8_9

3. Angluin, D.: On counting problems and the polynomial-time hierarchy. Theoret. Comput. Sci. **12**, 161–173 (1980)

4. Bacchus, F., Dalmao, S., Pitassi, T.: Algorithms and complexity results for #SAT and Bayesian inference. In: Proceedings of the 44th Symposium on Foundations of Computer Science, 11–14 October 2003, Cambridge, MA, USA, pp. 340–351 (2003)

5. Bellare, M., Goldreich, O., Petrank, E.: Uniform generation of np-witnesses using an NP-oracle. Inf. Comput. **163**(2), 510–526 (2000)

6. Biere, A., Heule, M., van Maaren, H., Walsh, T. (eds.): Handbook of Satisfiability, Frontiers in Artificial Intelligence and Applications, vol. 185. IOS Press (2009)

7. Bjørner, N., Phan, A.: νz - maximal satisfaction with Z3. In: Proceedings of the 6th International Symposium on Symbolic Computation in Software Science, pp. 1–9 (2014)

8. Chakraborty, S., Fremont, D.J., Meel, K.S., Seshia, S.A., Vardi, M.Y.: On parallel scalable uniform SAT witness generation. In: Baier, C., Tinelli, C. (eds.) TACAS 2015. LNCS, vol. 9035, pp. 304–319. Springer, Heidelberg (2015). https://doi.org/10.1007/978-3-662-46681-0_25

9. Chakraborty, S., Meel, K.S., Vardi, M.Y.: A scalable and nearly uniform generator of SAT witnesses. In: Sharygina, N., Veith, H. (eds.) CAV 2013. LNCS, vol. 8044, pp. 608–623. Springer, Heidelberg (2013). https://doi.org/10.1007/978-3-642-39799-8_40

10. Chakraborty, S., Meel, K.S., Vardi, M.Y.: Balancing scalability and uniformity in SAT witness generator. In: Proceedings of the 51st Annual Design Automation Conference (DAC), pp. 60:1–60:6 (2014)

11. Chen, G., Zhao, Z., Song, F., Chen, S., Fan, L., Liu, Y.: SEC4SR: a security analysis platform for speaker recognition. CoRR abs/2109.01766 (2021)

12. Cook, S.A.: The complexity of theorem-proving procedures. In: Proceedings of the 3rd Annual ACM Symposium on Theory of Computing, pp. 151–158 (1971)

13. DIMACS: Clique and coloring problems graph format (1993). http://archive.dimacs.rutgers.edu/pub/challenge/graph/doc/ccformat.tex. Accessed 16 Sept 2021

14. Dutra, R., Laeufer, K., Bachrach, J., Sen, K.: Efficient sampling of SAT solutions for testing. In: Proceedings of the 40th International Conference on Software Engineering, pp. 549–559 (2018)

15. Ermon, S., Gomes, C.P., Sabharwal, A., Selman, B.: Embed and project: discrete sampling with universal hashing. In: Proceedings of the 27th Annual Conference on Neural Information Processing Systems, pp. 2085–2093 (2013)

16. Ermon, S., Gomes, C.P., Selman, B.: Uniform solution sampling using a constraint solver as an oracle. In: Proceedings of the Twenty-Eighth Conference on Uncertainty in Artificial Intelligence, pp. 255–264 (2012)

17. Gomes, C.P., Sabharwal, A., Selman, B.: Near-uniform sampling of combinatorial spaces using XOR constraints. In: Proceedings of the 2th Annual Conference on Neural Information Processing Systems, pp. 481–488 (2006)

18. Guralnik, E., Aharoni, M., Birnbaum, A.J., Koyfman, A.: Simulation-based verification of floating-point division. IEEE Trans. Comput. **60**(2), 176–188 (2011)

19. Hubara, I., Courbariaux, M., Soudry, D., El-Yaniv, R., Bengio, Y.: Binarized neural networks. In: Proceedings of the Annual Conference on Neural Information Processing Systems, pp. 4107–4115 (2016)

20. Ivrii, A., Malik, S., Meel, K.S., Vardi, M.Y.: On computing minimal independent support and its applications to sampling and counting. Constraints **21**(1), 41–58 (2015). https://doi.org/10.1007/s10601-015-9204-z
21. Bayardo Jr., R.J., Schrag, R.: Using CSP look-back techniques to solve real-world SAT instances. In: Proceedings of the Fourteenth National Conference on Artificial Intelligence and Ninth Innovative Applications of Artificial Intelligence Conference, 27–31 July 1997, Providence, Rhode Island, USA, pp. 203–208 (1997)
22. Kitchen, N.: Markov chain Monte Carlo stimulus generation for constrained random simulation. Ph.D. thesis, University of California, Berkeley, USA (2010)
23. Kitchen, N., Kuehlmann, A.: Stimulus generation for constrained random simulation. In: Proceedings of the 2007 International Conference on Computer-Aided Design, pp. 258–265 (2007)
24. Korneev, S., Narodytska, N., Pulina, L., Tacchella, A., Bjorner, N., Sagiv, M.: Constrained image generation using binarized neural networks with decision procedures. In: Beyersdorff, O., Wintersteiger, C.M. (eds.) SAT 2018. LNCS, vol. 10929, pp. 438–449. Springer, Cham (2018). https://doi.org/10.1007/978-3-319-94144-8_27
25. Kukula, J.H., Shiple, T.R.: Building circuits from relations. In: Emerson, E.A., Sistla, A.P. (eds.) CAV 2000. LNCS, vol. 1855, pp. 113–123. Springer, Heidelberg (2000). https://doi.org/10.1007/10722167_12
26. Meel, K.S.: Constrained counting and sampling: bridging the gap between theory and practice. CoRR abs/1806.02239 (2018)
27. de Moura, L., Bjørner, N.: Z3: an efficient SMT solver. In: Ramakrishnan, C.R., Rehof, J. (eds.) TACAS 2008. LNCS, vol. 4963, pp. 337–340. Springer, Heidelberg (2008). https://doi.org/10.1007/978-3-540-78800-3_24
28. Narodytska, N.: Formal analysis of deep binarized neural networks. In: Proceedings of the 27th International Joint Conference on Artificial Intelligence, pp. 5692–5696 (2018)
29. Naveh, R., Metodi, A.: Beyond feasibility: CP usage in constrained-random functional hardware verification. In: Schulte, C. (ed.) CP 2013. LNCS, vol. 8124, pp. 823–831. Springer, Heidelberg (2013). https://doi.org/10.1007/978-3-642-40627-0_60
30. Naveh, Y., et al.: Constraint-based random stimuli generation for hardware verification. In: Proceedings of the 21st National Conference on Artificial Intelligence and the 18th Innovative Applications of Artificial Intelligence Conference, pp. 1720–1727 (2006)
31. Naveh, Y., et al.: Constraint-based random stimuli generation for hardware verification. AI Mag. **28**(3), 13 (2007)
32. Roth, D.: On the hardness of approximate reasoning. Artif. Intell. **82**(1–2), 273–302 (1996)
33. Silva, J.P.M., Sakallah, K.A.: GRASP: a search algorithm for propositional satisfiability. IEEE Trans. Comput. **48**(5), 506–521 (1999)
34. Silva, J.P.M., Sakallah, K.A.: Grasp–a new search algorithm for satisfiability. In: Kuehlmann, A. (ed.) The Best of ICCAD, pp. 73–89. Springer, Boston (2003). https://doi.org/10.1007/978-1-4615-0292-0_7
35. Sipser, M.: A complexity theoretic approach to randomness. In: Proceedings of the 15th Annual ACM Symposium on Theory of Computing, pp. 330–335 (1983)
36. Soos, M., Gocht, S., Meel, K.S.: Tinted, detached, and lazy CNF-XOR solving and its applications to counting and sampling. In: Lahiri, S.K., Wang, C. (eds.) CAV 2020. LNCS, vol. 12224, pp. 463–484. Springer, Cham (2020). https://doi.org/10.1007/978-3-030-53288-8_22

37. Soos, M., Nohl, K., Castelluccia, C.: Extending SAT solvers to cryptographic problems. In: Kullmann, O. (ed.) SAT 2009. LNCS, vol. 5584, pp. 244–257. Springer, Heidelberg (2009). https://doi.org/10.1007/978-3-642-02777-2_24

38. Sörensson, N., Eén, N.: MiniSat: a SAT solver with conflict-clause minimization. Solver Description (2005)

39. Valiant, L.G.: The complexity of enumeration and reliability problems. SIAM J. Comput. 8(3), 410–421 (1979)

40. Vorobyov, K., Krishnan, P.: Combining static analysis and constraint solving for automatic test case generation. In: Proceedings of the 5th IEEE International Conference on Software Testing, Verification and Validation, pp. 915–920 (2012)

41. Wei, W., Erenrich, J., Selman, B.: Towards efficient sampling: exploiting random walk strategies. In: Proceedings of the 19th National Conference on Artificial Intelligence, 16th Conference on Innovative Applications of Artificial Intelligence, pp. 670–676 (2004)

42. Wei, W., Selman, B.: A new approach to model counting. In: Bacchus, F., Walsh, T. (eds.) SAT 2005. LNCS, vol. 3569, pp. 324–339. Springer, Heidelberg (2005). https://doi.org/10.1007/11499107_24

43. Yuan, J., Aziz, A., Pixley, C., Albin, K.: Simplifying boolean constraint solving for random simulation-vector generation. IEEE Trans. Comput. Aided Des. Integr. Circ. Syst. 23(3), 412–420 (2004)

44. Zhang, Y., Zhao, Z., Chen, G., Song, F., Chen, T.: BDD4BNN: a BDD-based quantitative analysis framework for binarized neural networks. In: Proceedings of the 33rd International Conference on Computer Aided Verification, pp. 175–200 (2021)

45. Zhang, Y., Li, J., Zhang, M., Pu, G., Song, F.: Optimizing backbone filtering. In: Proceedings of the 11th International Symposium on Theoretical Aspects of Software Engineering, pp. 1–8 (2017)

46. Zhang, Y., Zhang, M., Pu, G., Song, F., Li, J.: Towards backbone computing: a greedy-whitening based approach. AI Commun. 31(3), 267–280 (2018)

47. Zhao, Y., Bian, J., Deng, S., Kong, Z.: Random stimulus generation with self-tuning. In: Proceedings of the 13th International Conference on Computers Supported Cooperative Work in Design, pp. 62–65. IEEE (2009)

48. Zhao, Z., Chen, G., Wang, J., Yang, Y., Song, F., Sun, J.: Attack as defense: characterizing adversarial examples using robustness. In: Proceedings of the 30th ACM SIGSOFT International Symposium on Software Testing and Analysis, pp. 42–55 (2021)

API Usage Pattern Search Based on Model Checking

Xue-er Ding[1](✉), Jun Niu[1,2](✉), and Jia Wang[1](✉)

[1] Faculty of Electrical Engineering and Computer Science, Ningbo University, Ningbo 315211, China
dingxuer@yeah.net, niujun@nbu.edu.cn
[2] Key Laboratory of Embedded System and Service Computing Ministry of Education, Tongji University, Shanghai 201804, China

Abstract. Reusing existing class libraries can improve the productivity of software development. API usage patterns are useful resources for programmers in reusing class libraries. Existing approaches often exploit API graphs to model semantic relations between API elements of class libraries, and traversal graphs to capture API usage patterns. However, those approaches cannot describe the number of parameters and the number of overload methods, and may not search for various API usage patterns. In this paper, we propose an automatic and complete approach to searching for API usage patterns by model checking technique. We introduce a novel kind of API transition system model to completely describe the relations between all API elements of existing class libraries. We obtain API usage constraints from queries, namely the numbers and types of input and output objects and class types transformed based on APIs replacement model, and give the logical characterizations of the constraints by suitable CTL* (computation tree logic) formulas. Then, we can obtain suitable API usage patterns by model checking the logical formulas in related API transition system models based on model checker NuSMV. The experiments indicate that, in contrast to existing approaches, our approach can automatically and effectively search for various API usage patterns.

Keywords: Code reusage · API usage pattern · Model checking · API transition system · Computation tree logic CTL*

1 Introduction

With the widespread employments of computers, increasing large-scale software systems appear in reality. Their development and maintenance costs increase with their sizes and complexities [1]. Reusing existing class libraries can improve software qualities and development efficiencies [2]. In recent years, developing software by reusing class libraries has received considerable attention from both academia and industry [3].

In general, class libraries refer to reusable classes consisting of the definitions of their member variables and methods. When working with class libraries, programmers often choose suitable methods provided by libraries (called API methods) and organize those API methods to implement a certain functionality [4]. A suitable calling sequences of API methods are called an API usage pattern. Earlier studies show that API usage patterns are useful resources for programmers in reusing existing class libraries [5].

However, the existing manual search approaches to obtaining API usage patterns are inefficient and error-prone [6]. For instance, as a graphical interactive class library commonly used in Eclipse, the GEF has 350,000 lines of codes and more than 60,000 API methods. When programmers search for their desired API usage patterns from this library, they have to read and understand a large number of reference documents. It has been reported that programmers usually spend more than 40% of their programming time searching and understanding the usages of existing APIs [7]. If API usage patterns can be automatically identified, the workload of searching, understanding, combining, and debugging will be greatly reduced, and thus it will reduce the error probability [8, 9]. Hence, automatic API usage pattern search has attracted more attention, and has become one of the research hotspots in code reusage.

Currently, there are two kinds of search approaches of API usage patterns. The first is based on frequent-sequence mining [10, 11]. They transform code snippets in the source code repository into API calling sequences and divide the sequences into different clusters. Each cluster has similar sequences, representing a common API usage pattern. Then, they search for relevant API usage patterns by comparing the similarities between queries provided by users and clusters. Thus, these approaches can reduce the redundancy of patterns and improve the efficiency of pattern discovery. However, there are still several major issues. For instance, an imbalanced usage occurs when an API usage pattern appears more frequently than other usage patterns. So, it will increase the possibility that other API usage patterns are ignored and reduce the completeness of patterns. As noted by Mendez et al., that imbalanced usage is common in Java and other source code ecosystems [12]. Thus, existing approaches based on frequent-sequence mining might not be suitable for API usage patterns search.

The second kind of search approach of API usage patterns is based on API graph models [13–17]. These approaches model semantic relations between all API elements (classes and methods) in class libraries as graphs, to extract complete API usage patterns. Given the queries represented as pairs of input and output types, they obtain reachable subgraphs from input type to output type in graph models. Each subgraph corresponds to a method calling sequence that constitutes a target pattern. These approaches can avoid the imbalance that may appear in the first kind of approaches, and has higher applicability and search efficiency. However, there also exist three key shortcomings. First, these approaches only support a single input type in queries and cannot cope with multiple input objects. Second, when analyzing and constructing graph models, they lack quantitative analysis between API elements such as the number of parameters of methods, and cannot treat overloaded methods. Also, existing traversal algorithms can only handle methods with a single parameter in the target pattern [13].

In the last three decades, as a remarkable formal method, model checking technique has been widely applied in various areas, such as software, hardware, protocol verification and abnormal data detection [18, 19]. Model checking is usually used for the verification of temporal properties of complex systems. The input of a model checking algorithm consists of a formal model and a property to be verified, usually expressed as a logic formula. The model checking procedure automatically traverses all states of the model, to check whether the model satisfies the property [20, 21]. In API usage patterns search, API graph models represent the semantic relations between all API elements of source codes, and the constraints represented as pairs of input and output types can also be organized as properties of interest, thus model checking technique can be applied to the searches of API usage patterns. In this case, one can construct formal models to model the semantic relationships between API elements in class libraries, and further mine semantic information of API elements to improve the effect of API usage pattern search.

In this paper, we propose an API usage pattern search approach based on model checking technique. We exploit model checking to effectively handle various API usage patterns, especially those that contain API methods with multiple parameters. Furthermore, to comprehensively describe the relations between API elements in class libraries, we propose a novel kind of API transition system model corresponding to the semantic representations of class libraries. Figure 1 shows the complete process of our approach. First, we exploit program analysis technique to extract API elements of class libraries and build transition system models that describe semantic relations between API elements. Second, we transform query statements each consisting of a desired pair of input and output types and natural language descriptions into matching rules, and formalize these rules by computation tree logic CTL* formulae. Then we take the transition system models and CTL* formulae as the inputs of the model checker NuSMV to obtain desired API usage patterns that satisfy the CTL* formulae.

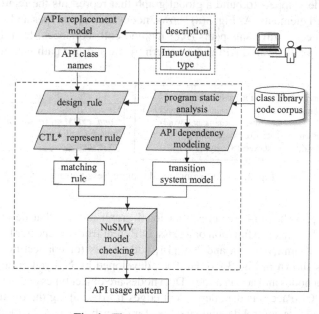

Fig. 1. The process of the approach.

The contributions of this paper are as follows.

- It introduces a novel kind of transition system model to describe the semantic dependencies of API elements in class libraries. Different from existing works, this paper further analyzes the numerical features between API elements, uses the labeling function to represent multiple parameters of API methods, and exploits the concept of clone to distinguish overloaded methods.
- It proposes an approach to searching for API usage patterns based on model checking technique. This approach formulates formalized matching rules to express queries and replaces the traditional graph traversal algorithm with model checking technique, to automatically and effectively search for various API usage patterns.

2 Related Work

In recent years, many researchers have studied the API usage pattern search approaches based on graph models. These studies are divided into two categories. One integrates source code snippets to build a global graph model, while the other exploits a series of single code snippets such as a function or a class to build local graph models.

To describe the various graph models of existing approaches intuitively, we take a code snippet as an example in Fig. 2. The left side in Fig. 2 is the source code that connects the database and queries table data, and the right side represents the involved object types. Prospector developed by Mandelin et al. [13] uses API method signatures and source code snippets to build a global graph that represents the relations between all included API elements. As Fig. 3(a) shows, nodes are object types and edges are API methods. Prospector traversals paths (API method call sequences) from input type to output type to obtain desired API usage pattern by the shortest path search algorithm.

```
String dburl,usename,password,query;          Str a₁,a₂,a₃,a₄;
Connection cn=DriverManager.getConnection     Conn c=DM.m₁ (a₁,a₂,a₃);
          (dburl,usename,password);            Stmt d=c.m₂( );
Statement st=cn.CreatStatement( );             RS e=d.m₃(a₄);
ResultSet rs=st.executeQuery(query);
```

$Str\ a_1,a_2,a_3,a_4;$
$Conn\ c=DM.m_1\ (a_1,a_2,a_3);$
$Stmt\ d=c.m_2(\ );$
$RS\ e=d.m_3(a_4);$

Fig. 2. Code example and type representation.

Several approaches [14–16] construct local graph models that describe relations between API elements in a function or a class. Different from Prospector [13], ParseWeb developed by Thummalapenta and Xie [14] adds edges for connecting methods and parameters, as shown in Fig. 3 (b). GraPacc developed by Nguyen et al. [15] divides nodes into data nodes and action nodes. Data nodes are object types and action nodes are API methods. GraPacc sets data dependent edges for describing the relations between object types and sets control dependent edges for describing called methods sequences, as shown in Fig. 3 (c). In APISynth developed by Lv Chen et al. [16], the nodes consist of methods, input and output types of methods and usage frequencies of methods (QoS). The edges connect adjacent nodes, indicating that the output type of method in a node is

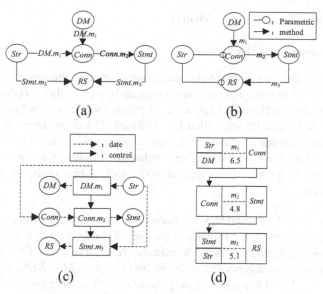

Fig. 3. Examples of existing graph models.

the input type of method in the next node, as shown in Fig. 3 (d). Similar to Prospector [13], ParseWeb and APISynth exploit the graph traversal algorithm to extract the shortest method sequence from input type to output type. APISynth uses the tool Grouminer to mine common API usage patterns and matches patterns related to queries.

In general, API usage pattern search approaches based on graph models are helpful for programmers to obtain suitable method sequences, whereas they have two key shortcomings. Firstly, existing graph models lack numerical relations between API elements such as the number of parameters. Secondly, the path search algorithm commonly used in existing approaches cannot automatically match the pattern containing methods with multiple parameters. Thus, these approaches require manual operations. Manual operations easily cause errors, thereby reducing the search accuracy.

In addition, there are some related researches focusing on searching for API usage patterns. Saied et al. extract method sequences from source code snippets by program analysis technique, and exploit mining frequent items algorithm to mine API usage patterns [10]. Niu et al., represent source code snippets as a network of object usages and their co-existence relations, and identify representative object usages by clustering similar object usages in the network [8]. These approaches rely on clustering technique and easily ignore uncommon API usage patterns. Raghothaman et al. extract API classes and methods related to queries based on clickthrough data from the Bing search engine, and exploit structured call sequences to capture usage patterns of extracted APIs [22]. Gu et al. build a neural language model named RNN Encoder-Decoder to generate API usage sequences for a given API-related natural language query. Whereas the approach based on deep learning has low interpretability [23].

3 API Transition System Model

3.1 Class Library API Dependency

In general, class libraries in oriented-object context indicate the sets of reusable codes that possess the definitions of classes, interfaces, and their member variables or methods (functions). In this section, we explore the dependency relations between class types and methods in a class library, called Class library API dependency (*CLAD*). These dependency relations can be classified into three categories, namely call relations (*call*), parameter relations (*par*) and return (*ret*) relations. Further, we also consider some numerical relations between types and methods, such as the number of parameters or overloaded methods.

Definition 1. The API dependency relations of a classes library can be represented as a tuple $CLAD = (C, M, Rel, Ln)$, where C is a set of class types, M is a set of methods, $Rel: C \times M \to \{call, par, ret\}$ is the dependency relation function, Ln is the numerical relation function between types and methods: for cC and $m \in M$, if $Rel(c, m) \in \{call, ret\}$, then $Ln(c, m) \to (1)^T$; if $Rel(c, m) \in \{par\}$, then $Ln(c, m) \to (n_1 \ n_2 \cdots n_i)^T$ with $n \in \mathbb{N}^+$, where n_i represents the number of the parameter with class type c in the i-th overloaded method.

For example, the class library *java. sql* in JAVA 2 exists dependency relations between the classes **Connection**, **Statement** and the method *createStatement*, as shown in Table 1. For simplicity, **Connection**, **Statement** and *createStatement* are abbreviated as *Conn*, *Stmt*, *creS*, respectively. We use (C, M, Rel, Ln) to represent the dependency between these elements. Here, we have $C = \{Conn, Stmt, int\}$ and $M = \{creS\}$. In addition, we have $Rel (Conn, creS) = call$ and $Ln (Conn, creS) = (1)^T$, representing that calling method *creS* needs only one caller type *Conn*. We have $Rel (Stmt, creS) = ret$ and $Ln (Stmt, creS) = (1)^T$, representing that only one type *Stmt* is returned after calling method *creS*. We have $Rel (int, creS) = par$ and $Ln (int, creS) = (0 \ 2 \ 3)^T$, representing that *creS* are overloaded methods and the numbers of parameters with type *int* in overloaded methods are 0, 2, 3, respectively.

Table 1. Relations between partial API elements in the class **Connection**.

Caller type	Returnee type	Method
Connection	**Statement**	createStatement ()
		createStatement (int resultSetType, int resultSetConcurrency)
		createStatement (int resultSetType, int resultSetConcurrency, int resultSetHoldability)

3.2 API Transition System

To search for API usage patterns by model checking, we propose a formal API Transition System (*ATS*) model to describe API dependencies of class libraries. In this section, we explain in detail how an *ATS* model can represent class library API dependency.

In program statements, an API method calling sequence indicates a conversion process of class types or some basic data types such as *int*, *float* and *double*, reflecting class libraries API dependency. For example, given a method calling statement, to some extent, we can say that the returnee type might be determined by its caller type and parameter types. We observe that this conversion process of class types is similar to the intuitive behavior of a transition system [18]. Thus, we can exploit a transition system model to represent the conversion process of types in class libraries. Specifically, a transition system involves three elements: states, propositions and transitions. Each state of a transition system describes a specific stage of the behavior process of the system. Propositions indicate the main features of states. Transitions correspond to actions that change states [24]. As described above, we can treat API methods as transitions, and the current configuration of class types as states. In addition, we label caller types and parameter types with specified propositions.

To further express the numerical relations between the API elements of class libraries, we need to add some variables and labeling functions to a basic transition system model. A model *ATS* describes a *CLAD* as follows: (1) The transition relations indicate that the dependency relations between class types and methods are call or return; (2) Variables appearing in propositions indicate that class types are the parameters of methods; (3) The labeling function is used to indicate the number of parameters.

Definition 2. An *ATS* is a 8-tuple $ATS = (S, S_0, T, \rightarrow, K, AP, [.], L)$, where S is a set of states, $S_0 \in S$ is the set of initial states, T is a set of transition actions, $\rightarrow \subseteq S \times T \times S$ is the transition relation, K is a set of variables used to label states, AP is a set of atomic propositions used to represent the constraints of states, $[.]: AP \rightarrow (K \rightarrow [b, \infty])$ is a number labeling function that, for $ap \in AP$, assigns to each variable appearing in ap a non-negative integer interval $[ap](k)$ in $[b, \infty]$ with $b \in \mathbb{N}^+$, $L: S \rightarrow 2^{AP}$ is used to label the constraints of states.

Let (C, M, Rel, Ln) be the API dependency of a class library, and $(S, S_0, T, \rightarrow, K, AP, [.], L)$ be its *ATS* model. The set S_0 is used to denote the possible class types that are just the callers of some methods in class libraries. Here, S_0 corresponds to the input types provided by users, thus S_0 is initialized to $\emptyset$. The set T donates the methods in class libraries. And the set S denotes the callers and returnees of methods. For any $m \in M$, if $c_1, c_2 \in C$, $Rel(c_1, m) = call$ and $Rel(c_2, m) = ret$, then $_{tm} \in T$, $s_{c1}, s_{c2} \in S$, $s_{c1} \overset{t_m}{\rightarrow} s_{c2}$, $k_{c1} \in K$, $ap_{c1} \in AP$, $[ap_{c1}]_m(k_{c1}) \in [1, \infty)$, where s_{c1}, s_{c2} represent the state whose class type label is c_1 and c_2, respectively, k_{c1} denotes the variable related to c_1, ap_{c1} represents the proposition related to c_1, and $[ap_{c1}]_m(k_{c1})$ represents the value range of k_{c1} in ap_{c1} (the range is $[1, \infty)$, because the number of the caller of a method is 1).

If $c_3 \in C$ and $Rel(c_3, m) = par$, $k_{c3} \in K$, $ap_{c3} \in AP$, $[ap_{c3}]_m(k_{c3}) \in [Ln(c_3)_m, \infty)$, where k_{c3} and ap_{c3} represent variables and propositions related to c_3 respectively, and the lowest value of k_{c3} in proposition ap_{c3} is $Ln(c_3)_m$ which represents the number of parameter c_3 in the method m. Let C_c be the set of callers, if $c \in C_c$ and $Rel(c, m) =$

call, then $L(s_c) \in 2^{AP}$, where $L(s_c)$ represents a mapping from state s_c to propositions in AP at s_c and proposition $ap \in AP$ is composed of variable k and $[ap]m(k)$.

However, *AST* models may not accurately describe API dependencies at a high semantic level. For instance, the proposition ap_c cannot express all numbers of parameter c of method m which are overload methods. Only one transition relation $s_{c_1} \xrightarrow{t_m} s_{c_2}$ cannot describe different API methods converting type c_1 to type c_2. To solve these problems, here we discuss them by a special concept of "*clone*".

Overloaded Method. Java, generally speaking, method overloading refers to the situation that some methods with the same method name but different parameter lists. Specifically, it can be divided into the following situations. The types of parameters are different; the number of parameters is different (a different number must constitute an overload); there are multiple and different types of parameters, and their order is different to constitute an overload. For simplicity, we do not consider the last situation above in this paper. Given there exist n overloaded methods for a method m, and the i-th overloaded method has d_i return types. Let *om* be the number of all possible overloading situations. For the overloaded method m, we clone it into multiple method m_1, $m_2, \cdots, m_n$, and there exist corresponding cloned transitions $t_1, t_2, \cdots, t_{om}$ related to these cloned methods. For all overloading situations, we also need to clone the states of the caller to distinguish the constraints of the parameters of the methods. If *Rel* $(c, m) = call$ and *Rel* $(c', m) = par$, we clone the state s related to the class type c to the states $s_{c_1}, s_{c_2}, \cdots, s_{c_{om}}$. The propositions of the cloned states and the labeling function are obvious, and we omit them here.

Different Methods for Type Conversion. If there exist n methods that can convert the class type c to c', we also need to clone the state related to c into n cloned states. The definitions of the other elements are similar to the situation of overloaded method.

Overall, this paper formulates the mapping of elements in class libraries to elements in *ATS*, as shown in Table 2.

3.3   Constructing API Transition System

The construction process of an API Transition System contains two phases. The first phase analyzes the source codes of class libraries to extract dependency relations between API elements. The second phase transforms the dependency relations into API graph model *ATS*.

Here we take Java class libraries as examples. For Java code snippets, the corresponding abstract syntax tree contains all code elements (class types, methods, etc.) and their relations (*call*, *ret*, *par*, etc.). Thus, to extract dependency relations between API elements, we generate the abstract syntax trees corresponding to Java source codes by program static analysis tool Spoon[1] and Javassit[2], and then exploit the Depth First Search algorithm to traverse the branches and nodes. According to the mapping rules from the

---

[1] http://spoon.gforge.inria.fr/.

[2] https://sourceforge.net/projects/jboss/files/Javassist/.

Table 2. The mapping of library elements to *ATS* elements.

Library elements	ATS elements	Semantic description
Method M	Transition action set T	T represents a set of API methods
Class type C	Variable set K	Variables records the numbers of the callers and parameters of methods
	State set S	States specify the callers and returnees of methods and constraints
	Proposition set AP	Propositions represent the constraints of the numbers of callers and parameters of methods
Type $c1$-method m-type $c2$ Condtion: $Rel(c_1,m) = call \cup$ $Rel(c_2,m) = ret$	Transition relation $s_{c_1} \xrightarrow{t_m} s_{c_2}$	The class type c_1 is the caller of method t_m and c_2 is its returnee type
Type c_1-method m Condition: $Rel\,(c_1, m) = call$	Labeling function$[ap_{c1}]_m(k_{c1})$	$[ap_{c1}]_m(k_{c1})$ represents the number of caller types c_1 to call method t_m, and $[ap_{c1}]_m(k_{c1}) \geq 1$
Type c_3-method m Condition: $Rel\,(c_3, m) = par$	Labeling function$[ap_{c3}]_m(k_{c3})$	$[ap_{c3}]_m(k_{c3})$ represents the number of parameter c_3 to execute method t_m, and $[ap_{c3}]_m(k_{c3}) \geq o$, where o is the number of parameter c_3
Type C_c condition: C_c is a set of caller types	Function L	L represents the propositions in states corresponding to type C_c
Special case: Method m is an overloaded method	Cloned transition action set t_m	$t_m = \{t_{m_1}, t_{m_2}, \cdots t_{m_n \times d}\}$ represents cloned actions of method m, n is the number of overloaded methods, and d is the number of returnees
	Cloned state set s_c	$s_c = \{s_{c_1}, s_{c_2}, \cdots, s_{c_n}\}$ represents cloned states of method m, where c is the caller
	Cloned proposition set a_c	$a_c = \{a_{c_1}, a_{c_2}, \cdots, a_{c_n}\}$ represents cloned propositions of method m, where c is the parameter

(continued)

Table 2. (*continued*)

Library elements	ATS elements	Semantic description
	Token function$[a_c]m(k_c)$	$[a_c]m(k_c)$represents the different number of parameter c in overloaded methods m
Special case: different methods can convert type c to c_r	Cloned state set s_c	$s_c = \{s_{c_1}, s_{c_2}, \cdots, s_{c_n}\}$ represents cloned states of different methods $m_1, m_2, \cdots m_n$, n is the number of methods
	Transition action set T	$t_{m_1}, t_{m_2}, \cdots, t_{m_{n\times d}} \in T, d$ represents the number of returned type states

elements in class libraries to the elements in API Transition System (in Sect. 3.2), we develop the following algorithm that can transform *CLAD* into *ATS*.

Algorithm1 BuildingAPITransitionSystem

Input： Class library API dependencies *CLAD*

Output: API Transition System $ATS= (S, S_0, T, \rightarrow, K, AP, [.], L)$

    assume $CLAD = (C, M, Rel, L)$

    $S:=\{s_0\}$ $s_0:=\varnothing$ $T:=\varnothing$ $\rightarrow:=\varnothing$ $K:=\varnothing$ $AP:=\varnothing$ ▷Initialize the element of *ATS*

    for all $m \in M$ do

      $T:=T \cup \{m\}$ ▷For each method m, create a corresponding transition t

    while $m \neq \varnothing$ do

      choose $m \in M$ do

      $M:=M-\{m\}$

      for all $c_i, c_j \in C$ do

      if $rel(c_i,m)=cal\&rel(c_j,m)=ret\&rel(c_p,m)=par$ do

        ▷Determine the caller type, return type, and parameter type of each method

      $S:=S \cup \{c_i\} \cup \{c_j\}$

        ▷For each caller and return type, create a corresponding state s

      $\rightarrow:= \rightarrow \cup \{< c_i,m,c_j >\}$ ▷Add directed arc

      $K:=K \cup \{c_i\} \cup \{c_p\}$

        ▷For each caller and parameter type, create a corresponding variable k

      for all $c \in c_i,c_p$ do

      $[a](k)_m:=L(c)_m$

      $AP:=AP \cup \{(k, [a](k)_m)\}$

        ▷ Each tuple in AP contains a k and the value of k under method m

  define func L as $L(s,ap):=s(ap'),ap' \in AP{:}k \in s \cup rel(k,m) \in par,m \in <s,m,s'>$

      ▷ Assign propositions to each state s

  return *ATS*

Example 1. A partial of the transition model *ATS* of the library *java. sql* is shown in Fig. 4. Intuitively, we label states with class types and parameters, and their quantitative constraints in the form of propositions. The directed edges are labeled with the names of the methods from the callers of the methods to their returnees. For a state that indicates a caller of a certain method, its propositions represent the caller and the number of parameters in this method. Furthermore, to distinguish between two special situations in Sect. 3.2, we mark cloned overloaded methods and the cloned callers of these methods in blue, and mark different methods that can convert a specific type to another type and cloned callers of these methods in yellow. We use blue and yellow concentric circles to indicate cloned states which are callers of overloaded methods and callers of methods converting a specific type to another type. For example, since the caller and returnee of the method *creatStatement* are state **Connection** and **Statement** respectively, there exist transitions from the state indicating the class **Connection** to the state indicating the state **Statement**. The method *creatStatement* is overloaded by 3 times and its returnee class **Statement** is cloned by 2 times, thus this method is cloned by 6 times, and the caller **Connection** is cloned by 3 times, not including the state with label Conn4. Since the numbers of the *int* parameter in overloading methods *creatStatement* are 0, 2 and 3, the propositions in cloned states related to the class **Connection** are $Conn \geq 1$, $Conn \geq 1\&int \geq 2$ and $Conn \geq 1\&int \geq 3$, respectively. For simplicity, we abbreviate the class type names in Fig. 4.

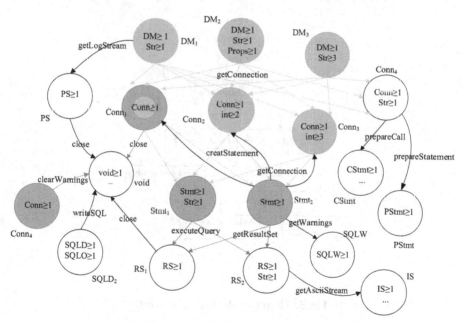

Fig. 4. Partial *ATS* model of API dependency in the *java.sql* library.

4   Formalization of the Matching Rules of Queries

In this section, we establish the matching rules to denote the search requirements and then to obtain suitable API usage patterns based on *ATS*. The construction process of the matching rules contains the semantics description and the formalization of rules. Specifically, given a query that consists of the description of the input and output types, we construct an APIs replacement model to locate the API classes related to the description, and combine these API classes with input/output types to build the final matching rules. Then, we formalize the rules by the computation tree logic CTL* [18].

4.1 Semantic Descriptions of Rules

We hope to understand the query requirements provided by users in natural language descriptions. The transition model *ATS* just describes the process of type conversion, and it cannot understand the natural language descriptions semantically. Hence, we build an APIs replacement model to convert natural language descriptions into the constraints on input and output types related to the elements in *ATS* model.

4.1.1 APIs Replacement Model

We follow the method proposed by Raghothaman et al., using clickthrough data to find relevant API names [22]. As Fig. 5 shows, it consists of preprocessing text and constructing the replacement model.

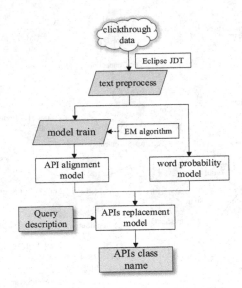

Fig. 5. Flowchart of APIs replacement.

Preprocessing Text. Firstly, we collect the set of pairs (Q, URL) from search engines, indicating the *URL* links that users click in response to the query Q. Secondly, we extract code snippets on web pages through HTML tags such as $<$ pre $>$ and $<$ code $>$. Thirdly, we exploit the tool Eclipse JDT to extract class types from code snippets. Finally, we split a single pair (Q, URL) into the set of pairs (Q, R), where R represents the set of class types.

Constructing Model. Let r be a class type related to the query Q, the probability of r being the replacement term, is given by:

$$Pr(r|Q) = Pr(r|q_1, q_2, \cdots, q_n) = \sum_{i=1}^{n} Pr(r|q_i) \cdot Pr(q_i|Q)$$

The API replacement model $Pr(r|Q)$ is composed of API alignment model $Pr(r|q_i)$ and word probability model $Pr(q_i|Q)$, where $Q = [q_1, q_2, ..., q_n]$ represents the query containing the words $q_1, q_2, \cdots, q_n$. $Pr(r|q_i)$ quantifies the connection between a word and an API, and indicates the probability of class type i given a query word q_i. $Pr(q_i|Q)$ quantifies the probability of a word appearing in the query, and indicates the unsmoothed unigram probability of the query word q_i in the query Q.

Since a data pair (Q, R) cannot establish a direct connection between a word $q \in Q$ and a class type $r \in R$, we use a standard procedure for training alignment model by applying an expectation maximization (EM) algorithm. The EM algorithm first initializes $Pr(r|q_i)$ to random values for each r and q, and then iteratively updates the probabilities to maximize the likelihood of generating the training data. This probability quantifies how likely the word q is to appear in the query Q and is calculated as follows:

$$Pr(q|Q) = \frac{\alpha_q}{\Sigma_{q' \in Q} \alpha_{q'}}$$

$$\alpha_q = \frac{\text{\# of times q occurs in query log}}{\text{Total word count in query log}}$$

4.1.2 Description of Rules

After converting the descriptions to class types, we need to combine class types with query types to generate matching rules.

Definition 3. A query type is a 2-tuple (*Type_in, Type_out*), where *Type_in* represents the set of input types, and *Type_out* represents the output type.

An API usage pattern is a sequence of API methods where participant methods belong to different API classes.

Definition 4. An API usage pattern is a sequence of API methods $<m_{a,1}, m_{b,2}, \cdots, m_{n,i}>$, $i \in \mathbb{N}^+$, $i \geq 2$, where the second subscript of a method $m_{n,i}$ denotes the order number of the method, and the first subscript represents the API class the method belongs to.

In general, the returnee of a method in a pattern is the caller of its successor method. For instance, the returnee of method $m_{a,1}$ is b. For an API usage pattern $p = <m_{a,1}, m_{b,2}, \cdots, m_{n,i}>$ and a query $q = (Type\_in, Type\_out)$, satisfies queried type, if a belongs to *Type_in* and the returnee of $m_{n,i}$ is *Type_out*, we can say that the pattern p satisfies q.

As described above, users desire to find a method sequence from input type to output type, thus we aim to match a transition path tp that can convert the types in *Type_in* to the type *Type_out* from *ATS* model (The initial state set S_0 in *ATS* are the caller types in *Type_in*, and the final state in *ATS* is *Type_out*). Since a description from a user and a query (*Type_in, Type_out*) indicate the same API usage pattern, some class types corresponding to the description are likely to be included in the transition path from input types to output type. They may be the middle states *MS* (state *Type_in* reaches state *Type_out* through state APIs) or the middle proposition *MP* (some parameters of methods in transition path *Tp* are APIs). For a middle state, we need to further determine whether it passes transition path *tp*. For a middle proposition, we regarded it as *Type_in*. In conclusion, we formulate the following rules: (1) Graph model *ATS* has state *Type_out*, state or proposition *Type_in*; (2) *ATS* satisfies proposition *Type_in*, and can convert state *Type_in* to *Type_out* through the transition path *Tp*; (3) The transition path *Tp* passes *MS*.

4.2 Characterization of Query Rules by CTL*

CTL* is a powerful temporal logic used to describe temporal properties of transition system models [25, 26]. This logic consists of path quantifiers and temporal operators [27]. The path quantifiers A (for all paths) and E (there exists a path) can specify the branch structures features, and the temporal operators X(next), F(eventually), G(globally) and U(until) are used to specify some temporal properties on paths.

In this paper, we use CTL* formulae to characterize matching rules, and then detect whether there exist transferable method sequences that satisfy the formulae in *ATS*. Table 3 shows some examples of CTL* formulas corresponding to matching rules. The left side in Table 3 are input types, output types and class types converted by description. The right side represents the CTL* formulas related to types. For the first query consisting of input types *DriverManager*, *String*, output type *Boolean* and converted type *Properties*, we aim to find an existing sequence converting *DriverManager*, *String* and *Properties* to *Boolean* from *ATS* model (because *Properties* is the middle proposition, it can be regarded as input type). Thus, we construct the CTL* formula containing types, the number of types and relations of types to describe this existing sequence.

This paper exploits the model checker NuSMV[3] to search for API usage patterns. NuSMV developed by McMillan et.al is a tool that can effectively analyze and verify logical properties of concurrent systems.

To automatically detect whether matching rules are satisfied in *ATS* models, we convert *ATS* and CTL* formulae about the reversals of matching rules into SMV language as the input of NuSMV. If the given rule is satisfied in *ATS*, the output of NuSMV is "True". Otherwise, NuSMV will provide a counterexample path that does not satisfy.

5 Evaluation

To evaluate our approach, we design two experiments. In the first experiment, we verify whether our approach can search for the desired API usage patterns, and measure the search accuracy of our approach and other approaches. In the second, we demonstrate whether our approach can effectively solve the problems that cannot be solved by the other methods, and discuss the influence of technical points involved in our approach.

---

[3] http://nusmv.fbk.eu/.

Table 3. CTL* representation examples of matching rules.

Type_in/Type_out APIs (MS, MP)	CTL* formula
***DriverManager, String/ boolean Properties* (MP)**	a. (DriverManager = 1 ∨ String = 1∨Properties = 1) ⋀ E(trueU(boolean = 1))
	b. (DriverManager = 1&String = 1&Properties = 1) → EF (boolean = 1)
***DriverManager, String/ Statement Connection* (MS)**	a. (DriverManager = 1 ∨ String = 1) ⋀ E(trueU(Connection = 1 ⋀ E(trueU (Statement = 1))))
	b. (DriverManager = 1 ∨ String = 1) → EF(Connection = 1 → EF(Statement = 1))
***DriverManager, String, String/ResultSet Connection, Statement* (MS)**	a. (DriverManager = 1 ∨ String = 2) ⋀ E(trueU((Connection = 1 ⋀ E(trueU(Statement = 1 ⋀ E(trueU(ResultSet = 1))))) ∨ (Statement = 1 ⋀ E(trueU(Connection = 1 ⋀ E(trueU (ResultSet = 1)))))))
	b. (DriverManager = 1&String = 1) → EF(Connection = 1 → EF(Statement = 1 → EF(ResultSet = 1)))|(Statement = 1 → EF(Connection = 1 → EF(ResultSet = 1))))

5.1 Setup

We compare our approach with frequent-pattern-mining based the approach MLUP [10], global-graph-model based the approach Prospector [13], and local-graph-model GraPacc [15].

To ensure fairness, we build graph models based on the same Java packages and class libraries used in the compared approaches. Specifically, in the first expcriment, we compare the class library GEF with Prospector and MLUP, and the Java SDK Utility (*java. util, java. io*) with GraPacc. In the second experiment, we use the library *java.sql* and *java. nio. file*.

In the first experiment, we use 30 query pairs in the form of (*Type_in, Type_out*), including 20 queries in [13] and 10 queries about complex programming tasks. In the second, we extract 10 popular questions from Stack Overflow[4] and the pairs of the input/output types in answered code examples as queries (in Table 4). If there exist some types of arrays as the class types in some query pairs (e.g. line 6, 8 in Table 4), it implies that there exist multiple classes with the same types, and this can be achieved by adding some numerical constraints, which is discussed in Sect. 3.

In order to uniformly measure the relevance of the search results, we use two precision metrics commonly used in information retrieval: top-1 precision($P@1$) [28, 29] and mean average precision (*MAP*) [30]. Descriptions and definitions of the metrics are as follows:

---

[4] https://stackoverflow.com/.

Table 4. Benchmark queries.

No	Description	Type_in/Type_out
1	Create and write to a(text) file	String, String, Path/void
2	Connect Java to a MySQL database	DriverManager, String, String/ResultSet
3	Iterate through a HashMap	Map/void
4	How to append text to an existing file in Java?	String/PrintWriter
5	convert a stack trace to a string	StringWriter/String
6	How can I generate an MD5 hash?	String/byte []
7	Calculating the difference between two Java date instances	date, date/long
8	determine whether an array contains a particular value	String [], String/boolean
9	Parse JSON in Java	String/JSONArray
10	How to upload files to server using JSP Servlet	HttpServletRequest, HttpServletResponse/void

$P@1$: This metric represents the relevance of the first result. Relevance in our study is either 1 for relevant or 0 for irrelevant.

MAP: The mean average precision is for a set of queries and is computed as follows:

$$MAP = \frac{\sum_{i=1}^{Q} AveP(i)}{Q}$$

$$AveP = \frac{\sum_{k=1}^{n}(P(k) \times rel_k)}{\text{the number of relevant documents}}$$

where n is the number of results and rel_k is the relevance of the kth result. $P(k)$ is the weight of rank k in the list of related results. For instance, if a list has two relevant results that appear at ranks 1 and 3, then $P(1) = 1.00$ and $P(3) = 0.67$.

5.2 Results

5.2.1 Relevance Assessment

Based on the queries in the literature [13], we compare the search results of our approach, Prospector and MLUP, as shown in Table 5. In addition, we compare the search results of our approach and GraPacc, as shown in Table 6. In Tables 5 and 6, the columns marked "P@1" and rows marked "*MAP*" show the precision of our approach is the significantly highest among MLUP, Prospector and GraPacc. We explain as follows: (1) MLUP largely depends on the usage frequencies of patterns in the corpus. For example, we find that a pattern satisfying query (TableViewer, Table) is only used once. The pattern cannot be recognized because of its low usage frequency. (2) When suitable patterns contain methods with parameters, Prospector requires additional manual operations, resulting in many irrelevant results. (3) In addition, the graph models of Prospector and CraPacc do not consider quantitative relations between API elements, thus describe semantic information of class libraries insufficiently. In this paper, the *ATS* models completely consider the quantitative dependence between API elements in class libraries. Moreover, by combining model checking technique, our approach automatically identifies various patterns in any form of queries, to avoid manual intervention that often appears in existing approaches based on the graph traversal search algorithm.

Table 5. Evaluation results of the queries from [13].

Query		P@1		
Type_in	Type_out	Prospector	MLUP	Our approach
InputStream	BufferedReader	1	1	1
String	MappedByteBuffer	1	1	1
TableViewer	Table	1	0	1
IWorkbench	IEditorPart	1	1	1
ScrollingGraphicalViewer	FigureCanvas	1	0	1
KeyEvent	Shell	1	1	1
Enumeration	Iterator	1	0	1
SelectionChangedEvent	ISelection	1	0	1
ImageRegistry	ImageDescriptor	1	0	1
Map	Iterator	1	1	1
IViewPart	MenuManager	1	1	1
TableViewer	TableColumn	0	1	1
IEditorSite	ISelectionService	0	0	1
String	BufferedReader	0	0	1
IWorkbenchPage	IStructuredSelection	0	0	0
IWorkbenchPage	IDocumentProvider	0	1	1
IFile	String	0	1	1
IWorkbenchWindow	IViewPart	0	0	1
AbstractGraphicalEditPart	ConnectionLayer	0	0	1
IWorkspace	IFile	0	0	0
MAP		0.55	0.45	0.9

Table 6. Evaluation results of the queries from Java SDK Utility.

| Query | | P@1 | |
Type_in	Type_out	GraPacc	Our approach
FileReader	BufferedReader	1	1
InputStream	BufferedReader	0	1
LinkedHashMap	Iterator	0	1
ArrayList	Iterator	1	1
FileWriter	PrintWriter	0	1
File	Scanner	0	0
FileInputStream	DataInputStream	1	1
Pattern	Matcher	1	1
GregorianCalendar	ZonedDateTime	0	0
Console	PrintWriter	1	1
MAP		0.5	0.8

5.2.2 Usability and Technique Assessment

To verify whether our approach can solve multiple-input-type queries that are not involved in other approaches, we conduct retrieval experiments on the graph models *ATS* by the queries in Table 4. Experimental results are shown in Table 7.

Table 7. Evaluation results of queries from Table 4.

| No | API classes corresponding to descriptions | P@1 | |
		Before replacement	After replacement
1	Files	1	1
2	Connection, Statement	0	1
3	Iterator	1	1
4	FileWriter, BufferedWriter	0	1
5	PrintWriter	1	1
6	MessageDigest	0	0
7	TimeUnit	1	1
8	Arrays	1	1
9	JSONobject	0	0
10	InputStream	0	1
MAP		0.5	0.8

We explain our approach intuitively based on the query 2 in Table 4. The search process about this query are as follows: Firstly, we convert the description of the query 2 to {*Connection, Statement*} through APIs replacement model. Secondly, we combine {*Connection, Statement*} with input/output types {*DriverManager, String, String/ResultSet*}to make matching rules, and exploit CTL* formula representing inverted rules. Finally, we use model checker NuSMV to check CTL* formula in ATS model. The result of NuSMV is shown in Fig. 6 (the omitted part is the variables with value 0).

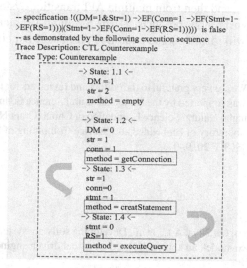

```
-- specification !((DM=1&Str=1) ->EF(Conn=1 ->EF(Stmt=1-
>EF(RS=1))))|(Stmt=1->EF(Conn=1->EF(RS=1)))))  is false
-- as demonstrated by the following execution sequence
Trace Description: CTL Counterexample
Trace Type: Counterexample
    -> State: 1.1 <-
        DM = 1
        str = 1
        method = empty
        ...
    -> State: 1.2 <-
        DM = 0
        str = 1
        conn = 1
        method = getConnection
    -> State: 1.3 <-
        str =1
        conn=0
        stmt = 1
        method = creatStatement
    -> State: 1.4 <-
        stmt = 0
        RS=1
        method = executeQuery
```

Fig. 6. Search result for the query "Connect Java to a MySQL database".

Figure 6 shows that the CTL* formula is not satisfied in model *ATS*, thus NuSMV provides a counterexample trace. According to the transition process (marked by the dashed box), we can identify the method sequence (namely an API usage pattern), where solid red boxes indicate specific methods and arrows indicate their order. After the empirical analysis, the API usage pattern satisfics the query 2. Furthermore, as shown in Table 7, our approach can effectively handle multiple forms of queries, including multiple-input-types. As a result, our approach has higher applicability than existing approaches. Table 7 also illustrates the necessity of the APIs replacement model. The columns "Before replacement" and "After replacement" show that the conversion from the descriptions of queries to API class types will make search results more accurate.

6 Conclusion

The API usage patterns of class libraries can help users to understand or learn the usage of some new class libraries, or provide programmers with helpful suggestions to improve the productivity when coding. In this paper, we propose a new approach to searching for API usage patterns. We develop a novel kind of API transition system model *ATS* to model the semantic dependency relations between API elements of class libraries. We use the logic CTL* to formalize the matching rules of API usage patterns abstracted from the queries provided by programmers, and exploit model checking technique to automatically obtain desired API usage patterns. Experiments shows that our approach is effective. Compared with the existing approaches, our approach has higher applicability.

In the future, we will strengthen our approach from two aspects: 1) To achieve some specific business logics when coding, the desired API methods may be span multiple class libraries. This also implies that the dependency relations of API methods will no longer be limited in a single class library. In that case, we need to search for patterns from multiple class libraries, and then from multiple API transition system models, possibly by computing their synchronous products. 2) The resulting API method sequences may be redundant, so we will identify some undesired API usage patterns by strengthening some constraints.

Acknowledgements. We are very grateful to the editors and reviewers for their comments on this manuscript. This work was supported by the National Natural Science Foundation of China under Grant 61672384, the Ningbo Natural Science Foundation of China (Grant No. 2019A610088), the Open Subject of Key Laboratory of Embedded and Service Computing of Ministry of Education of China (Grant No. ESSCKF 2019–07).

References

1. Osvaldo, S.S., Lopes, D., Silva, A.C., et al.: Developing software systems to big data platform based on mapreduce model: an approach based on model driven engineering. Inf. Soft. Tech. **7**(6), 30–48 (2017)
2. Mkitalo, N., Taivalsaari, A., Kiviluoto, A., et al.: On opportunistic software reuse. Computing **10**(2), 2385–2408 (2020)
3. Desouza, K.C., Awazu, Y., Tiwana, A.: Four dynamics for bringing use back into software reuse. Commun. ACM **49**(1), 96–100 (2015)
4. Shen, Q., Wu, S., Zou, Y., et al.: From API to NLI: a new interface for library reuse. J. Syst. Softw. **169**(110), 7–28 (2020)
5. Kula, R.G., German, D.M., Ouni, A., et al.: Do developers update their library dependencies. Empir. Softw. Eng. **4**(23), 384–417 (2018)
6. Zhong, H., Mei, H.: An empirical study on API usages. IEEE Trans. Softw. Eng. **45**(4), 319–334 (2019)
7. Saied, M.A., Sahraoui, H., Dufour, B.: An observational study on API usage constraints and their documentation. In: 2015 IEEE 22nd International Conference on Software Analysis, Evolution, and Reengineering (SANER). IEEE, pp. 33–42 (2015)
8. Niu, H., Keivanloo, I., Zou, Y., et al.: API usage pattern recommendation for software development. J. Syst. Softw. **12**(9), 127–139 (2017)
9. Dit, B., Revelle, M., Gethers, M., et al.: Feature location in source code: a taxonomy and survey. J. Softw. Maint. Evol. Res. Pract. **25**(1), 53–95 (2013)
10. Saied, M.A., Benomar, O., Abdeen, H., et al.: Mining multi-level API usage patterns. In: 2015 IEEE 22nd International Conference on Software Analysis, Evolution, and Reengineering (SANER). IEEE, pp. 23–32 (2015)
11. Zhong, H., Xie, T., Zhang, L., et al.: MAPO: mining and recommending API usage patterns. Proc Ecoop **56**(53), 318–343 (2009)

12. Mendez, D., Baudry, B., Monperrus, M.: Empirical evidence of large-scale diversity in API usage of objected-oriented software. In: Proceedings of 13th IEEE International Working Conference on Source Code Analysis and Manipulation (SCAM), pp. 43–52 (2013)
13. Mandelin, D., Xu, L., Bodik, R., et al.: Jungloid mining: helping to navigate the API jungle. Program. Lang. Des. Implementation, ACM Sigplan Not. **40**(6), 48–61, (2005)
14. Thummalapenta, S., Xie, T.: Parseweb: a programmer assistant for reusing open source code on the web. In: Proceeding soft the twenty-second IEEE/ACM international conference on Automated software engineering. ACM, New York, pp. 204–213 (2007)
15. Nguyen, A.T., Nguyen, H.A., Nguyen, T.T., et al.: GraPacc: a graph-based pattern-oriented, context-sensitive code completion tool. In: International Conference on Software Engineering. IEEE, NJ, 1407–1410 (2012)
16. Chen, L., Jiang, W., Songlin, H.: An API recommendation system based on a new graph model. Chin. J. Comput. **395**(11), 2172–2187 (2015)
17. Reps, T.W., et al.: Component-based synthesis for complex APIs. In: POPL 2017. ACM, pp. 15–21 (2017)
18. Kaile, S., Abdul, S., Xiangyu, L.: Model checking temporal logics of knowledge via OBDDs1. Comput. J. (4), 403–420
19. Agha, G., Palmskog, K.: A survey of statistical model checking. ACM Trans. Model. Comput. Simul. **28**(1), 1–39 (2018)
20. Gol, E.A., Bartocci, E., Belta, C.: A formal methods approach to pattern synthesis in reaction diffusion systems. Eprint Arxiv **20**(15), 108–113 (2014)
21. Cappart, Q., Limbree, C., Schaus, P., et al.: Dependability analysis of control systems using systemC and statistical model checking. Comput. Sci. **20**(18), 61–68 (2016)
22. Raghothaman, M., Wei, Y., Hamadi, Y.: SWIM: Synthesizing what I mean. In: Proceedings of the 38th International Conference on Software Engineering (ICSE), IEEE, pp. 357–367 (2016)
23. Gu, X., Zhang, H., Zhang, D., et al.: Deep API learning. In: Proceedings of the 2016 24th ACM SIGSOFT International Symposium on Foundations of Software Engineering. ACM, pp. 13–18 (2016)
24. Beek, M.H., Fantechi, A., Gnesi, S., et al.: Modelling and analysing variability in product families: Model checking of modal transition systems with variability constraints. J. Logic Algebraic Program. **85**(2), 287–315 (2016)
25. Khamespanah, E., Khosravi, R., Sirjani, M.: An efficient TCTL model checking algorithm and a reduction technique for verification of timed actor models. Sci. Comput. Program. **153**(15), 1–29 (2018)
26. Camilli, M., Bellettini, C., Capra, L., Monga, M.: CTL model checking in the cloud using MapReduce. In: 16th International Symposium on Symbolic and Numeric Algorithms for Scientific Computing, IEEE, pp. 333–340 (2014)
27. Bozzano, M., Cimatti, A., Lisagor, O., et al.: Safety assessment of AltaR9ica models via symbolic model checking. Ence Comput. Program. **98**(4), 464–483 (2015)
28. Nie, L., Jiang, H., Ren, Z., et al.: Query expansion based on crowd knowledge for code search. IEEE Trans. Serv. Comput. **9**(5), 771–783 (2017)
29. Stolee, K.T., Elbaum, S., Dobos, D.: Solving the search for source code. ACM Trans. Softw. Eng. Methodol. (TOSEM) **23**(3), 26–67 (2014)
30. Stolee, K.T., Elbaum, S., Dwyer, M.B.: Code search with input/output queries: generalizing, ranking, and assessment. J. Syst. Softw. **116**(4), 35–48 (2016)

Author Index

Printed in the United States
by Baker & Taylor Publisher Services

Printed in the United States
by Baker & Taylor Publisher Services